AFRICA

AFRICA

VOLUME 1

AFRICAN HISTORY
BEFORE 1885

Edited by

Toyin Falola

Carolina Academic Press
Durham, North Carolina

Library of Congress Cataloging-in-Publication Data

Africa / edited by Toyin Falola.
   p.   cm.
   Includes bibliographical references and index.
   ISBN 0-89089-768-9 (v. 1)—ISBN 0-89089-769-7 (v. 2)
   1. Africa—History—To 1884. I. Falola, Toyin.

   DT20 .A61785 2000
   960—dc21

                           00-035789

Carolina Academic Press
700 Kent Street
Durham, North Carolina 27701
Telephone (919) 489-7486
Fax (919) 493-5668
E-mail: cap@cap-press.com
www.cap-press.com

For Olabisi Florence, Dolapo Omobola,
Bisola Omolola, and Oloruntoyin Omoyeni

Contents

Preface and Acknowledgments

This text is intended to introduce Africa to college students and the general public. It presents in a simplified manner different aspects of African history. The book does not generalize about the continent; rather it reconstructs the history of many societies at different historical periods. Aspects of cultures and key institutions of society are presented in a companion volume titled *African Cultures and Societies Before 1885*. Both books meet the requirements of history and culture courses in most schools, and address those issues of interest to the general public. The choice of topics is dictated both by relevance and by the need to satisfy classroom requirements.

The book is divided into five parts. The first describes the geography of the continent and the role of the environment in its history. The second chapter is about how the continent has been studied and presented in books and the media by scholars and writers. In part B, there are two chapters on the early period of African history. Here, the place of archaeology looms large. Part C takes each region in turn, describing many of the great kingdoms and outstanding events. Part D looks at the history of the nineteenth century, a period much closer in time to the present era. The book ends with a section on the contacts between Africa and Europe, a relationship that redefined the history of Africa after 1885.

A section overview introduces each part, with a summary of the main issues and ideas. The review questions at the end of every chapter test both broad and specific knowledge.

The choice of the contributors is primarily based on their competence as teachers in explaining history to college students and beginners, and their skill in synthesizing a large body of data and ideas. The relevance and comprehensibility of the chapters have been tested by anonymous undergraduate students in two schools. I am grateful to all the contributors, students, and readers. I received valuable support from many students and scholars who offered excellent suggestions for the book's title, organization, and contents. In preparing for the press, valuable support from Steven Salm and Saheed Adejumobi ensured the completion of the project. Without the indefatigable assistance of Steven Salm, this project would have taken a much longer time to complete. Joel Tishken, my loyal friend, checked all the illustrations and suggested new ones. Dr. Ann O'Hear copy-edited the manuscript.

Toyin Falola
The University of Texas at Austin

List of Illustrations and Maps

Notes on the Authors

Saheed A. Adejumobi holds B.A. and M.A. degrees in history and is currently a doctoral candidate at the University of Texas at Austin. He has contributed to other publications on Africa. His interests include ethnicity, nationalism, and African diasporic cultural politics.

Julius Adekunle holds a Ph.D. from Dalhousie University, Canada. He has been a college teacher of history since the 1970s, and has written many essays on different aspects of precolonial Africa. He is preparing for press *A History of West Africa*.

Funso Afolayan holds a Ph.D. in African history from Obafemi Awolowo University, Ile-Ife, Nigeria. In addition to research publications in Europe, Africa and the United states, he is co-author of *Yoruba Sacred Kingship: A Power Unto the Gods* (1996). He has held a number of research and teaching positions, at Obafemi Awolowo University, Nigeria, at Amherst College, and in the Department of History and African and Afro-American Studies Program of Washington University in St. Louis. He currently teaches African and World History at the University of New Hampshire, Durham. He is completing a joint study with Toyin Falola on *The Yoruba in the Nineteenth Century*.

William C. Barnett graduated from Yale University in 1988 with a B.A. in History. He taught United States, African, Latin American, and World History at Brewster Academy in New Hampshire for three years. He earned an M.A. in History in 1990 from the University of Texas at Austin and he is currently a Ph.D. student at the University of Wisconsin–Madison. Barnet's speciality is environmental history, and he has written on a variety of regions.

Jeremiah Dibua, Ph.D., teaches African history at Morgan State University. He has taught in two Nigerian colleges — Edo State University, Ekpoma and University of Benin, Benin City — and the North Carolina State University, Raleigh, NC. His area of specialization is African history. He has published numerous articles in scholarly journals and contributed chapters to books. Dr. Dibua has been teaching African history for over twelve years.

Toyin Falola, Ph.D., has been teaching since the 1970s in different countries. Author of many books and articles, editor of journals and a monograph series, he is a professor of history at the University of Texas at Austin. Falola has participated in the drafting of history syllabi for two countries and has contributed to numerous texts on African history.

Joseph Inikori is professor of history at the University of Rochester, New York. Born in Nigeria, he took his B.A. and Ph.D. degrees at the University of Ibadan, and he has taught at that university and at Ahmadu Bello University. He has been a Fellow at the London School of Economics and the University of Birmingham. Among his many publications on slavery and the slave trade are *Forced Migration: The Impact of the Export Slave Trade on African Societies* (1982), *The Chaining of a Continent: Export Demand for Captives and the History of Africa South of the Sahara 1450–1870* (1992), and *The Atlantic Slave Trade: Effects on Economies, Societies, and Peoples in Africa, the Americas, and Europe* (1992).

Patrick U. Mbajekwe, an experienced teacher, holds M.A. from the University of Lagos, and he is currently a doctoral student at Emory University.

Chidiebere Nwaubani is with the History Department, University of Colorado at Boulder; he was previously a faculty member at Imo State University, Okigwe, Nigeria. His degrees are from the Universities of Ilorin, Ibadan, and Toronto. A recipient of many academic awards and distinctions, he was a Visiting Fellow of the British Academy in summer 1997. He has published in several journals on subjects including the philosophy of history, history of the Igbo, British decolonization in Africa, and the political economy of contemporary Africa. He is currently revising his Ph.D. for publication, to be titled, "The United States and Decolonization in West Africa, 1950–1960."

Adebayo Oyebade teaches in the Department of History, Tennessee State University, Nashville. Formerly he was a lecturer in African history at Ogun State University, Nigeria. He obtained his Ph.D. in history from Temple University where he was a Fulbright scholar. He has contributed chapters to books on African history and has published articles in learned journals, including the *Journal of Black Studies and African Economic History.* He is the co-editor of *Africa After the Cold War: Changing Perspectives on Security* (1998). In addition to teaching, Oyebade is also a poet.

Joel Tishken holds an M.A. in history, and he is currently working on his Ph.D. program in World History at the University of Texas at Austin. Tishken has acquired experience as a teacher at the college level. He has contributed to other publications and written reviews for *African Economic History.*

Jacqueline Woodfork has worked for many years as an administrator in the United States and Africa. After completing her M.A. degree she has embarked upon a Ph.D. program at the University of Texas at Austin. She is researching aspects of French imperialism in Africa.

AFRICA

PART A

BACKGROUND KNOWLEDGE

Section Overview

The two essays in this section introduce the reader to the geography of Africa and to some approaches to writing about its history. Africa, like all other continents, is always in transition. Its map, fortunes, and history have changed over time. African history reveals both continuity and change—many traditions and institutions have always been carried forward, but changes and new ideas are constant.

Africa, the second largest continent, is bigger than most maps tend to portray it. Geographically, it is the most central, with most of its land mass in the tropics. Today it is divided into more than fifty countries, with a population of over 660 million. In the period covered by this book, nations, groups and languages were numerous.

Environment influenced the people's way of life as they struggled to adapt. The survival of communities and individuals was tied to the land, as the majority of the population worked as farmers and herders. The fauna coexisted with humans. Where there was the need for space, food and other animal products, people encroached upon the fauna. The fauna supplied valuable materials for building, food, medicine, and other products. They also had to be controlled when they offered danger, as in areas with the tsetse fly that killed cattle.

The geography shows both diversity and unity. The continent is diverse by ethnicities, religions, and languages and different agents of imperial control. The countries of North Africa (Morocco, Algeria, Tunisia, Egypt, and Libya) often claim to be different from sub-Saharan Africa because they have been greatly influenced by Islam and they share ties with southwest Asia and the Mediterranean. There are regional variations in ecology, climate and topography. Some groups live in the forest, others in the desert or savanna.

There were many similarities in past histories and cultures. Descent groups formed the building blocks of society. Individual rights were less important than community rights. Many aspects of culture were common, such as occupations, respect for elders and authority, religious beliefs, attitude to land, and social groups constructed on kinship.

For centuries, Africa was misconceptualized by the outside world which promoted many ignorant ideas. To some it was a "dark continent" inhabited by savages. To others, it had no history. The trans-Atlantic slave trade and European imperialism encouraged racist ideas in which Africans were regarded as inferiors. Many of these views are intended to justify the exploitation of a continent and the imposition of imperial control. Not only is Africa's history one of the most dynamic in human civilization, its peoples have also contributed substantially both to their own development and to that of other continents.

One of the intellectual achievements of the twentieth century is the unraveling of the history of Africa. Arabic and European sources are complemented with rich oral traditions and archaeological findings with which to reconstruct the past. Defenders of the African past have also come up with perspectives with which to understand it. A nationalist historiography emerged after the Second World War with the aim of restoring the glory of Africa's past. Some other perspectives, like the recent controversial one on Afrocentricity, not only elaborate on African history but argue in addition that a great deal of Western civilization has its roots in Africa. Theoretical studies such as post-modernism and post-colonial literature have made a compelling case for locating Africa at the center of knowledge and enhancing the voices that have previously been ignored or marginalized.

Chapter 1

The Study of Africa in Historical Perspective

Adebayo Oyebade

Introduction

Africa's place as a prime contributor to the history of human development and civilization is generally accepted today. Across the ages, the continent played host to diverse cultures and striking civilizations. For instance, Africa was the home of such enduring civilizations as Kush, Aksum, and ancient Egypt in the Nile Valley. Indeed, ancient Egypt is believed to be the world's longest-lasting great civilization, enduring for well over two thousand years. In the Western Sudan, Ghana, Mali, and Songhai flourished as great empires. Great Zimbabwe was a magnificent civilization in southern Africa.

Nineteenth-century European scholarship questioned the now undisputed fact of Africa's contribution to human progress. In the Eurocentric intellectual tradition of that period, precolonial Africa was conceived as a "dark continent" which neither contributed to civilization, nor was touched by it. In European thought, as we shall see, Africa was painted as immersed so deep in barbarism and chaos that it could not have left in its past a history of any significance. Africa was thus defined out of history.

Of course, it would be overstating the fact to conclude that the Eurocentric conception of Africa as a "dark continent" does not exist any longer. The notion of an Africa with wild animals and dark jungles still lingers in many minds, untutored in the truth of the Africa past. Yet to many people—those who are sufficiently interested in an objective and critical study of Africa, scholars who have been involved in research into African history and are aware of the facts—the validity of Africa's historical past is no fresh news. The ever-growing bulk of scholarly literature on African history based on an array of sources that include written records, oral tradition, and archaeological evidence, have established the subject as a valid enterprise in intellectual inquiry. Indeed, since the mid-twentieth century, such great strides have been made in the historical study of Africa that today African history constitutes an integral part of the broader history of civilization.

This chapter will attempt a critical examination of how Africa has been conceptualized in the history of ideas across the ages, and how the study of its history has changed over time. It will discuss salient issues such as the antiquity of African history, historical consciousness, and the preservation of history in precolonial Africa. The chapter will also examine racism and the Eurocentric conception of Africa, the evolution of Africa-centered perspectives of history as represented both in the continent and in the diaspora, and the rise of recent conceptual frameworks such as Afrocentrism.

The Idea of History

Contrary to the Eurocentric thought that denied Africa its history, the continent has a rich historical past dating from long before the advent of Europeans. Africans had always had a clear conception of history and a notion of the past as a tangible reality worthy of preservation. What were the essential characteristics of historical reality among Africans prior to European contact?

First, history was conceived as the knowledge not only of the past, but also of the present. Historical processes in Africa, as in some other cultures of the world, were seen as a continuum stretching from the earliest times to the present. The present was an uninterrupted continuation of the past, and a bridge to the future. Hence, history involved the study of all aspects of society's past and present behavior. It was the study of people in their environment and of the institutions that govern their relationship with others—social, political, economic, and religious.

Second, Africans were also conscious of the historical significance of occurring and recurring events. The idea of history was of such paramount importance that every effort was made to preserve it for future generations, although not in a written form. Much of the historical preservation was accomplished through oral tradition. Today oral tradition constitutes an important historical source for the reconstruction of precolonial African history.

The beginning of oral history in Africa can, perhaps, be dated to the origin of African communities themselves. Africans preserved their history via various forms of oral tradition, as verbally communicated histories. The forms include myths and legends, folk tales, poetry, proverbs and riddles, praise songs, praise names, and religious and secular songs. Oral tradition could also be in form of enactment such as ceremonies and rituals. Whatever the form, oral tradition provides historical information about aspects of the history and culture of African peoples. Myths and legends, for example, often contain useful information about the origin of states and communities, the evolution and development of social and political institutions, the nature of religious and economic activities, and diplomatic relations between communities. The validity of traditional history as an authentic source of reconstructing African history is no longer in question. African historians have demonstrated through research that oral tradition can provide accurate historical accounts and when properly handled, can constitute an invaluable source for reconstructing history. Thus, as precolonial African history has shown, a lack of archival tradition does not preclude the existence of history. Oral preservation was ultimately the bedrock of history, and such history transmitted down the generations by word of mouth is no less valid than as if it were written. A great deal of the oral tradition of many African societies has now been reduced to written form by scholars. As will be shown, much of the written historical literature on many African societies owes a great deal to traditional accounts.

The third essential characteristic of precolonial African history is that it had a definite purpose. History was not an abstract concept. It was not a purposeless acquisition of knowledge of past and present events. Rather, history was relevant, having a purpose necessary for the survival of a community's traditions. History primarily served as a socializing agent, playing a vital role in day-to-day living, particularly in the education of the individual. History, therefore, constituted the pivot of the socialization process. It was a means through which every person was educated in the codes of conduct of the society, in the norms, values, and ethics of the culture. It was through the knowledge of history that each community defined itself and its relationship to other communities. History provided the basis for the appreciation and understanding of the institutions of the society, and for the smooth functioning of such institutions.

The "Dark Continent": Eurocentric Conception Of Africa

The conceptual idea of Africa as a continent without civilization or significant historical achievement was principally a by-product of the rise of racist scholarship in Europe. It was essentially a creation of Western thought and a Eurocentric framework of explanation. In the latter half of the nineteenth century and the early twentieth century, pseudo-scientific, racist postulations gained prominence in European thought and defined the black race as inferior. "Scientific racism," supposedly derived from empirical research, depicted people of African race as genetically inferior to Europeans. Lacking an understanding of African ways of life, Europeans saw African culture as backward, lagging behind in the march toward progress which other cultures had already made. Thus, unable to appreciate the complexities of the cultures of Africa which were different from those of Europe, Western thought simply concluded that the continent was still in the dark ages. Hence, Africa was a "dark continent."

The propagation of this racist and negative stereotype of Africa and its peoples was largely the handwork of Europeans who wrote about Africa. Some of these Europeans were travelers, explorers, traders, and missionaries who visited Africa and wrote accounts of their visits and their perception of the continent[1]. But their perception was marred by racial prejudice. They labored to represent the continent as a land of wild animals, and its people as primitive, incapable of building a civilization. This conception of Africa is vividly expressed in Lord Chesterfield's Letter to His Sons, published in 1901. In it, Lord Chesterfield wrote:

---

1. For instance, as a result of his visit to Africa, explorer Henry Morton Stanley wrote Through the Dark Continent, originally published in London in 1899, by G. Newness. The book displayed the typical stereotype of Africa and Africans.

> The Africans are the most ignorant and unpolished people in the world, little better than the lions, tigers, and leopards and other wild beasts, which that country produces in good numbers.[2]

The propagation of the "dark continent" stereotype of Africa was not confined to Europe. It was no less virulent in the racially segregated United States, especially in the south. Popular writings, motion pictures, and of course, racial theories produced by white Americans reinforced this stereotype. American popular literature in the form of books, magazines, journals, pamphlets, and comics, as well as film and stage presentations, constantly propagated the idea of an Africa irreparably lost in barbarism. These constituted the principal avenues by which most Americans form their ideas about Africa.

The pseudo-intellectual basis for the "dark continent" ideology was provided by scholars engaged in supposedly critical discourse on the cultures and peoples of Africa. Historians, anthropologists, and ethnologists produced "scholarly" works that denied the reality of African history, thus lending credence to the idea of a "dark Africa" before its penetration by Europeans. The basis for the denial of an African past by European scholars was the apparent lack of written records in much of the continent. Margery Perham, British political commentator, put this succinctly when she declared that "until the very recent penetration of Europeans the greater part of the continent was without... writing and so without history."[3] In essence, in Western intellectual thought, the period before the advent of Europeans in Africa was prehistoric.

Western scholars not only agreed that African history started at the point of European contact with Africa, they also agreed that such history was that of the white man in the continent. Before the colonial era in Africa, the European conception of African history was nothing more than a catalogue of activities of Europeans in Africa. It was the history of Europeans' travels, hunting expeditions, trade, and missionary activities. Africans were often invisible and were rarely featured within their own history. References to Africans were often derogatory.

Nevertheless, as Africa entered the colonial era the need to write African history that was more focused on the people became apparent. Imperial authorities felt that for colonial policy to succeed, the histories of the indigenous peoples must be known. In Nigeria, for example, colonial administrators such as Lord Lugard and Sir H.R. Palmer urged subordinate officials to compile notes on the history of Nigerian groups. The efforts to commit to writing aspects of the histories of the subject peoples led to the writing by colonial officials of an African history that was at least not entirely preoccupied with European activities.

Although colonial officials were the most prolific of those who wrote about Africa in the colonial period, a number of works were also produced by other proponents of and apologies for colonialism. Even while focusing on African peoples, the premise of colonial historiography was still basically racist and hegemonic. In the colonialist literature, the negative stereotype of Africans was still

2. Quoted in Robin Hallet, The Penetration of Africa: European Enterprise and Exploration Principally in Northern and Western Africa up to 1870, vol. 1 (London: Routledge and Kegan Paul, 1965), 37.

3. Margery Perham, "The British Problem in Africa," Foreign Affairs, July 1951: 638.

very much espoused by European writers. They stressed and romanticized the alleged backwardness of Africa and depicted Africans in horrifying terms. In a description of the people of southern Nigeria, for example, Maurice Bruce referred to them as "superstition-ridden people of the coast" who indulged in the "horrors of human sacrifice and cannibalism."[4]

By propagating a negative image of Africa, the colonialist historiography sought to justify the presence of Europeans in the continent. They argued that it was the dismal situation in Africa that prompted Europeans to embark on a civilizing mission. A British historian, D.G.O. Ayerst, alleged that frequent wars and outrageous slave raiding in Africa were some of the reasons which "made the people of Europe ready to undertake what they regarded as a civilizing mission in Africa."[5] In the same vein, King Leopold of Belgium was said to have been so moved by the terrible condition of the people in Africa that he called a conference at Brussels in 1876 where a charitable international African association was formed with the aim of civilizing and saving the people of the Congo. While purporting to write the history of African peoples, the overriding intention of the colonialist historiography is clear. It was an attempt not only to establish the validity of the European presence in Africa, but also to legitimize the colonial subjugation of the continent. European colonial officials and their imperialist collaborators wrote "African history" in a way that attempted to justify colonialism.

European colonial writing did yield a large volume of works on Africa, especially from colonial officials. Although these works were ostensibly histories of African peoples, they were in reality no more than pseudo-anthropological studies. Indeed, many of these writers still had the pre-conceived idea that a historical study of African peoples could not be undertaken.

Perhaps the most important legacy of the Western idea of Africa articulated in the literature produced from the eighteenth to the twentieth centuries was that it laid an enduring foundation for the sustenance of the "dark continent" ideology. The legacy of this ideology is so profound that it has never totally disappeared. Even at a time when Western historical tradition had begun to accept the validity of authentic African history, the noted British historian, Hugh Trevor-Roper, still held on to the myth of an Africa without history. Trevor-Roper stated in an article published in 1963:

> Perhaps in the future there will be some African history to teach. But at the present there is none; there is only the history of Europeans in Africa. The rest is darkness…and darkness is not the subject of history.[6]

During the public school desegregation fight in the United States in the 1960s, white opponents of school integration borrowed ideas from the racist assumptions of the "dark continent" ideology. Henry Garret, a college professor, expressed his opposition to integration by noting that "over the past 5,000 years, the history of black Africa is blank" and since, in his opinion, Africans did not

---

4. Maurice Bruce, The Shaping of the Modern World, 1870-1939, vol. 1 (London: Hutchinson, 1958), 605.

5. D.G.O. Ayerst, Europe in the Nineteenth Century (Cambridge: Cambridge University Press, 1940), 294.

6. Hugh Trevor-Roper, "The Rise of Christian Europe," The Listener, 28 November, 1963.

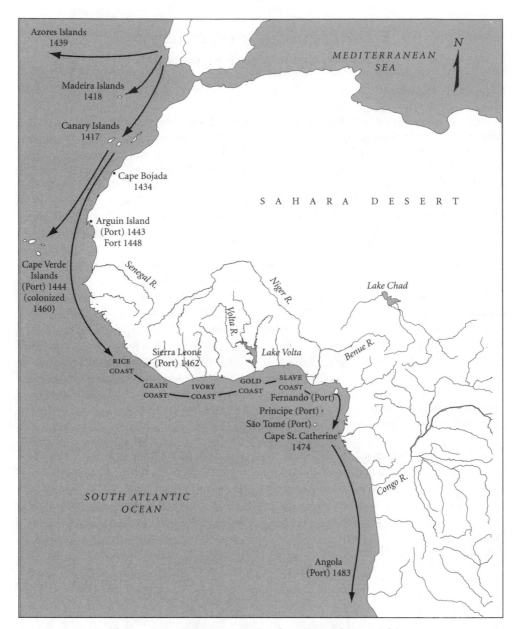

Figure 1-1. Portuguese Exploration of West Africa

contribute to civilization because they "had no written language; no numerals; no calendar or system of measurement," there was no basis for the integration of white and black children.[7] Despite the great strides that have been made in the knowledge of Africa today, the idea of Africa and Africans is still colored by the "dark continent" stereotype.

_____

7. Quoted in Sanford J. Ungar, Africa: The People and Politics of an Emerging Continent (New York: Simon and Schuster, 1989), 23.

The Rise of Africa-Centered Perspectives of History

Local Histories

During the colonial period when Europeans were busy writing their own version of African history, local African historians were writing their own version as well. The distinction between European and African colonial historical literature was obvious, based primarily on the purpose of writing and the perspective adopted. While European writers approached their subject from a framework that is basically Eurocentric, local African historians wrote from the African point of view. In essence, it was African colonial writing that began the tradition of the Africa-centered perspective of history.

It is important to recognize who the local historians were, and their motivation for committing to writing the histories of the indigenous African peoples and societies of which they wrote. The local historians were literate Africans who, during the colonial period, felt the need to write the history of their people.[8] Their medium of expression was not limited to the European languages alone. Apart from English, French, and other European languages, they wrote in Arabic and in various African languages as well. For them, there were two main motives for writing the indigenous histories of their people. First, they wanted to establish the fact that African societies had a vibrant history before the European incursion into the continent. They wanted to prove that these societies were custodians of historical achievements. The local historians were in effect the first to revolt against the Eurocentric idea of an Africa detached from history.

Second, local African historians were inspired to write by patriotic motives. They saw the preservation of the history of their communities as necessary in order to avoid the risk of its being completely forgotten. Writers fired by patriotic motives sought to commit to writing the history and culture of their people that was being threatened by the growing influence of Euro-Christian culture and civilization. This motivation is clearly expressed by Samuel Johnson, an example par excellence of a local African historian. In his History of the Yorubas, a monumental work on the Yoruba of Western Nigeria which was published in 1921, Johnson stated:

> Educated natives of Yoruba were well acquainted with the history of England and with that of Rome and Greece, but of the history of their own country they know nothing. This reproach is one of the author's objects to remove.[9]

The importance of African colonial writing has not often been well appreciated. This is probably because the local writers were not historians trained in the techniques and methods of scholarly study. Indeed, they lacked the techniques

---

8. Notable among them were Samuel Johnson of Nigeria, Carl Reindorf of the Gold Coast (Ghana), James Africanus Horton of Sierra Leone, Apolo Kagwa of Uganda, and Otomba Payne of Nigeria.

9. Samuel Johnson, History of the Yorubas (Lagos: C.M.S., 1921), preface. For a study of Samuel Johnson, see Toyin Falola, ed., Pioneer, Patriot, and Patriarchy: Samuel Johnson and the Yoruba People (Madison: University of Wisconsin-Madison, 1994).

such as the systematic collection of source materials and critical evaluation and interpretation of evidence. In most cases, the works they produced, which were mainly ethnographic, relied heavily and almost exclusively on oral traditions. As a result of their lack of academic training, at least by western standards, the collection and evaluation of oral tradition could hardly pass the test of the rigors of historical scholarship.

Nevertheless, colonial African historiography represented the pioneering effort to achieve an African perspective. Unlike the European writers, who lacked a basic knowledge and understanding of the history and culture of African communities they wrote about, local African historians were very much at home with their subject. Being proficient in the language of the culture of which they wrote, and having a unique relationship with the community, they stood at a better vantage point than their European counterparts. Thus, despite its demerits, colonial African historiography laid the groundwork for authentic African history. Its interpretation of historical events introduced a new approach to the analysis of African history. The pioneering works of the local historians became so valuable that modern academic historians have had to depend on them as a useful source for their more authoritative academic studies. Therefore, in terms of contribution to the development of the study of African history, these local historians were no less important than the academically equipped African historians who were to take over from them the mantle of producing a more Africa-centered history of the continent in the postcolonial period.

Academic Histories

The study of African history entered a new phase in the closing years of the colonial period. By the 1950s, the era of the struggle for independence in Africa, this new phase had begun to take shape. It was an era that saw not only the decolonization of Africa but the decolonization of African history as well. For the first time the study of African history was elevated to a pedestal of intellectual discourse. It became a credible subject of academic pursuit.

What is the basic characteristic of academic historiography? As opposed to popular literature, it is the writing of history based on scholarly research findings. Such history has to be a product of an elaborate methodology that insists on thorough investigation of issues with a view to arriving at a creditable conclusion. Sometimes, this methodology calls for the employment of the tools of other disciplines. The results of research in academic history are disseminated through the publication of books, journals, and monographs.

The development of the scholarly study of African history in the 1950s and 1960s owes a great deal to the establishment of institutions of higher education in many parts of Africa. In West Africa, the University College of Ibadan, (later to become the University of Ibadan), was founded in Nigeria in 1948. In the same year, the University College of the Gold Coast, (which later became the University of Ghana) was established at Legon, Ghana. Both universities paved the way for other institutions in Anglophone West Africa that emerged in the 1960s. These included, in Nigeria, the University of Nigeria at Nsukka (1960), the University of Lagos (1962), and the University of Ife (1961), (renamed Obafemi Awolowo University in 1987). In Francophone West Africa, a higher institution in Senegal became the University of Dakar in 1957 (later renamed Cheikh Anta Diop University). In Cote d'Ivoire, the University of Abidjan was established in 1964. In East Africa, notable early institutions were the University of Nairobi in Kenya, established in 1956, and the University of Dar es Salaam, in Tanzania, founded in 1964. Makerere University in Uganda, originally a technical institution established in 1922, became a full-fledged university in 1970.[10] In these institutions, students received training in the techniques of academic history. Although many of the institutions had no courses in African history during this early era, they still produced some of the leading African historians who were later to champion the academic study of African history. Thus, this small circle of African scholars, some of who had pursued specialized studies leading to doctorate degrees, was to become a formidable force in the creation of academic historiography in Africa.

When these highly trained scholars took faculty positions in African universities, they were confronted by departments of history where the curriculum was still basically Europe-centered. For example, at the University College of Ibadan, an affiliate of the University of London until 1962, students studied mainly European and British history. According to one of the pioneers of academic historiography in Africa, J.F. Ade Ajayi, by November 1950 the only courses available at the university were in British history, European history and the history of the colonization of Africa.[11] The reason for the focus on Europe in the curriculum had to do with the teaching faculty which was dominated by Europeans. Western historical scholarship had not yet fully accepted African history as fit for academic enterprise.

But the nonexistence of African history in the history curriculum of the African universities was always unacceptable to the few African teachers. This small group, therefore, called for a reorientation of the history syllabus in order to truly serve the purpose of the history department in an African university. At Ibadan, this effort was led by Kenneth Dike, who has been described as the "father of modern African historiography."[12] Within a relatively short period, Ibadan had begun to offer courses in African history.

After the curriculum had been transformed with the infusion of courses in African history, the next challenge was the availability of suitable textbooks. African scholars realized that they could not rely on books written by European writers with Eurocentric perspectives to teach African history. They realized that if they were to sustain and effectively teach the new courses in African history there was an urgent need for books written by Africans from African points of view. One of the earliest books to emerge out of this effort was Kenneth Dike's Trade and Politics in the Niger Delta, 1830-1885, published by Oxford University Press in 1956. The publication of this book was an important landmark in the evolution of academic historiography and the development of Africa-centerdness in the writing of African history. The book not only opened the gate for further publications by African scholars, but, more importantly, it demonstrated beyond any doubt the usefulness of local sources in historical research. Oral tradition had

---

10. Fourah Bay College in Sierra Leone, founded by the Church Missionary Society (CMS) in 1827, was the forerunner of these institutions. However, initially it was no more than an institution designed to train the clergy.

11. J.F. Ade Ajayi, "Towards a More Enduring Sense of History: A Tribute to K.O. Dike," Journal of the Historical Society of Nigeria, LXII, nos. 3 & 4 (1984-1985).

12. Ibid.

never been accepted as a valid source of historical reconstruction by European writers, but Dike's work proved this fallacious. The book, in fact, came out of Dike's doctoral dissertation—one of the first dissertations partly based on oral tradition to be accepted by a British University. In a review of the book, the Manchester Guardian concluded that:

> The period has been written on from the British side. Dr. Dike gives a lucid and convincing account of it from the African side...It is an important contribution to commonwealth history, perhaps the most penetrating and mature study so far contributed by an African scholar.[13]

Complementing Dike's book was S.O. Biobaku's The Egba and Their Neighbors, 1842-1872 published in 1957, a year after Dike's. With both books, a solid foundation had been laid for a host of other scholarly works written by African academic historians to follow.[14]

By the mid-1960s, a course of study in African history had been clearly and firmly established in African universities and other tertiary institutions. The study of various aspects of African history from prehistory to modern times was adequately supported by a growing number of textbooks written by African scholars. A number of European Africanist historians including Basil Davidson, Thurstan Shaw, Thomas Hodgkin, J. D. Fage, Michael Crowder, J. D. Omer-Cooper, A. F. C. Ryder, Robin Law, Roland Oliver, and many others also produced highly acclaimed books on African history.

One of the dimensions of the growth of academic study of African history in African institutions was the emergence of various schools of thought such as the Ibadan, Legon, Makerere, and IFAN (Institut Fondamental de l'Afrique Noire) schools. The contributions of these schools to the development of the study of African history cannot be overemphasized. Their primary concern was the development of a scholarly research program in the history and cultures of Africa, and also a data resource collection to aid this program. The Ibadan Historical School, for example, devoted its resources to researching the precolonial and colonial history of Africa in general, and that of Nigeria in particular. It began a program of research leading to monographs—namely the Ibadan Series. An impressive number of scholarly texts came out of this series.[15]

The Legon, Makerere, and IFAN schools also followed the tradition of Ibadan in scholarly research and documentation of African history, and in publishing research findings. The Legon History Series produced outstanding books dealing primarily with precolonial Ghana, but also with various other aspects of African his-

---

13. Quoted in Nigerian Year Book (Lagos: Government Printer, 1959), 111.

14. A good example of such works is J.F. Ade Ajayi, Christian Missions in Nigeria, 1841-1891: The Making of a New Elite (London: Longman, 1965).

15. A few examples of these works include Murray Last, The Sokoto Caliphate (New York: Humanities Press, 1967); Obaro Ikime, Niger Delta Rivalry: Itsekiri-Urhobo Relations and the European Presence, 1884–1936 (New York: Humanities Press, 1969); S.A. Akintoye, Revolution and Power Politics in Yorubaland, 1840–1893 (London: Longman, 1971); R.A. Adeleye, Power and Diplomacy in Northern Nigeria, 1804–1906: The Sokoto Caliphate and its Enemies (London: Longman, 1971); B.O. Oluruntimehin, The Segu Tukulor Empire (London: Longman, 1972); and P.M. Mutibwa, The Malagasy and the Europeans: Madagascar's Foreign Relations, 1861–1895 (London: Longman, 1974).

tory.[16] While the primary attention of the Makerere school was on the history of East Africa, that of IFAN was on Francophone Africa. All these schools of thought devoted their resources to developing research into the history of African peoples.

As a way of enhancing scholarship, African scholars also established professional bodies such as the Historical Society of Nigeria and the Historical Society of Ghana. These associations held annual conferences where scholars came together to present academic papers. The associations also sponsored academic publications which became one of the avenues for scholars to disseminate the results of their researches. For instance, the Historical Society of Nigeria began to publish the Journal of the Historical Society of Nigeria and Tarikh.

Since the 1956 publication of the trail blazing Trade and Politics in the Niger Delta, the volume of works on virtually all periods of African history and all regions of the continent has increased tremendously. It is due to these works that the academic study of African history has been firmly established and its rapid growth ensured. Unlike the ethnographic and superficial analysis of Africa by the early European writers, and the non-critical, story-type accounts of the local chroniclers, the historical scholarship produced from the late 1950s has laid a proper claim to academic history. Its qualification is based on its careful and critical research methodology.

One important product of the tradition of academic history in Africa is that it has given new interpretations to themes treated previously from a Eurocentric perspective. Old themes have been revisited and reinterpreted and new conclusions arrived at. Much of the credit for this revision can be ascribed to a strand of academic historians which emerged in the 1970s. These had a different orientation from their predecessors who were pioneers of academic African history. Many of them, influenced by the radical technique of political economy, adopted a Marxian approach in their analysis of African history. While the early set of scholars succeeded in establishing the validity of the academic study of Africa, the new cadre of African historians revised, redefined, and reinterpreted African history.

The colonial and postcolonial history of Africa has particularly received the attention of revisionism. Political economic historians have argued that to explain colonialism as a progressive theme in African history, as it was characterized by European scholarship, is to trivialize, or fail to see in its totality, the complex nature of the colonial experience. On the contrary, revisionist historians argued that colonialism effectively impoverished Africa while it developed Europe.[17] These scholars have drawn a casual connection between European imperialism and underdevelopment in Africa. Their analysis repudiates the claim of contemporary modernizers that the West is the universal model of modernism; that new states, including emerging African states, must look toward the industrialized nations of the West and borrow their values in order to develop. Rather, the radical African historians have consistently argued that the emerging states possessed the internal dynamics necessary for development. To them, indeed, modernization or development is a product of internal dialectics or class struggle, and is not attainable through the acquisition of foreign values. Scholars of this persuasion, in fact, be-

---

16. An example is M.A. Kwamena-Poh's Government and Politics in the Akuapem State,1730–1850 (London: Longman, 1973).

17. See the series of essays in Toyin Falola, ed., Britain and Nigeria: Exploration or Development? (London: Zed Books, 1987).

lieve that the alliance of some African states with the West is the foundation of their continued underdevelopment.[18]

Afrocentricity

The study of African history received an important boost from outside the continent in the 1960s. While the tradition of academic history was being developed in the continent in the opening years of the 1960s, African Studies as a discipline was beginning to emerge in American colleges and universities. Within this new discipline (sometimes referred to as Black Studies or African-American Studies), African history became an important component.

The impetus for the rise of African Studies was provided by two momentous events of the early 1960s. The emergence of sovereign states in the continent led to a gradual change in perception of the continent by African-Americans who had hitherto held the Eurocentric view of barbaric Africa. The result of the new perception was to engender a renewed interest in the history of the continent.

The U.S. civil rights movement of the 1960s also contributed to the rise of African Studies. Although the movement was principally a struggle for civil rights for Black America, one of its important intellectual legacies was the inclusion of African history and culture in the college curriculum. The demand for civil rights by African-Americans went hand in hand with the insistence that the history of Africa be incorporated into the learning process. Consequently, courses in African history began to be widely offered in colleges across the United States, either taught within an African Studies program, or as a unit of the curriculum in the history department.

In the last thirty years, African Studies as an academic discipline has matured so well in the United States that it has become a leading discipline in academia. Not only has it made tremendous growth quantitatively (going by the number of African Studies programs), it has also made significant qualitative strides. Perhaps more than the proliferation of programs, it is its qualitative growth in terms of the development of theoretical frameworks of analysis that confers legitimacy on it as an academic discourse.

Theory building and the formulation of conceptual frameworks have, indeed, been a part of the development of African Studies. Afrocentrism (sometimes called Afrocentricity) is perhaps the most controversial paradigm for the study of Africa to have come out of the Black intellectual tradition in recent times. This concept, which has gained currency particularly among many Black scholars in the United States, is conceived essentially as a critique of European hegemony in scholarship. Molefi Kete Asante, the leading scholar of the Afrocentric paradigm, states that "my work has increasingly constituted a radical critique of the Eurocentric ideology that masquerades as a universal view."[19]

The hegemonic character of the Eurocentric mode of explanation, Afrocentric scholars contend, is necessarily detrimental to the study of the history of Africa,

---

18. One of the greatest apostles of this idea was the Guyanese historian, Walter Rodney. See his How Europe Underdeveloped Africa (Washington, D.C.: Howard University Press, 1097), 6.

19. Molefi Kete Asante, The Afrocentric Idea (Philadelphia: Temple University Press, 1997), 6.

and that of its diaspora. Within the Eurocentric tradition, Afrocentrists argue that the black historical experience is presented as a by-product of European culture and therefore tangential to the historical process. The effect of this is that Africans and peoples of African descent are precluded from having a sense of the historicity of the African experience, and of the contributions of blacks to human civilization.

What is the theoretical grounding of the Afrocentric theory as a paradigm for historical inquiry? The Afrocentric method of history, as conceptualized by its main proponents, is predicated on a central theoretical assumption. This is that, for a historical analysis of the African world to be meaningful and valid, it must begin with Africa as the core of discourse. In other words, Afrocentrism places Africa at the nucleus of any scholarly exposition of African history. In the Afrocentric philosophy, such exposition must derive its intellectual foundation from ancient Egypt, believed to be the first human civilization to attain greatness. Ancient Egypt, (or Kemet as is frequently referred to by Afrocentrists), thus becomes for Afrocentric scholars a classical reference point for the study of Africa. One Afrocentric historian, Tsehloane Keto, articulates this when he argues that "an Africa centered perspective of history cannot be sustained without its connection to the African culture of Ancient Egypt."[20]

The claim of ancient Egypt as a classical reference point for African history is not entirely new. It was Cheikh Anta Diop, the Senegalese historian and Egyptologist often regarded by Afrocentrists as their "intellectual ancestor," who first laid the groundwork for reclaiming ancient Egypt for Africa. Diop's major work, The African Origin of Civilization, is devoted to proving that the "ancient Egyptians were Negroes," and that "ancient Egypt was a Negro civilization."[21] This is a teaching that contradicts the popular wisdom of Western scholarship. But to Diop, the making of the ancient Egyptian civilization was the work of Africans. It is thus appropriate and necessary to connect African history with ancient Egypt. Diop argues:

> The history of Black Africa will remain suspended in air and cannot be written correctly until African historians dare to connect it with the history of Egypt...it will be impossible to build African humanities, a body of African human sciences, so long as that relationship does not appear legitimate.[22]

Afrocentrism, as a theoretical contribution to the historiography of African history, has not escaped virulent criticism. The bone of contention does not appear to be the philosophical foundation of the paradigm. Not many critics would quarrel with an approach which insists that the study of Africa must be carried on within a perspective that places the continent at the center stage of analysis. Indeed, to many scholars there is nothing particularly new about this call for centeredness in the study of Africa. Much of the scholarship about Africa since the 1960s is considered Africa-centered in perspective.

---

20. See Tsheloane Keto, The Africa-Centered Perspective on History (Blackwood: K.A. Publications, 1989), 23.

21. Cheikh Anta Diop, The African Origin of Civilization: Myth and Reality (New York: Lawrence Hill, 1974), xiv.

22. Ibid., xiv.

The controversy over Afrocentric history rather has to do with methods and claims. Afrocentrists have stressed the primacy of classical Egypt in the study of Africa. The utility of this is that the linkage with ancient Egypt provides intellectual muscle to African studies the way classical Greece provides an inspiration to scholarship about Europe. However, there has never been a consensus among scholars of antiquity that ancient Egypt was an authentically Black African civilization as claimed by Afrocentrists. At best, some scholars have contended that ancient Egypt was a racially mixed culture, and that the Egyptians themselves were not racially conscious as modern society is.[23]

There are other Afrocentric claims about Ancient Egypt that irk opponents of the theory. Afrocentrists posit that the source of Egyptian culture can be located somewhere further south of Egypt, in Black Africa. As well as this, a dimension of Diop's thesis, to which many Afrocentrists also subscribe, is that classical Greece is a product of ancient Egypt. In other words, Egypt was the mother of the ancient Greek culture, the progenitor of European civilization. Therefore, by implication, Europe owes its civilization to Africa. Diop craftily points this out when he asserts that "instead of presenting itself to history as an insolvent debtor [the] black world is the very initiator of the western civilization."[24]

The thesis of the Afrocentric scholars about ancient Egypt received a great boost with the publication of Martin Bernal's Black Athena.[25] Bernal, a Cornell professor of government, offers strong evidence of ancient Egypt's influence on ancient Greek civilization. Bernal argues that Eurocentric writers have over the centuries, deliberately left such evidence unacknowledged in classical studies. However, while most scholars of the classical world would agree that ancient Egypt did influence classical Greece, they would contend that such influence was minimal, that it was not fundamental to the building of Greek civilization.[26] Others would argue that both Egypt and Greece had mutual influences on each other; that it was not a case of one-way traffic whereby the Greeks wholly obtained or "stole" their art, philosophy, religion, and science from the Egyptians.

The rebuttal of the Afrocentric interpretation of history, in the final analysis, rests squarely on what many critics regard as its subjective claims. These, they note, are reflected not only in the fundamental Afrocentric claim about ancient Egypt, but also in other hypotheses. One of the basic claims of Afrocentrism which critics regard as historically baseless is the assertion of the presence of Africans in the American continent before Christopher Columbus. Again, Diop appears to be one of the first scholars to express these "possibilities of pre-Columbian relations between Africa and America."[27] But Ivan Van Sertima, a Rutgers' scholar and an authority on African civilizations, has been at the forefront of this subject. In 1976, Ivan Van Sertima published They Came Before

---

23. See for example, Mary Lefkowitz, Not Out of Africa: How Afrocentrism Became an Excuse to Teach Myth as History (New York: Basic Books, 1996).

24. Diop, African Origin, xiv. See also Asante's works, Afrocentricity (Trenton: Africa World Press, 1988), 38-39; and Kemet, Afrocentricity, and Knowledge (Trenton: Africa World Press, 1990).

25. Martin Bernal, Black Athena: The Afroasiatic Roots of Classical Civilization: The Fabrication of Ancient Greece, 1785–1985 (New Brunswick: Rutgers University Press, 1987).

26. This idea is also articulated in Lefkowwitz's Not Out of Africa.

27. Diop, African Origin, xvii.

Columbus: The African Presence in America, in which he forcefully argues the black presence in America prior to Columbus' voyage. He finds evidence in "practically every field of study" including botanical, linguistic, cartographic, oceanographic, skeletal, epigraphic, and also eyewitness accounts.[28] Many Afrocentric scholars accept Ivan Van Sertima's postulation of a black presence in the Americas before Columbus.[29] However, this theory has not been widely accepted among students of American history.

For critics of Afrocentrism, the central element of critique is the question of intellectual objectivity. To many, the Afrocentric project is manipulative of history, ideologically motivated, and designed to serve a political end. Many scholars have accused Afrocentrists of creating "myth as history," in order to realize a political agenda of replacing the white superiority doctrine with a black model. One critic, Diane Ravitch of Teachers College, Columbia, concludes that "Afrocentrism intends to replace the discredited white supremacy of the past with its equally disreputable theory of African supremacy."[30]

Despite the criticism of Afrocentrism, it has become a formidable presence in the historiography of Africa and the diaspora. It is making a great impact on the academic environment, particularly in African-American intellectual circles. Indeed, an increasing number of black scholars continue to regard Afrocentrism as the way toward the rescue of African and African-American Studies from peripheralization. Leading scholars of the Afrocentric theory spare no effort to correct what they regard as the misconceptions of their critics. They argue that there is nothing ethnocentric or hegemonic about the Afrocentric model. Asante concludes that "it does not valorize the African view while downgrading others."[31]

Conclusion

The history of the idea of Africa was shaped by misconceived European thought. Unfortunately, this thought, the "dark continent" conception, dominated the terrain of scholarship for a long time. It has, nevertheless, been exploded by almost half a century of historical writing about Africa. Today African history is known not to be a recent phenomenon which originated with the coming of the Europeans to the continent. The historical consciousness and recognition of the functional purpose of history clearly evident in Africa prior to European contact have been acknowledged. African history is as old as African communities and peoples.

The writings on African history produced in the last half century have ensured that no longer will the African past be treated as a unit of European explo-

---

28. See Ivan Van Sertima, "African Science Before the Birth of the 'New World'," The Black Collegian, January-February 1992: 70-71.

29. See for example, Molefi Kete Asante, "Toward an Afrocentric University," Africa and the World, no. 1s (1988): 49.

30. Diane Ravitch, "Multiculturalism: An Exchange," The American Scholar 60 (1991): 267. Also expressing the same idea is Arthur Schlessinger's The Disuniting of America (New York: Norton, 1992).

31. Molefi Kete Asante, "Multiculturalism: An Exchange," The American Scholar 60 (1991): 270.

which are one of the most basic elements of geography, are one example of the in-accurate views of Africa. The traditional Mercator map, made by a sixteenth-cen-tury European and still popular, portrays the continents of the Northern Hemi-sphere as far larger than they actually are, relative to Africa and South America. The accurate Peters Projection map shows the true size of Africa relative to the European nations which colonized it, and a direct comparison of the two maps indicates one of the ethnocentric views that continues to be passed on.[2]

The common perception that Africa really means sub-Saharan Black Africa is a second example of a way of thinking about African geography that is shaped by colonialism and ethnocentrism. Geographers and historians frequently categorize North Africa as part of the Middle East rather than Africa, and when students are taught about ancient Egypt, this great culture is rarely presented as an African achievement. The argument traditionally made by European scholars is that the Sa-hara Desert cut the Mediterranean coast off from the rest of Africa, and that North Africa's cultural achievements have nothing to do with sub-Saharan Africa. In this argument, Egypt and the Middle East are linked with Asia and Europe, and Africa's ancient historical connections to the Mediterranean world are denied. From a strictly geographical point of view, the idea that North Africa should be considered part of the Middle East is absurd, but the practice continues. A system of racial clas-sifications underlies this idea, as the assertion that North Africa was part of the Middle East allowed Europeans to see Africa as the land of the Blacks, while the Middle East was the home of the Arabs. Africa is now home to people of all races, but the legacies of racial classifications and colonialist ideas persist.[3]

Americans and Europeans often hold skewed ideas of the African landscape, as their visual images represent extreme situations rather than typical scenes. Many people equate Africa's geography with images of tropical jungles taken from Tarzan movies or National Geographic specials on wildlife. A more recent visual image of Africa comes from television news footage of hungry drought vic-tims in arid landscapes like Ethiopia and Somalia. These two contrasting images do exist in reality, but they are not typical of the landscapes that Africans experi-ence. Less than one-fifth of Africa is rain forest, as these wet, tropical environ-ments are only found near the equator in the low river basins of West and Central Africa, and few people live there. Huge areas of Africa are indeed desert, but they are sparsely inhabited. The majority of Africans live not in rain forest or desert but in savanna regions, the grassland plains that stretch across great expanses of the continent. The semiarid areas where savannas border deserts can, in times of drought, fail to provide sustenance for their residents, as in the recent tragedies in the Horn of Africa. The largest of the semidesert regions is called the sahel, and it forms a belt of semiarid land that runs south of the Sahara from West Africa to the Red Sea. With adequate rain, the savannas can support an abundance of life, including the elephants, zebras, lions, and giraffes which make African wildlife parks into famous tourist destinations.[4]

2. Ali A. Mazrui, The Africans: A Triple Heritage (Boston: Little, Brown and Company, 1986), 23-24, 30-31; Roland Oliver and J.D. Fage, A Short History of Africa, 6th ed. (New York: Penguin Books, 1990), 1-2.

3. Mazrui, The Africans, 12-16, 23-38.

4. Joel Samoff, "Triumphalism, Tarzan, and Other Influences: Teaching About Africa in the 1990s," in Patricia Alden, et al., African Studies and the Undergraduate Curriculum

The grasslands of national parks such as the Serengeti offer a more accurate view of Africa's dominant natural environment than do rain forests and deserts, but something central is missing. These savanna regions are usually presented to people outside Africa as the home of animals rather than people. Americans and Europeans rarely see typical African village landscapes or images of the farmers, cattle herders, and townspeople who make up most of Africa's population. It is even more uncommon for Africa's large towns and cities to be represented to non-Africans. Instead, African geography is presented for its natural beauty or for its extreme conditions. When African people are covered in the media, the stories usually involve natural disasters such as drought, or major political or military conflicts. This chapter seeks to give a more balanced view of Africa and Africans, describing both everyday landscapes and extreme conditions.[5]

The richness and beauty of African landscapes and wildlife is undeniable, and the continent possesses geographic marvels that are unsurpassed anywhere on earth. Africa is home to the Nile, the world's longest river, and the Sahara Desert, the largest hot, arid region on earth. It is indeed a continent of great extremes, where ice-capped mountains straddle the equator, only hours away from tropical beaches and scorching deserts. The diversity of African landscapes, ranging from the Congo's rain forests to the Sahara Desert, and from snowy Mount Kilimanjaro to the vast Serengeti plains, is truly remarkable. All of these dramatic contrasts make Africa a place of ecological treasures, but it is at the same time a landscape characterized by life and death struggles. The dramatic extremes of drought and flood or heat and cold can be deadly to both animals and humans.[6]

Africa's people have met these environmental challenges through a wide variety of adaptations and innovations. The ecological adjustments to the landscape can be traced all the way back to the origins of the human species. Archaeologists believe that human beings took their first steps on the savannas of East Africa, well over one million years ago, and learned to survive by hunting and gathering. Human society was revolutionized over seven thousand years ago when food production began. The domestication of livestock and the development of agriculture probably first occurred in the Middle East, but both innovations soon spread to northern Africa and then further south. This revolution led to perhaps the most remarkable of all ancient civilizations, the Egyptian kingdoms that lasted nearly three thousand years. Northern Africa's Nile Valley was the setting for these Egyptian dynasties, and the great cultural achievements of this complex urban civilization were supported by farmlands irrigated by the Nile's waters.[7]

(Boulder: Lynne Rienner Publishers, 1994), 35-80; James L. Newman, *The Peopling of Africa: A Geographic Interpretation* (New Haven: Yale University Press, 1995), 119-120, 137, 202-205; Mazrui, *The Africans*, 41-61; Fred Burke, *Africa: World Regional Studies* (Boston: Houghton Mifflin Company, 1991), 1-10; Louise Crane, et al., *Africa: History, Culture, Geography* (Englewood Cliffs, N.J.: Globe Book Company, 1989), 26-29, 204-205, 246, 263.

    5. Douglas H. Johnson and David M. Anderson, eds., *The Ecology of Survival: Case Studies from Northeast African History* (Boulder: Westview Press, 1988), 1-24; Samoff, "Triumphalism, Tarzan, and Other Influences," in Alden, et al., *African Studies and the Undergraduate Curriculum*, 35-80; Crane, et al., *Africa: History, Culture, Geography*, 26-29, 41-47, 246, 263; Burke, *Africa: World Regional Studies*, 1-10.

    6. Iliffe, *Africans*, 1-5; Newman, *The Peopling of Africa*, 202-205; Mazrui, *The Africans*, 41-61; Crane, et al., *Africa: History, Culture, Geography*, 1-19.

est regions, rain's leaching of nutrients from the soil means that farmland only lasts for a few years, and then new forest areas must be cleared to replace the exhausted soil. Barriers such as deserts complicate the movements of pastoralists and farmers, especially since the Sahara stretches across the entire continent. Nomadic groups often inhabit the borders of Africa's climate and vegetation zones, with many people living on the margins of productive land, hoping that the rains will not fail.[23]

Africa also faces a separate set of ecological challenges that are only indirectly related to the central problems of water, aridity, and poor soil. In addition to being an unpredictable and challenging landscape in terms of climate, the African landscape is also home to a variety of debilitating diseases. The emerging field of environmental history, which combines human and biological history, has revealed the profound impact that diseases and micro-organisms can have on human populations.[24] Certain insects can also bring pestilence to the land, and locusts are a serious problem in North Africa and the Horn. Diseases are more common in tropical areas than deserts, however, and West and Central Africa's coastal regions are perfect sites in which micro-organisms can thrive. These humid, tropical, low-lying areas are home to diseases such as malaria, yellow fever, bilharzia, and river blindness. Tropical illnesses like river blindness can force whole communities to completely abandon potentially productive river basins. Insect vectors carry many of Africa's most widespread diseases, including malaria and sleeping sickness. Malaria is a problem across the width of Africa between the tropics, and it is a chronic disease for many Africans. Sleeping sickness, carried by the tsetse fly, affects people in forest regions, and it too can render large areas unfit for habitation. Rinderpest, a related fly-borne disease that attacks cattle, also significantly limits the regions that can be used for livestock herding. All of these diseases limit the productivity of African peoples, and better health care, water, and sanitation systems are needed to reduce the adverse impact of these environmental problems. These diseases are not visible on maps, but they are another important element in forming the ecological complexity and diversity of the African continent.[25]

---

23. Mazrui, *The Africans*, 63-76; Burke, *Africa: World Regional Studies*, 14-19, 29-31; Crane, et al., *Africa: History, Culture, Geography*, 41-43.

24. For an introduction to environmental history, see William Cronon, "The Uses of Environmental History," *Environmental History Review*, volume 17, Fall 1993; Beinart and Coates, *Environment and History*, 1-13; Crosby, *The Columbian Exchange* and *Ecological Imperialism*, 1-7. On Africa's environmental history, see Gregory Maddox, James L. Giblin, and Isaria N. Kimambo, eds., *Custodians of the Land: Ecology and Culture in the History of Tanzania* (Athens: Ohio University Press, 1996); Douglas H. Johnson and David M. Anderson, eds., *The Ecology of Survival: Case Studies from Northeast African History* (Boulder: Westview Press, 1988); James L. Webb, *Desert Frontier: Ecological and Economic Changes alongthe Western Sahel, 1600-1850* (Madison: University of Wisconsin Press, 1995); and George E. Brooks, *Landlords and Strangers: Ecology, Society, and Trade in Western Africa, 1000-1630* (Boulder: Westview Press, 1993).

25. John Ford, *The Role of the Trypanosomiases in African Ecology: A Study of the Tsetse Fly Problem* (Oxford: Clarendon Press, 1971), 1-11, 86-90, 493-496; Maddox, Giblin, and Kimambo, eds., *Custodians of the Land*, 127-148; Iliffe, *Africans*, 1-5, 65-69; Crosby, *Ecological Imperialism*, 132-144; Griffiths, *An Atlas of African Affairs*, 22-25; Newman, *The Peopling of Africa*, 119-120; Crane, et al., *Africa: History, Culture, Geography*, 17-19.

The Peoples of Africa: Innovation and Adaptation

Birthplace of Humanity

The diverse and challenging geography of Africa has shaped the human species that first evolved on that continent in very significant ways. All of humanity shares a common genetic identity that was formed on African soil, so the earliest adaptations of our prehistoric ancestors are a part of all human beings. Many of the most crucial adaptations and innovations in human history were responses made to Africa's environmental conditions. Our earliest ancestors faced· severe challenges on the African landscape several million years ago, particularly from predators such as lions, leopards, and hyenas. These predators were faster, stronger, and better equipped to kill, but the early hominids evolved in unique ways to meet these challenges. Bipedal locomotion freed the forelimbs for carrying objects and eventually for the use of tools and fire, while the need for group co-operation led to the critical developments of language and culture.[26]

African prehistory and the story of human evolution will be discussed in detail in the next chapter, but it is important to understand the links between Africa's geography and early human history. Scientists believe that the earliest hominids originated in eastern Africa, splitting off from apes and chimpanzees perhaps as late as five million years ago. Archaeologists have studied two to four million-year-old australopithecine fossils from eastern African sites ranging from Ethiopia to South Africa. The greatest concentration of remains come from present-day Kenya and Tanzania, and a number of experts have suggested that the ecologically diverse geography of the East African Rift Valley region was a stimulus for the evolution process. These early foragers and scavengers needed to be near sources of water, and the region is filled with lakes, which also contained fish and attracted wildlife. The broad savannas encouraged bipedal movement, as standing upright enabled early hominids to see farther and travel more quickly. A wide variety of plant, fish, and animal foods were also available in the extremely varied region of savannas, mountain rain forests, and lakes.[27]

Other hominids classified within the genus *Homo* overlapped with the australopithecines in the rich East African environment that has been called the cradle of humanity. *Homo habilis* and the later and more successful *Homo erectus* appear to have also originally inhabited this Rift Valley region beginning roughly two million years ago. The increased intelligence linked to the larger brain of *Homo erectus* was probably the key to making possible the expansion of the human geographic range beyond eastern Africa. *Homo erectus* was able to move northward into North Africa and Europe and eastward into Asia, in part because the Sahara was significantly greener than it is today, and the Nile offered a route to the Mediterranean and the Arabian peninsula even in dry periods. The dates of these movements are still uncertain, as is the transition from *Homo erectus* to

---

26. Oliver and Fage, *A Short History of Africa*, 1-9; Newman, *The Peopling of Africa*, 11-21.

27. Newman, *The Peopling of Africa*, 11-21, 202-203; Oliver and Fage, *A Short History of Africa*, 1-9.

Figure 2-4. A Goods Train on the Side of the Rift Valley in Kenya

Homo sapiens, but scientists are in agreement that eastern Africa was the site of the birth of humanity and the beginnings of human culture.[28]

Birthplace of Civilization

Africa was also the site of the world's first great civilization, but a huge span of time came between the adaptations of Rift Valley hominids and the civilization of Egypt. During the million-year period commonly called the Stone Age, the diverse environments of the African continent were slowly populated. Stone tools are the best sources of information that archeologists have about the gradual evolution of human culture during this time span. Old Stone Age sites can be found from Africa's Mediterranean coast to the Cape of Good Hope, but they are clustered around water sources in savanna and open woodland areas. Hunting and tool-making techniques improved slowly through the Middle Stone Age, and by the Late Stone Age, human economies were increasingly specialized to specific ecological conditions. Humans gradually adapted to mountain, woodland, and desert-edge environments, and learned to fish and to exploit specific wild plants and animals.[29]

The next great leap in human evolution and environmental adaptation was the domestication of plants and animals. Fishing may well have brought communities together into fixed sites earlier than farming, but agriculture truly transformed human culture. The agricultural revolution led to significantly higher pop-

28. Newman, *The Peopling of Africa*, 14-21; Oliver and Fage, *A Short History of Africa*, 1-9.

29. Newman, *The Peopling of Africa*, 22-39, 202-203; Oliver and Fage, *A Short History of Africa*, 1-9.

ulations and greater cultural development, but it was a gradual process. Most experts believe that agriculture developed first in southwestern Asia, and spread to northern Africa by cultural diffusion. Clear evidence of farming has been found near the Nile in Egypt from approximately seven thousand years ago, and in Ethiopia from about five thousand years ago. Wheat and barley were cultivated at the early Egyptian sites, which also had domesticated animals including cattle, sheep, and goats. These crops and livestock were the same species as those used in southwestern Asia, but Africans soon began domesticating indigenous plants and animals. The earliest Ethiopian sites were settings for the domestication of finger millet and teff, grains which are still important in Africa, and northern Africans also domesticated indigenous African cattle.[30]

Agriculture led to population increases, larger sedentary settlements, and the need for more organized cultural institutions. The achievements of the ancient Egyptians are the world's greatest example of the impact of agriculture on human society. Egypt's Nile Valley communities were unified approximately five thousand years ago, and the rule of the pharaohs lasted an incredible three thousand years. The stability and wealth of the Egyptian dynasties depended on the water and fertile silt of the Nile River, and the great monuments of this society are still standing, preserved by their solidity and the arid climate. Egyptians learned to control the Nile's annual floods, and their irrigation systems enabled them to harvest multiple crops. Egypt's cultural achievements were stunning, as the society's cities, economy, religion, government, and arts reached remarkable heights.[31]

Egypt was uniquely blessed with the Nile River, but similar cultural developments soon followed on a smaller scale in other regions. Complex civilizations such as Aksum and Kush emerged in Nubia, closer to the sources of the Nile. Agriculture and sophisticated societies also developed in West Africa, where sorghum, bulrush millet, and local rice and yams were first domesticated. River valleys were again crucial, as the Senegal and Niger Rivers in particular supplied the settings for large agricultural communities. The combination of agriculture and trade eventually led to the Nok, Ghana, Mali, and Songhai civilizations of West Africa. Egypt and all of these other early African kingdoms will be discussed in greater detail in later chapters, but it is important to note their common themes of river valley agriculture and ecological adaptation.[32]

Hunters, Pastoralists, and Farmers

The domestication of plants and animals revolutionized human culture, but many regions of Africa never developed the complex urban civilizations that were built primarily upon the base of irrigated agriculture in river valleys. The majority of the African continent simply does not possess sufficient water or fertile soil to support such societies. Africans have always had to adapt to the limits of their local environments, and in most regions less-centralized societies were the norm.

---

30. Iliffe, *Africans*, 12-17; Newman, *The Peopling of Africa*, 31-38, 203-204; Oliver and Fage, *A Short History of Africa*, 10-20.

31. Iliffe, *Africans*, 18-26; Mazrui, *The Africans*, 41-49; Newman, *The Peopling of Africa*, 40-45, 202-205; Oliver and Fage, *A Short History of Africa*, 21-26.

32. Newman, *The Peopling of Africa*, 40-49, 54-59; Iliffe, *Africans*, 26-36; Oliver and Fage, *A Short History of Africa*, 24-30; Burke, *Africa: World Regional Studies*, 35-50, 67-90.

ships took young Africans and their productive labor away from the African continent forever.[43]

Colonial Africa

The entire colonial history of Africa was defined by these same exploitative economic systems in which outsiders gained control of Africa's peoples and natural resources. European nations occupied African regions and restructured the relationships between African peoples and their natural environment. Africans had skillfully adapted their lifestyles to the challenging landscape so that they could make a living in almost any environment, but this fragile ecological balance was shattered by the impact of the Atlantic slave trade and then by European colonial rule. The slave trade, carried out in order to supply Europe's American colonies with cheap labor, destroyed existing systems of international trade in Africa. The African continent was stripped of millions of potentially productive people, and the goods received in exchange were usually guns, alcohol, and cheap manufactured goods. None of the European products were of significant value, and the slave trade and its guns brought greatly increased warfare to Africa's coast and interior. Societies that once co-operated were swept into hostile relations. For some African societies, the best way to maintain power amidst the constant slave raids was to participate in this process, and these groups often became economically dependent on the slave trade.[44]

After the trans-Atlantic slave trade ended in the mid-nineteenth century, European colonial powers began occupying extensive regions of Africa. At first these European nations sought to control strategic points or economically desirable areas, but by the 1880s their imperial rivalries led to their division of the entire continent. England and France claimed the largest sections, but Portugal, Germany, Belgium, and Italy also rushed into Africa. The geographic boundaries of today's African nations often follow the boundaries decided by European rulers during this "scramble for Africa." These artificial boundaries are one of the most troublesome problems for independent Africa, as the almost randomly drawn lines divide many ethnic groups that wish to be united. Europeans justified their occupation of Africa with claims that they were bringing civilization and Christianity and ending the continent's warfare, but in fact they were there to exploit the continent's diverse ecological resources. The main motive of the colonial powers was economic gain, as they sought raw materials and markets for their own industrial goods.[45]

Some of the commodities that Europeans sought, such as gold, had long been part of African trade patterns, but other products were new and altered the African landscape. The Europeans took over control of African regions and economies. They used force when they met resistance, and they did not seek to

---

43. Newman, *The Peopling of Africa*, 109-116, 177-192, 203-205; Mazrui, *The Africans*, 159-177; Iliffe, *Africans*, 49-55, 81-85, 118-120.

44. Mazrui, *The Africans*, 99-113, 149-177; Newman, *The Peopling of Africa*, 149-157; Iliffe, *Africans*, 127-158.

45. Iliffe, *Africans*, 187-211; Griffiths, *An Atlas of African Affairs*, 64-69; Mazrui, *The Africans*, 99-113; Davidson, *Modern Africa*, 260-269.

balance their use of the natural environment or to meet the interests of the African population. European nations required Africans in cool highland locations to begin harvesting cocoa, coffee, and tea, often demanding that all the best agricultural areas be used for these luxury export crops. Rubber and palm oil became important raw materials for European industry, and these products also took precedence over food production. Forest landscapes were dramatically changed, as rubber plantations, hardwood timber harvesting, and agricultural clearing all increased rapidly. Europeans desired ivory and relished the adventure of hunting African game to such an extent that they greatly reduced wildlife populations, and societies that depended on hunting suffered.[46]

These massive colonial intrusions into the carefully balanced relationships between Africans and their environment frequently had devastating effects on African people as well as on the continent itself. Belgian King Leopold's reign of terror ravaged the people of the Congo, as hundreds of thousands died working on rubber plantations without being allowed to grow food. The British were not as cold and brutal as Leopold, but their advances into East Africa also set off devastating ecological crises. It is believed that Europeans were unintentionally responsible for the appalling rinderpest and smallpox epidemics that swept through Maasai and other pastoralist communities in the 1880s, killing 90 percent of the cattle and perhaps half of the people in some areas. Local disease control broke down in many regions occupied by colonial powers. Africans were pushed or ordered into disease-ridden areas, and the time-proven African methods of dealing with illnesses such as sleeping sickness were rejected by colonial authorities who believed that they understood Africa's ecology better than Africans did.[47]

Independent Africa

African nations began winning their independence from colonial rule in the 1950s, and this process continued across four decades, culminating in the fall of South Africa's apartheid system in the 1990s. The independent nations are thus still in their infancy, but it is important to understand how the relationships between Africans and the natural environment have changed with this critical political shift. Unfortunately, an examination of the economies of different African regions suggests that African peoples have not yet been able to gain control of Africa's natural resources and end the exploitation of their continent by outsiders. Ecological relationships have not remained static, but important colonial patterns persist, as luxury crops like coffee, tea, and cocoa are still grown for export on much of the continent's best farmland. The beneficiaries of Africa's natural and human resources are no longer European kings, but international corporations and small African elites have assumed a similar role. The wealth from South Africa's gold and diamond mines, Nigeria's oil wells, and Congo's copper mines has flowed out of Africa, enriching American, European, and White South African corporations and their investors. These neo-colonial systems have al-

---

46. Iliffe, *Africans*, 202-208; Mazrui, *The Africans*, 159-177; Burke, *Africa: World Regional Studies*, 179-193.

47. Johnson and Anderson, eds., *The Ecology of Survival*, 47-112; Iliffe, *Africans*, 203-204, 208-211; Mazrui, *The Africans*, 159-160; Burke, *Africa: World Regional Studies*, 193.

tion growth, economic competition, or the use of their land for export crops, and these border areas are ecologically vulnerable. Africa faces many difficult choices, as export crops and wildlife parks for tourists bring in important foreign currency for development, but these uses of the land also reduce the land available for food production. Africa's land use policies need to be carefully managed, and any changes made must be ecologically sustainable. Africa needs more food, more industry, more infrastructure, and more education; and greater unity and stability are required to successfully face these challenges.[51]

The recent end of the Cold War suggests greater hope for peace and unity in Africa, as does the achievement of democracy in South Africa. Now that South Africa's efforts to destabilize neighboring nations have ended, and the superpowers are no longer building up the military forces of African nations to use these countries as Cold War pawns, African nations may be able to work together to solve mutual problems. However, some African peoples are still divided by ethnic tensions, which have caused terrible conflicts in areas such as Sudan and Rwanda. Ethnic conflict is certainly not unique for Africa, as it has erupted in Eastern Europe recently, and some experts view these African wars as the legacy of colonial Europe's divide-and-conquer strategies. The ethnic tensions between Rwanda's Hutu and Tutsi peoples, for example, are largely due to colonial policies that placed the minority Tutsi above the Hutu. Similarly, Sudan's ongoing civil wars are the result of arbitrary colonial boundaries, which forced very different peoples and ecological regions into one huge nation. It is important to note that Africa's most serious famines have been directly related to ethnic warfare in Sudan, Somalia, and Ethiopia, as war interrupts food production and distribution. If these ethnic tensions can be reduced as time heals the scars of colonialism, Africa will have made great strides towards peace, unity, and the reduction of famine.[52]

Africa's ecological and economic problems are extremely challenging, but Africans have a long history of surviving harsh conditions. The history of African peoples and the African continent is an incredible story of environmental adaptation and innovation. As we move beyond the year 2000, it should be recognized that Africans built long-lasting, rich, and complex societies in difficult environments over five thousand years ago. Viewed on this scale, the colonial occupation of Africa was only a brief interruption in a long period of African sovereignty over the continent. European colonial powers defeated and replaced most of the indigenous peoples of North America, South America, and Australia, but Africans withstood the colonial invasions and returned to rule their continent. African nations might be seen as both the youngest and the oldest human societies on earth, and these newly independent nations need time to implement the wisdom that is part of their rich cultural heritage.[53]

---

51. Beinart and Coates, *Environment and History*, 72-90; Mazrui, *The Africans*, 201-237; Davidson, *Modern Africa*, 218-245; Iliffe, *Africans*, 243-270; Griffiths, *An Atlas of African Affairs*, 152-157; Crane, et al., *Africa: History, Culture, Geography*, 17-19, 41-47, 246-252.

52. Mazrui, *The Africans*, 107-113, 261-293; Davidson, *Modern Africa*, 246-278; Beinart and Coates, *Environment and History*, 98-111; Burke, *Africa: World Regional Studies*, 115-116, 261-265; Crane, et al., *Africa: History, Culture, Geography*, 252-255.

53. Crosby, *Ecological Imperialism*, 132-144; Iliffe, *Africans*, 1-5; Mazrui, *The Africans*, 11-21; Maddox, Giblin, and Kimambo, eds., *Custodians of the Land*, 1-6; Davidson, *Modern Africa*, 260-270; Oliver and Fage, *A Short History of Africa*, 1-2.

Efforts by non-Africans to solve the continent's development problems have usually failed, and it appears that it is time for African solutions. There are several elements within the African cultural heritage that suggest hope for success. Africa has undergone ecological and social decline while the belief systems of colonial powers determined the relationships between people and the land, but these exploitative, accumulationist beliefs can be rejected. Africans can achieve greater unity, peace, and stability if they move away from the competitive Western ideologies of racism and nationalism, and return to the more fluid and inclusive African concepts of ethnicity and group identity. Africans need unity and balance with the environment as much as unity between peoples, and there are also cultural traditions that support this goal. Religious and cultural beliefs across the African continent share the concept that humans and religious spirits are not separate from the land. This holistic approach to the relationship between people and the environment is very different from the Western ethos that supports maximizing environmental exploitation. The African belief in the unity of humans and the environment can be a cornerstone in developing economic and ecological practices that are sustainable and are for the benefit of Africans. Regaining a balanced relationship between Africans and the African continent is a great challenge, but the peoples of Africa have shown their ability to adapt time and time again.[54]

Review Questions

1. In what ways does the geological history of the African continent's formation continue to shape life in Africa? What role has the Great Rift Valley played in African history?
2. Why is Africa less densely populated than Europe and the United States? In light of Africa's population growth, do you expect that this will still be true in the future?
3. What geographical conditions promoted or discouraged the development of early civilizations? What was the role of trade routes in these early societies?
4. How is ethnicity related to geography and to economic methods such as hunting, herding, and farming? In what ways is ethnicity likely to change amidst modern Africa's urban migration trends?
5. How would acceleration of current trends in Africa's changing climate affect Africans? To what extent could technology improve on Africa's uneven distribution of water?
6. How do Africa's landforms and climate affect economic development today? What natural resources might independent Africa exploit more profitably?

---

54. Mazrui, *The Africans*, 11-21, 41-61, 239-259; Newman, *The Peopling of Africa*, 202-205; Maddox, Giblin, and Kimambo, eds., *Custodians of the Land*, 1-6, 69-97; Ford, *The Role of the Trypanosomiases*, 1-11, 481-496; Davidson, *Modern Africa*, 260-278.

Section Overview

Africa has yielded considerable information on the evolution of humankind, and many archaelogists now believe that it is the cradle of humankind and one of the earliest centers of world civilization. Three chapters in this volume examine different aspects of this early period, the two in part B and the one on the Bantu expansion in Part C.

Chapter 3 examines myths of origins and scientific evidence on evolution. This evolutionary story began about four million years ago, with evidence about the australopithecines, regarded as the earliest hominids. The tool-making hominids emerged two to five million years ago. Known as Homo habilis, they lived in small encampments, gathered wild fruits for food, used small stone tools and had bigger brains than their predecessors. Hominids were different from other primates because of their larger brains, and as they developed further, because of bipedalism, the ability to walk on two feet. Homo habilis was in turn succeeded by Homo erectus about 1.8 million years ago. These had larger brains, better stone tools, an erect posture, and were able to make fire and travel greater distances. Homo erectus was superceded by Homo sapiens which appeared 150,000 to 200,000 years ago and developed rapidly thereafter. Homo sapiens were able to use sophisticated stone tools, and they lived in the forest region as well as in the savanna. With Homo sapiens, the history of Africa began to unfold more rapidly.

Chapter 4 describes the civilizations of Egypt, Kush, and Aksum. Egypt can proudly claim to be one of the first advanced civilizations in world history. It survived for a long time, with a history divided into several epochs. The Old Kingdom (ca.3100-2180 B.C.) developed a divine kingship in the pharaohs and a complex set of religious ideas. The pharaohs were powerful and they collected tribute from their subjects. Grand architecture was constructed, as evidenced in the pyramids, and the knowledge of mathematics also grew. Egypt grew to become an empire, with control of commerce and agriculture. The fortunes of Egypt fluctuated as it engaged in wars with its neighbors. Kush and Aksum are other examples of ancient civilizations discussed in this chapter.

Chapter 5 in Part C describes the peopling of sub-Saharan Africa by the Bantu. Over a long period, Bantu-speaking peoples carried their ideas from the area of Nigeria and the Cameroons to other parts of sub-Saharan Africa. The Bantu absorbed many Stone Age cultures and spread the knowledge of agriculture and iron, as well as advanced political and social organization. They have been credited with the formation of such important kingdoms as Kongo and Zimbabwe.

As genetic, linguistic, and archaeological research improves, so too will our knowledge of early Africa. Meanwhile, we have firm evidence on agriculture, the

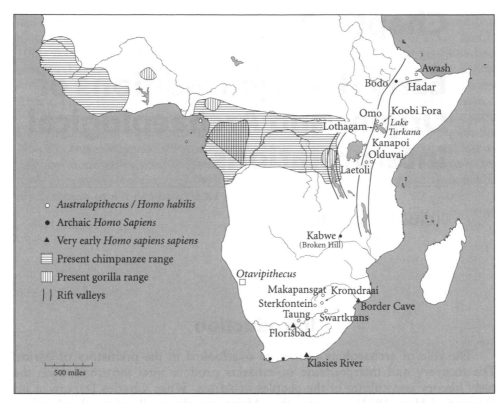

Figure 3-1. Archaeological Sites for Discoveries in Human Evolution

tions are sacred and constitute the history, culture, and indeed the totality of African people's existence. In that respect, they cannot be entirely ignored.

In this chapter an attempt will be made to present both archaeological and African interpretations of the origins of humans. This is a rare approach to the study of the early history and culture of Africa because previous works have focused primarily on the prehistory of Africa from archaeological perspective. While the objective of the approach in this chapter is not to reconcile the traditional and archaeological interpretations, it is to show that Africans have their own explanation of the origins of humans. However, because of the abundance of scientific and universally accepted evidence, emphasis will be placed on archaeological interpretations.

Archaeological Discoveries and Interpretations

Paleoanthropologists believe that the earliest humans (hominids) had close relationship with the great apes, the chimpanzee, and gorilla (pongids) most of which were found in central Africa. Charles Darwin pointed out that "it is probable that Africa was formerly inhabited by extinct apes closely allied to the gorilla and chimpanzee."[2] The split between hominids and pongids took place during the late Miocene (about 10-5 million years ago).[3] Clifford Jolly states that "from rocks of this age [Miocene] have been found the earliest fossils representing the primates of sub-Saharan Africa, the home of many living monkeys and apes and the probable place of the origin of the human family."[4] In search of the "missing link," archaeologists have excavated many sites in East and South Africa with amazing results. Fossils have been found, analyzed, and dated thereby enlightening the understanding of the history and culture of the early people of Africa.

The search for the origins of humans is carried out through the study and interpretation of fossils. In the 1850s, scientists found only two fossils; one was that of an ape and the other was a near-human bone called the Neanderthal man.[5] The Neanderthal man was classified as later archaic *Homo sapiens* with the striking features of a large brain, stone tools and weapons, hunting, artwork, and burying of the dead. Eugene Dubois (1858-1940) in 1891 found the first remains of *Homo erectus* from the fossiliferous gravels in Java, Asia. Dubois believed that his discovery provided the "missing link" between humans and apes.[6]

In 1924 some fossilized bones of australopithecines were discovered, studied, and interpreted by Raymond Dart, a paleontologist and professor of anatomy at the University of the Witwatersrand in Johannesburg, South Africa. A skull, which represented early humankind, was discovered at Taung. The skull was different from either the Neanderthal or *H. erectus*. Dart named it *Australopithecus africanus* ("The South African Ape" or "Southern Ape from Africa"). *Australopithecus africanus* with a larger brain than that of a modern ape was dated about 2-3 million years ago.[7] Australopithecines have been found also in Tanzania, Kenya, and southern Ethiopia. Later discoveries show that *Australopithecus afarensis* fossils found at Hadar in Ethiopia lived between 3 and 4 million years ago.[8] A later species of the genus *Authralopithecus* was *A. aethiopicus*. In the 1930s, Robert Broom found adult samples of *A. robustus*. Both *A. robustus* and *A. africanus* belonged to the hominid family.[9]

2. Charles Darwin, *The Origin of Species and Descent of Man* (New York: Random House, 1936), 520.

3. Robert Jurmain, et al., *Introduction to Physical Anthropology*, 7th ed. (Belmont, CA: West/Wadsworth, 1997), 316-321.

4. Clifford Jolly, "Prehistoric Humans," *Academic American Encyclopedia*, Vol. 15 (Connecticut: Danbury, 1994), 516.

5. Neanderthal is named after the Neander Valley in Germany where the fossils were first found in 1856. Robert Jurmain, et al., *Essentials of Physical Anthropology* 3rd ed. (Belmont, CA: West/Wadsworth, 1998), 306-309; Bernard G. Campbell, *Humankind Emerging*, 6th ed. (New York: Harper Collins Publishers, 1992), 24.

6. Jurmain, *Essentials of Physical Anthropology*, 281-282.

7. Campbell, *Humankind Emerging*, 187.

8. Mary Leakey, 1974-1977 also found *A. afarensis* at Laetoli. Kenneth L. Feder, *The Past in Perspective: An Introduction to Human Prehistory* (Mountainview: Mayfield Publishing Company, 1996), 89.

9. Joseph O. Vogel, "Search for Human Origins in Africa: A Historical Note," in Joseph O. Vogel, ed., *Encyclopedia of Precolonial Africa* (Walnut Creek: AltaMira Press, 1997), 84-90.

Africa, migrated to, and completely replaced the populations in Europe and Asia. The second believes in partial replacement, and the third proposes multiregional evolution.[22] *Homo sapiens sapiens* manufactured complicated tools and weapons of wood, stone, and metal. They made handles for tools, ornaments for their bodies, and lived in larger and complex communities. Adaptation to ecological and climatic dictates also led to differences and improvement in toolkits.

In 1978, Mary Leakey discovered the fossilized footprints of hominids at Laetoli. The three sets of hominid footprints formed a trail more than 75-80 feet long. They were found in a layer of volcanic tuff in sediments dated between 3.59 and 3.77 million years ago.[23] Mary Leakey was convinced that the footprints existed about half a million years before the fossils that Johanson had unearthed in the Afar region of Ethiopia in 1973.[24] Archaeologists have found more footprints to prove that bipedal locomotion was an important characteristic of early hominids. Aside from the footprints, Louis and Mary Leakey discovered thousands of stone tools made, used, and left behind by the early people at the Olduvai Gorge in Tanzania.

Archaeology has facilitated the study of the early human beings not only in Africa but also in other parts of the world. As Richard Leakey put it, "Archaeologists have assembled a wealth of data on early human technology in Africa that tells us a great deal about the appearance of man."[25] With all the archaeological evidence at our disposal, it is possible to trace the technology of the early humans.

The Stone Age

Tool-making activities dominated the early stages of human history. It was one of the hallmarks of human development in technology, especially in Africa. Foraging for food by human beings as well as animals such as chimpanzees led to the manufacturing of tools. Stone tools were associated with Homo habilis. The Stone Age is used to designate the period when stones were important in the development of human technology. The Stone Age has been divided into three: Paleolithic (Old Stone), Mesolithic (Middle Stone), and Neolithic (New Stone). In studying these periods, some problems have emerged. First, there is the difficulty in presenting the events of the ancient times in a neat chronological sequence. Second, there is no uniform development of technology and civilizations of the world.

The emergence of tool technology took place during the Paleolithic (Old Stone) Age. The Paleolithic period diffused over much of the world, beginning from Africa. The period has been sub-divided into three—the Upper, Middle, and Lower Paleolithic. The three have been defined by the invention of new techniques of stone tools. During the Upper Paleolithic, the technique for manufactur-

---

22. Jurmain, et al., *Essentials of Physical Anthropology*, 324-328.
23. Mary D. Leakey and R.H. Hay, "Pliocene Footprints in Lateolil Beds at Lateoli, Northern Tanzania," *Nature*, 278 (1979): 317-323; Mary D. Leakey, "Footprints in the Ashes of Time," *National Geographic* (April 1979); Roland Oliver, *The African Experience* (New York: Harper Collins Publishers, 1991), 8.
24. Mary D. Leakey, "Footprints in the Ashes of Time," *National Geographic* (April 1979): 446-457.
25. Leakey, "African Fossil Man," 440.

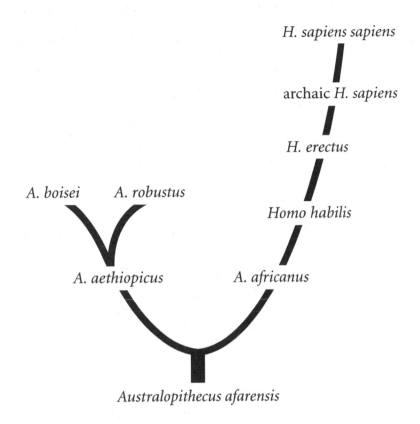

Figure 3-2. Evolutionary Tree

ing was stone blades, although flakes too were produced. These new tools increased efficiency in hunting and gathering. The Upper Paleolithic people discovered which plant to eat and which animal to kill for meat. They, however, did not develop the concept of planting or domesticating animals. Archaeologists and anthropologists suggest that the people of this Age lived in small nomadic bands.

The Oldowan Culture

In 1959, the Leakeys recovered some tools from the Olduvai Gorge. They were believed to be the oldest tools made by either *H. habilis* or *H. rudolfensis*. They called the finds the Oldowan Culture. According to Louis Leakey, the Oldowan culture is the oldest well-authenticated stone-age culture that has yet been discovered in the world. He emphasized the making of tools because "it was this step which lifted 'near-man' from the purely animal level to that of human status." [26] The period was characterized by bifacial flaking technology. Some of the Oldowan stone tools such as the choppers, scrapers, chisels, cleavers, hammer stones, and flakes were simple and did not perform specialized functions. All of

---

26. Leakey, *The Progress and Evolution*, 3.

the economy, especially in hunting and fishing.[33] Microliths were made about 35,000 years ago at various sites such as the Olduvai Gorge, Mumba-Hohle in northern Tanzania, and Matupi Cave in Zaire.[34] In West Africa, microlithic centers have been found at Iwo Eleru, Mejiro Cave, and the rock-shelters at Rop in Nigeria, the Bosumpra Cave in Ghana, the Shum Laka in Cameroon, and Kourounkorokalé in Mali.[35] Other stone tools of the Late Stone Age included knives, scrapers, anvils, grinding stones, hammer stones, and saws. The bone tools discovered in the Katanda region of Zaire, compare with the European Upper Paleolithic technology.[36]

Iron Age

The development of food-production in contrast to foraging called for the use of metal-based implements. Metals such as copper, bronze, and iron were used. Africa did not experience the Copper or Bronze Age. However, there was a large deposit of copper at Akjoujt in Mauritania, central Mali, Niger, Angola, and Central African Copperbelt in South Africa. Copper was used mainly for decorative objects such as bracelets and it was later associated with political power. It also became an important article of trade in the indigenous commercial networks.[37] Bronze was used in northern Africa, especially along the Mediterranean.[38] Thurstan Shaw suggests that Africa jumped from the Stone to the Iron Age because the desiccation of the Sahara broke the connection between Egypt and sub-Saharan Africa and "the link was not re-established until... some three thousand years later."[39]

During the Iron Age, which spread between 500 B. C. and A. D. 500, iron-based equipment such as axes, hoes, knives, arrows, spears, and razors were produced thereby transforming the economic system and culture of the early people. As agricultural communities increased, it became necessary to produce powerful, durable, and handy implements, which were used to clear rough and rugged lands.

Indigenous iron working in Africa involved two activities: smelting and smithing. The procedure for iron smelting is complex. There is an argument that the smelting of iron was introduced to Africa from Anatolia (modern Turkey) from about 1500 B. C.[40] A contrary argument is that iron smelting was an independent development in Africa because iron ore was plenty and various types of ore were exploited. The Nok civilization, which flourished in 500 B. C. in central

---

33. Shaw, "The Prehistory," 622.

34. Lawrence H. Robbins, "Eastern African Advanced Foragers," in Vogel, *Encyclopedia of Prehistory of Africa*, 341.

35. The Late Stone Age is divided into three periods-the Upper, Middle, and Lower Stone Age. Several sites of the three periods are mentioned by Holl, "Western Africa," 305-312 and Shaw, "The Prehistory," 624.

36. Jurmain, *Essentials of Physical anthropology*, 343-344.

37. Michael S. Bisson, "Copper Metallurgy," in Vogel, *Encyclopedia of Prehistory of Africa*, 125-132.

38. Kevin Shillington, *History of Africa* (New York, St. Martin's Press, 1995), 37.

39. Thurstan Shaw, "The Prehistory of West Africa," in J.F. Ade. Ajayi and Michael Crowder, eds., *History of West Africa*, vol. 1 (London: Longman, 1976), 61.

40. Shillington, *History of Africa*, 39.

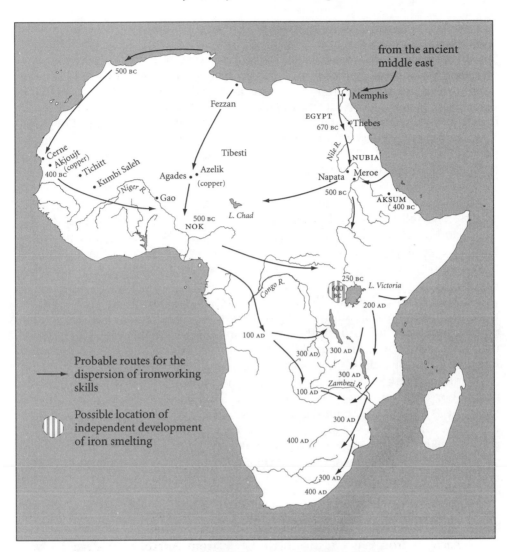

Figure 3-5. The Spread of Iron Working in Africa

Nigeria, diffused to other parts of West Africa where there was no contact with the outside world in the early part of the Iron Age. Iron smelting industries were established at Taruga (central Nigeria) in the fifth to the third centuries B. C.[41] Archaeological excavations recovered terracotta figurines in the Nok region, which suggests that the makers were iron smelters. Other early Iron Age sites in West Africa were Djenne in the Niger Delta, Agadez, and Do Dimi in the Sahel region.[42] The continuity of the culture of the Neolithic peoples and the early Iron

41. C.T. Shaw, "The Prehistory of West Africa," in Ki-Zerbo, *Methodology and African Prehistory*, 628-629.

42. Graham Connah, *African Civilizations: Precolonial Cities and States in Tropical Africa: An Archaeological Perspective* (Cambridge: Cambridge University Press, 1993), 113-114.

Age populations made the rapid spread of iron technology possible in West Africa.[43]

Another site of independent development of iron smelting was the kingdom of Kush. Meroe was both the political headquarter and the industrial center of Kush. Meroe played an important role in the diffusion of iron working in Africa.[44] Archaeological excavations indicate that metallurgical technology developed in Axum where iron and bronze artifacts have been recovered. In Egypt, the role of iron in agriculture and commerce became important during the period of the Saite kings (663-525 B.C.)[45] Iron was mined and smelted in Ethiopia and there were communities that used iron in the region around the Great Lakes. A recent survey by Pierre de Maret and G. Thiry indicates that the first appearance of iron in Central Africa was among villagers and it diffused slowly among other groups. They also indicate that agricultural populations in modern Rwanda, Burundi, and the Kivu region of Zaire (Democratic Republic of Congo) emerged as productive iron-smelters. It is, however, difficult to arrive at a specific date of the spread of iron technology in Africa because a spectrum of dates has been suggested.[46]

In East Africa, Roland Oliver used pottery types and patterns to trace the spread of iron by the Bantu-speaking people. Their farming and pottery occupations required the use of iron thus, the technology was spread in the course of their migration. Oliver associated the growth and diffusion of pottery in Rwanda, Burundi, Kivu, Uganda, and western Kenya with the Early Iron Age.[47]

A recent linguistic study of loan words in Bantu reveals that the early Bantu people borrowed iron working from Central Sudanic speakers.[48] Archaeological excavations by Peter Schmidt on the western shore of Lake Victoria have recovered some furnace pits. He argued that the Buhaya, a Bantu-speaking agricultural people inhabiting the Kagera region of Lake Victoria, are one of the groups of people with a living iron working tradition in Africa. They practiced iron smelting in 200-600 B. C., the same period when iron technology flourished in the Nok culture.[49]

The use of iron brought about significant changes in technology and the economic system of African peoples, whether it was introduced or it developed inde-

---

43. Scott MacEachern, "Western African Iron Age," in Vogel, *Encyclopedia of Prehistory of Africa*, 426-429.

44. Bruce Williams, "Egypt and sub-Saharan Africa: Their Interaction," in Vogel, *Encyclopedia of Prehistory of Africa*, 465-472.

45. Elizabeth Isichei, *A History of African Societies to 1870* (Cambridge, Cambridge University Press, 1997), 70-71.

46. Pierre de Maret and G. Thiry, "How Old is the Iron Age in Central Africa?" in Peter R. Schmidt, ed., *The Culture and Technology of African Iron Production* (Gainesville, University Press of Florida, 1996), 29-30.

47. Roland Oliver, "The Emergence of Bantu Africa," in Fage, ed., *The Cambridge History*, 366-87.

48. Peter R. Schmidt, *Iron Technology in East Africa: Symbolism, Science, and Archaeology* (Bloomington: Indiana University Press, 1997), 15, cited in David Schoenbrun, "Early History of Eastern Africa's Great Lakes Region: Linguistic, Ecological, and Archaeological Approaches ca. 500 B.C. to ca. A.D. 1000," Ph.D. dissertation (University of California, Los Angeles), 268.

49. Peter R. Schmidt and S. Terry Childs, "Ancient African Iron Production," *American Scientist* (November-December 1995): 524-33.

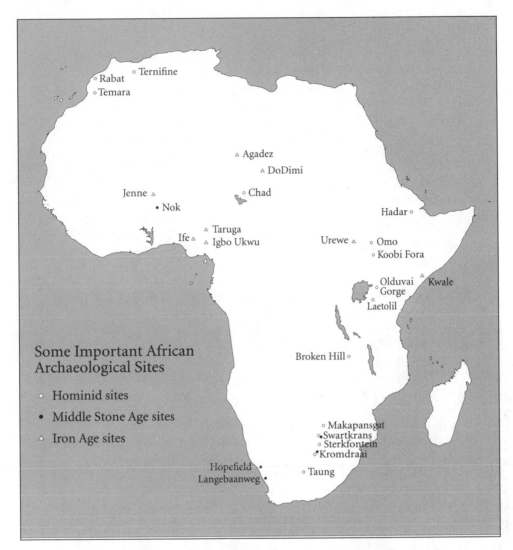

Figure 3-6. Some Important African Archaeological Sites

pendently. It strengthened and facilitated the practice of agriculture and commerce. Iron smelters and blacksmiths produced hoes, knives, and diggers, which were used for farming, arrowheads, spears, and swords, which were weapons used especially against wild animals. Thus, iron was used for tools and weapons. The possession of iron materials was a status symbol, particularly among blacksmiths and rulers. Broadly, iron performed socio-political and economic functions.

Agriculture and Pastoralism

Towards the end of the Late Stone Age, there was a gradual transition from hunting and gathering to a production economy with the practice of agriculture and pastoralism. Improved metallurgy with the adoption of iron implements and microlithic technologies played a major role in the transition. Along with farming arose permanent settlements and large communities. Settlements were located around fertile areas and rivers such as the Nile, Niger, Gambia, Senegal, Congo, and Zambezi. Lake Chad in West Africa and the Great Lakes in Central Africa accommodated agricultural communities. Societies began to adapt to varied environments that permitted food production and diversification of the economy. As a result of increase in population, more food was produced.

Egypt, West Africa, and the Ethiopian highlands were cores of agricultural development. In these places, most of the food crops were cereals and vegetables such as wheat, sorghum, barley, millet, melons, beans, African rice (*Oryza glaberrima*), *Tef*, and *fonio*. Root crops such as African yams were also cultivated. In West Africa, cowpeas and black beniseed were grown and vegetable oils were obtained from oil-palm and shea butter trees. Graham Connah suggests that agricultural system began in West Africa in the first millennium A. D. when rotational bush-fallow cultivation was adopted. [50] Some of these crops were also found in the Nile valley, especially in Khartoum where microlithic tools and polished axes were used.

While the domestication of plants was an indigenous development in Africa, animal domestication, especially sheep and goats, was a result of influences from South-West Asia.[51] J. E. G. Sutton contends that the raising of sheep, followed by goats and cattle developed among East African peoples between the third and the second millennium.[52] The Tuareg of the Sahara, the Fulani of West Africa, and the Maasai of East Africa are nomadic people with great skills in domesticating animals such as sheep, horses, donkeys, goats, and cattle. Some Bantu groups, according to A.L. Mabogunje, combined animal husbandry with plant cultivation to the mutual advantage of both, and in Rwanda there was a symbiotic economic relationship where the Tutsi kept cattle and the Hutu practiced agriculture.[53]

Archaeological evidence suggests that irrigation system was adopted in pharaonic Egypt and the middle Nile to support agriculture and to protect people's shelter. Dike-building, canal-digging, and artificial dams were some of the techniques employed to check the annual inundation of the land. It is to be noted that "floods may be either too great—destroying everything in their passage—or too slight—failing to provide adequate irrigation."[54] In Upper Nubia, particularly on the Kerma plateau, vestiges of irrigation works have been found. The mechanisms used were the *shaduf*, which were later replaced by the *saqiya*. A. A. Hakem stated that the introduction of *saqiya* had a significant impact on agriculture, especially in Dongola because it saved more time and labor than the *shaduf*.[55] In most of the areas that experienced annual flooding, grains and cereals such as barley, wheat, peas, maize, and beans were cultivated. Cucumbers, lentils, and melons were also planted. Soil conservation was practiced through intercrop-

50. Connah, *African Civilizations*, 140-141.

51. Ibid., 4.

52. J.E.G. Sutton, "The Prehistory of East Africa," in Ki-Zerbo, *Methodology and African Prehistory*, 481.

53. A.L. Mabogunje, "Historical Geography: Economic Aspects," in Ki-Zerbo, *Methodology and African Prehistory*, 342.

54. G. Mokhtar, "Introduction," in G. Mokhtar, ed. *Ancient Civilizations of Africa, General History of Africa*, vol II (Berkeley, University of California Press, 1981), 12-13.

55. A.A. Hakem, "The Civilization of Napata and Meroe," in Mokhtar, *Ancient Civilizations of Africa*, 308-310.

ping and crop rotation. Irrigation system was also practiced in southern Ethiopia, northern Tanzania, and Kenya.

Crafts such as pottery and wood-carving supplemented agriculture and animal husbandry. Archaeological excavations along the coast of West Africa suggest that a complex structure of ironworking, wood-carving, and pottery was developed during the first millennium B. C. when foragers began to interact with farmers. The emergence of pottery was another innovation in technology among the ancient societies of Africa. Two pottery industries at Punpun and Kintampo in Ghana had developed by 1400 B. C.[56] Both sites show evidence of intermixture of material culture between the Saharan and forest people. Apart from pottery and rich deposits of iron ore that facilitated iron smelting and food production, there is evidence of domestication of animals at Kintampo by the Akan people.[57] However, the Bantu-speaking people were said to be responsible for the spread or ironworking and pottery in sub-Saharan Africa during their migrations. The Eastern stream of the Bantu spread the Urewe and Kwale styles of pottery designs.[58]

In tracing the origins of humans and the development of technology, archaeology has provided tremendous information. Prehistoric societies of Africa interacted, borrowed ideas, and evolved agricultural, economic, and social patterns, which became significant aspects of human transition to historic times. Through archaeological studies, it is possible to identify similarities in agricultural tools and crops that existed from one region to another.

African Interpretation of Human Origins

Oral traditions in Africa are numerous and widely diverse in contents. They provide limited information, especially when dealing with the remote past. Much of what is contained in the traditions is associated with religious beliefs and practices. Writing on the spirituality of African peoples, Peter Paris contends: "undoubtedly, African societies on the continent have produced extremely complex cosmologies in their many and varied attempts to explain and relate the three realms of reality: spirit, history, and nature."[59]

The African philosophy of life is separate and distinct from the Western perspective. Like other cultures of the world, African societies deal with the issue of how humans came into existence. To this end, they narrate traditions that support creation and they place human beings as central figures among all other creatures. A major problem that arises from the traditions of origins is their historical validity and acceptability. Historians deal with facts that have rational interpretation, which African traditions of origins do not provide. The concept of creation is a universal phenomenon. In his *Myths of the World*, Michael Jordan asserts that

56. Francis Musonda, "Foragers and Farmers: Their Interaction," in Vogel, *Encyclopedia of Prehistory of Africa*, 398-403.

57. Connah, *African Civilizations*, 130, 140.

58. For the process of how pottery was manufactured, see Richard A. Krause, "Pottery Manufacture," and the spread of pottery, Joseph O. Vogel, "Bantu Expansion," in Vogel, *Encyclopedia of Prehistory of Africa*, 115-124.

59. Peter J. Paris, *The Spirituality of African Peoples: The Search for a Common Moral Discourse* (Minneapolis: Fortress Press, 1995), 34.

chapter, both views have been presented. While traditions rationalize the origins of humans in terms of creation, scientific interpretations emphasize the theory of evolution. The objective was not to resolve the opposing views but to represent African interpretation. Instead of engaging in a reconciliation of the two conflicting approaches (an attempt which might end up merely in the formulation of unresolvable theories), a worthwhile exercise is to concentrate on what early human beings have bequeathed on modern societies. Obviously, scientific evidence does not fit with a religious view in which God and the ancestors are the ultimate powers in a cyclical, ahistoric universe. African philosophy of life may differ in certain ways from other people's or stands in contradistinction with scientific explanation, nevertheless, it is imperative to acknowledge and respect the belief systems in order that their history and culture would become meaningful. While traditions of origins are universal, archaeological interpretation is a more widely recognized and accepted approach to the study of the prehistory of Africa.

Review Questions

1. What historical values can we derive from African traditions of origins?
2. What similarities or differences exist in African traditions of origins from myths of other places?
3. How has the theory of evolution helped in tracing the origins of man?
4. Discuss the importance of agricultural revolution in the early history of Africa.
5. What is the main proof of the existence of man in Africa?
6. Discuss the contributions of the following to the study of evolution:
   a) Charles Darwin
   b) Raymond Dart
   c) Louis and Mary Leakey
   d) Donald Johanson

Additional Reading

Bahn, Paul G., ed. *Cambridge Illustrated History of Archaeology*, Cambridge: Cambridge University Press, 1996.

Connah, Graham. *African Civilizations*. Cambridge: Cambridge University Press, 1993.

Fage, J.D. *A History of Africa*. London: Routledge, 1995.

Idowu, Bolaji. *Olodumare: God In Yoruba Belief*. Brooklyn: A&B Books Publishers, 1994.

Martin, Phyllis M. and Patrick O'Meara. *Africa*. Bloomington: Indiana University Press, 1995

Schmidt, Peter R., ed. *The Culture and Technology of African Iron Production*. Gainesville: University Press of Florida, 1996.

Schmidt, Peter R. *Iron Technology in East Africa: Symbolism, Science, and Archaeology*. Bloomington: Indiana University Press, 1997.

Wenke, Robert J. *Patterns in Prehistory: Humankind's First Three Million Years*, 4th ed. New York: Oxford University Press, 1999.

Chapter 4

Civilizations of the Upper Nile and North Africa

Funso Afolayan

This chapter examines the development of early civilizations in the regions of the Upper Nile and North Africa. It looks at the rise, historical formation, structures, politics, culture, trade, religion, achievements, external relations, and fall of the ancient civilizations of Egypt, Kush, Aksum, and Carthage. The advent and the consequences of Greco-Roman domination and of Christianity in North Africa before the rise of Islam are also examined.

Ancient Egypt: Foundations and Historical Development

The Neolithic Revolution

Environmental factors set the stage for the emergence of the civilization of ancient Egypt. The story began in the area known as the Fertile Crescent, covering the region stretching from Mesopotamia, through Palestine to Upper Egypt. It was in this region, about twelve thousand years ago, towards the end of the Late Stone Age period, that the genus *homo sapiens sapiens*, or man the hunter and food gatherer, became a farmer and domesticator of animals. This was the Neolithic Revolution, an agricultural transformation that had momentous consequences for subsequent human history. Farming and pastoralism ensured more regular and more predictable food production, resulting in larger surpluses. With food supply assured, man the wanderer became man the settler. Increased food production and more varied diet led to population expansion. Surplus food production freed segments of the population to engage and specialize in non-material pursuits such as art, music, and politics. The result of all these developments was the emergence of permanent settlements, the growth of trade, and the establishment of more elaborate socio-political organizations. Available evidence shows that by 10,000 B.C. the inhabitants of Nubia and Lower Egypt were already beginning to experiment with the planting of wild barley and other crops. By 6,000 B.C., millet and sorghum, two cereals of African origin, were being harvested in the Nile Valley.[1]

---

1. On the history of the neolithic revolution in Africa see J.R. Harlan, J.M.J. de Wet and A.B.L., Stemler, eds., *Origins of African plant domestication*, (The Hague: Mouton, 1976)

Climatic factors favored the crystallization of the Neolithic revolution in the Nile Valley of Egypt. Surrounded by the driest and most extensive desert in the world, the valley of the Nile was always a major magnet for groups and individuals fleeing from the forbidding arid regions to the west and east. This process of immigration was further accentuated by the gradual but progressive desiccation of the Sahara. The Sahara, which, prior to the fourth millennium B.C., had enjoyed a moist climate as well as a lush green habitat teeming with wetland and aquatic plants and animals, experienced a major but decisive climatic change. The rains stopped falling, the many rivers and their numerous tributaries stopped flowing, the extensive lakes began to dry up (with a few surviving as scattered oases), while the ever-encroaching desert smothered virtually all marine and animal life. While a few held on precariously to life in the oases, the vast majority of the survivors simply took to their heels, migrating in many directions to escape the drought and desiccation. The valley of the Nile, with its ever-verdant flood plain, was a natural attraction. Increased population pressure in the Nile Valley meant a more intensive exploitation of the resources of the river. It is, therefore, not surprising that the emergence of major civilizations in the Nile Valley coincided with the onset of the desiccation of the Sahara.

"The Gift of the River"

After a visit to Egypt, Herodotus, the famous Greek historian, described Egypt as the "Gift of the Nile." No statement could be more accurate in underscoring the nature and the basis of the development of civilizations in the Nile Valley. Like its peers in the Euphrates, Indus, and Yellow River Valleys, Egypt was above all a river civilization. The Nile was Egypt; Egypt was the Nile. It was conceived, born, nourished, and sustained by the Great River. In arts, science, economy, religion, culture, and politics, the Nile gave Egypt its unique features and its enduring characteristics. Celebrated throughout Egypt's long history as the benevolent deity, with its never-failing bounty, the Nile set the rhythm of Egyptian life.[2]

Deriving its source from inner Africa, in Lake Victoria-Nyasa, the largest lake on this oldest continent, traversing a distance of 4,600 miles and flowing relentlessly through arid and desolate regions before discharging its water into the Mediterranean, the Nile is the longest river in the world. It is fed by three major sources. The first, known as the White Nile, rises in Uganda bringing much water from the interlacustrine lakes, Victoria, Albert, and Edward. At Khartoum it is joined by the Blue Nile, tumbling down from the mountains of Ethiopia, fed by melting snow and heavy relief rains and bringing with it fertile mud, washed off the highlands of Ethiopia. Further north, the swelling deluge is augmented by the Atbarah River, also rolling down from the Ethiopian Highlands. From Khartoum to Aswan, the Nile is interrupted by six major rapids, known as the cataracts, that made navigation difficult. Thereafter from Aswan to the sea and for the last 750 miles, there is no interruption, except for the last hundred miles when the river fans out in numerous branches whose triangular shape so resembled the Greek letter for "delta," that it was given that name. This last stretch between the first

---

and J.D. Clark, *The Prehistory of Africa*, (Westport: Greenwood Press, 1984).

2. On the significance of the Nile in ancient Egypt, see Lionel Casson, *Ancient Egypt* (Alexandria: Time-Life Books, 1977), 29-49.

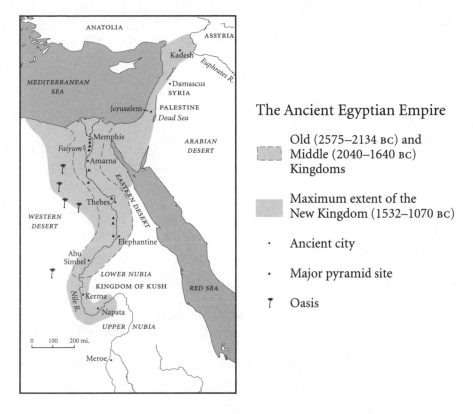

The Ancient Egyptian Empire

Old (2575–2134 BC) and
Middle (2040–1640 BC)
Kingdoms

Maximum extent of the
New Kingdom (1532–1070 BC)

· Ancient city

▲ Major pyramid site

Ŧ Oasis

Figure 4-1. The Ancient Egyptian Empire

cataract and the sea became the seat of the ancient civilization of Egypt. The part close to the Delta was known as Lower Egypt, while the part to the south, located on higher ground, where the Nile is bordered on both sides by arid cliffs, became known as Upper Egypt.

Every year, swollen by the torrential rains of Ethiopia, the Nile floods its banks. It is this annual, regular, predictable inundation that is at the root of the rise and prosperity of ancient Egypt. "When the Nile inundates the land," Herodotus wrote in the fifth century B.C., "all of Egypt becomes a sea, and only the towns remain above water, looking like the Islands of the Aegean. At such times shipping no longer follows the stream, but goes straight across the country. Anyone for example, traveling from Naucratis to Memphis sails right along the pyramids."[3] As the waters recede, they leave behind a rich layer of fertile silt, which the Egyptians called "black land," to distinguish it from the sterile "red land" of the desert.

The Era of Dynasties and Kingdoms

The history of ancient Egypt is usually divided into seven eras: the Archaic Period (ca.3100-2685 B.C.), the Old Kingdom (ca.2685-2200 B.C.), the First Inter-

---

3. Herodotus, *The Histories* (Harmondsworth: Penguin, 1954), quoted in Casson, *Ancient Egypt*, 29-30.

mediate Period (ca.2200-2050 B.C.), the Middle Kingdom (ca.2050-1786 B.C.), the Second Intermediate Period (ca.1786-1560 B.C.), the New Kingdom (ca.1560-1087 B.C.,) and the Late Period (ca.1087-332 B.C.).[4] The process of state formation began long before the Archaic Period. As more and more people crowded into the Nile Valley, they began to engage in settled farming. Soon they added copper to their stone tool assemblage. With time they developed a system of writing known as hieroglyphics (a Greek word for "priestly carving"). Made up of pictorial symbols, the hieroglyphics included twenty-four consonants but no way of indicating vowels. It is not very clear how this invention came about. It could have received inspiration from Mesopotamia. However, the Egyptian hieroglyphics, with their peculiarly African motifs, are so very different from the Mesopotamia cuneiform that they must have been largely an indigenous Egyptian invention. Writing permitted a record-keeping system, more efficient administration, and a more effective organization and mobilization of Egyptian society and resources. It prepared the way for the emergence of more powerful and more centralized societies in the region.

By 4,000 B.C. a series of regional states had taken root in the area. By 3,500 B.C. two major kingdoms had become dominant, one in Upper Egypt, the other in Lower Egypt. The struggle for mastery between the two went on inconclusively for four centuries, before it was eventually and decisively resolved in favor of Upper Egypt. In 3100 B.C. Narmer (probably the same one referred to as Menes in some records), the king of the south, invaded and successfully conquered the Northern Kingdom of Lower Egypt. He established the first in a series of thirty dynasties. He became the first of the pharaohs (kings) and united under his supreme authority all the lands of Upper and Lower Egypt from the first cataract to the Mediterranean. Unity provided the peace and stability necessary for the free flow of traffic along the Nile and the effective control and mobilization of the entire populace for agricultural and construction purposes. The energies that were previously directed to fueling local squabbles were now effectively coordinated for irrigation projects. South of the apex of the Delta and midway between Upper and Lower Egypt, Menes built the city of Memphis, which became the capital of the kingdom, the seat and tomb sites of the eighteen pharaohs of the First and Second Dynasties. The early dynastic period saw Egyptian writing, and technical, artistic, and administrative capabilities acquire their classic forms and styles. As regional authorities declined, power became progressively centralized in the kingship.

The Old Kingdom, 2685–2200 B.C.

The Old Kingdom began around 2700 B.C., with the rise of the Third Dynasty. It was a period of economic expansion and trade, all of which greatly increased the power and status of the god-king, giving him supreme authority over all his subjects. The brains of the nobility were combined with the brawn of the

---

4. The major sources for the reconstruction of the history of dynastic Egypt which follows are A. Abu Bakr, "Pharaonic Egypt," in G. Mokhtar, ed., *Ancient Civilizations of Africa.* UNESCO General History of Africa, Vol. 2 (London: Heinemann, 1981), 84-111; John Baines and Jaromir Malek, *Atlas of Ancient Egypt* (New York: Facts On File, 1980), 8-64; Casson, *Ancient Egypt*, 11-60; and *The Age of God-Kings, TimeFrame 3000-1500 BC*, (Alexandria: Time-Life Books, 1988), 55-97.

Figure 4-2. The Rosetta Stone

peasantry to raise a colossal and eternal home fit only for the god-king. This was the era of the great pyramids, which have endured through the centuries, striking evidence of astonishing technical mastery, state power, and royal absolutism. The first of these great tombs was the Step Pyramid, built for Djoser (2630-2611), the first pharaoh of the Third Dynasty. This was an astonishing feat, for it was the first monumental stone structure in the world. It was soon followed by the trio of pyramid tombs built to honor and house the three powerful kings of the Fourth Dynasty: Khufu, Khafre, and Menkaure. These are the most famous of the eighty or so pyramids that have survived. Individually and collectively, they proclaimed the exalted status of the pharaoh and made Egypt a land of wonder and admiration.[5]

The era of the Old Kingdom was one of peace. Warfare was limited. There was no standing army or national militia. Local militias existed, but they were commanded by civil officials. Hastily organized militias were called into service

5. Casson, *Ancient Egypt*, 52; and D. Stewart, *The Pyramids and Sphinx*, (New York: Newsweek: Wonders of Man Series, 1971).

reigning concurrently from two separate and competing capitals. The Thirteenth Dynasty, based at Thebes and controlling much of Upper Egypt, produced sixty kings, while from the western Delta town of Xois, the Fourteenth Dynasty boasted of seventy-six rulers all of whom claimed to be pharaohs.

Internal decadence was compounded by external subjugation. For the first time in its long history, Egypt had to endure the pangs and humiliation of foreign domination. The Hyksos (a Greek term derived from an Egyptian phrase meaning "princes of foreign countries"[6]) took advantage of the chaotic state of the Nile Valley to seize control and establish themselves in the Delta as a major power in the region. Using horse-drawn chariots and armed with new weapons largely unknown in Egypt, body armor, new types of scimitars and daggers, and composite bows of wood and horn, they quickly overcame the weak resistance of the Egyptians with their unwieldy man-sized shields, small axes and relatively feeble arrows.

Though Egyptian traditions remember the Hyksos as merciless tyrants, their era was not without benefits. They strove to Egyptianize themselves by adopting Egyptian names and promoting Egyptian culture. New technical innovations combined to rescue Egypt from military and technological backwardness. New techniques of bronze working were introduced. Improvements occurred in pot making and weaving on the vertical loom. Food production was boosted through the introduction of hump-backed cattle (*zebu*) as well as new vegetable and fruit crops. However, in spite of their superior military accouterments, the Hyksos were unable to control the whole country. They held sway over Memphis, but had no grip over Thebes where, from about the middle of the sixteenth century B.C., a new and vigorous dynasty, the Eighteenth, emerged. With the aid of its newly set up and powerful army, ironically equipped with the weapons introduced by the foreigners, Egypt clashed repeatedly and violently with the Hyksos rulers before storming their fortress at Avaris in 1567 B.C., breaking their power, expelling the alien rulers from the country, and terminating their century-long domination of Lower Egypt.

The New Kingdom, 1560–1087 B.C.

The expulsion of the Hyksos set the stage for the emergence of the New Kingdom. Under Ahmosis I, who expelled the Hyksos, and his two successors, Egypt entered a period of prosperity. The country was once again united under a single monarchy. The experience of foreign domination ensured that the new era would be one of militarism and imperial expansion. Having secured the control of the Delta, Ahmosis pursued the retreating Hyksos to Palestine, where after a three year siege he conquered their stronghold of Sharuhen. The new policy of aggression continued under Thutmosis I, who subdued Palestine and Syria, sweeping everything before him across the Euphrates, before confronting and defeating the kingdom of Mitanni in Mesopotamia. In the Sudan, Thutmosis's extraordinary military exploits took him as far as the fourth cataract, where he secured the effective subjugation of Nubia or Kush and the opening of trade routes to inner

---

6. See T.G.H. James, *An Introduction to Ancient Egypt* (New York: Harper and Row, 1979), 55.

Africa. To the west of the Delta, successful campaigns were prosecuted against the Libyans, who were making predatory forays into Egypt.

A lull in militarism followed the short rule of Thutmose II, whose half-sister and wife, Hatshepsut, became regent to the young Thutmose III. However, Hatshepsut soon seized the initiative, establishing herself firmly as pharaoh. Her highly eventful twenty-two-years reign was one of political consolidation, economic buoyancy, and technological advancements. Agriculture expanded and trade boomed. Foreign contacts and local prosperity produced an explosion of artistic activities. Vast, unusual, and beautiful temples were erected to honor the god Amon. In the newly delineated Valley of the Kings, rock-cut tomb-chambers provided splendid resting places for the god-kings and their nobles, whose accomplishments were proudly, lavishly, and indelibly inscribed on the walls of monuments and on commemorative steles and scarabs, to serve, in the words of Ramses III, as "a lesson for a million generations."[7]

Notable rulers of the New Kingdom included the youthful Tutankhamen, whose attempt to exalt the worship of Amun over that of Aten provoked widespread resistance that proved disruptive for the empire. Under the Nineteenth Dynasty, established by Ramses I, Egypt reached the peak of its power. Through a policy of strong administration and firm diplomacy, Egypt asserted and consolidated its hegemony in Nubia and elsewhere. Through prodigious construction of colossal temples, obelisks, and statues, Ramses II in the course of a long reign (1279-1212 B.C.), fostered his reputation as the greatest Egyptian king of all time. He married eight wives (not counting numerous concubines), and sired close to two hundred children. Undoubtedly a king of kings; deified in his lifetime, he made the name Ramses synonymous with kingship for centuries.[8]

Ramses was succeeded by several other rulers, many of whom shared his name but lacked his strong personality and self-confidence. Weak rulers and royal intrigues, combined with incessant incursions by Libyans and other Mediterranean peoples, resulted in widespread disorder and periodic civil wars. The priestly class came increasingly to challenge the prerogatives of the pharaoh. Powerful priests and military generals proclaimed themselves pharaoh. Nubia, Palestine, and Asia Minor declared their independence as Egypt came under a succession of dynasties of foreign origins, from Libya, Nubia, and elsewhere. The Assyrian conquest of 671 ended Egyptian dominance and isolation. Thereafter, Egypt became actively involved in all the politics of international relations as it sought to exploit and maintain a balance of power in the struggle for supremacy among the newly emerging powers of antiquity, the Hittites, Assyria, Persia, Babylon, and Israel. The widespread employment of Greek and Carian mercenaries in trade and warfare from the fourth century onwards set the stage for the Greco-Roman conquest and domination of Egypt. In 332 B.C. the Greeks, led by Alexander, took Egypt without a struggle, inaugurating the two-and-a-half-century Ptolemaic era, marked by the proliferation of Greek deities and the hellenization of Egyptian culture. The advent of Roman rule and the death of Queen Cleopatra in 30 B.C. resulted eventually in Christianization. In 395 A.D., Egypt became part of the Byzantine empire.

---

7. Quoted in Casson, *Ancient Egypt*, 68.

8. On Ramses II see M.D. Lemonick, "Secrets of the Lost Tomb," *TIME*, (May 29, 1995): 48-54; and Baines and Malek, *Atlas of Ancient Egypt*, 46.

Figure 4-3. The Colossus of Ramses II

Time Line of the Kingdoms, Dynasties, Rulers and Principal Events of Ancient Egypt

3100–2685 B.C.	*Early Dynastic Period* (Dynasties 1-2) Development of central authority and kingship, Narmer
2685–2200 B.C.	*Old Kingdom* (Dynasties 3-6) Step Pyramid at Saqqara by Djoser (2630-2611), Great Pyramid at Giza by Khufu (2551-2528); expansion of trade and ascendancy of regional princes
2200–2050 B.C.	*First Intermediate Period* (Dynasties 7-10) Collapse of central authority and decline of trade
2050–1786 B.C.	*Middle Kingdom* (Dynasties 11-12) Restoration of central authority, revival of pyramid building, irrigated agriculture, trade expansion to the red sea and inner Africa; conquest of Nubia to the second Cataract;

1786–1560 B.C.	*Second Intermediate Period* (Dynasties 13-16) Collapse of central authority; Hyksos chariot invaders from Western Asia
1560–1087 B.C.	*New Kingdom* (Dynasties 17-20) Expulsion of the Hyksos by Thebban Kings, royal rock tombs in the Valley of the Kings; massive statues and temples, Imperial development: large standing army, conquest of Palestine, Syria and Nubia to the fourth cataract; war with the Hittites of Turkey and with Libyans; Exodus of Isrealites under Moses; Rulers: Ahmosis (1550–1525) Hatshepsut (1503–1482), Akhenaton (1353–1332), Tuthmosis I (1504–1492), Tutankhamun (1333–1323) and Ramses II (1279–1213)
1087–332 B.C.	*Late Period* (Dynasties 21-30) Series of revolts and successions of invasions and dominations by Libyans, Nubians, Assyrians, Persians (525 B.C.) and by the Greeks under Alexander of Macedona in 332 B.C.
332 B.C.–639 A.D.	*Greco-Roman Era* Ptolemaic dynasty; Queen Cleopatra (d. 30 B.C.); Advent of Christianity; Monasticism and the Desert Fathers; Saint Augustine of Hippo (354-430 AD); Vandals invasion (400 AD); Byzantine invasion (533 AD); Arab-Islamic conquest (639 AD)[9]

Government and Politics:
The Pharaoh and His People

At the apex of Egyptian government was the Pharaoh, who was both god and king. The myth and legends explaining the emergence of the god-king established and legitimated his claim to mystical powers. The most popular of these myths speaks of Horus, who was the son of Osiris, the king of Egypt and the god of nature who controlled the flow of the Nile. In a bitter power struggle, Osiris was brought down by his murderously jealous brother, Seth, who dismembered Osiris and scattered his body parts all over the land. However, Isis, Osiris' sister and faithful wife, with the assistance of Anubis, the god of mummification and the gate-keeper to the underworld, used her life-giving power to put together the scattered pieces, resurrecting her husband, who thereafter became the lord of the afterworld. Horus, with the assistance of the earth-god, Geb, was able to avenge his father's death, though not before losing an eye in the contest. Seth was demoted, becoming the god of the netherworld, where the light never shines and flowers never bloom. Every pharaoh reigned as the incarnation of the falcon-god Horus in this world, and at his death became Osiris in the afterworld.

---

9. For the dates in the Time Line see Baines and Malek, *Atlas of Ancient Egypt*, 36-37; James, *An Introduction*, 262-266; and K. Shillington, *History of Africa*, (New York: St. Martin's Press, 1995), 20-21.

Succession was usually by primogeniture, though the designation and recognition of the new king by the oracles of the sun-god Re, and later those of Amon, outweighed dynastic legitimacy. The emergence over the centuries of several dynasties of diverse origins showed that the hereditary principle, inherent in the mythical model of Osiris and Horus, was often vitiated by countervailing circumstances. The rituals of installation made each reign a new beginning. Though Egyptian custom made no provision for female "kings," four women became pharaohs. These were Nitokris and Sebeknefru, whose reigns marked the end of dynasties, and Hatshepsut and Tauosre, who are remembered as usurpers. Similarly there were mothers, wives, and daughters of kings, who exercised considerable influence and were showered with honors. Notable among such are Teye, the wife of Amenhotep, and Nefertari, the first wife of Ramses II. Generally, Egyptian women enjoyed far more rights and occupied a higher status than their counterparts in Mesopotamia, Greece, and Rome. Though excluded from the bureaucracy, women could engage in most other occupations. They could own property, including land, engage in financial transactions, own slaves, and witness documents. They paid tax and had the same right to divorce as their husbands. The two sexes received the same funerary rituals.

As the personification of the gods, the pharaoh was the soul of the state, the lord of the land, the master of the fields, the controller of the Nile which he caused to flow unceasingly by his magical power and eternal godliness. Divinely omniscient, he was the mighty and terrible one, who ensured order in the universe. "He is a god," wrote a late fifteenth century B.C. chief minister, "by whose dealings one lives, the father and mother of all men, alone by himself, without an equal."[10] As the commander of all Egyptians and the dispenser of all justice, his word was law and his summons must be unquestioningly obeyed. The legal system was uncodified. Unlike much of sub-Saharan Africa, its orientation was individualistic, not communal. It was based on custom and usage as embodied in the king. As "the dispenser of wealth and the regulator of trade," the king was, as a tomb inscription proclaimed, the "superintendent of all things which heaven gives and the earth produces."[11]

As a matter of practical necessity, the pharaoh was assisted by a host of officials, who ranked below him in descending order of power. Nobles, deputies, priests, scribes, artisans, laborers, and peasants were the instruments of the god-king in the fulfillment of his many functions to ensure the flow of the Nile, the yield of the fields, the flourishing of trade, the worship of the gods, the dispensing of justice, the success of the army, the supervision and construction of public and artistic works, and the maintenance of the peace. At the top of this administrative hierarchy was the vizier, whose numerous titles indicated his many functions and tremendous power. He was the hereditary prince, the chief royal steward, the seal-bearer of and sole companion to the king. Among his thirty listed functions, he was the prime minister, the minister of justice and of war, the chief of police, and the general overseer of the fields, the herds, construction, tax, and tributes. He saw the king each morning and had the keys to all the palace gates. As the voice and visible representative of the pharaoh in all matters relating to the exercise of

---

10. Quoted in J.M. Roberts, *The Penguin History of the World* (London and New York: Penguin Books, 1995), 68.
11. Quoted in *The Age of God-Kings,* 84.

Figure 4-4. Pharaoh Tutankhamun

divine authority, justice, and appointments, he was expected to be fair and equitable, showing no partiality to the poor or the rich. Next to the vizier was the chancellor, who was followed in rank by the nomarchs. These provincial governors exercised considerable leverage in their nomes and were, by and large, loyal to their monarch. However, on occasion, their relative distance from the capital and their sense of autonomy and self-assurance led to the formation of subversive alliances to challenge the prerogatives of the king.

The War Machine: Militarism and the Building of an Empire

The defense of the state was the personal responsibility of the king. Defeats and victories were attributed to him. For much of its history, Egypt was not an expansionist state. Shielded by the deserts to the east and west and protected by the cataracts to the south and the Mediterranean Sea to the north, Egyptian civilization flourished for centuries in relative security and independence. To its south were the Nubians who were constantly warring among themselves; while to the west and north were the peoples of Libya and Asia Minor, who lacked the unity and organization to cause a major problem. Thus, for much of Egypt's long history there was no power to threaten its independence or challenge its supremacy. Lacking an active expansionist policy, Egyptian armies from after the time of Menes were deployed mainly for economic and construction projects. Teams of elite troops, desert scouts, and specialized paramilitary corps supervised the movement of restive Bedouins, the quarrying and transportation of stones for the pyramids, and the prospecting and exploitation of minerals, most especially gold from Nubia, Sinai, and elsewhere. However, following the experience of foreign invasion under the Hyksos, Egypt developed into a military and expansionist state, committed to building an empire.

The era of the New Kingdom was one of international conflicts. New powers began to emerge, especially in Asia Minor, whose warlike temperament and expansionist tendencies Egypt could not for long ignore. Under the Eighteenth and Nineteenth Dynasties, a war machine, served by a large and complex bureaucracy and marked by an unprecedented expansion of the professional army, developed. Fresh and fierce troops recruited from abroad supplemented the disciplined standing army, trained to fight on land and on sea. Once Egypt became an expansionist state, there was no turning back. All the energies of the state and of its god-king became geared towards war. Rulers gloried in their victories, and boastfully exhibited their captives and spoils. In times of war, the pharaoh could literally mobilize the entire land for battle. The Egyptian arsenal consisted of an assortment of weapons, such as the bow and arrow, sharp-edged scimitars and axes, and short-stabbing close-combat bronze daggers. The army was divided into two branches, the archers, who fought on foot, and the horsemen, who fought in speeding chariots, drawn by seasoned horses, that in the words of Ramses III, "quivered in all their limbs, prepared to crush the foreign countries under their hoofs."[12]

Economy and Society

Agriculture was the basis of the society's subsistence. It was dependent on the regular annual flooding of the Nile. To maximize the use of the flood water, irrigation was extensively practiced. The shaduf water-raising system involved the use of dams, dikes, canals, wells, big catch basins, embankments, and pits, to trap, control, and distribute the water and silt. The shortness of the agricultural cycle permitted only one crop a year, but this made plenty of manpower available for major construction projects. There were three seasons in the year, all determined by the Nile. The first was "inundation," approximately from June to September, when the fields were flooded, and no farming could be done. But this was also the period for the hauling of stones for construction projects. The next season, the "emergence," began in October and continued till February, when the water receded, leaving behind a moist fertile soil, on which planting would be immediately carried out. This would be followed by the season of drought which

---

12. Quoted in Casson, *Ancient Egypt*, 65.

lasted till June. This was the time of harvesting and threshing. It was also a time to engage in feasts and celebrate religious festivals.

The Nile was ubiquitous in Egyptian life. It fed the populace. It facilitated easy movement of people, and the haulage of timber, stones, and minerals. Canals were dug to bypass the cataracts; boats, canoes, and barges were used to move people and cargoes. The northward flow of the river and the southward blowing of the wind combined to make navigation an almost effortless exercise. The Nile provided a perfect artery of communication, and its seven-armed Delta a web of waterways. The Nile determined all real estate values and tax assessments. A nilometer was devised to gauge the level of the flood, and to divide the land into those who regularly received the flood, and could pay higher taxes, those who sometimes did, and those who seldom benefited from the flood, and would thus pay the least. Though there were periods of famine like the seven lean years, associated with Joseph the Dreamer, and recorded in the Hebrew Bible, such time were few and far between. And in any case, the development of an-all year shaduf irrigation and of granaries, especially from the Middle Kingdom period onwards, lessened the problem.

Generally, the Nile ensured such a bountiful yield of grain that it made Egypt the food-basket of the ancient world. The major crops were wheat, barley, and grapes. Bread and wine formed the staple diet. Other crops were beans, lettuce, cucumbers, dates, figs, and olive oil. Cattle raising was also practiced, though on a limited scale, to furnish the tables of the gods with meat offerings and to supplement the diet of the populace, especially the rich. Horses and camels were used as beasts of burden, while the ass and the cat were successfully domesticated. Meat supplies came from cattle, sheep, oxen, wildfowl, goats, and pigs. Fishing in the shallows and goose and hare hunting were also popular.

Surrounding the Nile were the deserts, barren and inhospitable, where the murderous deity, Seth, reigned supreme. But they were also of much economic importance. The deserts offered a wide range of useful mineral resources. Notable among these were black and green dyes from the Arabian Desert. Hard stone was quarried from Aswan, Arabia, Sinai, and Nubia, and used for building and sculptural projects. Semi-precious stones such as turquoise came from Sinai, and carnelian and amethysts from Nubia. Gold came from Nubia and the Arabian Desert. More highly prized than silver, it was considered the symbol of perfect immortality. No wonder it was used lavishly in royal funerary rituals. The innermost of the three coffins of Tutankhamen was made of solid gold and weighed 242 pounds. Copper came from Sinai and Asia. Nevertheless, Egypt appears to have lagged behind the Near East in the development of metal-working techniques. Wood, flint and hard stone remained the major materials in agricultural and sculptural occupations. In manufacturing, Egypt produced and exported linen textiles of unequaled fineness.

The Nile furnished Egypt with another commodity, which was to have revolutionary consequences in the ancient world. This was the papyrus, a tall bulrush that grew along the banks of the Nile and most profusely in the swamps of the Delta. From the stalks of this reed, used also for fibers, ropes, sails, clothing, and footwear, the Egyptians fashioned the first paper, and the most convenient writing material anywhere in the world. Infinitely more serviceable and lightweight than the clay tablets of Mesopotamia, it revolutionized book- and record-keeping and helped disseminate the knowledge of writing and of new ideas to the rest of the world. For the Egyptians, it remained a most valuable export, over which they maintained a lucrative trade monopoly till the twelfth century A. D.

Available evidence shows that foreign trade, mining, quarrying, production, and distribution were state-controlled activities. Though in theory, all powers of decision-making and control of material resources stemmed from the king, in practice, power and responsibilities were delegated to a whole hierarchy of officials. These officials were often rewarded with lands and titles, some of which became hereditary in their families. Land was also allotted to deities and their priests, nobles, and warriors. The emphasis on the divine legitimacy of kingship and the need to maintain the worship of the gods obliged the king to share his political and economic power with the temples and the priests who serviced them. Militarism drew the king out of his isolation, manifesting his humanness and weakening his sacral aura more than ever before. Concurrently, the wealth and the influence of the priestly class grew. An elaborate guild system organized the artisans into various groups. These included bakers, potters, brewers, sculptors, goldsmiths, draftsmen, and shepherds.

A civil service emerged, staffed by officials recruited for their mastery of writing and technical skills. Noted for their efficiency, these scribes, tax-assessors, accountants, agronomists, engineers, porters, ritualists, and others, depending on their rank and office, exercised great power, acquired much wealth, and lived in comfort and affluence. Egypt developed an international reputation for its sophisticated management skills and its remarkable techniques in secretarial work and accountancy. Though there were frequent references to slaves, and rulers boasted of their numerous war captives, taken especially from Syria and Asia Minor, the servile class does not appear to have constituted a major labor force in Egypt. The peasantry remained the backbone of the economy. They provided the labor supply both for agriculture and construction, and, in the days of the empire, the fighting force for expansion and national security.

Religion and the Afterlife: Funerary Beliefs and Practices

For the Egyptians, there was no separation of religion and the state. Religion permeated all aspects of life, socially, politically, and economically. Every detail of life, from the victory of the pharaoh in war and the flooding of the Nile to the loss of a job or death of a domestic fowl, was explained through reference to the disposition of the gods. Diseases, drought, and other calamities were explained as the wrath of the gods. Egyptian cosmology presented a coherent and splendid image of the world, expressed in myths, rituals, art, language, and literature. While there were many ideas on the origin of the cosmos, the most popular conceived of the universe as being an expression of the mind and the utterance of Ptah, the god of Memphis. The earthen world emerged out of the chaos of primeval waters in the same way that the fertile land emerged every year out of the Nile flood. It was the sun-god Re who fertilized the earth daily, ensured procreation, and controlled the ebb and flow of the Nile. The sun's daily rise (resurrection) and setting (death) mysteriously regenerated the earth, dispersing the primordial darkness, in a daily and archetypal act reminiscent of the original creation.

Figure 4-5. Queen Nefertiti

Dating to pre-pharaonic times, a strong reverence for and emphasis on the wonders of nature and on the fearsome and admirable qualities of animals predominated. Hence, animals featured widely in the Egyptian pantheon. The falcon, boar, cat, crocodile, cobra, bull, ram, lion, frog, fish, and crocodile became symbols of divine entities. Gradually, however, this zoomorphic representation was anthropomorphized, fusing the ideas of nature, animal, and man in the conceptualization of the gods. The most powerful and pervasive was the sun-god, Re. But dominating Egyptian mythology were Osiris, the god of earth and vegetation, who reigned supreme in the afterworld, and caused the Nile to flood and the grain to grow; Horus, the falcon-headed god, who controlled life in this world; Seth, the beastial big-eared deity of deserts and storms, who dominated the netherworld; and Isis, whose love and fidelity to her husband, her life-giving virtue, and her protection of children, made her the most popular goddess. During the Middle Kingdom, Amun, the god of Thebes, the air, and the unseen was raised to a position of pre-eminence that he occupied, largely unassailed, for the rest of Egyptian history.

gins of the ancient Egyptians,[15] few will deny that Egypt left a profound and enduring legacy for the modern world.

Having broken through into the Neolithic Revolution, characterized by agricultural innovations, urbanization, and demographic expansion, a new social system, associated with increased specialization of labor, came into being. Major developments occurred in the area of material culture. The most striking of these
was in the art of stone cutting. Like most innovations in Egypt, once acquired
during the predynastic period, it was refined, enriched, and subsequently transmitted with little modification from one generation to the next, throughout the
long period of Egyptian history. The Egyptians developed great skills and dexterity in stone craftsmanship. Using different varieties of stone, from the softest, such
as limestone and sandstone, to the hardest, such as granite and basalt, they carved
highly impressive stone vases and steles, and made stone sculpting a fascinating
art. By the time of the Old Kingdom, they had developed a remarkable tradition
in stone masonry, expressed in the hewing of tombs from solid rocks and the erec-
tion of other monumental structures like the pyramids and the lion-faced Sphinx.

Egyptian stone-carving techniques spread to the Mediterranean world, leaving a permanent imprint on Cretan and Minoan vases and finding powerful expression in the statuary of the Roman Empire. In mining, Egyptians explored and
exploited the various resources of their country and empire. They fashioned various tools and weapons such as axes, chisels, mallets, and adzes as well as bows,
arrows, daggers, and shields. They worked gold, silver, copper, and other precious
and semi-precious stones with great skill, developing jewelry making into an art,
which if they did not invent, they greatly refined and improved on. More than any
other place, Egypt, through tomb-wall pictorial representations and models of
workshops, has provided us with a wealth of information on the stages of development and techniques of ancient art. Using locally grown flax, they became accomplished in hand spinning and linen making. The women, who dominated the
textile trade, could handle two spindles simultaneously and with great skill. They
used both horizontal and vertical looms. By the time of the pharaohs, clothes of
superior quality, indeed the finest anywhere in the world, were being woven in
and exported from Egypt, bringing the pharaoh huge revenues.

Other craft products were ceramics, leather ware, ivory combs, mirrors, reed
mats and ropes, silver vases, and wooden coffins. The Egyptians became adept at
shipbuilding and could boast of great expertise in sailing and in naval warfare.
Equipped with adjustable yards and sails, Egyptian vessels were more maneuver-
able and manipulable in terms of speed and movement than those of any other

15. On the relationship between dynastic Egypt and African civilizations, see the writings of Cheikh Anta Diop, especially *The African Origins of Western Civilization: Myth or
Reality* (New York: Lawrence Hill, 1974), in which he argued for a black African origin for
the Egyptian civilization; and the rejoinder and review by Raymond Mauny, in *Bulletin de
l'Institut Francais d'Afrique Noire* 22, Series B (1960): 544-551, where he insisted that Egypt
should be seen as a melting pot of diverse ethnic and cultural influences. The unrelenting controversies over the African origin of the ancient Egyptians and the Egyptian origin of the
Greek "miracle," appear to have much to do with cultural and political appropriation and
the intersection of the issues of racial identity, Eurocentrism and Afrocentrism. See V.Y.
Mudimbe, *The Invention of Africa: Gnosis, Philosophy, and the Order of Knowledge*
(Bloomington: Indiana University Press, 1988); and Wyatt MacGaffey, "Who Owns Ancient
Egypt?" *Journal of African History* 32, no. 3 (1991): 515-519.

nation of the time. In furniture making, they built four-legged tables and chairs, two innovations that spread and endured to become part of virtually every household in the modern world. Glass making appears to have been invented independently in Egypt, Mesopotamia, and China. Egypt, however, appears to have refined and spread the technique, especially from the time of the Phoenicians, who adopted the skill and disseminated it throughout Europe and the Mediterranean world. The development of paper from the Nile reed plant, papyrus, made Egypt the paper-mill of the world. The word paper derived from an Egyptian word *paperaa*, meaning "that of a king," since paper production was for long a royal monopoly.[16] Cut, placed together in successive layers, pressed, and dried, the papyrus reed was made into large sheets and scrolls. Despite its fragility, it was a practical means of record-keeping bequeathed to other ancient civilizations and the modern world by Egypt. Papyrus was later adopted by the Greeks, the Romans, the Byzantines, the Hebrews, and the Arabs. Combined with the knowledge of writing, its revolutionary consequences in human communication remained unsurpassed for five thousand years, until the advent of the computer.

Scientific Achievements: Mummification, Surgery, and Medicine

In the field of science, the Egyptians left a major legacy to the world. Their belief in life after death, dependent on the perfect preservation of the body of the deceased, led them to develop the science of mummification. To preserve the body, they removed the brain and the intestines and then applied natron, a chemical preservative, made up of sodium carbonate, sodium bicarbonate, salt, and sodium sulphate. All this demonstrates their knowledge of human anatomy and their awareness of the chemical functions of many substances. They succeeded in preserving virtually intact the bodies of many of their rulers, such as Ramses II and Tutankhamen.

In the areas of surgery and medicine, the Egyptians made some of their most valuable contributions to history. A papyrus treatise, later named the Smith Papyrus, composed about 2500 B.C., shows their remarkable knowledge of surgery and pathology. This treatise, the oldest book on surgery anywhere in the world, systematically examined forty-eight cases, giving precise and incisive clinical descriptions, clear diagnoses, and methods of treatments. Extant records and examination of mummies have revealed the great skills of Egyptian surgeons. They successfully stitched up wounds, worked on lesions of the bones and contusions of cervical and spinal vertebrae, and set many fractures of the skull, limbs, nose, ribs, humerus, jaw, and collar-bone. They filled dental cavities and used gold wires to harness shaky teeth.

Like other ancient peoples, the Egyptians associated sickness with the work of malevolent spirits, and sometimes prescribed incredible magical remedies for their cures. But they were also highly rational and scientific in their attitude and approach. Their methodical observation of symptoms, accurate diagnosis, and careful prescription have passed on to posterity, and are widely used today as standard medical procedures. They diagnosed and competently treated a myriad of

---

16. James, *An Introduction*, 92-93.

ailments ranging from stomach disorders, skin cancer, coryza, laryngitis, angina pectoris, and constipation, to diabetes, bronchitis, bilharzia, ophthamia, and hemorrhoids. Their pharmacopoeia involved the use of a wide variety of herbs and chemicals. In surgery, medicine, and pharmacology, Egypt enjoyed great prestige in the ancient world. Egyptian doctors were widely employed and were always in demand in foreign lands. Their medicines, medical techniques, and instruments were adopted in Africa, Asia, Greece, and Rome. Many Greek physicians came to study medicine in Egypt and it is on record that Hippocrates, the famed founder of modern medicine, was indebted to the library of the Imhotep temple at Memphis. Imhotep was the vizier, architect, and physician of Djoser, whose outstanding achievements led to his deification by the Egyptians as Imouthes and his subsequent assimilation into the Greek pantheon as Askelepios, the Greek god of medicine.[17]

Mathematics and Astronomy

The need for accurate measurements of their enormous buildings, the level of the flood water, the size of a field, the volume of grain in a silo, the need to determine the number of bricks for a building, and the requirements of tax assessment, administrative organization, and efficiency led to major advancements in mathematics. The Egyptians developed a method of numeration, based on the decimal system, which involved counting by ones, tens, hundreds, and thousands, all numbers for which they had specific symbols. Practical necessities dictated the nature, the extent, and the limits of Egyptian science. It was an empirical science meant to solve different forms of material problems routinely confronted by officials in the daily performance of their duties. A highly practical people, the Egyptians made little use of abstract symbols. This limited their expertise in algebra. Classical writers, however, agreed that geometry was invented by the Egyptians. They led the way in teaching the world how to calculate perfectly the area of a circle (their greatest success), and that of a square and a triangle, as well as the volume of a cylinder and of a pyramid.

The Egyptians' preoccupation with religion and their need to accurately predict the seasons made them great astronomers. They observed and precisely identified several major constellations. The accurate alignment of the four faces of their pyramids with the four cardinal points of the solar system (the Great Pyramid deviates from the true North by less than one degree), convincingly affirms their reputation as accomplished astronomers. Thus they were the first to discover the length of the solar year and to fashion a useful, practical, and serviceable calendar. Once again, the inspiration came from the Nile. From as early as 4241 B.C. they broke their Nile year into twelve months of thirty days each, at the end of which they added five days to make the 365-day year. While the Greeks and the Babylonians hung on clumsily to the lunar year, the Egyptians discovered quite early that their flood year could not be made to conform to the phases of the moon. Though still fascinated by the moon, they declared their independence of it in their everyday lives. In their ceaseless and precise astronomical observations of

---

17. For a fuller but succinct discussion of the scientific achievements of ancient Egypt see R. El-Nadoury, "The Legacy of Pharaonic Egypt," in Mokhtar, ed., *Ancient Civilizations*, 155-183.

the heavens, they found that Sirius, the Dog Star and the brightest star in the fir-
mament, rose once a year in the morning with the sun. This became the beginning
of the Egyptian year. The Egyptian calendar proved so valuable that it was
adopted by Julius Caesar to make his Julian calendar, which was still in use till the
sixteenth century. The need for instruments to measure accurately the time spent
on irrigation and other projects led the Egyptians, as early as 1580 B.C., to devise
a sun rod and a water clock that were later taken over and perfected by the
Greeks to become the precursors of the modern clocks.[18]

Arts and Architecture

Egyptian arts and architecture clearly reflected their beliefs about life and the
afterlife. Their homes, made of mud bricks and built on low ground, could not
survive for too long, and were often covered by the silt from the annual Nile flood.
More attention was paid to the afterlife, entrance to which was predicated on the
perfect preservation of the body. To ensure this, the Egyptians soon abandoned the
prehistoric practice of burial in shallow graves covered with sand or heaps of
stones that could be blown away by the desert wind or ravaged by scavenging
jackals. They began to construct *mastabas*. These were bench-like, flat-topped,
slope-sided graves made out of mud bricks and later limestone and other stone.
The *mastabas* soon gave way to the pyramids, the greatest of which was built by
Khufu (c.2600 B.C.). Noted as one of the seven wonders of the ancient world (and
the only one of the seven still extant), the Great Pyramid of Giza measured 480
feet in height. The pyramids were executed with superb skill and organizing genius. Using the simplest tools, the Egyptians were able to quarry and move huge
blocks of limestone and granite on rollers and sleds and along the Nile by barge.

By the time of the Middle Kingdom, as the emphasis shifted from the glorifica-
tion of the god-king to honoring him along with other gods, funerary monuments,
more ambitious and complex, were built around or hewn out of cliffs. The New
Kingdom witnessed the proliferation of mortuary temples dedicated to the cult of
the dead pharaoh. The most impressive of these was the one that Queen Hatshepsut built for herself at Deir el Bahri. Executed as a single unit, it was a triumph of
setting and design, with skillfully wrought columns of varying shapes, adroitly integrated with nearly two hundred statues and relief carvings glorifying the queen's
divinity and accomplishments. Similarly, massive walled temples of the gods, built
of sandstone, sprouted all over the country. This development reached its peak
during the reign of Ramses II, one of whose statues of himself, hewn out of heavy
red granite and weighing over a thousand tons, rose to more than fifty-seven feet in
height. Each of his four giant statues that dominate the facade of one of his temples
at Abu Simbel is sixty-five feet tall. Noted for their massiveness, instead of their
aesthetic grace, these new constructions appeared to affirm Egyptian pride and
self-confidence in their largely unchallenged dominance of the ancient world. [19]

---

18. For more information on how and why the Egyptians were the first to declare their
independence of the moon and devise a solar calender, see D.J. Boorstin, *The Discoverers*
(New York: Random House, 1983): 5-7

19. Casson, *Ancient Egypt*, 119-122. On art and architecture in ancient Egypt see K.
Michalowski, *Art of Ancient Egypt* (New York: Harry N. Abrams, Inc., 1970); and D. Stewart, *The Pyramids*.

Very early in their history, Egyptians made sculpture an important artistic medium. Concerned with eternity rather than fleeting emotions, Egyptian statues were largely devoid of motion and passion. The statues, however, were impressive portraits of character and majesty. The vicissitudes of Egyptian history were clearly reflected in changes in artistic expression. The pharaohs of the stable era of the Old Kingdom were presented as sleek, muscular, serene, confident, and majestic. After the chaos of the First Intermediate Period, the rulers of the Middle Kingdom betrayed in their faces weariness and sternness. By the time of the New Kingdom, characterized by imperial conquests and prosperity, the faces of the pharaohs indicated arrogant self-consciousness in pose and grandiosity in scale.[20] The commitment to conventional forms was also shown in charming paintings and decorations, in furniture making and exquisite fashioning of beds, chairs, boats, canopies, chariots, coffins, and cosmetic tools as well as in ornaments and jewelry designs. The Egyptians developed great dexterity in faience and bead making as well as in joinery and veneering. Their great technical skills were shown in their digging of canals, and the building of dikes and dams. They raised huge colonnades, columns, obelisks, and steles, whose influence can be discerned in later Greco-Roman arts. Most scholars agree that Greek sculptors of the seventh and sixth centuries B.C traveled to Egypt to learn the art of stone carving. The Egyptians' penchant for domestic pools and gardens appears to have passed to the Romans. With regard to inner Africa, Egyptian architectural traditions traveled south, appearing in Meroe and later Napata.

Temperamentally conservative, religiously committed to tradition, patronized and sponsored by the pharaoh, Egypt developed an artistic vision which, in spite of variations in details, remained relatively changeless for millennia. By placing an emphasis on continuity and stability, Egyptians created a splendid and enduring artistic culture, leaving for later generations a legacy of sophistication and grandeur.

The Nubian Corridor: Kush and Meroe

Kush

To the south of Egypt lay Nubia, a region of more than passing interest to the state builders of ancient Egypt. There were two reasons for this. The Nile River, the lifeline of ancient Egypt, traversed this region. Its two major sources joined together here. It is not surprising that successive rulers of Egypt were aware of developments in this region so vital to the survival of Egypt itself. Equally important were the famed mineral resources believed to exist in abundance in this region. Of these the most important was gold. To Egypt, this was the land of gold and the region eventually took its name from the Egyptians' word for that precious metal, *nub*. Trade relations developed very early between Egypt and its less centralized neighbors to the south. However, the emergence of Egypt as a major imperial power during the New Kingdom led to the military conquest of Nubia about 1500 B.C. For the five centuries that Egyptian control lasted, Nubia became progressively Egyptianized in religion, language, and writing skills.

---

20. Baines and Malek, *Atlas of Ancient Egypt*, 56; and Casson, *Ancient Egypt*, 123.

Equally important was its museum, named after Muses, the deity of the scientific mind. Built and maintained by royal patronage, the museum's enormous library contained well over two hundred thousand volumes. Unparalleled in the ancient world, and serviced by illustrious scholars, this library became the chief means for the preservation and the transmission of the cultural heritage of the Hellenistic world. To this cultural repository we owe the survival of the works of men of letters such as Aeschylus and Aristophanes, and historians such as Herodotus and Thucydides. In the sciences, Alexandria again led the way, providing an environment conducive to major breakthroughs, as evidenced in the works of scholars such as Eratosthenes, the father of scientific geography, who for many years was the chief librarian of Alexandria. Other scholars included the geographer, Strabo, who gave us the oldest and the most comprehensive systematic account of the geography of Egypt; the famous mathematician, Euclid; Archimedes of Syracuse, who studied in Egypt; and Apollonius of Perga, who studied and worked in Egypt, and became known as the founder of trigonometry. The turbulence associated with the early years of the Roman Empire began to take its toll on the museum and library of Alexandria. Torched by soldiers of Julius Caesar, this center of learning entered a period of progressive decline and ruin, from which it never recovered.[27]

In religion, considerable synthesis occurred. Certain Greek gods were paired or even fused with Egyptian gods believed to possess similar characteristics. A new trinity emerged: Serapis, from Osir-Hapi, emerged as the father-god; Isis became the mother-goddess; and Harpocrates assumed the position of the son-god. The worship of these deities spread far and wide, conquering the islands of the Aegean Sea and gaining adherents as far as away as Babylon and India. The mother-goddess, Isis, however, soon became the greatest of all the gods of the Hellenistic world. She was widely celebrated as the deity of love and fertility, and a hymn to her declares: "I am she whom women call goddess. I ordained that women should be loved by men, brought wife and husband together, and invented marriage. I ordained that women should bear children, and that children should love their parents."[28] It is not surprising that while other deities disappeared with the triumph of Christianity, Isis survived, re-emerging in the form of the Madonna.

The impact of the advent of Greek culture on the Egyptian people and society must, however, not be overemphasized. For the majority of the population, especially those in the countryside, life continued as in previous times. The new administration left the bureaucratic structures affecting the ordinary people little changed. Their presence was reflected more in their efficient means of tax extraction, meant to support the luxury-loving elite domiciled in Alexandria. Soon, however, Hellenistic cultural influences began to spread to the west, affecting the Maghrib and Western Europe. Commerce, dominated by merchants of Greek and Levantine origins, became the major instrument of diffusion. Along the shores of the Mediterranean, trading posts sprang up. Established and manned by Greek traders, these soon developed into city-states. As enclaves of Greek culture, they became the centers for the dissemination of Hellenistic ideas.

27. Riad, "Egypt," 191-195.
28. W.W. Tarn, *Hellenistic Civilization* (London: E. Arnold and Co., 1930): 324.

Phoenicians and Carthage

For the Maghrib, the disseminators of the Egyptian and Hellenistic cultures were the Phoenicians from Palestine, who from about 1000 B.C. began to trade along the coast of North Africa and Spain. They exchanged a variety of articles for gold, silver, copper, and lead. By 800 B.C., they had established a string of trading stations along the southern shore of the Mediterranean. The most important of these was Carthage ("New City"), founded in 814 B.C. Though settled mainly along the coast, the Phoenicians intermarried, interacted, and traded extensively with the indigenous Berbers and other groups, producing a new hybrid society, the Carthaginians. Dominating the northern end of the trans-Saharan trade and much of the trade of the Mediterranean, Carthage emerged by 600 B.C. as a major power in the region. Its rise appears to have stimulated the trans-Saharan trade, as extant rock-paintings in the desert show the development of many routes and the use of horse-drawn chariots during this period. From inner Africa, Carthage obtained gold, copper, salt, and slaves, in exchange for food, olive oil, and the knowledge of iron-smelting and manufacturing techniques. The consequences of iron use appeared to have been improved hunting, more efficient agriculture, population increase, permanent settlement, and the establishment of villages and states.

The attempt of Carthage to extend its dominance of the southern shores of the Mediterranean to the northern shore brought it into conflict with Rome, a new power that was rising to prominence following the death of Alexandria and the political (but not cultural) eclipse of his famous but short-lived Greek empire. After suffering a series of reversals, especially at the hands of the indefatigable Carthaginian general, Hannibal, Rome bounced back. Exploiting the rivalries between Carthage and the powerful Berber kingdoms of Numidia and Mauritania, it inflicted a crushing defeat on Carthage during the Second Punic War in 241 B.C. Forty years later in 202 B.C., with the aid of Masinissa, the ruler of Numidia, Rome again defeated Carthage reducing it and its adjacent territories into a Roman province called Africa, a name that would later come to be applied to the whole continent, but whose origin and etymology remain a puzzle.

Roman North Africa

Following its victory over Carthage, Rome allied with the Berber kingdoms of Numidia and Mauritania, two states with strong Greek and Phoenician cultural influences, who were able to maintain their independence for the next two centuries. Rome, however, soon became entangled in the struggle of the two Berber kingdoms for supremacy. Rome began to interfere actively in local Berber politics, undermining indigenous authority, and eventually conquering the two states in 150 A.D. Like the Greeks and the Phoenicians who came before them, the Romans had, by the beginning of the first century A.D., established a chain of military settlements along the North African coast. Settled by thousands of Roman immigrants, the coastal towns became noted for their large estates and plantations that were worked by *coloni* (with a status somewhat between "tenants" and "serfs"). The *coloni*, who as a rule supplied tributary labor to their masters or their masters' contractor-farmers, were sold with the land and were prohibited from leaving it. In addition, they had to pay a third of their crops in rent to the landlord or his estate manager. Rome took great pains to ensure the maximal agricultural exploitation of its African provinces through the production of wheat on the coastal plains and of olive oil on the high plains of the interior. North Africa became the granary of the Roman Empire, as its products were taxed and exported to support the city of Rome and the comfort of its upper classes.

Roman North Africa was stratified socially and territorially into three classes. In the coastal towns and cities lived the ruling class made up of administrators, aristocrats, merchants, and farmers. These were mainly Romans and Carthaginians, who lived on the great estates, and possessed large plantations and farms worked by slaves and tenants. Beyond the coastal settlements and on the high plains of the interior lived the Berber peasant farmers. These were taxed heavily and were rabidly anti-Roman. The third group was made up of the nomadic pastoralists, who lived further south and on the fringes of the Roman Empire. They were sometimes loyal to the occupying power but periodically raided their farms for food, especially in times of drought and in retaliation for attacks. To ensure more effective control of the nomads and the peasant farmers, the Romans introduced the use of the camel as an instrument for the pacification of the desert people. This, however, soon became counterproductive for the Romans. The camel soon got into the hands of the Berber nomads, increasing both their mobility and their predatory capabilities. From about the fourth century, pastoralists on the desert edge and cultivators on the high plains began to assert their autonomy, gradually and effectively shrinking the frontiers of the Roman Empire in the region. Roman cultural influence, however, remained strong, especially in architecture and religion. A new religious synthesis saw the adoption and transformation of Tanit, the Berber deity of Carthage, into Juno Caelestis, the Roman Queen of Heaven.[29]

Christianity in North Africa

The peak of Roman rule in North Africa coincided with the advent of a new religion from Palestine: Christianity. Brought by Jewish converts and others, the new faith was already established in Alexandria by the end of the first century A.D.[30] Initially subject to persecution by the Roman rulers, Christianity became the religion of the opposition. It traveled west, carried most probably by Greek and Roman intermediaries along the North African coast. By the end of the second century it was in Sicilli, where twelve Christians were martyred in 180 A.D. for refusing to sacrifice in honor of the Roman emperor. In 203, the legendary Saints Perpetua and Felicity and their companions were fed to the beasts at the

---

29. For an excellent survey of the Greco-Roman period see R. Law, "North Africa in the Hellenistic and Roman periods, 323 BC to AD 305," in J.D. Fage, ed., *Cambridge History of Africa, vol. 2: from c. 500 BC to AD 1050*, (Cambridge: Cambridge University Press, 1978), 148-209. See also the brief survey in Shillington, *History of Africa*, 62-71. On the resilience and survival of indigenous religions in Roman Egypt see D. Frankfurter, *Religion in Roman Egypt: Assimilation and Resistance* (Princeton: Princeton University Press, 1998).

30. For a lucid and fascinating introduction to Christianity in Africa and the main source for much of what follows see Isichei, *A History of Christianity, From Antiquity to the Present* (Grand Rapids: Wm. B. Eerdmans Publishing Co., 1995). See also W.H.C. Frend, "The Christian period in Mediterranean Africa c. AD 200 to 700," in Fage, ed., *Cambridge History of Africa*, vol. 2, 410-489.

Figure 4-7. Early Christian and Islamic Centers in Northern Africa

Carthage arena. Rome, although famed for its tolerant outlook, could not be indifferent to Christianity, with its monotheism and its subversive refusal to acknowledge the cult of the emperor many of who, in the traditions of the Pharaohs, desired to be worshipped as gods. However, sustained persecution and sporadic repression, which reached a frenzy under Emperor Diocletian in 302 A.D., only worked to fuel the expansion of the new faith. Christianity's offer of fellowship across social and racial barriers in a class society, its teaching of love and compassion, and its promise of bodily resurrection and eternal life became catalysts for its growth. Following in the tradition of the Greeks, the Egyptians perceived Christ as a great teacher noted for his wisdom and asceticism and worthy of emulation. Despised and hunted down by the Roman rulers, the Christians retreated to the dreary terrain beyond the Nile, where they adapted to an austere and hermitic existence. Celebrated by scholars as the Desert Fathers (though there were several women among them),[31] they virtually invented both the eremitical and the monastic way of life. They gave birth to the Christian institution of monasticism, an ordered life of religious devotion, clearly modeled after ancient Egyptian priestly asceticism.

The adoption of Christianity by Emperor Constantine as the official religion of the Roman empire in 312 A.D., followed later in the century by the persecution of the priests of traditional religions, paved the way for widespread conversions to Christianity. As it would become for Islam several centuries later, North Africa became the social nucleus and the intellectual spearhead of Christianity. It gave the church some of its early Fathers and leading theologians. The first was Origen (185-253 A.D.). Named after the ancient Egyptian deity, Horus, Origen soon distinguished himself as a universalist, a theologian of genius, an immensely learned scholar, and the first major thinker to successfully grapple with and articulate the problems of Christology. An intellectual celebrity and a consort to royalty, in pro-

---

31. See Helen Waddell, *The Desert Fathers* (London: Constable, 1977).

lific and influential writings and teachings he left a lasting legacy. One of his pupils was Gregory the Wonderworker. According to traditions, after an encounter with Origen, Gregory returned as a missionary to his homeland, Cappadocia, where he met only seventeen Christians; but by the time of his death, there were only seventeen pagans yet to be converted. Another of these catechetical pioneers was Tertullian (160-240 A.D.). A puritan and the first Christian theologian to write in Latin, Tertullian was a bundle of contradictions: he eulogized martyrdom, but died a natural death; he espoused virginity, but was happily married; he denounced classical learning though he wrote prodigiously; and he was unsparing in his criticism of heretical sects, though he soon became a member of the Montanistic order, a heretical sect given to fasting and ecstatic experiences. However, by far the most famous and the most prolific of the early church Fathers was Aurelius Augustus (354-430), of Berber descent and known to history as St. Augustine of Hippo in Numidia (eastern Algeria). More than any other thinker, St. Augustine was responsible for establishing the basic theological and doctrinal foundations of the Roman church and for preserving and transmitting to posterity the rich heritage of Latin culture. So prodigious was he in his literary and theological output that an inscription in a Spanish library insists that anyone with a claim to have read them all should be branded a liar.[32]

The close association of Christianity with Rome ensured that Latin, rather than Greek, would emerge as the language of African Christianity. The association created new problems. Social and ethnic differences within the Roman Empire began to crystallize into religious cleavages. With Alexandria being the intellectual center of early Christendom, Africa became inextricably entangled in all the heretical and schismatic controversies of the Christian world. Attempts to define the precise nature of Christ as God-Man and establish the meaning of the Trinity generated heated controversies that plagued Christendom for generations. Those with beliefs contrary to official doctrines were branded heretics and excommunicated. In North Africa, defiance of the Roman authority and of the official Roman Church was led by the Donatists, over the extent or the possibility of salvation by grace for a lapsed sinner without the need for martyrdom. Early in the fourth century, four hundred Donatist North African bishops and their churches were officially banned from the Catholic Church. Similarly, in Egypt, a new doctrine which argued that Christ had only one nature and was fully divine and that his human manifestation was a mere appearance and not a reality became dominant. This was contrary to the Chalcedonian and Catholic views of the duality of Christ's nature. In 451 A. D., Egyptian monophysitism was declared heretical. The public lynching, six years later, of the Patriarch of Alexandria for espousing the Chaceldonian doctrine of the Papacy dramatically and effectively sealed the severance of the Egyptian church from Rome. Monophysitism continued as the religion of the majority of the population, in the Coptic Church.[33]

---

32. On Saint Augustine and some of the early church fathers of Africa, see Isichei, *A History of Christianity*, 18-29. On Saint Augustine, see Augustine, *The Confessions*, (New York: Vintage Books, 1998); and the well-written biography by Peter Brown, *Augustine of Hippo* (London: Faber and Faber, 1967).

33. For a more detailed account of Egyptian monophysitism, see W.H.C. Frend, *The Rise of the Monophysite Movement* (Cambridge: Cambridge University Press, 1972).

Aksum

From Egypt, the Monophysite variant of Christianity spread to Nubia and Ethiopia. In Nubia, a distinctly indigenous Christian civilization developed, complete with bishoprics, churches, and monasteries. Archaeological evidence testifies to the prosperity of its Christian ruling class and the artistically creative, decoratively patterned pottery and magnificent paintings of its artists and craftsmen. Well beyond the reach of Roman rule, Nubian Christianity became culturally associated with Byzantium. The overwhelming influence of Coptic Egypt is evidenced in the strong adherence to the Monophysite faith. With the rise and triumph of Islam in Egypt, Egyptian influence was to substantially contribute to the Arabization of Nubia and the gradual but successful displacement of Christianity from the region, especially from the early fourteenth century.

It was in the Ethiopian kingdom of Aksum that Christianity was to reach the peak of its splendor in Africa, especially after the advent of Islam. Aksum began as one of the many trading settlements of the Sabean-speaking people of southeastern Arabia. Starting from about 600 B.C., they began to migrate across the Red Sea into Eritrea, largely in search of ivory for their Persian and Indian Ocean trades. They settled, intermarried, and intermingled with the local population. A new language, known as Ge'ez, with its own script, developed to replace their Sabean language. The prosperity of these Ge'ez-speaking people was based on trade. They built the thriving seaport of Adulis, which gave them command of the Red Sea. Their strategic location put them in a position to benefit from the trades of the Mediterranean, the Red Sea and the Indian Ocean. Tapping the human and material reservoirs of inner Africa, they exported ivory and slaves in exchange for silver, gold, oil, and wine. They minted their own coins and exported frankincense, myrrh, glass crystal, brass, and copper to Egypt and the Greco-Roman worlds. In their fertile area, they practiced irrigated and terraced agriculture, worked mainly by peasants. By the first century A.D. a kingdom centered on the city of Aksum emerged.

Our knowledge of Aksum comes from fragmentary traditions, classical writings, cave paintings, and numismatics, as well as from epigraphical and archaeological materials. In a history spanning a period of more than one thousand years, kings succeeded kings, many of them known to history only through their coinage. Two, however, are distinguished: Ezana, who converted to Christianity; and Kaleb, who immortalized his name through the many outstanding monuments he left behind. After breaking and taking over the power of the princes of the segmentary states of ancient Ethiopia, the rulers of the new kingdom had, by the third century, incorporated Saba (Yemen) in south Arabia. By the fourth century, the declining state of Meroe had been brought to submission. At the head of this kingdom was the Negus, the king of kings. He was assisted in administration by his retinue of relatives and royal officials and by the rulers of the vassal states, who paid regular tribute, and supervised and taxed foreign trade on behalf of the monarch. Archaeology has unearthed the remains of several cities that testify to the prosperity and power of Aksum, which by the third century had gained the reputation of being one of the leading kingdoms in the world. Its cities were dotted with palatial stone buildings, massive temples, and royal graves marked with tall and impressive stone steles; the tallest of these to survive rises to a height of thirty-three meters and weighs about seven hundred tons.[34]

Unlike Egypt, but like Nubia, Aksum remained beyond the military and political reach of the Roman Empire. It, however, forged commercial and cultural links with Rome and later with Constantinople. The "conquest" of Rome by Christianity in 312 A.D. was repeated two decades later in Aksum. Christianity appears to have come to Aksum from Alexandria. This origin ensured that the Ethiopian church would be Monophysite and allied with the Coptic Church of Egypt, which from the time of Athanasius, supplied its bishops and its canon laws. The conversion of Negus Abraha Ezana early in the fourth century, through the instrumentality of Frumentius, a shipwrecked young Christian trader from Tyre in Syria, made Christianity the official state religion from 333 A.D. It also paved the way for its triumph over the other competing cults in the royal courts of Aksum, and its gradual spread to the whole population through priests and monks who enjoyed royal patronage. Temples that were originally dedicated to indigenous deities such as Astar, Baher, Meder, and Mahrem became churches. Inscriptions on royal monuments, graves, and coins began to display Christian messages and motifs. In the fifth century, missionaries from Syria, known as the "Nine Saints," arrived in Aksum. They established monasteries and translated the scriptures into Ge'ez.[35]

However, from the late sixth century, Aksum began to decline. The rise of the new powers of Persia and Byzantium and the warfare between them dislocated trade and forced Aksum to become increasingly dependent on agriculture. The resultant over-exploitation of its land, forest, and ivory and mineral resources led to the deterioration of the environment and to declining productivity. Aksum escaped the military devastation of the Vandals, a northern Germanic horde, who occupied Carthage in 400 A.D. It was also beyond the reach of the Byzantine conquerors, who displaced the Vandals in 533, building a powerful navy in Carthage to defend their Mediterranean holdings. Aksum, however, could not escape the commercial dislocations occasioned by these invasions. The rise of Islam across the eastern frontier of Aksum, and of the state of Baghdad, led to the Persian conquest of Saba and the expulsion of the Aksumites from there. The diversion of trade from the Red Sea to the Persian Gulf dealt a crippling blow to the economy of Aksum. Already weakened by its fratricidal schism, and ravaged by a succession of devastating invasions, North African Christianity could not resist the united and determined approach of Islam. It disappeared almost overnight, leaving behind only the relics of its past glories in the Copts of Egypt. Aksum, however, survived the ingress of Islam, though at a high cost. Expelled from Saba, deprived of its lucrative trade on the Red Sea, surrounded by hostile and more powerful states, and perennially threatened by Islam, Aksum existed in isolation. Greek and Arab influences declined. Re-emerging as Ethiopia, the kingdom of the legendary Prester John of Africa and the Indies, Aksum became the main bastion

---

34. On Aksum see Y.M. Kobishanov, "Aksum: Political System, Economics and Culture, First to Fourth Century," in Mokhtar, ed., *Ancient Civilizations*, 381-400.

35. On the early history of Christianity in Ethiopia see S. Kaplan, *The Monastic Holy Man and the Christianization of Early Solomonic Ethiopia* (Wiesbaden: Franz Steiner Verlag, 1984); and D. Kessler, *The Falashas: The Forgotten Jews of Ethiopia* (London: Allen & Unwin, 1982).

of Christianity in Africa for many centuries after the triumph of Islam in North Africa and the virtual eclipse of Christianity on the continent before the advent of the Portuguese in the fifteenth century.

Review Questions

1. "The Gift of the Nile." How accurate is this description of the civilization of ancient Egypt?
2. "He (the pharaoh) is a god by whose dealings one lives, alone by himself, without an equal." (Pharaoh's Vizier, ca. 1500 BC) In the light of this statement, assess the significance of the institution of sacred kingship in the historical development of ancient Egypt.
3. What were the major achievements and legacies of pharaonic Egypt?
4. Compare and contrast the main features and the major achievements of the empires of Kush, Meroe, and Aksum.
5. With reference to specific examples, examine the significance of North Africa in the early development of Christianity.

Additional Reading

Bernal, Martin. *Black Athena: The Afro-Asiatic Roots of Classical Civilization.* London: Free Association Press, 1987.

Frend, W.H.C. *The Rise of Christianity.* London: Darton, Longman, and Todd, 1986.

Isichei, Elizabeth. *A History of Christianity in Africa, From Antiquity to the Present.* Grand Rapids: Wm. B. Eerdmans Publishing Co., 1995.

Mokhtar, G., ed. *Ancient Civilizations of Africa.* UNESCO General History of Africa, Vol. 2. Berkeley: University of California Press, 1981.

Shinnie, P.L., *Meroe: A Civilization of the Sudan.* London: Thames and Hudson, 1967.

PART C

Peoples and States

Section Overview

There was no area of Africa without major states or empires. The leading ones included:

Kush 100 B.C.–A.D. 300	Dahomey 1700–1900
Nubia 550–1400 A.D.	Darfur 1400–1800
Aksum 100–700 A.D.	Abyssinia 700–1974
Ghana 700–1240 A.D.	Bunyoro 1500–1900
Mali 1050–1500 A.D.	Buganda 1600–1970
Songhai 1350–1600 A.D.	Lunda 1500–1700
Kanem Borno 800–1900	Lozi 1650–1700
Hausa States 1000–1800	Karanga/Mutapa 1250–1700
Ife/Oyo 1400–1850	Swazi 1800–
Benin 1400–1800	Zulu 1800–
Asante 1700–1900	

This list omits many small states and segementary or non-centralized political systems.

This section provides many case-studies of states and societies. Chapter 5 is on South Africa, a continuation of the consequences of Bantu migration, and chapters 6 and 7 are on the states of West Africa, both those in the savanna and those in the forest. Chapter 8 covers East Africa, chapter 9 is on Central Africa, chapter 10 on Ethiopia, and chapter 11 on North Africa.

The states reveal varying levels and patterns of political organization, urbanization, and economic, social, and cultural institutions. Chapter 11 draws attention to societies without the complex institutions of empires. In centralized states (as in the empires), power was structured hierarchically, with a few people wielding enormous power and a bureaucracy collecting tax and running the administration. A king or an emperor was very powerful, with many rights and privileges. In non- centralized polities (such as the Igbo of Nigeria, the Nuer of the Sudan and the Kikuyu of Kenya), the exercise of power was diffused and groups such as elders and age-grade associations played prominent political functions.

The family was the basic unit of production. Division of labor was both by age and by gender. Women were active in farm work in many places, in addition to their many other occupations. Children received informal education in the home. In Islamic areas, Qur'anic schools offered a more formal system, with instruction in Arabic and emphasis on religious beliefs.

The states benefited from advanced agriculture, iron technology, and trade. Domestic production and trade sustained power. States in the forest such as Benin, Oyo, and Asante built their power on agriculture and local trade. Luba, Luanda, and Longo in southern Africa built their prosperity on metal work, agriculture, and trade in salt, metals, and foodstuffs. Karanga had a successful trade in gold—Great Zimbabwe, its capital, was a center of commerce that attracted goods from China and India.

Long-distance trade was important, for bringing wealth, ideas, and missionaries. The Sudanese empires of West Africa were connected with the trans-Saharan trade, and their control of trade routes became one factor leading to prosperity. With the use of the camel after the 7th century, the trans-Saharan trade increased in scale and cemented the relations between two regions of the continent. From West Africa came exports such as slaves, gold, ivory, ostrich feathers, and other products. Imports included books, textiles, armaments, and beads.

For East Africa, maritime commerce with Arabia, Persia, Oman, India, and China was important. Trade increased in volume after the eighth century, with the participation of Arab traders. Slaves, gold, and ivory were taken from East Africa. As chapter 8 shows, about forty coastal cities developed, and a Swahili culture, combining Arab and African civilizations, evolved and flourished in such places as Kilwa, Malindi, Mombasa, Zanzibar, Mogadishu, and Dar es Salaam.

Many were affected by the external contacts brought by Islam, Christianity, and interaction with the Europeans after the fifteenth century. Christianity spread in North Africa, as well as in Aksum in the northern Ethiopian highlands. From the sixth to the fifteenth centuries A.D., Nubia contained three Christian kingdoms. In the North east and East Africa, the Abyssinian or Ethiopian kingdom adopted Christianity. The churches of Lalibela, carved in solid rocks, were built during the 12th century.

Islam spread rapidly from the eighth century, reaching many places in North, West, and East Africa. Kingdoms such as Mali embraced Islam, integrating aspects of it with its politics, importing religious books from North Africa, and establishing Islamic universities at Djenne and Timbuktu.

Chapter 5

Bantu Expansion and Its Consequences

Funso Afolayan

In 1862, Wilhem Bleek, in the course of a visit to East Africa, identified the speakers of a group of languages in Africa as belonging to a single language family which he termed "Bantu."[1] This postulation derived from the structural similarities of the word for "people" in all these languages. Among the Duala, the word for "people" is *bato*, among the Bushong *baat*, the Fang *bot*, the Luba *bantu*, the Tio *baaru*, the Shona *vanhu*, the Rwanda *abatu*, the Herero *abandu*, the Swahili *watu*, the Kongo *bantu*, and the Mongo *banto*, to mention just a few. Hundreds of words from all these languages with similarities in meaning and regular phonetic patterns have been identified and listed by scholars to form a proto-Bantu glossary. In the last few years these languages have been studied, and they continue to be studied, for their morphological or grammatical concordances as well as their syntactical and phonological systems of agreements. Studies have confirmed, again and again, a single ancestry for virtually all the languages spoken by the peoples occupying the southern half of the African continent. Thus, from eastern Nigeria in the northwest and Somalia in the northeast, to Namibia and South Africa in the south, about six hundred languages have been identified as deriving from the same ancestral language known as proto-Bantu. The implications of this discovery for uncovering the processes of the peopling of the continent and the emergence of states, societies, and cultural formations are momentous. This chapter focuses on the origins of the Bantu and their expansion into much of Central, eastern, and southern Africa. The nature, antiquity, features, patterns, and major consequences of their expansion will be examined.

Sources and Methodology

Oral Tradition and Archaeology

Historians have relied on various types of evidence to unravel the possible origins, nature, antiquity, directions, and impact of Bantu expansion. The major sources of information are oral tradition, archaeology, and linguistics. Used cor-

---

1. W.H.I. Bleek, *A Comparative Grammar of South African Languages*, 2 vols. (Cape Town: Trubner, 1862-1869).

certain basic rules that must be followed in any classification of languages. The first rule is that languages must be classified on linguistic evidence alone. Second, the only significant resemblances are those resulting from the conjunction of similar forms with similar meanings. Third, for a genetic relationship between languages to be validly established, resemblances between them must be neither sporadic nor accidental, but must occur in large numbers and with a high degree of consistency. Finally, it must be recognized that genuine resemblances can also result from borrowing and do not always stem from genetic relationship. Disentangling genetic relationships from borrowing can be done through a rough distinction between "fundamental" and "cultural" vocabulary. Fundamental vocabulary includes pronouns and words for numerals and parts of the body; such words are more likely to be genetically derived and less likely to result from borrowing. Genetic classifications of languages are not inventions or arbitrary constructions. Instead they are patterns of relationships that should be evident and objective enough for well-trained linguists to recognize.[3]

Tree and Wave Models in Bantu Studies

Two models have been used by linguists to study the history of Bantu languages. The first of these is the family tree model, in which daughter languages split from mother languages. The tree model emphasizes migration or isolation from the mother community as the major impetus for change. It speaks of branches splitting at nodes, with each group of speakers branching off from the trunk or main language and moving away to form new languages. In this model, a multiplicity of origins is inconceivable, since a language can have only a single ancestor. Another drawback of the tree model is its inability to accommodate situations or scenarios in which three or more languages sprout simultaneously from the same node. It represents synchronic differentiation as successive splits of two branches each.

The second model speaks of clusters that differentiate. It assumes that changes spread out like waves from idiolects and dialects. Its emphasis is not on migrations but on innovations within and interactions between closely related languages. Continuing interactions between two or more different ancestral dialects can result in the development of a new, distinct language. This model observes that increased distances and reduced frequency of communication between stationary groups could result in the dialects at the periphery developing into new languages, distinct from and unintelligible to the people speaking the dialects spoken in the center of the circle; the dialect spoken at the center may also evolve into a new language. The wave model, unlike the tree model, permits multiple parentage for a single language, since the influencing languages are usually closely situated and related, all of them evolving from a single huge dialect continuum.

By studying the features that various languages have in common, one can trace a family or group of closely related languages back to the original parent language. A language genealogy or family tree can thus be established on a map or chart, showing the development of its branches and the nature and direction of

3. See Joseph Greenberg, *Studies in African Linguistic Classification* (New Haven: Compass Publishing, 1955); *The Languages of Africa* (Bloomington: Indiana University Press, 1970); and "Linguistic Evidence Regarding Bantu Origins," *Journal of African History* 13 (1973). See also Thomas Spear, *Kenya's Past* (Essex: Longman, 1981).

the movement of speakers from a common original language heartland. Phonetic change has been shown to be regular and not arbitrary. Consequently, linguists compare features of genetically similar looking languages to identify similarities as well as innovations in phonetic, morphological, lexical, and syntactic structures, as a means of documenting linguistic history. In Africa, scholars have combined the family tree and wave models to classify African languages and to establish the genealogy of the Bantu family of languages.[4]

For clarification, it is important to note that the word "Bantu" is not the name of any one particular language, but a linguistic term used to identify a group of closely related languages spoken over much of the southern half of the African continent.[5]

Bantu Origins and Proto-Bantu Origins

From the study of the vocabulary of proto-Bantu, linguists are generally agreed that the Bantu originated from the grassland area of Cameroun and the adjacent Benue region of southeastern Nigeria. It is in this region that the closest relatives of the proto-Bantu language can still be found. Notable among these are the Tiv and Efik languages of southeastern Nigeria and the Ekoi and Duala of southern Cameroon. Similarly, the greatest concentration or incidence of the compiled and validated proto-Bantu vocabularies is also found among some of the languages still spoken in this region. Malcolm Guthrie, who has devoted a lifetime to the study of the Bantu languages, was able to identify two thousand common word roots, particularly as measured in twenty-eight test languages, chosen for their wide geographical distribution across the Bantu zone and also for the quality of information available on them. Of the two thousand common words, he was able to identify at least 455 "general" word roots that could be said to have existed in proto-Bantu. His results also confirm the tendency of the Bantu languages to throw up pairs of synonyms and reflexes, one with an eastern and one with a western distribution, confirming the postulation of two concurrent movements in the dispersal of the Bantu speakers.[6]

In his search for the nucleus of the Bantu expansion, Guthrie directed his efforts at identifying the area with the highest retention of the "general" roots as the likely historical point of origin at which the proto-language first took shape and began to diversify. The balance of his evidence overwhelmingly points to the northwest of the Bantu language zone, linking Bantu to the languages of sub-Saharan West Africa, and the wider grouping classified by Greenberg as Niger-

---

4. For a fuller discussion of the tree and wave models see Colin Flight, "Trees and Traps," *History in Africa*, vol. 8 (1981): 43-66; and Jan Vansina, "New Linguistic Evidence and 'The Bantu Expansion,'" *Journal of African History*, 36 (1995): 173-195.

5. For a succinct articulation of the present state of linguistic research on the Bantu expansion see Vansina, "New Linguistic Evidence," 173-195.

6. See Malcolm Guthrie, *Comparative Bantu: An Introduction to the Comparative Linguistics and Prehistory of the Bantu Languages*, 4 vols. (Farnborough: Gregg, 1967-1971). For a completely different classification of the Bantu languages based on Guthrie's data, see Alick Henrici, "Numerical classification of Bantu languages," *African Language Studies*, 14 (1973).

there are reflexes in the Tiv language of central Nigeria, thus confirming once again the Benue-Cross River nucleus for proto-Bantu.[9]

Bantu Expansion

Linguistic Footprints

With the aid of two dating methods, glottochronology and lexicostatistics, linguists have provided a relative chronology for the dispersal of the Bantu. Proto-Bantu vocabularies attest to the making of pottery and the cultivation of root crops, two developments dated in archaeology for the Bantu cradle area to around 3000 B. C. This means that the proto-Bantu expansion must have begun some time after this date. The first stage involved the differentiation of the original Bantu language from the cluster of Bantoid languages spoken in western Cameroon. Thereafter, it expanded eastward and became established on the savanna fringe, north of the Zaire River, by about 500 B. C. While in this region, the group differentiated into several language clusters. Two of these were proto-West Bantu and proto-East Bantu. Simultaneously, a northwest cluster was also differentiating itself from West Bantu. This process of initial differentiation appears to have been completed by the beginning of the Christian Era. Thereafter, West and East Bantu also began to disperse. From their cradle in northern Congo, the speakers of West Bantu infiltrated the forests and swamps between the Sangha and Ubangi Rivers. From there they ascended the mainstream of the Congo-Lualaba, penetrating its southern tributaries, the Kasai, the Kwango, the Sankuru, and the Lubilash, before reaching the dry woodlands of southwestern Zaire. From here, they slowly expanded southward into the savanna grasslands of Angola and Namibia.

In the meantime the speakers of proto-East Bantu pushed southeastward from their cradle in the equatorial rain forests, reaching the middle Zambezi River. From there, they spread over the Makua area of Mozambique, and the Kilimanjaro and Great Lakes areas of East Africa. This dispersal must have occurred very slowly, since seven of the eight subgroups of the savanna Bantu appear to have developed along the southern fringes of the forest zone before their emergence into the savanna along the lower Congo River. Beyond the Great Lakes, the pace of expansion appeared to have accelerated, because most of the Bantu languages spoken from eastern to southern Africa belong to a single eastern highland sub-group of savanna Bantu. The fact that the languages belonging to the eastern Bantu block are more closely related to each other than those of the western Bantu is an indication that the expansion of the eastern groups started at a later date, but occurred more rapidly once it began. Linguists and archaeologists are generally agreed that the initial differentiation of the Bantu languages into eight or so constituent sub-groups took place in the course of the second millennium B.C, while the secondary diffusion of the Bantu languages through the savanna and the eastern highlands was well under way by the middle of the first millen-

---

9. The sources for the reconstructed proto-Bantu vocabularies are Guthrie, *Comparative Bantu*; and J. Vansina, *Paths in the Rainforests, Towards a History of Political Tradition in Equatorial Africa* (Madison: the University of Wisconsin Press, 1990), 267-301.

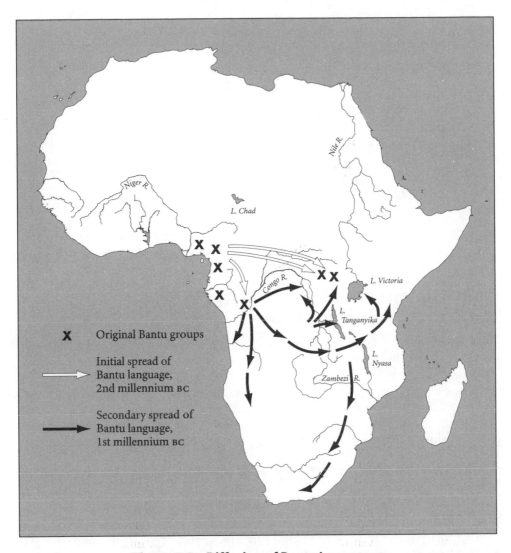

Figure 5-2. Diffusion of Bantu Languages

nium B.C. Dialects at the opposite end of the language continuum were usually the first to grow into new languages, followed later by the core of dialects at the center. This process of fission and sequence of differentiation was repeated again and again within each successive or emerging language, until the whole of the southern half of the African continent was infiltrated and colonized by speakers of Bantu languages. Some languages developing in border areas between two language clusters became heirs to double parentage.[10]

---

10. For a fuller discussion of the emergence and initial dispersal of the proto-Bantu speakers from the Benue-Cross Rivers complex, see Spear, *Kenya's Past*, 29-33; Vansina, "Bantu in the Crystal Ball," *History in Africa*, 6 and 7 (1979, 1980) and various essays in C. Ehret and M. Posnansky, *The Archaeological and Linguistic Reconstruction of African History* (Berkeley and Los Angeles: University of California Press, 1982).

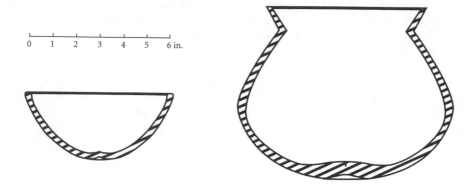

Figure 5-3. Urewe Pottery

Bantu Expansion and Early Iron Age Farming: The Archaeological Evidence

The division of the dispersal of the Bantu speakers into two broad fronts or streams is corroborated by archaeological evidence.[11] Archaeologists studying styles and methods of pottery decoration and furnace construction have divided the Bantu expansion into two broad streams, the eastern and western traditions. There are many strands of the eastern pottery tradition, of which two, Urewe (east central) and Kwale (eastern), are the most dominant. The east central pottery tradition appears to have had its origins in the Great Lakes region. Classified as Urewe ware and referred to as "dimple-based" pottery, its distinctive characteristic is an indenation on the base of its pots and bowls. Urewe pottery is also characterized by beveled rims, and a distinctive range of channeled decoration in festoons and spirals. The spread of the Urewe sites from the western shores of Lake Victoria, the northern end of Lake Albert, and through the western Rift Valley to Burundi, Rwanda, and Lake Tanganyika suggests that its makers were riverine peoples, used to fishing and living in thickly wooded country. In virtually all the sites where the Urewe pottery have been found, there was associated evidence of ironworking in the form of slag, charcoal, tuyeres, and furnaces. Urewe sites have been dated to between the second and fifth centuries A.D. and earlier. Half a dozen sites from northwestern Tanzania and Rwanda have yielded dates in the first half of the first millennium B.C.

The implication of these early dates could be that iron-working techniques were invented independently in this region and not adopted from Meroe, as previously believed. Also, the possibility of diffusion from another source not yet discovered by archaeologists can not be ruled out. Nonetheless, the evidence shows that it is to Urewe that we must go if we will unravel the mystery of the origin of

---

11. For the archaeological evidence see M. Posnansky, "Bantu Genesis: Archaeological Reflections," *JAH,* 9, 1 (1968); D.W. Phillipson, "The Chronology of the Iron Age in Bantu Africa," *JAH,* 16, 3 (1975); and Kevin Shillington, *History of Africa* (New York: St. Martin's Press, 1995), 49-61.

pottery traditions in Africa south of the equator. Leaving behind its dimple-base feature, the Urewe tradition spread to southern Zaire and western Zambia. Here it shed its typical channel decoration, while retaining its vessel shapes and necks and its everted and beveled rims, before penetrating into the southern part of the continent. In every place, it remains invariably associated with iron-working sites which have yielded dates that are chronological in sequence from north to south.

As with the linguistic evidence, the archaeological data indicate that the pace of the geographical spread of iron-working populations became more rapid in the area to the south of the interlacustrine region. One explanation for the rapid movement of people would be the nature of the environment. The Congo-Zambezi watershed, with its many tributary-rivers, well stocked with fish, its alluvial land, rich in copper and iron and well-suited for agriculture, and its forests generating fuel for iron smelting, was highly favorable for Early Iron Age farming settlement. Furthermore, to the south of the Congo basin were extensive grazing lands, to which it appears that Early Iron Age migrants brought the first herds of cattle and sheep before introducing them to southern Africa. Archaeological excavations by Brian Fagan in central Zambia show that the introduction of livestock to this region was gradual. It was not until several centuries later that the advent of the era of the great herds, introduced by specialized pastoralists, transformed the economic history of the region. In the meantime, from the few holdings of the early farmers, cattle and sheep appear to have passed into the hands of the Khoikhoi hunter gatherers, who retreated with them into the plains of northern Botswana, on the edge of the Kalahari Desert, an area too arid for the wetland farmers to follow them into.

Closely related to the Urewe style and contemporaneous with it is the Kwale ware found in sites scattered unevenly in southern Kenya, northern Tanzania, and the hilly country southeast of Kilimanjaro. Balked in its eastward expansion by the presence of another set of ceramic and metallurgical traditions associated with the Kushites of southern Somalia, the Kwale ceramic tradition veered south, penetrating the coastal plains of the Maputo region of Mozambique. The southward push of the Early Iron Age fishermen-farmers was very rapid, extending over a distance of more than one thousand miles in less than two hundred years. The rapid pace was no doubt facilitated by ease of movement along the coast and the accessibility provided by the river valleys for penetration into southern Malawi and eastern Zimbabwe. The spread of the Kwale ware sites betrays the preference of its makers for the deep, fertile soils of mountain slopes and escarpments and the margins of the forests. They were predominantly farmers and fisherfolks. The majority of the Kwale sites show no sign of cattle keeping. Only at the southern edge of their spread, and on sites dated to the fifth or sixth century A.D. onwards, have archaeologists unearthed evidence of pastoral food production. Since this was usually in places where the Kwale merged into the Urewe east central stream, cattle most probably came from this fusion. Between the third and the seventh centuries A.D., Early Iron Age farmers of the Urewe tradition had settled the Malawi lake region and penetrated the river valleys of Zululand, Natal, and Transkei in southern Africa.

Archaeological excavations and findings are uneven for the western zone. Findings in the Kinshasa region of Zaire date iron working in this region to the first or second centuries A.D. The savanna woodland south of the Zaire forest has provided rich evidence of copper and iron smelting dating to the fourth century

A.D. Intensive archaeological research in Zambia has unearthed three main pottery traditions in this east central African region, dated to between the third and the seventh centuries. Between the third and fifth centuries, Bantu farmers of the western pottery tradition penetrated beyond the Zambezi and the Limpopo river valleys, into the region of Great Zimbabwe, Botswana, and the Transvaal highveld of South Africa. In one of these sites, located on the edge of the eastern Transvaal escarpment, fascinating and highly refined terracotta heads, dated to ca.500 A.D., were recovered. They were probably used for religious and ceremonial purposes. This remarkable finding demonstrates the existence of well-settled and highly organized communities in this region by the fifth century A.D. South of the Zambezi and over much of central southern Africa, the division between eastern and western Bantu breaks down. Over much of this region, considerable intermixing and intermeshing of ideas between the various peoples, languages, and ceramic traditions must have occurred. Indeed, archaeologists are already beginning to speak of the likelihood of a third or "central" stream for the diffusion of early Iron Age traditions into the plateau region of Zimbabwe.

Dynamics of Expansion

Early attempts to explain the expansion of the Bantu resulted in theories of population explosion, followed by rapid migration and military conquests. As early as 1913, Sir Harry Johnston, in a paper read to the Royal Anthropological Institute, argued that "All Bantu Africa of today, except the heartland of the Congo forest and the regions south of the Zambezi, must have been more or less thickly populated before the Bantu impressed with extraordinary rapidity and completeness their own type of language on the tribes they conquered."[12] Many years later, another prominent Africanist, C.C. Wrigley, unequivocally asserted: "I see these people, not as agriculturists spreading over a virtually empty land, but as a dominant minority, specialized to hunting with the spear, constantly attracting new adherents by their fabulous prestige as suppliers of meat, constantly throwing off new bands of migratory adventurers, until the whole southern sub-continent was iron-using and Bantu-speaking."[13]

Demography and Ecology

The theory of overpopulation cannot be sustained. According to this argument, the desiccation of the Sahara around 2,500 B.C. resulted in a southward immigration which led to a population explosion in the Benue-Cross River area. Out of this came the Bantu with their sedentary, farming, and iron-using culture, which gave them an advantage over the nomadic autochthons. There are many problems with this position. So far, we have no archaeological evidence to sup-

---

12. H.H. Johnston, "A Survey of the Ethnography of Africa: And the Former Racial and Tribal Migrations of that Continent," *Journal of the Royal Anthropological Institute*, 43 (1913): 391-392.
13. C.C. Wrigley, "Speculations on the Economic Prehistory of Africa," *Journal of African History*, 1 (1960): 201.

port any mass migration from the Sahara to the central Nigerian area. The theory is also flawed because of its failure to recognize that a language, like water ripples, can spread without involving the migration of people. Third, it is problematic to reduce developments covering several millennia, and involving many discrete dispersals, into a single huge migration. Further, available evidence shows that the transformation from a hunting and a food gathering economy to an agricultural one was not a sudden or dramatic development. It occurred gradually over an extended period of time and was, therefore, not likely to have inspired a phenomenal demographic revolution that could have provoked a mass migration into, and a conquest of, new lands.

No monocausal explanation will do justice to the multidimensional nature of Bantu expansion. Apparently the people moved for various reasons. Given the prevailing methods of food production, new lands were always needed to replace already exhausted soil, which could then be left fallow. Through a process of natural drift, farmers moved to fresh sites once or twice a decade. New and uncharted farming and grazing lands were always available beyond the frontiers of the area already occupied. The attraction of unexplored and virgin lands near rivers and other natural clearings, away from areas already settled and tilled, remained a powerful pull to migration. Other natural factors such as drought, epidemics and even war should not be ruled out as stimuli. Nor should the spirit of adventure be discarded as a powerful motivation for the young, the restless, and the ambitious, many of whom probably struck out in different directions to claim new lands for themselves and their followers.

There is no evidence to support the idea that the Bantu expansion ever assumed the form of an exodus involving thousands of people, moving across the continent *en masse* like a conquering horde. For the most part, the movement involved small numbers of people who moved from one settlement to another. Also, this was also not a linear, a unidirectional, or a perpetual forward movement. While the general direction of motion was mostly southward, movement must have occurred in all directions as groups moved back and forth, making advances and suffering reverses. This process must have been repeated again and again by successive generations. The nature, timing, and direction of movement fluctuated widely in response to the great variety of natural habitats the Bantu had to deal with. The immediate attraction was naturally to the more readily accessible, fertile, and well-watered regions, such as the forest savanna margin of Gabon-Congo, the extensive Zaire River basin and the Great Lakes region of East Africa. Other areas such as the disease infested swamps of the great rivers, the sandy and arid Bateke plateaus, and the Kalahari Desert were avoided. The attraction was always towards vacant or sparsely populated lands, hence north-east Kenya and Somalia, already inhabited by earlier Nilo-Kushitic migrants, were not favored destinations, forcing the eastern Bantu groups to veer south when they came in contact with these pre-existing groups. Moving into regions that were thinly populated by small and isolated roving bands of Stone Age hunter-gatherers, the Bantu farmers had considerable freedom of action to select areas best suited for grazing and cultivation. Without the need to leave the land to fallow or fight over space, new generations easily moved on to new sites.

The Bantu had to adapt themselves to a variety of habitats. Those who colonized the river valleys and the lake regions developed an aquatic culture, the forest dwellers established a forest economy, while the grassland inhabitants adapted themselves to a grassland ecology. None of these was monolithic, as people moved in and out of ecological zones, acquiring new habits and transmitting their own.

Thus the Bantu expansion was neither a rapid nor a massive movement. Indeed, it can hardly even be described as a migration. should be seen as a slow, gradual, piecemeal infiltration and colonization of a whole sub-continent, involving small numbers of people at any time, and continuing over a very long period of time, probably extending back to the first millennium before the Christian Era.

The Adoption of Metallurgy

It used to be assumed that possession of the knowledge of iron smelting was principally responsible for the expansion and the success of the Bantu over pre-existing groups who had no such knowledge. This point must not be overemphasized. There is no proto-Bantu word for iron. Instead there are at least fifty roots for the word in the Bantu languages. These words are not entirely congruent with each other. Some of them were borrowed from non-Bantu languages, while some derive from Bantu words for "white," "stone," "stone block," or "rock." The implication of this is that the speakers of proto-Bantu did not possess the knowledge of iron working before leaving their original homeland in the Benue-Cross River region. The earliest date for iron working in sub-Saharan Africa is from the Great Lakes region of East Africa, and is dated to 800 B.C. The Nok culture site at Taruga in central Nigeria is dated to the fifth century. The ancient city of Meroe on the middle Nile was already a flourishing iron-making center by the 6th century B.C. Iron smelting sites dating to the fifth century have been identified in northern Gabon. However, because of the complexities of the processes involved, it is unlikely that iron-smelting techniques were invented independently in northern Gabon. The balance of evidence seems to indicate that the Bantu acquired the knowledge of iron-working after the completion of their initial expansion from the Benue-Cross River region. The range of terms relating to iron smelting and their pattern of distribution point to the Great Lakes region as the probable origin of the diffusion of iron working for the Bantu world.[14]

Once acquired, the knowledge of metallurgy became a decisive instrument in the hands of the Bantu, facilitating their expansion into new areas and their mastery of the different ecological environments they had to confront. They appear to have spread the knowledge of metal-working to the southern and central parts of the continent. Metals became the mediators of social and political relations. They were used for currencies, as repositories of , and as prestige goods such as jewelry that became objects of trade, marriage, and political exchange. Those who possessed the knowledge of metallurgy had at their disposal a valuable instrument for the acquisition of wealth. This could in turn be converted to the acquisition of followers as well as to gaining economic and political power and privileges. But the working of iron did not mark a sudden radical transformation in the ecosystem. While its impact on agriculture was revolutionary, it was gradual. Good quality

---

14. Guthrie, *Comparative Bantu*, vol. 1, 132-140; B.M. Fagan, *Southern Africa During the Iron Age* (London, 1965); and F. Van Noten, "The Early Iron Age in the Interlacustrine Region: The Diffusion of Iron Technology," *Azania,* 14 (1979): 61-80.

iron ores were not universally available, and only a small quantity of the metal appears to have been initially produced in Bantu Africa. There is little conclusive evidence of the superiority of a primitive iron technology over a Stone Age technology whose assemblage of tool kits included ground and polished axes and adzes. No doubt the availability of metal tools like the bush-knife improved the clearing of soft vegetation, and the iron sickle did the same for the harvesting of cereals. Nevertheless, in many parts of the region, the digging stick continued to be used, in spite of the knowledge of cutlasses, axes and hoes, while most forest and bush clearing continued to be done by fire. Grinding stones and stone scrapers for preparing skins also continued in use.

In pastoralism, besides the use of the new weapons for the protection of the stock from wild animals, stock raising could flourish with little or no use of iron technology. If the immediate impact of the introduction of metallurgy was modest in agriculture, it was probably far-reaching in hunting and fishing. The possession of iron weapons such as spear-heads and metal harpoons must have improved efficiency of hunters, enabling them to convert a wide range of wild animals, including large mammals like elephants and hippopotami, into food. With regard to fishing, the advent of iron allowed and even stimulated a more efficient and intensive exploitation of the resources of rivers, lakes, and coastal waters. This would mean increased population, and the establishment of new settlements to maximize the advantages of the new technology in river valleys, on lake shores, and in coastal areas. In the military sphere, iron-tipped spears and arrows made war more lethal, but they did not render stone- or bone-tipped poisoned arrows, or wooden spears and clubs, obsolete or less effective nor their users less aggressive.[15]

Vegeculture and the Coming of the Banana

The knowledge of agriculture was a major asset for the Bantu. Linguistic evidence shows that they were already farmers in their proto-Bantu homeland. From this base they moved out as Late Stone Age food producers, who lived by fishing and small-scale gardening in their waterside settlements. Hunting and foraging continued among the Bantu speakers. However, their expansion at the expense of other language groups was not based on superior methods of hunting and gathering. It appears to have been based on the development of a food-producing economy. This economy was initially associated with the ground and polished stone axes and hoes that were still used in various Bantu settlements along the forest margins. Before long, however, iron was added to the tool-kit of the Bantu farmers, especially as they emerged from the northern forests into the open savanna to the south, a region in much of which food production did not begin until the Iron Age. Through a process of linguistic sieving and comparison of common words, or cognates, linguists have been able to establish that the proto-Bantu were fishermen and root cultivators. Guthrie's analysis of the "general" roots relating to the environment shows the presence of well-attested words for "forest patch" and "thicket," but none for "grassland" or "unbroken forest." There are many words for wild fauna, but none for any of the animals of the open savanna, such as the

---

15. For a pioneering exploration of the dynamics of the Bantu expansion, see R. Oliver, "The problem of the Bantu expansion," *JAH*, 7 (1966): 361-76.

lion, zebra, or ostrich. The reconstructed proto-Bantu glossary contains common words for fishhooks, fish traps, dugout canoes, and paddles. A great variety of crops were cultivated, depending on the local environment. The forest Bantu planted yams and harvested beans, as well as a variety of vegetables and palm products. There is also a word for "fig tree," a plant of the savanna or forest margin. Living in the forest automatically excluded grain cultivation and cattle herding. Hence, like most of their close relatives in the tsetse fly-ridden region of Cameroon and southeastern Nigeria, the forest Bantu kept goats, but had no word for cattle. Similarly, they had no common words for grains, bananas, pastoralism, iron working, or pottery, with the implication that these were either little grown or practiced, or more probably were adopted in the course of their expansion southeastward.

Taken together, all this evidence indicates that the proto-Bantu lived in a forest or forest margin environment, with many rivers, a wet climate, and an economy based on fishing and vegeculture, where crop planting rather than cereal sowing was the norm. Archaeological evidence indicates that sorghum, millet, and cattle were already domesticated in eastern Africa, before the arrival of Bantu speakers in the area. It is not surprising that many of the Bantu words for irrigation, fertilization, sorghum, eleusine, cattle, and pastoralism were borrowings from the Kushitic languages spoken in the area prior to the coming of the Bantu speakers.

The introduction of the banana from Southeast Asia and/or India had far reaching effects on the Bantu expansion. Botanical and linguistic evidence indicates that the introduction of bananas into Africa was a complex historical process involving multiple diffusions over a wide area, probably passing through the Nile Valley and the Great Lakes before reaching equatorial Africa and then to West Africa, over an extended period of time. The advent of the banana has also been connected with the oceanic voyages of Indonesian traders and migrants who colonized the island of Madagascar at the beginning of the Christian Era, before passing the banana inland through the region of Lake Malawi and up the Western Rift Valley into the interlacustrine region and beyond. This is the most plausible route produced by Guthrie's analysis of the pattern of distribution of the word root, *tooke,* for "banana." Two varieties of bananas are found in Africa. The most prevalent is the plantain, larger in size, usually baked or made into flour, and dominant in West and Central Africa. Fifty-eight cultivars of the plantain are cultivated in the Zaire basin alone. The second variety is the sweet banana, smaller in size, and dominant in East Africa.[16]

The yield of bananas is ten times that of the yam and is comparable only to the yield of manioc or cassava. Unlike yam it is resistant to the epidemiological hazards of the evergreen rain forests and it does not require a dry season to flourish. Once planted, it requires little care. It self-propagates and regenerates itself continuously for generations, eating up weeds and other plants, surviving floods and droughts, and colonizing forests and forest margins, especially river valleys

---

16. On the coming of bananas, see D. N. McMaster, "Speculations on the Coming of the Banana to Uganda," *Journal of Tropical Geography,* 16 (1962): 57-69; and David Schoenbrun, "Cattle Herds and Banana Gardens: The Historical Geography of the Western Great Lakes Region, *ca.* A.D. 800-1500," *African Archaeological Review*, 2 (Cambridge: Cambridge University Press, 1993), 39-72.

and swamps. Before long the banana ousted the yam as the staple crop of the region. Bantu farmers could now produce food surpluses to exchange for the fruits and meat of the hunters and food gatherers. Intensification of food production meant increased population, more economic and occupational specialization for the farming folks, and the establishment of more permanent settlements. Bananas produced a flurry of colonization and expansion as well as an economic and demographical revolution with far-reaching consequences. This revolution was further accelerated by the introduction from South America of staple food plants such as maize, cassava or manioc and sweet potatoes. Complementing their mastery of agricultural technology was the Bantu possession of pottery which allowed them to cook the food and thus achieve better nutrition.

Consequences of the Bantu Expansion

Bantu Farmers and the Autochthons

To understand the impact of the Bantu food producers on the hunters and food gatherers, it is necessary to briefly examine the state of the autochthons at the advent of the farmers. Notable among the foragers were the Sandawe and Hadza of Tanzania, the Twa of Rwanda, Burundi, and Zaire, and the Khoikhoi and San of southern Africa.[17] For want of countervailing evidence, the languages of all these groups have been grouped together in one language family, Khoisan, probably the oldest language family in Africa. The precise nature of the genetic connections between these various groups is not clear. The closeness of the Sandawe language to that of the Khoi has led scholars to infer that both belonged to a single language group, whose speakers became separated as a result of the eastward expansion of the Bantu from equatorial Africa. Similarly, scholars are increasingly leaning to the conclusion that two of the groups, the Khoikhoi and the San, actually belonged to the same group which, over the centuries, became differentiated into two as a result of occupational diversification. A section of them, who adopted cattle either from the early Bantu migrants or from the vanguard of Nilo-Kushitic migrants, became known as Khoikhoi. These were the "Hottentots" of European writings, though many of the indigenous names of their constituent groups have survived.

The Khoikhoi remained the dominant group over much of the western half of southern Africa and central Tanzania, in the east, before the advent of the Bantu. The others, who continued to subsist on hunting and foraging, became the San, described in European writings as "Bushmen," or "Bosjesman," "Sonqua" or "!kung" (meaning "person"). They remained scattered over a wide area of the eastern half of southern Africa. The two groups remained physically and linguistically related, speaking similar click-sound languages and having much in common in their material and subsistence culture.

---

17. On the history of these pre-Bantu groups, see J. Desmond Clark, *The Prehistory of Southern Africa* (Baltimore: Penguin Books, 1959); and Paul Maylam, *A History of the African People of South Africa: From the Early Iron Age to the 1970s* (New York: St. Martins, 1986).

We know more today about the Khoisan than we do about all the other groups put together. This is due to a combination of fortuitous circumstances. The Khoisan were spread over a large area of the sub-continent, from Central Africa to the Cape of Good Hope, where they were already domiciled at the advent of the Portuguese in the late fifteenth century. Consequently, archaeological excavation has unearthed artifactual remains of plant and animal food residue associated with the Khoisan. We also have impressive evidence from rock paintings and engravings, believed to be the handiwork of the Khoisan, that have provided valuable information on the social, economic, demographic, technological, and religious history of the group. In addition, we have ample historical documentation on the Khoisan from European traders who began active, though sometimes conflictual, trading and military interactions with them, from the sixteenth century onwards. The relative stability of the southern African environment during the last few centuries also meant that the group has experienced limited occupational variation over the years.

Available evidence shows that at the advent of the Bantu, the Khoisan were already in the Late Stone Age. They lived by fruit gathering, scavenging, and hunting. Fishing and the exploitation of other marine resources led to the use of fiber-nets, funnel-shaped reed-basket traps and rock and tidal fish-traps. They used bows and poisoned arrows, forked wooden objects, and pointed sticks. With the aid of digging sticks they harvested the roots and tubers of wild plants and dug large pits for storage and for trapping large game. Leather work provided rudimentary clothing, water bags, ropes, and bow strings. Their diet included collectible items such as rootstalks, plant corms, fruits, honey, and insects. They supplemented their diet with small animals like tortoises and rats, and marine resources such as fish, seals, lobsters, and different types of shellfish. They brewed wine from local umbelliferous plants. Rock paintings and contemporary European records show that women played crucial roles in the society. While men dominated hunting, women were responsible for child rearing and for much of the food collecting that provided the bulk of the day-to-day staples of the community. Food and water supplies remained subject to seasonal fluctuations in climate that resulted in periodic migration, seasonal occupancy of sites, and the fission and fusion of groups following the patterns dictated by changes in food supplies. The size of Khoisan settlements varied from small family groups to large gatherings of usually related kinship groups. The size depended on the human resources requirements for efficient exploitation of the environment.

The Khoikhoi became noted for their pastoral way of life. Milk and vegetables became their staple diet while, like the San, they supplemented their diet by hunting and food gathering. Contemporary records attest to the fact that, like most pastoral societies, they were often loath to kill their stock, except on special occasions. Compared with the San, they appear to have built larger huts, were organized in larger hordes, lived in consistently larger settlements, and made use of pottery and metal that were, in all probabilities, adopted from the Bantu. Relations between the Khoikhoi and the San were characterized by both conflict and cooperation. The San on occasions raided the livestock of the Khoikhoi, while at times serving as clients, marriage partners, and guides for them. The evidence shows that the Khoisan lived in highly organized small groups, either as foragers or as pastoralists. There is no evidence that they were on the brink of disaster, either at the advent of the Bantu or of the Europeans later in the fifteenth century, the two groups of invaders that were to significantly and irreversibly transform the demographic and social fate of the Khoisan.

Thus, as Vansina aptly notes, the autochthons were not peripatetic peoples on the verge of extinction. Indeed, vis-a-vis the newcomers, the autochthons were not always at a disadvantage. They were often initially more numerous, though more scattered, than the newcomers. They also possessed a knowledge of the habitats that the newcomers did not have. Traditions of the Bantu speak of the presence of autochthons everywhere. The farmers held profoundly ambivalent views about them. On this, a leading scholar of the Bantu expansion wrote:

> They were a despised, uncivilized, subhuman race, unfit for sexual congress with any farming woman. Yet they were the fountain of civilization: the first in the land; the inventors of fire; the teachers about habitats; the wise healers with medicinal plants; sometimes even the first metallurgists; and, on occasion, the first farmers.[18]

The Bantu Triumph: Assimilation, Adaptation, and Acculturation

The establishment of permanent settlements gave the farmers a decisive and strategic edge over their less sedentary neighbors. While the population of the Bantu villages appears to not have been very large, they were usually larger than the more numerous but scattered bands of foragers among whom they came to settle. San hunting bands did not usually number more than thirty to fifty persons. This made them more vulnerable to absorption and assimilation than the Khoikhoi whose hordes, at times, numbered from two to three thousand. The Khoikhoi pastoralists were, however, generally unstable populations as they moved up and down in search of green pasture. The more compact, semipermanent village of the farmers became the focal point for everyone in the vicinity. As a reference point for trade and group actions, it served as a magnet attracting foragers and other migrants to visit and settle. As farmers and stock raisers, the Bantu had a more reliable source of food supply. The cohesiveness of the farmers ensured the survival of their languages and culture over that of the foragers. As foragers frequented the larger villages of the farmers, they became bilingual. Trading interaction and intermarriage resulted in some of the foragers settling permanently with the villagers and eventually abandoning their own language.

In most cases, the interaction of the two groups was usually characterized by peaceful and mutual exchanges of skills and products. In story after story, the aboriginals were the people who taught the newcomers the secret of coping with their new habitat. Skills of hunting, trapping, and medicine diffused from the autochthons to the newcomers. Foragers exchanged their game and fruit for the food products and iron tools of the farmers in mutually beneficial transactions. The two groups also exchanged women. Though most of the autochthons eventually became assimilated, the process was not as rapid as the traditions imply. Archaeological findings indicate that both communities continued to live side by side for centuries. The autochthons had other choices. Those who were not pre-

---

18. Vansina, *Paths in the Rainforests*, 56.

pared to become farmers could stand their ground, fight for a time, or simply intensify their relations with the villagers. Others chose to remain wholly independent of the food producers by moving beyond the immediate reach of the farmers or into inaccessible swamps or inhospitable arid lands like the Kalahari, unattractive to the Bantu population of mixed farmers. Many groups survived till the twentieth century, in southern Angola, northern Namibia, and Botswana, tenaciously ignoring agriculture and precariously living by hunting and gathering. Others were able to preserve their language and culture, though not without some changes and adjustments, by partial or wholesale adoption of food production and stock raising. The ingenuity of the Khoikhoi hunters is demonstrated in their successful adoption of a pastoral economy, while at the same time preserving their linguistic and cultural identities.

Ultimately, however, the hunter-gatherers lost out in the competition. They became drawn into dependent relationships with the farmers. In most cases, they lost their languages so thoroughly that only faint traces of them can still be discerned. The gradual incorporation of many Khoisan into the expanding Bantu population explains the presence of many Khoisan click sounds in the languages of many Bantu groups, such as the Zulu, Swazi, Sotho, and Tsonga. There were also cases in which Bantu speakers abandoned their languages and adopted the speech of others. The Bergdamara and the Coroka of Namibia and Angola, who today speak Khoisan, probably abandoned their Bantu language over a thousand years ago. In the same way, scholars have made much of the fact that the Nguni and Sotho-Tswana words for "cow," "milk" and "fat-tailed sheep" appear to have been derived from Khoi roots.[19] The evidence is too tenuous to conclude that these Bantu groups adopted cattle from the Khoi; more probably, they adopted the cattle terminology of their neighboring pastoral specialists, with whom they had considerable interaction. Similarly, though the Kikuyu are Bantu in speech patterns and agricultural practices, their socio-political system based on age-sets, their practice of circumcision, and their aversion to fish appear to have been adopted from the pre-existing Kushitic groups they met in East Africa upon their arrival.

By the end of the first millennium A.D., the Bantu-speaking food producers appeared to have occupied much of sub-equatorial Africa. Virtually all the linguistic sub-groups had differentiated into individual languages. Linguistic stability and elaboration, rather than diversification and expansion, became the feature of Bantu history during the second millennium A.D. Though settlements remained sparse by A.D. 1000, the population continued to multiply. Individual mobility remained high, while population movements continued, though the demographic movement of the new era was smaller in scale and frequency. It was also characterized largely by cyclic drift within a given territory, since the supply of fertile, empty land was no longer inexhaustible. Triggered largely by overpopulation in the more favored habitats and provoked by resultant competition for the control of resources, trade, and power, emigration continued and produced new socio-political configurations all over the region. Linguistic and archaeological evidence indicates that the new communities were linked by trade. Stimulated by the distances between the locations of deposits of valuable resources, such as iron

---

19. Monica Wilson and Leonard Thompson, eds., *The Oxford History of South Africa*, *Vol.1: South Africa to 1870* (New York: Oxford University Press, 1971), 104.

ores, copper, gold, and salt, an extensive network of local and regional trade began to develop. The presence of a wide variety of exotic objects, connected with the Early Iron Age Bantu farmers, such as beads, seashells, and porcelain attests to some forms of tentative and indirect economic interaction with the commercial worlds of the Indian Ocean and the Far East. By the end of the first millennium A.D., internal and external dynamics worked together to produce commercial prosperity and political centralization; this was evident, for instance, in the spectacular civilization of Zimbabwe (ca.1100-c.1500 A.D.).

Bantu settlements were usually small. Houses were built with poles, clay, and grass. They were small and arranged in a circular pattern with a fenced livestock pen in the middle. Typically, socio-political organization was based on kinship, and the extended family was the most important unit of organization. Division of labor was usually along gender lines. The men were in charge of livestock, hunting, and trade as well as diplomatic and political affairs. Women's spheres of interest included agriculture, cooking, and child rearing. The gender asymmetry is further exemplified in the fact that men were usually buried within and beneath the central livestock enclosure, while women and children were buried on the outer edge of the village.

Challenges, Problems, and Gaps in Bantu Studies

Much progress has been made in the attempts to resolve the Bantu enigma, but much work remains to be done. Progress has been made in archaeology in the areas of East and southern Africa, but much of Central Africa, like much of the continent itself, is still an archaeological wilderness. This is particularly evident in the fact that scholars have been unable to reach any definitive conclusion as to the origin and spread of iron-working techniques. Questions such as how, when, where, and from whom did the Bantu acquire the knowledge of iron working are yet to be resolved. We still do not know how and when iron technology superseded Stone Age technology in much of the region. Our information on the adoption of pastoralism by the Khoikhoi has also remained largely speculative. Was this directly from the Nilo-Kushitic groups? Did they acquire the practice before the advent of the Bantu, or was it through the agency of early or later Bantu immigrants? The situation is not helped by the fact that the linguistic evidence, both on technical innovations and on pastoralism, is full of pitfalls.

Though linguistics has contributed substantially to our understanding of the Bantu expansion, it also suffers from major limitations. We presently have a proto-Bantu glossary of over five hundred word roots with regular phonetic patterns drawn from twenty eight "test languages" out of the more than six hundred Bantu languages. The limitation of this sample is evident. Half of the Bantu languages have not been studied and thus have no vocabularies compiled for them. Only a handful of the languages have had dictionaries produced or their grammatical structures studied. We have few options if each of the Bantu languages is to be placed in its proper historical perspective. For definitive conclusions to be reached, the minimum requirements will be the production of accurate linguistic notation, a comprehensive set of dictionaries, and an outline of the grammatical structure of each language. Another difficulty is the fact that, unlike the Indo-European languages, the Bantu languages did not evolve as blocks of languages, but through a process of differentiation. This makes comparison of blocks of languages difficult, implying that each language will have to be studied and contextualized linguistically and historically on its own. The issue of linguistic dating remains problematic. The situation is compounded by the extent of the time period we are dealing with: processes of language differentiation stretching across several millennia. Archaeology has given us fairly definite dates, though the margins of error for most of them remain quite wide. But even these dates cannot be linked directly with languages and peoples without much methodological intervention and speculative inference.

We must also watch out for and avoid the error of juxtaposing and confusing language, culture, and race. These are three distinct, though often interrelated entities; but there is no necessary correlation between them. Similarities of language need not imply similarities of culture and race. We have cases where the three elements overlap, but evidence abounds that renders invalid any definite equation of language, race, and culture. There are groups who are Bantu in origin, but who abandoned their languages and adopted the languages and culture of the non-Bantu groups they came in contact with. There are also cases of non-Bantu groups and hunting and trapping communities who abandoned their languages for those of the newcomers. Some of these groups lost their languages but managed to preserve their cultures, while others lost both.

The same point can also be made with reference to the physical types of the present-day Bantu speakers. As a result of their West African provenance, it is generally assumed that the Bantu were negroid. The evidence, however, indicates that as a result of centuries of interaction with their neighbors, the Bantu speakers of today vary considerably, from the Pygmies of the Congo rain forest, through the tall, thin peoples of the equatorial savanna. Scholars interested in the history of African languages and of the peopling of the African continent must recognize the salience of other variables beside migration that are at work in socio-linguistic formations. Intervening variables, like social and physical environment and a whole range of socio-linguistic mechanisms such as commercial and religious links, demographic balance, and socio-cultural power relations must always be taken into consideration. These variables have often been more decisive in the engendering of language and culture than biology. Thus, much progress notwithstanding, the controversy regarding the nature of the Bantu expansion is not entirely resolved. Indeed, many problems remain, and there are many lacunae in our knowledge of this historically significant phenomenon.

Conclusions: The Bantu Impact

The Bantu expansion was one of the greatest migrations in human history. Its gradual nature should not make us underestimate its significance in, and consequences for, African history. It is clear that some of the early assumptions on this expansion can no longer be sustained. The impression created in the oral traditions that the expansion was a recent phenomenon is not substantiated either by archaeological or by linguistic evidence. Indeed, it began a long time ago. The Niger-Congo languages began to differentiate about eight thousand years ago. About five thousand years ago, the proto-Bantu language itself appears to have emerged. Separating itself from its closest relatives in the Benue-Cross River region, it expanded eastward, most probably as a single language, to the northern fringe of the Congo equatorial rain forest. It was in this region that proto-Bantu differentiated itself into a cluster of languages which, from the beginning of the first millennium B.C., began a gradual but successful expansion into much of Africa south of the Equator. Those within the forest pushed southward along the river valleys and the coast with their vegeculture. Those living north of the forest became adept at cereal agriculture and stock raising. The addition of grain cultivation to their previous forest agriculture facilitated the expansion of the proto-East Bantu into the savannas of eastern and southern Africa, previously dominated by hunting and gathering peoples. We have also seen that the Bantu expansion was not marked by large scale expansion and military conquest by iron-using "Hamites," sweeping in massive waves across the land of the relatively weaker pre-existing foragers who knew nothing of metallurgy. Rather, it was a slow, steady, and effective infiltration of new and thinly populated regions, by pockets of sedentary farmers. While the possession of iron proved useful to the Bantu and accelerated their colonization of the continent, there is little evidence to show that metallurgy was instrumental in the initial expansion. The Bantu do not appear to have acquired the knowledge of iron working until their expansion was already at an advanced stage.

Whatever the origin and dynamics of Bantu expansion, its consequences were far-reaching. It was responsible for the proliferation of languages and the imposition of a near total linguistic unity over much of Central, eastern, and southern Africa, a region today dominated by more than six hundred languages of the Bantu language family. It is the most widely spoken language group in Africa. The expansion thus resulted in the Bantuzisation of Central, eastern and southern Africa, over which the Bantu imposed their ancestral traditions. This resulted in a major socio-political transformation. As farmers, they initiated an agricultural revolution through the spread of new crops, new farming techniques, and pastoralism to central and southern Africa. The Bantu have also been held responsible for the diffusion of new ideas such as iron-smelting, pottery making and cooking to much of the region. Bantu sedentarism and the introduction of more stable sources of food supply led to demographic expansion. This was manifested in the establishment of more permanent settlements and the development of more organized and complex societies, requiring the establishment of more elaborate socio-political institutions. New ideas of socio-political organization, new patterns of settlement, and new forms of trade exchange and cultural formation came into being.

The impact of the Bantu on pre-existing groups varied depending on the time, the environment, and the level of development of the group concerned. Initially, it was often one of co-operation and collaboration, but there were also periods of conflict. The end result of the encounter was invariably the conquest, displacement, the near-extinction, and assimilation of the pre-existing groups, such as the Khoikhoi and the San. From their northwestern homeland in the Benue-Cross River region, the Bantu had come with a single ancestral tradition. Over the centuries, and in the course of their phenomenal expansion, peopling, and Bantuzisation of sub-equatorial Africa, their ancestral heritage, the way of life and thought of their ancestors, was gradually and creatively enriched and transformed. The evidence shows that it is in the ability of the Bantu to assimilate and adapt to different habitats, rather than their ability to displace other groups, that an explanation both for the cultural differences between the various Bantu groups and for their population increase and expansion to much of sub-equatorial Africa can be situated. In virtually every case, interactions between the East and West Bantu groups and with the autochthons, as well as with the equally advanced and well-organized migrant groups like the Nilotes and Kushites in East Africa, produced a wide range of different socio-cultural syntheses.

Review Questions

1. Critically examine the strength and the weaknesses of the major sources for the reconstruction of the history of Bantu expansion.
2. From the available evidence, is there a consensus that there *was* a Bantu expansion?
3. "A race of metal-equipped warriors, relentlessly sweeping everything before them." How accurate is this description of the dynamics and the main features of the Bantu expansion in Africa before 1000 A.D?
4. Account for the triumph and the major consequences of Bantu expansion in East, Central, and southern Africa before 1000 A.D.
5. Examine the major problems and the challenges involved in the study of the history of Bantu expansion in sub-equatorial Africa.

Additional Readings

Fage, J.D. and R. Oliver, eds. *Papers in African Prehistory*. 1970.

Greenberg, Joseph. *The Languages of Africa*. Bloomington: Indiana University Press, 1970.

Lwanga-Lunyiigo, S. and Jan Vansina. "The Bantu-speaking peoples and their expansion," in M. Elfasi and I Hrbek, eds., *Africa from the Seventh to the Eleventh Century, UNESCO General History of Africa*. Vol. 3. London: Heinemann, 1988, 140-162.

Oliver, Roland and Brian M. Fagan. "The Emergence of Bantu Africa," in J.D. Fage, ed., *Cambridge History of Africa. Vol. 2, From c. 500 BC to AD 1050*. Cambridge: Cambridge University Press, 1978.

Phillipson, D.W. *African Archaeology*. Cambridge: Cambridge University Press, 1993.

Chapter 6

Sudanese Kingdoms of West Africa

J. I. Dibua

Introduction

The Sudan is derived from the Arabic word, *Bilad al-Sudan* (the land of the Black peoples), a term which early Arab geographers used to describe the West African savanna. This area occupies a unique position in the history of West Africa, in that it gave rise to some of the earliest states, kingdoms, and empires in the region. The most prominent of them were Ghana, Mali, Songhai, Kanem-Borno, and the Hausa states. Some of these kingdoms began to flourish from about the eighth century A.D. While to varying degrees the states in the central and eastern areas of the West African Sudan lasted till the nineteenth century or even the imposition of colonial rule in the early twentieth century, those in the west experienced a period of rise and fall. Ghana, the first of the Sudanese empires, thrived between the fifth century A.D. and the early thirteenth century. It was briefly overshadowed by the Susu state which was displaced by Mali Empire. Mali was in turn eclipsed by the Songhai Empire which lasted until 1591.

The West African Sudan was one of the earliest parts of sub-Saharan Africa to effect a transition from hunting and gathering to sedentary culture through the domestication of animals and the development of cultivation. One factor which contributed to this transition was the population pressure occasioned by the desiccation of the Sahara Desert. Up to about 5000 B.C., the area now occupied by the Sahara Desert was a fertile land traversed by a number of rivers, lakes, creeks, and streams. Because of its fertility, it supported a large population. But the Sahara started drying up, causing most of its inhabitants to move northward into the Maghrib and southward into the Sudan. The resultant population pressure, coupled with a number of other factors, necessitated increased sedentarization.

The vegetation of the savanna, particularly the grassland of the northern savanna (the sahel), made it very easy for the occupants, with their stone and later iron implements, to conquer, harness, and exploit the environment. In the Late Stone Age, sharp stone implements were used to clear the vegetation and till the soil. Of revolutionary significance was the development of iron technology in the

137

activities. This is clearly attested to by the fact that the people of the Songhai Empire were divided into three main professional groups, the Sorko who were fishermen, the Gow or Gabibi who were hunters, and the Do who were mixed farmers. Their products included fresh and dried fish, rice, corn, sorghum, and millet. The presence of craftsmen who produced farming tools, boats, and weapons greatly encouraged both the exploitation of their environment and the eventual incorporation of surrounding groups into the kingdom. Perhaps a unique advantage derived from location was the development of a powerful navy which played a major role in Songhai's expansion.

Lake Chad played a crucial role in the emergence of Kanem. The desiccation of the Sahara drew people from various directions towards the diminishing lake. The Chad area was home to diverse groups of hunters, farmers and pastoralists, as well as craftsmen. Apart from supporting the production of diverse items and hence the development of surplus accumulation and social differentiation, this convergence of various peoples and their attempts to adjust to the new environment created challenges and conflicts. These were resolved through the development of better tools and weapons and the foundation of Kanem by the Kanuri people who became the dominant group in the region.

The location of the Hausa states, which stretched from the sahel in the north to the southern savanna in the south, enabled them to produce a variety of crops. Much of Hausaland had rich and fertile soil. As a result the Hausa were able to support early sedentarization, and agriculture became the bedrock of their economy. The crops grown included millet, sorghum, various forms of grains, and rice. One important factor that supported the early settlement and development of states in this area was the presence of rich and fairly well-distributed deposits of iron ore. Since most of the deposits were in the southern savanna regions, close to wooded areas, it was relatively easy to get enough firewood and charcoal for smelting the ore. This resulted in the production of various domestic and farming implements, as well as weapons. In addition the strategic location of some areas in terms of defense attracted early settlement. The presence of all or most of these factors contributed to the early emergence of the nuclei of the Hausa states, such as Kano. Apart from the fact that the Kano area was very rich and fertile, Dalla Hill, the nucleus of the state, was useful in defense and contained rich iron ore deposits.

Of all the Sudanese kingdoms, Mali was the only one whose nucleus was completely located within the fertile southern savanna region. This favorable geographical location not only aided the rise of Mali, but turned it into one of the wealthiest Sudanese states with a highly diversified economic base. The location of Kangaba, the nucleus of the empire, together with its capital, Niane, in the southern savanna where rainfall was plentiful, as well as on the fertile plain of the Sankarani River (a tributary of the Niger), promoted agriculture and fishing. The primary occupations of the people were agriculture, hunting, and fishing. They produced regular surpluses of millet, sorghum, fonio, and rice. In addition, Kangaba was situated on the edge of the gold-producing regions of Bure and Bambuk. Hence, a major impetus for expansion was the control of these important goldfields. Indeed the early control of the gold-producing areas was important in the rise of Mali Empire.

Trade

Trade played a crucial role in the history of the Sudanese kingdoms. A major factor that stimulated their expansion was the need to control areas of production, as well as trade routes. Trade promoted the intense exploitation of the resources of the Sudan and was a primary source of surplus accumulation, social stratification, centralization, and expansion of kingdoms. It also contributed to the introduction of new ideas such as Islam. In addition, the immense benefits associated with trade led to competition and warfare among the Sudanese kingdoms. This had the dual effects of causing the fall of some of the kingdoms and spurring the expansion of others. There were three forms of trade: local trade; regional trade among the Sudanese, with the forest region to the south, and the Sahara to the north; and perhaps most important, the trans-Saharan trade with North Africa.

Local and regional trade provided the initial material basis for the development of the Sudanese kingdoms. The sahel was one of the earliest areas to benefit from these forms of trade. It was one of the earliest parts of the Sudan to develop agriculture through the domestication of sorghum, millet, and various grains. Although the majority of the people of the Sudan were farmers, there were also fishermen, hunters, and craftsmen. This, together with territorial specialization in the production of certain food crops, gold, iron, and other products, gave rise to an exchange economy which expanded over time. In addition, variations in terms of resources gave rise to trade between the inhabitants of the sahel and the Sahara on the one hand, and those of the southern savanna and the forest region on the other hand. It has been estimated that trade between the inhabitants of the Sudan and those of the Sahara started as early as 500 B.C.

The first people to take advantage of this local and regional trade were the Soninke. With their advantageous position in the sahel, they were able to obtain gold and staples like rice and dried fish from the southern savanna in exchange for salt and copper which they obtained from the Saharan dwellers. Hence, from the beginning, the Soninke people occupied a middleman position, a situation which was enhanced by the trans-Saharan trade.

The significance of local and regional trade for the rise and development of the Sudanese states can be even better illustrated with the examples of Mali and the Hausa states. As already noted, the heartland of Mali Empire was within the fertile southern savanna and the upper Niger flood plain. The significant agricultural surplus from this fertile area helped to promote an internal exchange economy, wealth accumulation, and social stratification. At its peak, Mali expanded to embrace large parts of the southern savanna and the sahel. The significance of this is that diverse items were produced in the empire. Different areas specialized in the production of different crops. The majority of the people produced the savanna crops of sorghum, millet, and fonio, while rice was produced in the Gambian valley and on the upper Niger floodplain. Many of those who lived along the Sankarani and Niger were fishermen. The occupants of the sahelian grassland, which during the period of the Mali Empire was less fertile, were pastoralists who specialized in keeping cattle, sheep, and goats. Thus, farmers, fishermen, and pastoralists exchanged their products. Indeed, the diversity of primary products stimulated trade between the various parts of the empire. For instance, rice from the

Gambia was exchanged for iron from the central areas. Millet and sorghum from the southern savanna were exchanged for animals from the sahel, while dried fish from the riverine areas was supplied to various parts of the empire.

The large surplus derived from these diverse products, together with gold from Bure and Bambuk, placed the people of Mali in a very favorable middleman position, between the Saharan dwellers to the north and the forest dwellers to the south. Gold and kola nuts from the forest region, together with agricultural products like sorghum and millet, and dried fish from the southern savanna, were exchanged for salt and copper from the Sahara. The emergence of the skilled and professional long-distance Wangara or Dyula traders from the principal ethnic groups (Malinke, Bambara, and Soninke) of Mali Empire, was largely due to this very favorable position.

The greater part of Hausaland was fertile and could support the cultivation of variety of crops. The majority of the people were farmers who cultivated items like millet, sorghum, rice, maize, peanuts, beans, onions, cotton, and indigo. Some engaged in fishing and hunting. There were also pastoralists (particularly the Fulani) who raised cattle, sheep, and goats. One significant trend in parts of Hausaland, like Kano and Katsina, was the symbiotic relationship that developed between farmers and pastoralists, by which, in exchange for food, the waste from cattle was used as fertilizer. This increased agricultural productivity.

The diverse economic base of Hausaland was further enhanced by a variety of crafts. The high technical quality of the items produced was generally acknowledged. The articles produced included various iron implements for agricultural, domestic, and military purposes; leather items like bags, sandals, harnesses, and saddles; tunics and cloth; and pottery and baskets. This diverse economic base supported a great deal of domestic and regional trade. This trade greatly contributed to the development of the Hausa states. In particular, the high quality of crafts led to considerable demand for them in other parts of West Africa. For instance, Hausaland supplied leather goods to the Akan in exchange for kola nuts and gold dust. Hausaland also used its own middleman position to promote trade with Borno and the Sahara dwellers to the north and the Nupe and Yoruba to the south. Millet, slaves, eunuchs, clothes, fabrics, leather goods, hides, iron, and kola nuts were supplied to Borno and the Sahara in exchange for horses, camels, paper, dates, henna, salt, and other items. Items like salt, cloth, swords, hides, horses, and leather goods were supplied to Borgu, Nupe, and Yorubaland to the south, in exchange for slaves and kola nuts among other items.

The immense contributions of local and regional trade to the development of the Sudanese states have not received sufficient emphasis. The impression usually created is that these states owe their development mainly to the trans-Saharan trade. Yet, as is clear from the preceeding discussion, domestic trade provided the material basis for the origin and initial development of the states. In fact, none of them owed their origin to the trans-Saharan trade. The states developed as responses to local geographical, environmental, and economic factors. But it cannot be denied that the trans-Saharan trade acted as a catalyst that helped to accelerate their development and expansion.

The trans-Saharan trade was carried on between traders from North Africa and their counterparts in the Sudan. But in fact it linked together North Africa, the Mediterranean world, Europe, the Sahara, the Sudan, and the forest region of West Africa. The trade, which started around the third century A.D., assumed a greater dimension from about the eight century. Although various articles were involved in the trade, the primary ones were horses and salt from North Africa and the Sahara, and gold and kola nuts from the South. Other items included textiles, copper, tea, coffee, sugar, cowries, writing paper, beads, and various European manufactured goods from North Africa and the Sahara; and millet, sorghum, gum, ivory, ostrich feathers, clothes, leather materials, and slaves and eunuchs from the Sudan and the forest region. It was the desire of rulers of the Sudanese states to have preponderant access to the primary imports (horses and salt), to have control over the main exports (gold and kola nuts), and to control the major routes and the important trading centers that provided a major impetus for expansion.

With its advantageous location in the sahel, it is not surprising that Ghana was the first of the Sudanese states to take advantage of the benefits of the trans-Saharan trade and embark on an expansionist course. Being ideally placed to play the role of middleman, Ghana expanded to control the surrounding communities that were the sources of some of the trade items. For example, it gained exclusive control over the gold-producing center of Bambuk and, by the eleventh century A.D., expanded northwards to impose its control over the Berber town of Awdaghost in the southwestern Sahara, which was an important trading center.

However, the activities of the Almoravids and the decline of Ghana from the late twelfth century made it unsafe for traders to continue to use the trade routes that terminated in Ghana. This resulted in the diversion of the main trade routes eastwards, with some of them terminating in the heartland of the Mali Empire. By then, Bure had become a new source of gold while Timbuktu and Djenne had become important trading centers. Mali expanded to embrace Bambuk and Bure, as well as Timbuktu and Djenne. The determination of Mali to control all of the important trading termini in the Western Sudan led it to extend its authority over Gao and Tadmekka to the northeast. In addition, the Wangara penetrated the forest region to open new sources of gold from the Akan and Lobi fields, as well as to gain more advantage in the kola nut trade.

The contributions of the trans-Saharan trade to the expansion of the Sudanese states can be further seen in the case of the Songhai Empire. Although Gao, the nucleus of Songhai, developed into a kingdom at about the same time as Ghana and was an important terminus of the trans-Saharan trade, it did not begin to expand and gain more advantage from the trade until the middle of the fifteenth century. One reason for this is that Gao was not as well-placed as Ghana and Mali to control the trade in gold and kola nuts. Not until the fourteenth and fifteenth centuries, when trade routes were extended to Hausaland, did the heartland of Songhai become focal point in the trade. Thus, apart from taking advantage of the decline of Mali to take over important trading centers like Timbuktu and Djenne, it expanded eastwards to exercise some form of control over parts of Hausaland and expanded northwards into the Sahara to impose its rule over the major trading and salt-producing center of Taghaza.

Kanem, which was the nucleus of Kanem-Borno Empire, was situated in the sahel, northeast of Lake Chad. It arose at about the same time as Ghana and Gao. Although before the fifteenth century the bulk of the trans-Saharan trade was concentrated in the western part of the Sudan, there was also a thriving trade from the Lake Chad region through the Central Sahara to North Africa. Fezzan, an important trading center in the Sahara, as well as Bilma, a salt-mining center, were located on these routes. It was the determination of Kanem to maximize the benefits from this trade that led it to bring these two areas under its control by the middle of the thirteenth century. By the end of the fourteenth century, the center of the empire was moved to Borno to the west of lake Chad. From there, the empire sought to extend its control over the trade in this area and, in particular, impose some form of authority over the eastern Hausaland.

Hausaland became fully integrated into the trans-Saharan trading network from about the fifteenth century. This contributed significantly to the expansion of some of the Hausa states. Katsina, which was the main entrepot of trade into the Hausaland, expanded north and south to bring neighboring groups under its control. Kano, because of the variety of its products, became an important center and sought to maximize this by bringing surrounding communities under its control. One reason that has been suggested for the struggle for supremacy in Hausaland between Katsina and Kano was the desire to control the trans-Saharan trade. To the south, Zaria was the gateway to the forest region and established trading links with Nupe, Borgu, and Yorubaland. It too expanded to bring its neighbors under its control.

An important advantage from the trans-Saharan trade was the wealth the leadership derived from it. For one thing, the Sudanese rulers and other members of the ruling class were actively involved in the trade. In Ghana, for example, the people could only sell gold dust while gold nuggets were reserved for the monarch. Another important source of wealth was the various taxes which were imposed on both imports and exports. Al-Bakri wrote that a tax of one dinar of gold was levied on every donkey-load of salt which was imported into Ghana and two dinars for a similar amount of salt exported out of the kingdom. Also five mithqals were levied on every imported load of copper. Similar taxes were levied in the other Sudanese states. The wealth derived from these sources helped to provide the means to prosecute wars of expansion, and to promote social differentiation, specialization, and efficient administration.

It should be noted that in spite of the role played by trade, only few of the Sudanese people were full-time traders. The majority were farmers and thus agriculture remained the mainstay of their economies.

Islam

Islam played an important role in the history of the Sudanese kingdoms. Although it was not responsible for the rise of any of the empires, it contributed significantly to their development and expansion. Islam was introduced into the Sudan from North Africa and was mainly a product of the trans-Saharan trade. It is believed that Islam spread into the Western Sudan by the second half of the tenth century, the Chad region by the eleventh century, and Hausaland between the twelfth and thirteenth centuries. By the end of the eleventh century some Sudanese rulers, notably those of Gao, Mali, and Kanem, had embraced Islam, but still the influence of the religion was restricted.

Since the introduction of Islam to the Sudan was essentially a product of the trans-Saharan trade, it should be expected that some of the groups on which it had its greatest impact were traders. Muslim traders from North Africa helped to spread the religion in the Sudan. Hence, the first set of Sudanese people to embrace Islam were traders who were converted through their relationships with the North Africans. Of note in this regard were the Soninke and Malinke traders, some of whom became the famous Wangara or Dyula long-distance traders. They, as already noted, were responsible for opening up markets in gold and kola nuts in the forest region and, in the process spread Islam not only to a large part of the Sudan, but also to parts of the forest. Other notable Sudanese long-distance traders who converted and helped to spread it to other parts of West Africa were the Kanuri and the Hausa. The fact that both the North African traders and many of their Sudanese counterparts came to share the same religion helped to further promote the trans-Saharan trade.

The importance of trade made the Sudanese rulers take steps to guarantee the security and freedom of worship of North African traders within their kingdoms. This was not the case only with those leaders who accepted Islam, like those of Mali, Songhai, Kanem- Borno, and the Hausa states, but also with those that did not accept Islam, such as those of Ghana before the twelfth century. For instance, in 1067 A.D., al-Bakri wrote that the capital of Ghana was divided into two parts, six miles apart. One part was made up of Muslims and had twelve mosques, while the other part was occupied by the king and his people who were adherents of the traditional religion, though even this part had a mosque for use by Muslims who visited the king. In fact, many large Sudanese towns, like Djenne, Timbuktu, Gazargamu, Katsina, and Kano, had a sizeable number of Muslim traders. These towns also attracted Muslim scholars and clerics who, apart from contributing to the spread of the religion, helped to promote Islamic literacy and scholarship.

The acceptance of Islam by some Sudanese rulers affected the histories of their states in various ways. Some of them, like Mansa Musa of Mali, Askiya Mohammed of Songhai, Dunama Dibalemi and Idris Aloma of Kanem-Borno, embarked on various jihads and, in the process, expanded the territorial extent of their kingdoms. Some of them went on pilgrimage to Mecca and returned with scholars, professionals, and ideas that helped to bring about changes in areas such as scholarship, administration, architecture, and warfare. In addition, it was believed that by going on pilgrimage such leaders acquired *baraka, a* form of spiritual power, which further helped to enhance their prestige and ensure the loyalty of Muslims among their subjects. Similarly, some of these leaders like Askiya Mohammed of Songhai and Ali Gaji of Kanem-Borno, sought and achieved appointment as caliphs of the Sudan - a position which made them the recognized leaders of the Muslims in the Sudan during their reigns.

The Muslim scholars and professionals who were employed as administrators and advisers helped to promote more efficient forms of administration in the Sudanese kingdoms. Of significance in this regard was al-Maghili's book on the Islamic form of administration, *The Obligation of Princes*, which he wrote for Muhammed Rumfa, the ruler of Kano, in the early 1490s. However, since most of the Muslim traders, scholars, and clerics lived in the urban centers and many of them were close to the seats of power, Islam in the Sudanese kingdoms remained primarily an urban religion and mainly for the ruling class, while the majority of the people remained traditionalists.

Although Islam contributed to the development and expansion of Sudanese kingdoms, it equally contributed to the decline and collapse of some of them. The constant skirmishes between the Muslim Berbers of the Sahara, particularly the Almoravids, and Ghana Empire in the second half of the eleventh century, contributed to the decline of the empire, especially since the resultant insecurity on the trade routes caused the diversion of trade from Ghana. The division between Muslims and non-Muslims (particularly among the ruling groups) in Songhai greatly contributed to its decline and collapse. It was the Sokoto jihad of the nineteenth century which brought about the collapse of the Hausa states.

The Empire of Ghana

Ghana was the first of the Sudanese kingdoms to rise to prominence. However, given the lack of written records and the antiquity of its rise, its early history is obscure. The importance of gold for the Arabs and Europe brought Ghana to the attention of the outside world by the eight century when it was described by al-Fazari as "the land of gold." Although Bambuk, the source of the gold, was not under its direct political control, Ghana controlled the trade in gold. The location of Ghana on the southern edge of the Sahara resulted in control over the trans-Saharan trade, particularly the important trading center of Awdaghost. Conflicts with Saharan Berbers and the need to promote security along the trade routes led Ghana to develop more effective defensive and offensive military strategies. At the height of its power in the eleventh century, Ghana had expanded west to the Senegal River, south to the boundaries of the gold-producing area of Bambuk, east to the River Niger and north to Awdaghost. From the accounts of various Arabic writers, Ghana was a very wealthy kingdom, whose central administration derived income from a number of sources.

The empire was loosely organized and broadly divided into two - metropolitan Ghana, which was the nucleus, and provincial Ghana which was made up of conquered vassal states. So long as the vassal kings recognized the authority of the central government and paid their annual tribute, they were allowed to control their own internal affairs. In order to ensure their continued loyalty, a son of each of the vassal kings was kept in the palace of the king of Ghana as hostage. But the king also endeavored to see that justice was fairly administered. According to al-Idrisi, he went out every day asking those who felt that they had suffered from injustice to come before him so that he could look into their cases.

By the end of the eleventh century, Ghana had started to experience a process of decline. Some of the factors that accounted for this decline were Islam, trade, and the environment, the same factors that had been important in its rise. While many Soninke traders and rulers of vassal states became Muslims, the king remained an adherent of the traditional religion. Most of the Muslim Soninke and vassal states were, therefore, not prepared to continue to pledge their loyalty to their non-Muslim ruler, thereby creating divisions within the empire.

The constant feud between the Muslim Sanhaja Berbers and the Ghana Empire did not help matters. This reached its peak in the second half of the eleventh century when the Almoravids (an Islamic religious movement that emerged among the Sanhaja Berbers and embarked on jihads) retook control of Awdaghost from Ghana in 1054 A.D., and by 1070 A.D. had established an empire which stretched from the northern boundaries of Ghana to the Magrib. It used to be claimed that the Almoravids overran Kumbi Saleh, the capital of Ghana, in 1076, but recent research has disproved this. But the conquest of Awdaghost and the diversion of trade routes to the east of Ghana beyond the control of its leaders deprived it of wealth and resources and weakened the central authority considerably.

Perhaps the greatest factor in the decline of the empire was environmental. Since it was located in the sahel which had been under continuous exploitation for a long time, the area became less fertile and could no longer support a large population. This was not helped by the fact that Berber pastoralists were pushing southwards into the area and were overgrazing the already-deteriorating environment. In the face of this environmental problem and deprived of wealth from the trans-Saharan trade, many Soninke had, by the beginning of the thirteenth century, started migrating southwards to form new settlements in the more fertile areas of the southern savanna.

Given these problems, the central authority became weak and could no longer impose its control over the vassal states which seized the opportunity to rebel. In 1203, one of them, the Susu state, under its leader Sumanguru Kante, declared its independence and overran the core area of Ghana. However, because of the tyrannical nature of Sumanguru's rule, his empire was ephemeral, and he was defeated in 1235 by Sundiata, who proceeded to establish the Empire of Mali.

Mali

The very favorable environment in which the heartland of Mali was located had by the tenth century, given rise to a number of Malinke chiefdoms in the western part of the southern savanna, around the upper Niger. By the twelfth century, Kangaba, which was situated in the valley of the Rivers Sankarani and Niger, had attained a form of ascendancy over the other Malinke chiefdoms. The immediate factors that accelerated the expansion of Mali into a large empire in the first half of the thirteenth century included the decline and collapse of Ghana, the discovery of new goldfields at Bure, the increased participation of Mali in the trans-Saharan trade, and the emergence of Sundiata as an able leader.

The decline of Ghana created a power vacuum which was initially filled by the Susu state. By the 1230s, Sumanguru had annexed the Malinke chiefdoms to the south of Susu. But Sumanguru was a tyrannical and oppressive leader, which united the Malinke in opposition to him. Sundiata, who was from the royal family of Kangaba, returned from exile and galvanized the Malinke opposition against Sumanguru whom he defeated at the battle of Kirina in 1235, thereby bringing an end to the Susu kingdom. After this victory, the leaders of the other Malinke chiefdoms recognized Sundiata as their leader and pledged allegiance to him. Sundiata then established Niane as the capital of Mali. In 1240, Sundiata sacked Kumbi Saleh and incorporated what was left of Ghana into the Mali kingdom. This marked the unquestioned emergence of Mali as the supreme kingdom in the Western Sudan.

Another factor which worked in favor of Mali during this early phase was the diversion of the trans-Saharan trade routes eastwards, with Walata replacing Awdaghost as the most important trading center in the southern Sahara, and some of the trade routes terminating in Mali. The emergence of Bure on the southern border of Mali as the new and most important source of gold further enhanced the position of Mali in the trans-Saharan trade. An important task for Sundiata and his immediate successors was to maximize Mali's benefits from the trade by conquering the gold-producing areas and important trading centers. Thus, by the time of Sundiata's death in 1255, he had incorporated the gold-producing areas of Bambuk and Bure into the empire, and had expanded west to include the upper valley of the Senegal and the Gambia, and north to include the termini of the trans-Saharan routes in the sahel. Mali, therefore, controlled all the internal trade routes over which gold was carried northwards for the trans-Saharan trade. At the time of Sundiata's death he had effectively established the Mali Empire. The tasks before his successors were to consolidate and build upon his work.

Sundiata was succeeded by his son Mansa Uli (1255-1270), who was an equally powerful leader and continued to expand the frontiers of the empire. However, after Uli's death Mali entered a period of instability which was characterized by succession disputes, and the deposition and assassination of kings who reigned for very brief periods. The level of instability was such that Sakura, a freed slave, was able to usurp the throne at one point. He was, however, a powerful leader who further expanded the frontiers of the empire and promoted trade. The conquests of Uli and Sakura brought the important commercial towns of Walata, Tadmekka, and Takedda in the southern Sahara, as well as Timbuktu and Gao on the middle Niger bend, under Mali's control. Thus the empire had virtually reached the limits of its expansion by the time Mansa Musa (1312-1337), the most famous ruler of Mali, came to the throne in 1312 A.D.

Mansa Musa came to the throne against the background of royal instability which had considerably weakened central administration. His first task was to strengthen the central administration and consolidate its hold over the entire empire. He strengthened the army and used it to reconquer those territories which had used the instability at the center as an opportunity to rebel and declare their independence. In order to ensure the continued loyalty of the military, the battalion commanders were given important posts in the royal court. Islam was accorded a prominent position in the court while literate Muslims were employed as interpreters, scribes, treasurers, and advisers. While some of the provinces were administered by Mansa Musa's appointees, others were left in the hands of their traditional rulers, so long as they recognized the central government and sent their annual tribute.

Given the peace and security that prevailed under Mansa Musa, the empire experienced great prosperity, as both internal and external trade flourished. As already mentioned, the Wangara helped to open up the Akan goldfields and more sources of kola nuts, thereby increasing the volume of trade which passed through the empire. Customs duties were imposed on all goods coming into or leaving the empire. Also, taxes were paid on the diverse agricultural items and crafts that were produced in the empire.

The greatest act for which Mansa Musa is known was his pilgrimage to Mecca from 1324-1325. He was said to have performed the pilgrimage with a caravan of one hundred camel-loads of gold. He spent so lavishly in Cairo and Mecca that the value of gold fell in Egypt and did not recover for a number of years. He even ran out of money and had to borrow at exorbitant interest rates before he could return home. Much have been written about the contribution of this pilgrimage to Mali in particular and the Western Sudan in general. For example, the pilgrimage brought Mali to the attention of the outside world, and it appeared on some European world maps in the fourteenth century. It attracted a number of Islamic scholars, professionals, and clerics, including al-Sahili whose new architectural designs helped to revolutionize the field in the Sudan. The scholars and traders who were attracted to Timbuktu helped to turn the town into an important educational and commercial center. These are significant contributions no doubt, but all things considered, this was a rather reckless and extravagant pilgrimage that amounted to an unnecessary waste of the resources of the empire. To say this is not to belittle the important contributions of Mansa Musa to the Mali Empire (he was certainly one of its greatest leaders) but to draw attention to the implications of praising the unedifyingly extravagant aspect of the pilgrimage. Despite Mansa Musa's attempts to promote Islam, the religion remained that of traders, the elite and the urban centers.

Mansa Musa was succeeded by his son, Mansa Maghan, who reigned for four years (1337-1341) and was succeeded by Mansa Musa's brother, Mansa Suleiman (1341-1359). Suleiman was an effective leader under whom the prosperity of the empire continued. However, after Suleiman's death, the empire witnessed an era of dynastic instability from which, this time, it never recovered. Hence, the period from the sixth decade of the fourteenth century was one of gradual decline. The vassal states seized this opportunity to rebel and declare independence. At the same time, Mali came under constant attack from the Mossi in the south and the Tuareg in the north. In 1433 the Tuareg captured and occupied Timbuktu. Mali's loss was Songhai's gain. Under Sunni Ali, Songhai replaced Mali as the dominant power in the Sudan. But unlike Ghana (and Songhai), which completely disintegrated, the Mali Empire only lost the non-Malinke groups as it shrank to its original nucleus in the Malinke heartland.

Songhai Empire

Gao, the nucleus of the Songhai Empire, emerged at about the same time with Ghana and Takrur. The location of Gao and Kukiya (the initial capital of Songhai) in the fertile Niger bend was an important advantage, making it possible for the area to support people with diverse occupations. This gave rise to an early exchange economy within the area. The Sorko were not only fishermen but had developed maritime warfare abilities. Hence, the initial course of Songhai's expansion was along the River Niger. Apart from the cavalry and the infantry, Songhai had the advantage of an effective naval force.

Although Gao was one of the earliest states in the Sudan and was an important terminus of the trans-Saharan trade, it was not until the fifteenth century that it began the process of transforming itself into a large empire. The reasons for this include the fact that unlike Ghana and Mali, Songhai was far removed from the sources of gold, the most important export of the Sudan, as well as the fact that it became a vassal state of Mali. It had to wait for an auspicious moment and the advent of able leaders who could exploit such a moment. This occurred with the decline of Mali; the increased participation of the Hausa states in the trans- Saha-

various forms of taxation and customs duties, while there was also a number of state-owned farms worked by slaves and craftsmen who produced various items for the central authority. Askiya Mohammed's major contribution to Songhai was that he completed and consolidated its transformation into a large and prosperous empire.

Askiya Mohammed's achievements notwithstanding, the empire began to have problems even during his lifetime. Even when he had become old and blind, he refused to hand over power, and in 1528 he was deposed by some of his sons. There ensued a period of royal instability, depositions, and assassinations among his descendants who were constantly vying for the throne. As with Mali, this sparked a period of decline. In 1588 the division in the empire between Muslims and traditionalists was clearly manifested in the civil war over the struggle for the throne between Askiya Ishaq II, who was supported by the traditionalists, and Sadiq, who was supported by the Muslims. Although Ishaq II emerged victorious, the empire came out from the war considerably weakened and divided. This was to act as an impetus for the final factor which brought about the collapse of Songhai, that is, the Moroccan invasion of 1591.

The cupidity of al-Mansur, the Moroccan sultan, had made him covet the wealth of the Western Sudan. He planned to attack the area and take control of the trade routes and the gold. He realized that he could not make such a move against a formidable empire, so in 1582 he sent a spy to Gao to report to him on events within the empire. He saw in the outcome of the 1588 civil war an opportunity to strike; so after some careful planning, he dispatched in 1591 a force of four thousand well-armed soldiers, the majority of them Andalusians, under the leadership of Judar Pasha, a young Spanish eunuch in the sultan's employ. Although Songhai was able to muster a large army greatly outnumbering the invaders, its spears, bows, and arrows were no match for the firearms of the invading force and at the battle of Tondibi in March 1591, the Songhai army was completely routed. The victorious invaders imposed a regime of savagery and terror which led to the disintegration of the economy and society of the Western Sudan and to the shift of the trans-Saharan trade routes eastwards into Kanem-Borno and Hausaland.

Kanem-Borno Empire

The circumstances that resulted in the emergence of the Kanem-Borno Empire were similar to those obtaining at the emergence of the early sahelian states of Takrur, Ghana, and Gao. The desiccation of the Sahara attracted people from various parts of the central Sahara to the Chad basin. This amalgam of people included farmers, fishermen, and pastoralists. By the beginning of the tenth century A.D., a group of negroid nomadic pastoralists, the Magumi, became ascendant and established the Safuwa dynasty which was to rule Kanem-Borno for a thousand years. This set in motion a gradual and prolonged process of welding the various peoples into a common cultural group which came to be known as the Kanuri. Some traditions of the Kanuri credit the origin of the Safuwa dynasty to a great Arab hero, Sayf b. Dhi Yazan, who, it was claimed, gained control of the Magumi and established the dynasty. These traditions are obviously not correct.

Apart from including elements of the discredited Hamitic hypothesis, they represent a general tendency among Muslim rulers in North Africa and the Sudan to trace their pedigree to great Arab heros as a way of winning prestige and respectability in the Muslim world. The Magumi were negroid nomads. It was the conflict that resulted from diverse people settling in the Chad basin that eventually gave rise to a resolution through the Magumi ascendancy.

However, in order to promote unity and win the acceptance of the various ethnic groups that made up Kanem, the Safuwa rulers pursued a deliberate policy of marrying non-Magumi women. It was from among the children of these non-Magumi women that successors to the throne were selected. This helped the Safuwa to win the support and acceptance of the other groups. Also, the introduction of the institution of devine kingship helped to promote the supremacy of the Safuwa. By the thirteenth century, Njimi had been established as the permanent capital of Kanem.

As in the Western Sudanese kingdoms, trade and Islam contributed to the expansion of the Kanuri empire. Islam was introduced through peaceful methods by traders from North Africa, and in the late eleventh century Mai Humai became the first Safuwa king to be converted to Islam. Succeeding rulers consolidated the position of Islam in the royal court and performed the pilgrimage. With the aid of a superior cavalry force, Kanem was able to bring the surrounding areas under its control. But it was not until the thirteenth century, in the reign of Dunama Dibalemi (1210-1248), that Kanem embarked on a deliberate and conscious policy of expansion. Dibalemi had a cavalry force of 4100 horsemen. Determined to bring the trade through the central Sahara under Kanem's control, he expanded the empire northwards into the desert to capture the important salt-producing and trading center of Bilma. At the same time, he engaged in wars with the neighboring So people, justifying them on the grounds of a jihad, although captives were sold as slaves in exchange for horses from North Africa. It was under Dunama Dibalemi that Kanem attained its peak.

After Dibalemi's reign, Kanem started experiencing a number of internal and external problems. Internally, there was royal instability in the form of succession disputes and assassinations of ruling kings. This weakened the central authority and some vassal states seized the opportunity to rebel. The Fezzan declared its independence from Kanem. By the fourteenth century, Kanem was experiencing fierce resistance and attacks from the So people west and south of Lake Chad. In the second part of the fourteenth century Kanem came under constant attacks from the Bulala, who were so successful that on occassions they occupied the center of Kanem and at least three kings were said to have met their deaths at the Bulala's hands.

The situation was compounded by economic problems. The location of Kanem in mostly desert and semidesert areas meant that the soil soon became exhausted from overgrazing and could no longer sustain a viable economy. Moreover, during the fourteenth century, Borno, which had been established as a tributary state of Kanem to the southwest of Lake Chad, seized the opportunity offered by the weakened central administration to assert its independence. It stopped paying tribute and began to bypass Kanem in the trans-Saharan trade. Kanem lost much of what it had derived from the trade. All these problems resulted in the collapse of the Kanem state towards the end of the fourteenth century. The Safuwa dynasty under Mai Umar b. Idris (1382-1387) decided to save the state from complete disintegration by relocating to the more strategic and fertile region of Borno.

In spite of this relocation, the first century of the Safuwa stay in Borno was full of problems and troubles. Dynastic instability continued and was accompanied by the revolts of powerful title holders while Bulala attacks remained unabated. In fact, two more kings (Sa'id and Kadai Afunu) died from Bulala attacks. Thus, the primary aim of moving to Borno, which was to reorganize the empire and build a strong economy, could not be realized during this period. On the contrary the very survival of the state was at stake.

Fortunately for Borno, the accession to the throne of Mai Ali Gaji (1465-1497) brought about an end to this period of instability and launched Borno towards greatness. One of Ali Gaji's achievements was the defeat of the Bulala in about 1471, temporarily putting a halt to their harassment. Perhaps his greatest achievement was the building of a well-fortified permanent capital, Birnin Gazargamu, for the empire. Apart from being well-fortified, Gazargamu was strategically placed to control a great part of the commerce to and from Hausaland. Ali Gaji was also an Islamizer who tried to strenghten the position of Islam in the royal court. He was invested with the title of caliph during his pilgrimage in about 1484 and from this time on successive Borno rulers claimed the title, caliph of the Sudan.

Ali Gaji's son and successor, Mai Idris Katakarmabe (ca. 1497-1519) built upon the policies of his father. The first threat he had to deal with was renewed Bulala attacks. He defeated the Bulala on two occassions and drove them out of Njimi which he occupied for a period. After concluding a treaty with the Bulala, he returned to Borno. But this peace was shortlived as occasional Bulala attacks continued until the reign of Idris Aloma in the second half of the sixteenth century. The kings that immediately succeeded Idris Katakarmabe continued to deal with the Bulala threats, embarked on some wars of expansion particularly along the southern border, tried to secure and control the trans-Saharan trade routes, and continued with the policy of Islamization. By the middle of the sixteenth century, Borno was developing as a great center of Islamic learning which was visited by scholars from all over the Islamic world. Moreover the claims of successive kings to the title of caliph was accepted by many Muslim scholars. It was this that was probably responsible for the sending of regular gifts, as opposed to tribute, by Muslim rulers in Hausaland to the Kanem-Borno rulers.

It is generally agreed that the Kanem-Borno Empire attained the peak of its glory in the reign of Mai Idris Aloma (ca.1569-ca.1600). His contributions included the introduction of new military technology and strategies, the ending of the Bulala threats, the expansion of the Kanem-Borno Empire to its limits, the building of a strong economy, and the Islamization of the empire. Since Idris Aloma saw the achievement of lasting peace as a *sine qua non* for the attainment of the objectives of Kanem-Borno, his first act was to introduce military innovations which would enable the empire to withstand the threats from various quarters. Apart from having a standing army made up of infantry and cavalry, he acquired Turkish muskets and musketeers, and introduced regular military drills. The acquisition of firearms and the introduction of military discipline gave his army supremacy over its enemies who still relied on the use of spears, bows, and arrows.

Having strengthened the military, he waged a series of wars against the Bulala whom he subdued; he finally achieved a lasting settlement with them. He used force to bring various groups who had continuously defied Borno's authority, like the Ngafata, the Talata, the Dugurti, the Kotoko, the So, the Buduma, the Bedde, and the Ngizim, under the empire's control. He asserted Borno's authority over the Ahir, the Tuareg of Demergu, the Teda of Jawana, and Bilma, all of whose in-cessant attacks had been disturbing the trans-Saharan trade. With the empire's control extended over all the major trade routes, Borno became the nerve center for both the east-west trade from Hausaland and the trans-Saharan trade. Gazargamu became the terminus for the Borno-Kawar-Tripoli trade route as well as for the main routes to Hausaland. Thus, Borno achieved a very strong and vi-able economy.

One of the activities of Idris Aloma on which much was written by Muslim scholars was his proselytizing. He was an Islamizer who campaigned relentlessly against lax morals, and he established Islamic juridical systems in Borno. He at-tempted to Islamize the royal court and he appointed Muslim scholars to adminis-trative positions. In fact the *ulama* (scholars) came to occupy very important and prestigious positions in Kanem-Borno. Under the conditions of peace and security that reigned, Islam grew and the empire became an important center of Islamic scholarship. But like Mansa Musa and Askiya Mohammed, Aloma could not com-pletely Islamize the central administration. Syncretism was prevalent and Islam re-mained mainly the religion of the elite, traders, and urban centers. Externally, Idris Aloma established diplomatic relations with foreign governments, such as the Ot-toman Empire and Morocco. By the time of his death in about 1600 A.D., Kanem-Borno had reached its apogee and his period is usually regarded as its golden age.

It used to be believed that Kanem-Borno declined soon after the death of Idris Aloma. But recent research has shown that this is not correct. On the contrary, the four immediate successors of Aloma in the seventeenth century consolidated his achievements and, since they were not involved in many wars, they used their time to promote more effective adminitration, commerce, and scholarship. Borno was a center of learning and culture, and the Kanuri culture and institutions spread to surrounding groups like the Hausa, where they were widely adopted.[3]

However in the eighteenth century, particularly from the mid eighteenth cen-tury, Kanem-Borno did enter a period of decline. Many of the kings were said to be indolent, corrupt, and increasingly syncretistic, while they lacked military fer-vor. As would be expected, many vassal states seized this opportunity to rebel. Raids from the Bedde disrupted the trade routes to Hausaland; Tuareg attacks dis-rupted the trans-Saharan trade and led to the capture of Bilma. Finally, the Fulani jihad of the ninteenth century resulted in the collapse of the Safuwa dynasty and its replacement by the Kanemi dynasty. Though the jihad further led to the loss of vassal states, the new dynasty succeeded in reorganizing metropolitan Borno and turned it into a strong Islamic community. It was only in the early twentieth cen-tury that Borno lost its independence to the British colonial invaders.

The Hausa States

Unlike the other parts of the Sudan already examined, Hausaland did not produce a single large empire. On the contrary, there existed a number of Hausa

---

3. In fact, Barkindo has argued that given the prosperity, educational, and cultural flow-ering of Borno in the seventeenth century, it is this century, rather than Idris Aloma's period, that should be regarded as the golden age of Kanem-Borno. See Barkindo (1992), 511.

states which were, for the most part, mutually antagonistic and competing with each other for supremacy. The fortunes of each state varied over time and no single state remained the most powerful throughout. Not much is known about the early history of the Hausa states. In fact, we do not have much information on this area until about the fifteenth century, and even then the amount of information we have on the individual states is uneven. But as previously noted, the greater part of Hausaland is located in the fertile savanna which, at a very early period, gave rise to a number of village settlements.

From about the eleventh century a form of revolution began in Hausaland which was manifested in the gradual transformation of some of these settlements into state-like organizations. This process of transformation is believed to have lasted till about the fifteenth century. It gave rise to the emergence of various centers of power. Closely associated with this revolution was the foundation of *birni* (cities) as new centers of political power. The factors that usually influenced the establishment of *birni* were economic, strategic, and defensive. Thus, a *birni* was always located in an area that could provide enough food to sustain the people during a period of prolonged siege, as well as being easily defensible. Because of these defense considerations, the *birni* was always a well-fortified walled city. The power of each Hausa ruler extended beyond the *birni* as the surounding communities looked to him for protection from external attack. In fact, during prolonged attacks, the surounding communities moved into the walled cities for protection. The territory of these states extended beyond the walled cities; hence it is not strictly correct to refer to them as city-states.

The leading Hausa states that emerged were Kano, Katsina, Kebbi, Gobir, Zamfara, and Zaria. With the possible exception of Kebbi, the trans-Saharan trade played an important role in their development and expansion. Katsina was an important trading terminus and the entrepot of the trans-Saharan trade into Hausaland. This, and the diverse resources of Kano, which included agriculture and manufacturing, turned it into the leading commercial center in the Hausaland. For its own part, Zaria controlled the trade with southern groups like the Nupe and the Yoruba. In addition, like the Wangara, many Hausa people became long-distance traders. Hausaland came to occupy an important position in the west-east trade in kola nuts and gold from the Akan, and the south-north trade in kola nuts and slaves.

Islam also played an important role in the history of the Hausa states. The introduction of Islam into Hausaland has been credited to the Wangarawa in the fourteenth century. It is now agreed that Islam in Hausaland predated the Wangarawa and was probably introduced as early as the twelfth century, but it did not become an important factor until the advent of the Wangarawa and the increasing participation of the Hausa states in the trans-Saharan trade during the fifteenth century. It was from the late fifteenth century that the rulers of some Hausa states, like Mohammad Rumfa of Kano and Mohammad Korau of Katsina, actively embraced and propagated Islam in their domains. Much is known about Mohammad Rumfa, who was perhaps the first ruler to give serious thought to the problems of governing a mutli-religious community in line with Islamic laws. Al-Maghili wrote him a treatise on Islamic administration. Through the patronage and activities of Hausa rulers, Muslim scholars and clerics from all over the Sudan were attracted to Hausaland, and cities like Kano and Katsina became centers of Islamic education. However, as in other parts of the Sudan, Islam did not gain much influence outside the royal courts and urban centers. It remained essentially a religion of the elite. Even among Muslim Hausa rulers, syncretism was prevalent and this gave rise to the jihad of the nineteenth century which brought about the collapse of the Hausa states.

An important theme in the history of the Hausa states was constant warfare. This included the internecine warfare between Kano and Katsina, lasting from the second half of the fifteenth century to 1651 when an enduring peace was finally signed. The *ulama* community in both Kano and Katsina played an important role in negotiating this peace. A common explanation that has been given for this warfare is that it was a struggle between the two states for the position of the trans-Saharan terminus, but D. Laya has pointed out that it was probably much more than that.[4] The warfare also represented a struggle for hegemony over eastern Hausaland. In the sixteenth and the seventeenth centuries, Kebbi was the dominant military power in Hausaland. It defeated Borno in 1561 and was also involved in wars with Zamfara and Gobir. In the eighteenth century there were wars between Zamfara and Gobir, while on different occasions both states were involved in wars with Katsina and Kano.

Administratively, each Hausa state was headed by a king known as the sarki, and under him was a retinue of fiefholders and officials. The Hausa states had access to varied resources and were therefore very rich, Kano being the richest. The central administrations derived revenue from a number of sources, including taxes (like custom duties, land tax, tax paid by craftsmen and traders, and cattle tax), gifts from government officials and dignitaries, and war booty. In the end, the Hausa states lost their independence to the Fulani jihadists of the nineteenth century who founded the Sokoto Caliphate.

Conclusion

The Sudanese kingdoms were remarkable in a number of ways. They all represented conscious attempts to take advantage of their environment, trade, and Islam to evolve large, centralized kingdoms. However, while the kingdoms in the west could not survive their internal and external problems, those in the central and eastern areas developed more resilience. One important factor which worked against the western states, particularly Ghana and Songhai, was location in the sahel, an area which became quickly depleted of resources. Kanem escaped such a fate by relocating to Borno. Moreover Kanem-Borno was fortunate not to have been confronted with a neighboring state that was bent on transforming itself into an empire. Among the Hausa states, there was a form of balance of power and, thus, no single one of them could impose its imperialism on the others for any lengthy period.

---

4. See Laya (1992), 458.

Chapter 7

Kingdoms of West Africa: Benin, Oyo, and Asante

Funso Afolayan

The major themes to be examined in this chapter are the rise of the kingdoms, their achievements and systems of government, the reasons for their long survivals, their external interactions, especially with Europeans, and finally their decline and fall.

Benin

Origins and Early Development

When the British invaded and conquered Benin in 1897, they brought to an end an empire that had flourished with much power and opulence for close to five hundred years. The rise of Benin to a position of prominence was an exception in the region. For the inhabitants of the lower Niger, small-scale socio-political formation was the norm. The village settlement was the basic political unit. The population of the village was usually organized into age-grades, which together with kinship and lineage organization became the basis of socio-political relations. Generally, succession and inheritance were patrilineal with an emphasis on primogeniture. Agriculture and also fishing, especially in the riverine and coastal areas, became the basis of economic existence. Over time, with increased population, competition for resources and the increasing sophistication of communities, kingship institutions developed, accompanied by the creation of title systems and the evolution of more complex socio-political units. This process reached by far its greatest advancement in Benin, which by the end of the fifteenth century had become the most powerful state in the forest region of West Africa.

Of the origins of the kingdom, we know very little, since the events of this early period are shrouded in mystery. Extant traditions recollect four phases of Benin history.[1] Stories connected with the first phase are highly speculative,

---

1. For details of these traditions and much of what follows see J.U. Egharevba, *A Short History of Benin* (Ibadan: Ibadan University Press, 1968), 1-10; A.F.C. Ryder, *Benin and the Europeans, 1485-1897* (New York: Humanities Press, 1969), 1-23; R.E. Bradbury, *The Benin Kingdom and the Edo-Speaking Peoples of South-Western Nigeria* (London: International African Institute, 1957); and *Benin Studies* (London: Oxford University Press, 1973), 17-75.

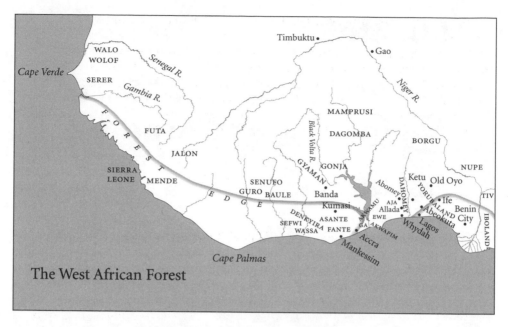

Figure 7-1. The West African Forest

speaking of dynasties of rulers whose names and achievements are lost in antiquity. The second phase was the era of the Ogiso dynasty. Established by one Obagodo, the Ogiso dynasty ruled Benin till the thirteenth century A.D. Thirty one Ogiso rulers appeared to have reigned before the dynasty came to an inglorious end under Owodo. Owodo's misrule and cruelties and the high-handedness of his only son and heir made him unpopular. This resulted in the banishment of his son to Ughoton in the southwest, where he established himself as the founder of a new dynasty. Owodo himself was removed and banished from the town. Thereafter, the chiefs determined to have nothing to do with the Ogiso family. They adopted a republican system of government, electing one of their members to the rulership of the state. This brief experimentation with republicanism was, however, a complete failure. Though the new system was meant to be non-hereditary and elective, one leader attempted surreptitiously to ensure the selection of his son to succeed him. The chiefs, after frustrating this subversion on the part of the ruler, were unable to agree on an alternative candidate among themselves for the throne. To break out of the deadlock, they sent to Oduduwa, the ruler of the ancient Yoruba city of Ile Ife, requesting a prince of the royal house. In response, Oduduwa sent his youngest son, Oranmiyan, who arrived in Benin with a party of followers, priests and craftsmen. Oranmiyan's advent inaugurated the fourth and final phase in the history of the Benin kingdom.

It is not clear in the traditions as to whether the Oranmiyan story is meant to conceal a story of conquest and political usurpation by a group of military invaders from the Yoruba country to the northeast. Nevertheless, the immigrant rulers appear to have brought with them new concepts and methods of government and new ideas of religion, warfare and craftsmanship. All these, in combination with indigenous ideas and practices, soon inaugurated a new era of political consolidation as well as conquest and imperialism in Benin history. The process of transformation was, however, neither easy nor sudden. The alien intrusion did not receive an unqualified welcome in the city, still recovering from the fissures created by recent political conflicts. So strong was the opposition that Oranmiyan and his party were for a long time kept outside the city while loyal chiefs attempted to establish control. Indeed, Oranmiyan eventually left the city in frustration, calling it a land of wrath, *ile-ibinu*, from which the city is said to have derived its name. Oranmiyan's son by an Edo woman became the oba, the Yoruba word for king, and the title by which the rulers of the new dynasty were known. The new rulers remained under the shadow of the principal Edo chiefs, the Uzama Nihinron, whose status was further enhanced by their position as hereditary kingmakers. It was not until the reign of the fourth Oba, Ewedo, that the stranglehold of the chiefs over the oba was broken.

Ewedo and the Consolidation of Royal Power

The reign of Ewedo marked the beginning of the consolidation of royal paramountcy in Benin history. The oba ceased to be merely *primus inter pares* in relation to the chiefs. He became a more powerful monarch and relegated the chiefs to subordinate positions. He compelled them to remain standing in his presence instead of being seated. The chiefs were henceforth prohibited from possessing or using the swords of state (*ada*) or conferring titles. To further establish his difference from the chiefs, Ewedo built an extensive new palace and instituted an elaborate system of palace organization and a hierarchy of chiefs to serve the palace.

The elaborate structure of palace officials which emerged was composed of three units. The most senior of these was the Iwebo, led by the Uwangue, which had charge of the oba's royal regalia, and later, responsibilities for trade and finance. The second group was the Iwegue, led by the Esere, and made up of personal attendants and courtiers of the king. The last group, the Ibiwe, led by the Osodin, had responsibility for the welfare of the oba's wives and children. Each group was quartered in a separate section of the palace. The consequence of this was rivalry and competition between the groups, giving a powerful and astute king considerable leverage as the final arbiter among his more powerful subjects who competed for his favors. The power of the oba to create new titles and offer non-hereditary titles to individuals of his choice enhanced his power and control over his subjects and chiefs. Loyalty and service to the king brought wealth, promotion, and influence. Falling out of favor with the king could mean demotion, execution, or in the case of the more powerful chiefs like the Uzama, banishment. Ewedo's internal reforms, however, do not appear to have irretrievably weakened the Uzama and the town chiefs, who continued to contest the authority of the kings who succeeded him.

Ewuare and the Foundation of the Benin Empire

The reign of Ewedo laid the foundation of a new era in the expansion of the Benin kingdom. New instruments of warfare such as horses, bows and swords appear to have been introduced at this time. These were accompanied by new meth-

Figure 7-2. The Oba of Benin in Procession

ods of organization which enabled Benin to effectively harness its resources for colonization. Benin, however, remained small and apart from a successful war against
the neighboring state of Udo, militarism was not a central feature of this period.
This situation, however, changed in the fifteenth century, when a new monarch,
Ewuare, seized the throne after a violent upheaval and succession dispute that was
settled only after considerable bloodshed, the killing of the ruling oba, and the
storming and burning down of the capital. Described in Benin tradition as "powerful, courageous and sagacious,"[2] Ewuare is credited with the transformation of the
town into a city, the monarch into an autocrat and the mini-kingdom into an empire. After securing himself on the throne, Ewuare redesigned and rebuilt the capital. The palace (*ogbe*) was separated from the town (*ore*) by a broad avenue.
Within the town were craftsmen and artisans such as diviners, physicians, carvers,
bards, carpenters, smiths, weavers and executioners. These were organized into
guilds and age grades, and were in turn, through their individual attachments to
one of the palace associations, integrated into the service of the king and the palace.

 Another important reform effected by Ewuare was the institution of the association of town chiefs, Eghaevbo n'Ore, who along with the existing palace chiefs,
Eghaevbo n'Ogbe, constituted the king's highest council with the duties of debating and deciding important matters of state, advising him in giving judgments,
and dealing with questions of war and peace. As individuals, these chiefs were
given responsibility for the administration and gathering of tribute from the villages and towns of the Benin kingdom. Ewuare's creation of the association of
town chiefs appears to have been inspired by the need to placate the town, especially after the civil upheaval that had marked his seizure of power. By closely as-
sociating the indigenous elements of his capital with the palace and actively involving their representatives in the administration of the state, he was attempting
to ensure their loyalty and the effective integration of town and palace in the state.

---

 2. J.U. Egharevba, *A Short History*, 13.

Over time, however, the group of town chiefs developed into what can be termed a permanent and official opposition to the palace. As *de facto* representatives of the non-royal population, they became significant in Benin politics as a legitimate counterweight to the palace. By the seveteenthth century, their leader, the Iyase, had become the commander of the Benin armies, and the leader and spokesman of the opposition. The Iyase became more or less the king's prime minister, with the prerogative, along with the other town chiefs, of arguing with or censuring the oba in public. Indeed at the death of any of the town chiefs, and as a ritual act symbolizing the oba's ultimate supremacy over every man in the state, the oba would send his men to claim the lower jaw of the deceased chief, "the jaw he had used to dispute with the oba." Nevertheless, the fact that these titles, unlike those of the Uzama, were non-hereditary and at the mercy of the king, gave the ruler considerable leverage in deploying his power of appointment and promotion to weaken and stifle opposition, reward services, and encourage and command loyalty.

As part of his attempt to ensure stability for the kingdom, Oba Ewuare grappled with the problem of regulating the succession to the throne. To confirm and enshrine the Edo principle of primogeniture, he decided to give formal recognition to his heir apparent in his lifetime. He bestowed on him the newly created title of Edaiken, made him a member of the Uzama, and gave him the rulership of his own village on the outskirts of the capital. Though the title of Edaiken survived, Ewuare's innovations could not resolve the rivalries and conflicts attendant on the struggle for succession to the most powerful office in the land.

Having taken care of internal dissension and established his unchallenged lordship of his people, Ewuare turned to military conquest. His achievements in this sphere ensured his reputation as the founder of the Benin Empire. He was able to harness the considerable energies of his people into an indefatigable war machine which became an effective instrument for the expansion of Benin and its establishment as the most formidable military power in the area. Tradition speaks of Ewuare's magical powers, his valor as a warrior, his gift of leadership and organization, and his undauntedness and resourcefulness as a military commander. Through successful annual military expeditions, recalcitrant subjects were brought to submission while the frontiers of the empire expanded to incorporate new lands and peoples. To the east, the western Igbo came under Benin's rulership; to the northeast, the empire expanded to include the Afenmai and other groups; to the northwest, many towns and villages of the Ekiti and Ikare and the important Yoruba kingdoms of Owo and Akure came to acknowledge Benin's suzerainty.

The century that followed Ewuare's reign was also a period of expansion, as his successors built upon what he had initiated. Ewuare's youngest son, Ozolua, further strengthened the army. Remembered in Benin tradition as Ozolua the Conqueror, he kept Benin's enemies and neighbors under sustained military pressure. He fought wars on many fronts and, by constant military successes, established the reputation of the Benin army as a superior and invincible force in the region. Personally leading his army and not known for retreat or surrender, he made the powerful kingdom of Ijebu feel his might, while he stubbornly fought the recalcitrant Ishan to a standstill before he was assassinated by his war-wearied and exhausted army. Ozolua's son and successor, Esigie, continued the military tradition of his father. He is remembered for his significant victory over the Igala

century, Benin's war machine began to reach boundaries beyond which it could not penetrate: the sea to the south, the Niger River to the east, the Nupe kingdom to the northeast, and the Oyo Empire to the northwest. The oba began to delegate the command of his armies to chiefs, especially the Iyase. The drowning of Ehengbuda in the course of an expedition which he led to the Lagos area led to a law prohibiting the oba from future command of the army. The oba became more restricted, living a secluded life in the palace. The military dimension of his power was de-emphasized as the supernatural elements of his person and the ritual functions of his office became the focus of attention. Virtually confined to his palace and hedged about with numerous taboos, the oba suffered a decline in power and prestige. Rarely permitted to venture beyond the palace without considerable ceremony, the oba became a captive of the whims and caprices of his chiefs. Compared to the famous kings of the sixteenth century, the seven obas of the seventeenth were weak, obscure, and effete, hardly distinguishable from one another. Exploiting their newly acquired power, the senior chiefs took direct charge of the succession, routinely ignoring the rule of primogeniture. They selected old and pliable candidates for the throne, ensuring short reigns and subservience of the oba to the chiefs.

The senior chiefs, however, failed to consolidate their gains into a permanent position of power or to transform the kingship into a constitutional monarchy. Mutual jealousies among the chiefs, their preoccupation with immediate gains, the attachment of the Edo to the principles and rituals of sacred kingship, and the resilience and resourcefulness of the monarchy ensured the eventual triumph of the monarchy over the chiefs. The chiefs remained mostly non-hereditary, still largely dependent on the king for their appointment, power, and promotion. When finally, at the end of the seventeenth century, a strong oba emerged, determined to seize the initiatives and reassert royal paramountcy over the chiefs, a protracted civil war could not be avoided. The oba, however, emerged victorious and stronger. Strategically deploying his power as the ultimate fountain of honor and influence and adroitly exploiting the fractious and competing claims of his principal chiefs, the oba was able to rally enough support for the monarchy to eventually break the stranglehold of the chiefs and expel the rebellious parties, led by the Iyase from the capital, while establishing his unchallenged supremacy in the state. The Iyase was divested of his duty as the commander of the army, a function which fell to the Ezomo, a member of the Uzama. The Iyase was replaced in his political function as leader of the opposition by the creation by Oba Akenzua of the Ologbotsere title, whose occupant henceforth became the most prominent Benin chief.

While the oba appears to have emerged triumphant in the conflict with his chiefs, the civil war set the stage for the steady but gradual decline of the empire. The oba did not entirely break out of his restriction to the palace. Increasing emphasis continued to be placed on his majesty and sacredness, as well as the ritual significance of his office as the soul of the nation and guarantor of its prosperity and protection. The oba continued to maintain his authority by continually manipulating the title system and playing upon the feuds and rivalries of his principal chiefs. The chiefs, however, remained active in succession disputes, royal rituals, and military matters, as commanders of the army, and in palace and state politics. They continued to challenge the prerogatives of the monarchy. Their incessant contest with the king created cleavages and fissures in the Benin body politics, that weakened the monarchy and eventually rendered the state weak and vulnerable.

Preoccupied with suppressing internal disruption, the oba was unable to maintain or strengthen his hold over his subject peoples. Taking advantage of the unrest in the capital, many of Benin's vassal states began to assert their independence. The Itsekiri and the Ijo, after establishing their independence, seized control of the important trade (with the Europeans) of the lower Benin River. Close to the center of the state, Ishan, Agbor, and Ugo, at different times, rose in rebellion. On the periphery of the empire, where vassals had been held to the center by a loose bond of nominal acknowledgment of loyalty, periodic tribute payment, and familial attachments, the ties began to loosen. However, as the periphery drifted from the center, the loose-knit, heterogeneous nature of the empire ensured that a revolt in one part did not occasion a wholesale and widespread repudiation of loyalty to Benin. But while Benin was still trying to recover and reassert its control over its vassal states, new forces arrived, let loose from the north and thesouth, putting much pressure on the already weakening fabric of the state. The outbreak, at the beginning of the nineteenth century, of the Fulani jihad in Hausaland to the north and its extension to the south created new centers of power in the Nupe and Yoruba countries, to the north of Benin. From Nupeland, the jihadists began to attack and seize control of many northern Edo settlements. Similarly, the breakup of the Oyo Empire provoked civil wars in the Yoruba country, drawing in the Ekiti, Owo, and Akoko areas still nominally committed to Benin.

In the meantime, from the coast a new presence, that of the British, was manifesting itself, with increasing militancy and imperialistic intentions. Assailed from all directions, the kingdom of Benin, which for centuries had welcomed and cultivated the friendship of foreigners, became suspicious of outsiders. It turned increasingly inward for security. With its enemies gradually closing in from all sides, the rulers of Benin sought solace in isolation, creating new titles to gain followers and counterbalance the resurgent powers of the chiefs, while desperately appealing to supernatural intervention to avert the total disintegration and collapse of the kingdom. All these proved of no avail. Nevertheless, at the time of the British invasion and conquest in 1897, the core of the kingdom was holding together and the prestige of the king remained largely unimpaired as he was able to rally the majority of the chiefs and people behind him. This ensured not only stiff resistance to the British incursion, but also compelled the new colonial masters to eventually restore the kingship and preserve the age-old monarchical system for the city-state.[3]

The Oyo Empire

The main focus here will be on the rise of Oyo vis-a-vis the other Yoruba states and most especially Ile Ife; the development of a cavalry army; Oyo's trading interactions with the north and the coast; the trans-Atlantic slave trade; the

3. On the history of Benin in the nineteenth century see Bradbury, *Benin Studies*, 76-84; Ryder, *Benin*, 239-294.

political organization of Oyo, based on a system of checks and balances; its imperial conquests and its final collapse.

Ile Ife and the Rise of Oyo

According to Yoruba traditions,[4] it was at Ife that the world was created. Ile Ife is regarded as the cradle of life, the ancient city where light and life dawned, where the spiritual and the temporal came together, where divinity impregnated the earth to produce the Yoruba cosmos, and where the first humans and deities descended from on high to colonize and inhabit the earth and establish the will of Olodumare, the Supreme God of the Yoruba. The primacy of Ile Ife in religion as well as in politics is generally acknowledged all over the Yoruba country. Featuring prominently in this early drama of state evolution was the figure of Oduduwa, the reputed progenitor of the Yoruba. Arriving in the Ife area, probably from a northeastern direction and at the head of a migrant group, Oduduwa, after overwhelming the pre-existing settlers, established himself as the new ruler.

Whatever we might make of this tradition, it would appear that Ile Ife was the seat of an early Yoruba settlement and that the advent of Oduduwa and his party marked the transformation of the little-known polity into a major kingdom. The political change was characterized by three prominent features: the establishment of a tradition of sacred kingship symbolized by the *ade ileke* or beaded crown, the building of a royal palace or *afin*, and the institution of the cult of *imule*. How long this process of transformation took is not clear in the traditions, but it appears to have taken years and involved much conflict and warfare, in which the immigrant group led by Oduduwa eventually triumphed over the autochtonous groups. The changes taking place in Ife soon began to produce far-reaching socio-political consequences in other parts of the Yoruba country. It would appear that from Ife, as a result of a multiplicity of factors such as demographical, ecological, and political pressures, bands of migrants, opportunists, warriors and other adventurers began to penetrate, migrate into, and invade other parts of Yoruba land. In many places, after supplanting the pre-existing groups, they appeared to have repeated, on different scales and with variations, the political achievements pioneered by Oduduwa at Ife. Ife continued to be important in the socio-political traditions of the new polities, as the cradle of the race, and the source of beaded crowns and the legitimization of the right to kingship.

Of the many Yoruba states that claim to have derived their origins and power from Ile Ife, the one that grew to become the most powerful and extensive was Oyo. Close to the Niger River and in the grassland region of northern Yorubaland, its geographical location gave Oyo decided advantages over its neighbors. Its fertile grasslands supported extensive and intensive agriculture, which became the mainstay of its people. Its strategic location, between the forest states and peoples in the south and the Sudanese peoples and states in the north, put it at the center of the trade between the two regions. Not only did Oyo gain and maintain control of the north-south trade passing through its territory, it benefited greatly

4. For details of these traditions see Samuel Johnson, *The History of the Yorubas* (Lagos: CMS Press), 1-25.

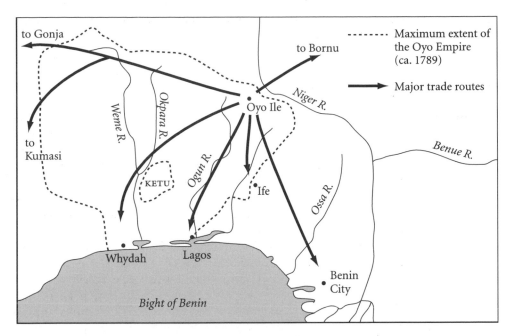

Figure 7-6. Oyo Empire, 1789

from this trade. On the coast, Oyo traders sold slaves and other items to European traders who had from the seventeenth century onwards become actively engaged in the slave trade. In return, Oyo obtained manufactured goods that it sold to its northern neighbors, the Nupe and Hausa, in exchange for salt, slaves, and horses. The last item became crucial for the development of Oyo's military power. Oyo became a cavalry state, a feature which sharply distinguished it from its Yoruba neighbors to the south and determined the nature and direction of its imperial expansion. Thus the empire expanded to incorporate the savanna regions of the Nupe, Borgu, and Dahomey, and the largely grassland regions of central and northern Yorubaland. In the hilly country of the Ekiti and the forested regions of Ijesa, not readily amenable to cavalry conquest, Oyo imperialism made little progress. Instead, this region became the major source for Oyo's human prestations, as the inhabitants became subjected to periodic slave raids to feed the demand for human cargo at the coast.

Military Conquest and Political Development

The rise of Oyo to prominence was neither sudden nor easy. Indeed from its inception, Oyo had to contend with the imperial ambitions of warlike neighbors, the Owu to the south, the Nupe to the northeast, and the Bariba of Borgu to the northwest. Following the establishment of the monarchy by Oranmiyan, the first alaafin or ruler believed in Oyo tradition to be the youngest son of Oduduwa and the inheritor of his title and throne at Ife, Oyo found itself tributary to Owu, the first major Yoruba state after Ife to establish its imperial power in central and northern Yorubaland. It was not until the reign of the third alaafin, Sango, that the power of Owu was broken. Oyo gained its independence and began its steady expansion. It flourished in the reigns of Aganju and Oluaso, two strong and long-lived rulers, and by the time of Alaafin Kori, probably in the fourteenth century, the kingdom had extended its influence about a hundred miles to the south. There it established the town of Ede to serve as a frontier post against the imperial designs of the forest but warlike Yoruba state of Ilesa. Troubles, however, continued and Oyo's relations with its vassal states as well as with its northern Nupe neighbors remained unsettled. Early in the 16th century, while the Oyo army was absent suppressing a revolt in one of the vassal states, a Nupe army invaded and sacked the capital. Alaafin Onigbogi fled with his chiefs and people to Borgu, where he took refuge and was offered protection by the ruler of Nikki. The alaafin and the royal court's exile lasted for close to a century. Their wanderings took them to Gbere, where Onigbogi died and Ofinran succeeded him; to Kusu, where Ofinran died; and to Igboho, where four alaafin reigned before the reoccupation of the capital at the beginning of the seventeenth century by Alaafin Abipa, after he had successfully frustrated the stratagems of his principal chiefs to prevent his return.

The experience of defeat and exile turned out, in fact, to be propitious for the kingdom. New ideas on religion, such as the Ifa divinatory corpus, and on militarism, were adopted and adapted by Oyo from its northern neighbors, most especially the Nupe and the Bariba. The army was reorganized to ensure that the capital would no longer be left defenseless and vulnerable. Having tasted the bitter pill of defeat, Oyo became more aggressive in its relations with its neighbors. The reoccupation of the capital was followed by a rapid expansion of the Oyo Empire. Under Obalokun and Ajagbo, two warlike alaafin, much of central and northern Yorubaland was incorporated into the empire, including the state of Owu which became tributary to Oyo. While Oyo could not extend its influence effectively into the forested regions of Ijesa and Ijebu, its attempt to impose its hegemony over the eastern Yoruba countries of Ekiti and Akoko brought it into collision with the powerful and expanding Edo empire of Benin. A peace agreement between the two powers recognized the eastern Yoruba town of Owo as the boundary between them.

Balked in its southeastward push, Oyo turned to the more open and less forested southwest, where it imposed its suzerainty over the Egba and their neighboring Egbado groups. As trade with the Europeans on the coast assumed more significance, Oyo established its imperial control over the western Yoruba states of Ketu and Iweme, and later Porto Novo on the coast. By the mid-seventeenth century, the Nupe and the Bariba, to the northeast and northwest respectively, appear to have come under Oyo domination, a relationship which remained largely unaltered till the late eighteenth century. In 1698, the Oyo army conquered Allada, the most important state of the Aja-speaking people. In 1730, after four successful military expeditions, the nascent but important Fon state of Dahomey was reduced to tributary status. Thereafter, until 1818, and apart from occasional intermissions, Dahomey paid to the alaafin an annual tribute of forty men, forty women, forty guns, and four hundred loads of cowries and corals. By the time of Ojigi's death in about 1735, Oyo had become the most powerful, the most extensive, and the most feared kingdom in the region. Its fame did not escape the attention of European traders and visitors on the coast. Writing in the late seventeenth century, William Bosman, a Dutch visitor, reported that this "Nation strikes Terror into all the circumjadcent Negroes."[5] Much the same impression was confirmed a century later in 1764 by Robert Norris, an English visitor in Dahomey, when he wrote, "The Dahomeans may possibly exaggerate, but the Eyeos are certainly a very populous, warlike and powerful nation."[6]

System of Government

A major source of strength for the Oyo Empire was its system of government. At the center of this empire was the alaafin. Regarded as a sacred ruler, he was saluted as "Kabiyesi, Oba Alaase, Ekeji Orisa," meaning "The One whose authority cannot be questioned, the King with authority, the companion of the Gods."[7] The elaborate rituals of his coronation and installation set him apart from other mortals. As the wearer of the beaded crown with fringes, he was the personification and reincarnation of all his ancestors who had worn that crown. As a semi-divine ruler, he became the link between the living and the dead in the community and the visible expression of the collective identity and social memory of his people. The alaafin, was, however, not an autocrat. While in theory his word was law and order and his court wasthe highest court of appeal, in practice, he had to rule with the advice of his chiefs. Hedged about with numerous taboos, bound by rules of precedent and practice, and ritually restricted to the palace, the alaafin became dependent on his principal chiefs and his coterie of palace officials.

While the extent of the power exercised by the alaafin depended to a great extent on his personality, he could hardly, unlike the more authoritarian monarchies of Benin and Dahomey, ignore the wishes and advice of his chiefs without imperiling his survival. The most important were the Oyomesi. Led by the Basorun, these were the seven kingmakers whose hereditary status as representatives of major lineages gave them considerable independence and the initiative to influence, restrain, and even remove the monarch. They provided a check on the royal tendency towards absolutism, compelling many alaafin in the course of the seventeenth and eighteenth centuries to commit suicide. To ensure fairness in their exercise of the power to remove the king, it became a requirement that one of their members, the Asamu, would also die with the king. This system of checks and balances became a major feature of the Oyo constitution during the imperial period. The breakdown of the system in the mid-eighteenth century, during the career of Basorun Gaha, set the stage for the gradual decline and eventual collapse of the empire. Describing the career of Gaha, Samuel Johnson, the famous Yoruba historian, wrote: "He lived to a good old age, and wielded his power ruthlessly. He was noted for having raised five kings to the throne, of whom he murdered four, and was himself murdered by the fifth."[8]

---

5. Quoted in Robert Smith, *Kingdoms of the Yoruba*, 3rd ed. (London: James Currey, 1988), 31.
6. Robert Norris, quoted in Thomas Hodgkin, *Nigerian Perspectives: An Historical Anthology* (London: Oxford University Press, 1975), 221.
7. John Pemberton III and Funso Afolayan, *Yoruba Sacred Kingship: A Power Like That of the Gods* (Washington and London: Smithsonian Institution Press, 1996), 73.
8. Samuel Johnson, *History* (Lagos: CMS, 1921), 178.

The Decline and Fall of Oyo

How and why did this great empire collapse? Historians are still debating the relative significance of the reasons for its collapse and fall.[9] Those who emphasize internal factors focus on the constitutional breakdown in the capital, which resulted from the perennial struggle for supremacy between the alaafin and his chiefs. In a political system stabilized by the balance of conflicts and interests between the principal players, the tilting of the balance in the mid-eighteenth century to the side of the chiefs did not augur well for the maintenance of stability in the state. Since the system appears to have been organized to contain and curtail royal absolutism, it had no answer to the assumption of authoritarianism on the part of the chiefs. Hence, in virtually all the major tussles between the alaafin and his chiefs, the latter won. This ascendancy of the chiefs reached its peak in the eighteenth century, when none of the alaafin died a natural death. All were compelled to commit suicide or are believed to have been poisoned. The attempt of Alaafin Abiodun in 1774 to seize the initiative and reassert royal paramountcy led him to bring in the armies of the provinces to redress the balance of power at the center. Though successful, this unprecedented step set a precedent for the future and, henceforth the provinces became a destabilizing force in the politics of the capital.

The first of the provincial rulers to exploit the weakened state of the center was Afonja, the Are Ona Kakamfo or commander in chief of the Oyo army and the ruler of the provincial town of Ilorin, who revolted against the alaafin. He was followed in his action by other notable provincial rulers like the Bale of Gbogun and the Onikoyi of Ikoyi. With Oyo disintegrating at the center, the vassal states on the periphery began to break away one after another. In 1783, Borgu broke away from its allegiance to Oyo, after inflicting a crushing defeat on the Oyo army. They were followed by the Nupe, who appear to have made good their independence from Oyo by 1791, and for a time subjected their erstwhile overlord to tributary status. In about 1796, the Egba, led by Lisabi, asserted their independence after carrying out a wholesale massacre of Oyo representatives and supporters in Egbaland. The attempts of the alaafin to extricate himself from the imbroglio with his chiefs and reassert his control over his rebellious vassals proved abortive. Oyo reeled from one defeat to the next before finally succumbing to the Fulani jihadists from Ilorin, who in alliance with Lanloke, the ruler of the northern Yoruba state of Ogodo, invaded and sacked the capital in 1835.

A major reason for the debacle was a decline in military strength. The preoccupation of the Oyo rulers and army with internal conflicts, and the reliance on the armies of vassal states, especially Dahomey, for some military activities resulted in the neglect of the army. The weakening of the army was further aggravated by the break away of Oyo's northern tributary states of Nupe and Borgu, which disrupted Oyo's northern trade, closing to it the northern markets from

---

9. For these debates see I.A. Akinjogbin, "The Prelude to the Yoruba Civil Wars of the Nineteenth Century," *Odu,* 2nd series, 1, 2 (1965): 24-46; R.C.C. Law, "The Constitutional Troubles of Oyo in the Eighteenth Century," *JAH,* 12 (1971): 25-44 and J.A. Atanda, "The Fall of the Old Oyo Empire: A Reconsideration of its Cause," *Journal of Historical Society of Nigeria,* 5, 4 (1971).

which it obtained its horses, the mainstay of its much feared cavalry. Parallel with this military decline was a decline in the economy. As the northern trade routes were disrupted, Oyo turned to the south, intensifying its dependence on the slave trade with the Europeans on the coast. The independence of the Egba and later of Dahomey, and the failure of Oyo to recover its losses, led to the decline of its influence in the coastal regions. The collapse of Porto Novo, Oyo's main outlet to the sea, as a result of incessant attacks from Dahomey between 1803 and 1805, shifted the center of the slave trade to the ports of Badagry and Lagos, well beyond the reach of the Oyo cavalry. To make matters worse the British, for reasons largely connected with their own commercial and imperial interests, abolished the slave trade in 1807. Thereafter, they stationed their naval squadron on the West African coast to stamp out the trade there.

In the meantime, on the northern periphery of the collapsing empire, new troubles were brewing. In 1804, a Fulani-led Islamic revivalist movement had broken out among the Hausa. Within a few years, the successful jihadists were in full control of much of the Central Sudan, and were pushing southward. The opportunity to carry their jihad across the Niger was provided by one of the alaafin's henchmen, Afonja, the rebellious Are Ona Kakanfo of the Oyo Empire. In his ambition to carve out a kingdom for himself, Afonja appealed to the Fulani jihadists for help against his master and overlord. Led by Alimi Salih, an itinerant Muslim preacher, the Fulani, rebellious Hausa and Nupe slaves in Oyo, and other adventurers flocked to the support and protection of the Alaafin's miscreant commander. Afonja's new friends and helpers, however, soon proved to be overbearing subjects. In 1823-1824, he attempted to check their excesses and extricate himself from their stranglehold but was killed in a hail of arrows and spears. The victorious Fulani took over Ilorin, and Abdulsalami, the son of Alimi, became the first ruler of the new emirate in the heart of Yoruba country. Thereafter, from Ilorin, the Fulani attacked and destroyed one Yoruba town after another, before eventually conquering Old Oyo itself in 1835, killing Alaafin Oluewu, and burning down the capital. It has remained in ruins ever since.

Even with the triumph of the Fulani and the desertion of the capital, the fate of Oyo might not have been sealed. Oyo had survived worse crises in the past. There is no reason to suppose that with the organization of a united resistance against the enemies and the emergence of a strong alaafin, Oyo would not have been able to rise to the occasion and rally itself to save the day. However, for Oyo and its subordinate Yoruba states, this was the worst of times. Instead of sinking their differences and uniting against their common enemies, the principal Oyo chiefs and the provincial rulers, as if anticipating the inevitable collapse of the empire, began to scheme and fight among themselves for the disposal of the carcass of the empire. The situation was not improved by the personality of the men who became alaafin during these years. These men were anything but strong and warlike. Awole, who succeeded Abiodun in 1789, was, in the words of Johnson, "too weak and too mild for the times."[10] Unable to control his army and at loggerheads with most of his principal chiefs, he was forced to commit suicide, to which he consented after pronouncing a solemn curse of carnage and enslavement on his people. His successor, Adebo, had little authority over anybody in

10. Johnson, *History*, 188.

the kingdom and he died, probably from frustration or poisoning, within a few months.

Adebo was followed by Maku, whose reign ended in disaster and suicide following his defeat in an expedition against the rebellious southeastern town of Iworo. A long interregnum followed, ending with the accession of the elderly Majotu. He was too weak to halt the disintegration of the empire. His successor, Amodo, was described by Johnson as "virtually the king of the capital only."[11] Worn out by apprehension, Amodo died before he could realize his plan to push back the Fulani. His successor, Oluewu, with the aid of fighters from Borgu, inflicted a major defeat on Ilorin showing at least that the jihadist forces were not invincible. The alaafin, however, could not follow up on his victory. Mutual jealousies and petty rivalries among his quarreling and ambitious chiefs sealed the fate of the alaafin and his capital. This ensured the defeat of the Oyo army at the next encounter with Ilorin, when the principal Yoruba chiefs and ambitious Oyo princes conspired to contrive the defeat of the alaafin and his Borgu allies, to guarantee their own succession to the alaafin's power and territory.

The destruction of Oyo and other northern Yoruba towns produced a major demographic change in Yorubaland. Northern Yorubaland became depopulated as refugees flooded south, increasing the population of old settlements like Ogbomoso, Epe, Ile Ife, and the town that became New Oyo, and establishing new ones like Ibadan, Ijaiye, and Abeokuta. The attempts of the Yoruba successor states to fill the vacuum created by the disappearance of the Oyo Empire led to incessant warfare which continued with varying degrees of intensity till the end of the nineteenth century. The most powerful of the successor states was the military and republican state of Ibadan. After defeating the Fulani at the Battle of Osogbo in 1839, Ibadan attempted to make good its claim to the leadership of the Yoruba country. Challenged by Kurunmi, who had established a military autocracy at Ijaiye, and frustrated in its attempt to reach the coast by the southern Yoruba states of Ijebu and Egba, Ibadan had to fight wars on many fronts. A clear testimony to the success of the new militarism established at Ibadan was its success in holding its own on all fronts, defeating and eliminating Ijaiye, fighting its adversaries in the northeast and in the southwest to a stand still, until the intervention of the British during the last decades of the nineteenth century.[12]

In the name of suppressing the slave trade and promoting Christian missionary activities and legitimate trade, the British had by 1851 established a foothold in the Yoruba port city of Lagos. In 1861, Lagos became a British colony. Frustrated by the wars in the interior and their destabilizing effects on the development of trade between Lagos and the Yoruba hinterland, the British became actively involved as arbitrators and peacemakers in the conflicts. Exhausted by nearly a century of warfare, raided by the Dahomeans from the west, harassed by the Fulani and the Nupe from the north, and unable to put their own houses in order, the Yoruba states and rulers were too weak and divided to resist British peacemaking overtures or to organize a concerted resistance to the conquering

---

11. Johnson, *History*, 217.

12. On nineteenth century Yorubaland see S.A. Akintoye, *Revolution and Power Politics in Yorubaland, 1840-1893* (London: Longman, 1971); T. Falola, *The Political Economy of a Pre-colonial African State: Ibadan, 1830-1900* (Ile Ife: University of Ife Press, 1984); and Akinjogbin, ed., *War and Peace in Yorubaland, 1793-1893* (Ibadan: Heinemann, 1998).

British army which seized control of one Yoruba state after another during the last decade of the nineteenth century.

The Asante Empire

This section focuses on Asante's situation in the gold-producing region of West Africa, the emergence of many states among the Akan; the harsh and unpopular rule of Denkyira; the development of Oyoko nationalism; and the leadership qualities and achievements of Asante's first three rulers. It will also examine the significance of the Golden Stool of Asante, the establishment of Kumasi as the capital, the adoption of a constitution for the union, the sacralization of the Asantehene's power and its reinforcement by the annual Odwira festival; Asante's military formations and wars of conquest, and its relations with its neighbors, especially the Fante and the Europeans on the coast.

The Akan and the Rise of Asante

The Asante belonged to the Akan-speaking peoples of southern Ghana. Their traditions indicate that they came from the Adanse-Amasie area.[13] It was here that they developed their matrilineal royal inheritance system. As a result of population pressure, land hunger, and political disturbances in their nucleus region, they began to disperse, migrating in several clan-groups northward, eventually establishing a number of small states in the area of present-day Kumasi by the middle of the sevententh century. Notable among these states were Mampon and Seniagya, established by the Bretuo clan groups; Abooso, Makom, and Agona, founded by the Asense; Domaa, Atwima and Tafo established by other Akan- or Guan-speaking peoples; and Asokore and Kwaaman founded by the Ekoona. The states of Dwaben, Kokofu, Nsuta, Bekwai, and Kumasi, established by the Oyoko clan groups, were the last to emerge in the area. They were also destined to become the builders of the most powerful empire in the region, which would by the end of the seventeenth century swallow up all the other states.

One major explanation for the concentration of migrants, settlers, and state founders in the Kumasi region was its proximity to the southern terminals of the trade routes to Mande areas in the northwest and Hausaland in the northeast. The desire to gain access to the lucrative northern trade and the production in this region of the two major commodities exported northward, gold and kolanuts, served as a magnet luring the poor, land-hungry migrants from the south. Equally important in the location of groups and individuals in this region was the emergence of Denkyira, Akyem, and Akwamu as powerful states in the hinterland of the Gold Coast. The disturbances and unsettlement associated with the military activities of these states led many groups, made up, in the words of T.E. Bowdich,

---

13. On the traditions of origins of the various Asante divisional states see R.S. Rattray, *Asanti Law and Constitution* (Oxford: Claredon Press, 1929), chs. 16-28; and C.C. Reindorf, *The History of the Gold Coast and Asante*, 2nd ed. (Accra: Ghana Universities Press, 1966).

Tutu. Anokye then informed the astonished audience that the Golden Stool, *Sika Dwa*, was from their ancestors. Henceforth, it would be the symbol of the union, the embodiment and repository of the collective soul (*sunsum*), the strength, the vitality, and the very survival of the nation. It must be guarded at all cost. Its possessor and occupant was to be recognized as the asantehene and should always come from the families of Obiri Yeboa and Osei Tutu. Displayed in public with much pomp and pageantry, the Golden Stool became, for the Asante, a powerful symbol of nationhood, unity, collective memory and cultural identity, provoking and evoking veneration, devotion, and loyalty. It provided a unifying ethic and became the major religious and symbolic focus, essential for the articulation, formalization, and consolidation of the Asante Union.[16]

To consolidate the union, and with the aid of a mixture of magic and diplomacy, Osei Tutu and Okomfo Anokye succeeded in persuading the other members of the union to recognize Kumasi, to which Osei Tutu had moved from Kwaman, as the permanent capital of the nation, and its ruler, the kumasihene as the supreme ruler of Asante, asantehene. To solidify the unity of the state, songs, recitals, national festivals, and ceremonies were organized and disseminated to emphasise commonalities in origin, history, identity, and destiny. The most important of these was the Odwira festival. Established by Osei Tutu and meant to annually rekindle "sentiments of solidarity and nationhood,"[17] it was attended by all the principal chiefs and provincial rulers in the state. It became an occasion for the settlement of disputes and misunderstandings, the propitiation of the memory of past kings, the ritual cleansing of the land, the expression of fealty and strengthening of allegiance, the offering of prayers for the nation, and the making of new laws and plans for the coming years. In the course of the festival, recalcitrant chiefs and other miscreants could be arraigned, judged, and sentenced by the asantehene, who could count on the collective sanction and support of the assembled chiefs to punish the offenders. Thus the annual festival became an effective instrument for checking subversion and strengthening of the union.

Forging a more perfect union also led to the devising of a constitution. At the head of the union was the Asantehene. Below him were the amanhene, the rulers of the divisions. In relation to the amanhene, the asantehene was *primus inter pares*. The amanhene had to take oaths of allegiance to the asantehene, swear to answer his call by day or night, contribute men to his fighting force, and even prosecute wars on his behalf, especially along their own frontiers. They also had to observe the king's regulations pertaining to trade, attend the annual Odwira festival, and send presents, tribute, and war tax to the king. They acknowledged the right of appeal from their own courts to that of the asantehene, the final court of appeal.

The amanhene, however, were not ciphers. In spite of their many obligations to the king they had their own compensatory rights, what Bowdich termed "pala-

---

16. For more information on the rise of the Asante state and the relationship between symbolism and power in precolonial Africa, see Naomi Chazan, "The Early State in Africa: The Asante Case," in S.N. Eisenstadt et al., eds., *The Early State in African Perspective* (Leiden: E.J. Brill, 1988), 60-97; and T.C. McCaskie, *State and Society in Pre-Colonial Asante* (Cambridge: Cambridge University Press), 1995.

17. K.A. Busia, *The Position of the Chief in the Modern Political System of Ashanti* (London: Oxford University Press, 1951), 101.

Figure 7-7. An Asante Group, Posed in Front of Their Compound

tine privileges."[18] They had absolute legal rights over their own divisional lands. These were not gifts from the king, having been acquired before the inauguration of the Asante Union. Though subject to the center in matters of national policy, the amanhene of the metropolitan region exercised a high degree of independence and initiative in the domestic affairs of their divisions. As Bowdich noted, "they possess distinct treasuries, levy tributes, administer justice, celebrate the great annual festival in their own capitals after they have assisted in that of Coomassie [Kumasi], and are alone permitted to wear the little silver circles like buckles, which distinguish the sandals of the king."[19] Since the armies of the divisions played a major role in the expansion of the empire, the amanhene were actively involved in the formulation of foreign policy. In the domestic and civil affairs of the nation, they usually deferred to the king; in matters of war, tribute, and peace, the king could not afford to ignore their counsel. It would appear that in theory, the asantehene could not depose one of the amanhene since he was not responsible for his selection, but as the asantehene increased in power and prestige, it became possible for him to, on occasion, use his enormous influence and leverage to contrive the removal of divisional chiefs who had fallen out of favor with him.

To counterbalance the power of the divisional chiefs, the asantehene created, and enhanced the position of the Kumasi chiefs. Kumasi chiefs were made overseers of the rulers of the distant and conquered provinces. Since they were directly responsible to the king for their titles as well as for the land they controlled, they became obligated to him. Further, as members of the Kumasi state

---

18. Bowdich, *Mission*, 256.

19. Bowdich, *An Essay on the Superstitions, Customs, and arts, common to the Ancient Egyptians, Abyssinians, and Ashantees* (Paris, 1821), 21.

pressed all revolts and rebellions. The situation, however, changed from the third decade of the nineteenth century, when the empire began a process of gradual decline.

The Decline and Fall of Asante

Many reasons have been suggested for the decline and collapse of the Asante Empire.[22] A major factor was administrative weakness of the central and provincial administrative systems. The asantehene was supreme only in the Kumasi state. In relation to the amanhene, he was first among equals; his moral status and influence derived from his occupancy of the Golden Stool. The amanhene remained virtually independent in their domestic affairs, while in imperial matters they were in a position to collectively constrain the asantehene to heed their advice. The power exercised by the king was not determined by well-established customs but by the personality, skill, and resourcefulness of the individual Asantehene. Unfortunately, most of the rulers of Asante in the nineteenth century were not as strong and competent as their predecessors. Thus, they were unable either to command the loyalty of all their peoples or to maintain the control of the conquered provinces, who began to break away in successful revolts during these years.

Equally important was the lack of power of the center over the provincial administration. The conquered provinces were not integrated effectively into the union. They were left under their indigenous rulers and were permitted to preserve their religions and socio-cultural traditions and festivals. They had no say in the Asante government and had no direct access to the asantehene except through one of the Kumasi chiefs. Perceiving their territories as sources for the collection of tribute and the gathering of troops for the king, they saw themselves as second-class members of the union. Consequently, they developed very little loyalty to Kumasi and did not identify themselves with the national sentiments associated with the Odwira festival and the Golden Stool. Apart from the threat of military intervention, the Asante rulers failed to evolve a system of socio-political control that could integrate the conquered units into a homogenous state. Lacking a sense of belonging, the vassal states seized every opportunity to assert their independence. That they were kept firmly under control till the early nineteenth century, was due largely to the strength of the metropolitan Asante army. The gradual weakening of this army from the mid-nineteenth century onwards set the stage for the breakup of the empire.

The weakening of the Asante army was the consequence of a combination of interrelated external factors that came to exercise a major influence on Asante. The evidence suggests that, left to themselves, the Asante could have succeeded in maintaining the integrity and independence of their empire till the end of the century. This was, however, not to happen. By the beginning of the nineteenth century, the British were already firmly established on the Gold Coast. Their commercial interests and their new commitment to the abolition of the slave trade and the spread of Christianity demanded active involvement in the politics and trade

---

22. On the decline and fall of Asante see F.C. Fuller, *A Vanished Dynasty: Ashanti* (London: John Murray, 1921) and Robert Edgerton, *The Fall of the Asante Empire* (New York: Free Press, 1995).

of the region. Through diplomacy, blackmail, and financial incentives, they succeeded in buying out the Danes and the Dutch, thus establishing a trade monopoly on the coast. The British were, however, unwilling to allow Asante domination of the coastal states and trade, which they felt would jeopardise their
commercial interests and monopoly in the region. To prevent this they began to
arm and support the coastal states, encouraging them to resist Asante. Between
1811 and 1826, the Asante army undertook a series of punitive expeditions to
suppress rebellions in Fante, Akyem, Wassa, and Denkyira. In some of these wars,
the British offerred logistic and military support to the coastal states.

The first major war between the British and the Asante occurred in 1824. The
British were defeated, and their governor, Sir Charles MacCarthy, was killed.
However, in the wars of 1874 and 1896, the British were successful, on the latter
occasion entering Kumasi and setting it on fire. These defeats and the resultant
disruption of the arms trade undermined the military supremacy of the Asante
army. The empire began to fall apart. One after the other, all the provincial states,
from Gonja and Dagomba in the north to Akyem, Denkyira, and Fante in the
south began to assert their independence, and this time they could neither be
stopped nor re-conquered. The Fante, not willing to exchange one master for another, organized themselves in 1868 into a confederation to preserve their independence from Asante as well as to establish a government which would "be to
ourselves a head, having no king under the British."[23] Rivalries among the chiefs
and the continued and active hostility of the British to the idea of an independent
confederation eventually brought the scheme to an end.

In July 1874, after their defeat of the Asante, the British annexed what is now
southern Ghana as a crown colony. In 1896, at the peak of the scramble for
Africa, in an attempt to forestall the French and the Germans, who were closing
in from the Ivory Coast and Togo respectively, the British invaded what was left
of Asante and northern Ghana. They entered Kumasi, and deposed and exiled
King Prempe along with members of his family and several prominent chiefs.
However, the Asante refused to surrender the Golden Stool. They mounted a
strong resistance to the British effort to seize it. Under the leadership of Yaa Asan-
tewa, the queen mother of Edweso, they laid siege to the British governor at Kumasi fort. It took four separate British expeditions before the resistance was finally suppressed. The British attempt to abolish the monarchy eventually failed.
In 1924, Prempe was brought back from his Seychelles Islands' exile and restored
to his throne.

Summary and Conclusions

For the region between the Volta and the lower Niger Rivers, the period between 1400 and 1800 was one of major developments and far-reaching innovations in state formation. It was also a time of remarkable ecological and cultural
adaptations. All over the region, the steady growth in population demanded more
creative and efficient use of available resources. Increased competition between

23. J.B. Webster, A.A. Boahen and M. Tidy, *The Revolutionary Years: West Africa since
1800* (Harlow: Longman, 1990), 161.

which put the alaafin in the hands of his chiefs. Through the Asante Union, the Asante succeeded in evolving political institutions that ensured the effective integration of the various component groups in the state without counterposing the king and his chiefs in structured opposition. In all these kingdoms, the rulers had to be efficient. They also, for reasons of convention and practical necessity, had to rule with the advice of their chiefs. Rulers who became unpopular or lost the confidence of their people could be removed constitutionally as in Oyo, or through open rebellion by the chiefs as in Benin. Royal succession practices varied from place to place. In Benin and Dahomey it was primogeniture; in Oyo it was rotational among competing ruling houses; while in Asante it was matrilineal. Benin and Oyo were plagued by fratricidal succession disputes, while Dahomey and Asante appear to have been largely spared.

None of these states lived in isolation. External relations remained central in their development. Ideas of religion, kingship, arts and crafts, commerce, and manufacture percolated from one state to the other. Trade opened access to goods and services not available locally. It gave rulers and chiefs the wealth and the resources to build their power and expand their states. All these states welcomed European traders and the access they provided to new and exotic goods. However, they became deeply enmeshed in the trans-Atlantic slave trade, an often profitable though nefarious occupation with major debilitating and distortive consequences. As European needs and interests changed from the forcible possession of the African person to the forcible possession of his land, a combination of internal and external dynamics ensured the eclipse of African independence and the establishment of European colonial rule by the end of the nineteenth century.

Review Questions

1. How important were ecological factors in the development of states and societies in the forest region of West Africa before the nineteenth century?
2. With reference to specific examples, assess the significance of the institution of kingship in the forest region of West Africa before 1800 A.D.
3. How accurate is the view that religion was peripheral to the development of states in West Africa before the nineteenth century?
4. Compare and contrast the political systems of Benin, Asante, and Oyo before the nineteenth century.
5. With reference to two examples, account for the strength and the resilience of West African forest kingdoms and also their failure to successfully resist European conquest and domination.

Additional Reading

Bradbury, R.E. *Benin Studies*. London: Oxford University Press, 1973.
Fynn, J.K. *Asante and Its Neighbours 1700-1807*. London: Longman, 1971.
Law, R.C.C. *The Oyo Empire, c. 1600-1836*. Oxford: Clarendon Press, 1977.

McCaskie, T.C. *State and Society in Pre-colonial Asante*. Cambridge: Cambridge University Press, 1995.

Ryder, A.F.C. *Benin and the Europeans, 1485-1897*. New York: Humanities Press, 1969.

Smith, Robert. *Kingdoms of the Yoruba*. 3rd ed. London: James Currey, 1988.

Wilks, Ivor. *Asante in the Nineteenth Century*. Cambridge: University Press, 1975.

Chapter 8

East African States

Julius O. Adekunle

Introduction

Between the second and the fifteenth centuries A.D., the East African coast became famous for its flourishing economy. The history of the territory stretching from Mogadishu in the north to Cape Delgado in the south is replete with information on the commercial development of the region and its attractiveness to foreign merchants. The settlements along the coast rapidly developed into commercial city-states because of their strategic location, which connected them to the outside world. Some of the cities such as Mogadishu, Kilwa, Sofala, Pemba, Pate, Mombasa, and Manda evolved as a result of trade. One after the other, they assumed leadership, effectively controlling the inter-regional trade with production centers in the hinterland. With their varying periods of prosperity, these states provide ample illustrations of the process of rise and decline common to African kingdoms and states. While reconstructing the history of the East African coast, foreign influences on these city-states must be acknowledged. The presence of the Arab, Persian, Indonesian, and Indian merchants facilitated trade. The Indian Ocean played an important role in enhancing the network of trade by connecting East African states with the outside world.

Written documents, oral tradition, and archaeology provide a great deal of information on the coast vis-à-vis the economic development of the states prior to the penetration of the Portuguese in the fifteenth century. Most of the early written documents are travelers' accounts; extreme caution is required in the use of the information they furnish because some are superficial and inaccurate. Chronicles of the city-states, which provide the most detailed information, are based essentially upon oral tradition. When taken together, these sources present very spotty and often contradictory accounts. Nonetheless, they have been very useful in reconstructing the political and economic history of early East African states, especially of those events not included in oral tradition. The primary interest of the foreigners along the coast was the development of commerce; thus they sought to control the trade in gold, ivory, ambergris, and slaves. Both the Arabs and the Persians were deeply involved in the East African coastal trade. Both contributed to the evolution of Swahili culture and employed Islam as a strong instrument of commercial and social interaction. When trade developed, Islamization followed from the seventh century onward. The Indonesians, Chinese, and Indi-

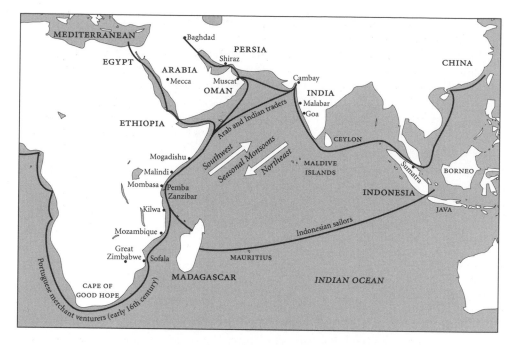

Figure 8-1. Indian Ocean Trading Networks

ans also established trade links with the early East African states. The Portuguese arrived in the fifteenth century and dominated the economy until the nineteenth century. In discussing the developments on the East African coast, it is appropriate to examine the early sources and the impact of foreigners on trade, culture, and religion.

Early Sources of Information

Fragmentary evidence from early written materials assists in recovering a significant part of the economic history of the East African coast. Beginning with the *Periplus of the Erythrean Sea*, a Greek commercial record written in the second century A.D., and the *Geography of Ptolemy* of the fourth century, the major theme was the thriving commerce along the coast. The *Periplus*[1] supplied information on the scattered ports and mentioned several emporia that had been established where custom duties were continually paid. These sources reveal the existence of well-organized commercial arrangements along the coast. Foreign merchants had begun to visit the coast for strictly commercial purposes by the second century. Various commodities were exchanged for frankincense and ivory.

---

* The author acknowledges the Creativity-in-Aid Committee of Monmouth University, West Long Branch, New Jersey for providing the funding for this research project.

1. Cited in Gervase Mathew, "The East African Coast Until the Coming of the Portuguese," in Roland Oliver and Gervase Mathew, eds., *History of East Africa* (London: Oxford University Press, 1963), 95-96.

There was a commercial link with the land of Punt (in the Horn of Africa), from which incense was supplied.

Between the second and fourth centuries, Opone in the north and Rhapta in the south served as the primary market centers, the emporia, where essential economic transactions were conducted. While cinnamon and tortoise shells were supplied in Opone, ivory was abundant in Rhapta. Menouthias, a thickly wooded island, was another trading settlement.[2] Adulis, the Aksumite port, became a renowned commercial base for the procument of ivory, rhinoceros horns, and tortoise shells. Until the fourth century, Egyptian economic connections with the East African coast through Adulis were significant owing to the supply of elephants for warfare.[3] During the same period, the Arab and Indian merchants accelerated their commercial activities in incense and spices. Through Adulis, alien merchants gained access to the kingdom of Aksum where iron smelting had developed considerably. Greek merchants also established commercial relations with Zanzibar and Cape Delgado, but their movements were periodic. Owing to the seasonal monsoon winds, they traveled to the south in the winter and sailed back in the summer. None of the documents mentions either gold or slaves, thus suggesting that they did not constitute major exports in the early centuries of commercial relations.

The trading organizations in the emporia differed one from another. For instance, Opone's economy was more developed than Phapta's because more ships reached there and more commodities were supplied. Nevertheless, Rhapta remained a commercial center as well as a political power in the region until the sixth century. Other commercial centers such as Nikon, where Ptolemaic coins from Egypt were found, and Essina (Somalia) had begun to spring up. Indeed, Nikon served as a commercial gateway for advancing into the interior. There developed a network of trade routes, which linked the empire of Aksum to the emporium at Nikon. While the *Periplus* described the original inhabitants of the coast, as very tall people, Ptolemy labelled them "Ethiopians" and "man eaters" and the Arabs called them Zanj.[4] Possibly these people were Bantu speakers. The *Periplus* mentioned the Ethiopian-Somali peoples who were also called Zanj. But ninth-century Chinese writers contrasted Somali nomads and black cultivators of Mo lin (Malindi), while the Arab al-Masudi in the tenth century referred to Blacks near Juba (the Kenya-Somali border).[5]

2. G.S.P. Freeman-Grenville, *The East African Coast: Selected Documents from the First to the Earlier Nineteenth Century* (London: Rex Collings, 1975), 1.

3. R.C.C. Law, "North Africa in the Hellenistic and Roman Periods, 323 B.C. to A.D. 305," in J.D. Fage, ed., *The Cambridge History of Africa: From c. 500 B.C. to A.D. 1050*, vol. 2 (Cambridge: Cambridge University Press, 1978), 164.

4. The term "Zanj" or "Zenj" has often been vaguely applied to designate the Black peoples of East Africa. J.E.G. Sutton, "The East African Coast: An Historical and Archaeological Review," *Historical Association of Tanzania*, Paper No. 1 (1966), 6-7. Neville Chittick suggests that the Zenj were Bantu-speaking people who had occupied the east African coast in the first centuries. Neviile Chittick, "The Coast Before the Arrival of the Portuguese," in B.A. Ogot, ed., *Zamani: A Survey of East African History* (Nairobi, Kenya: Longman, first published 1968, reprinted 1980), 102-104. Also consult H. Neville Chittick and Robert I. Rotberg, eds., *East Africa and the Orient: Cultural Syntheses in Pre-Colonial Times* (New York: Africana Publishing Company, 1975), 20-21.

5. R. Oliver and J.D. Fage, *A Short History of Africa*, 6th ed. with revisions (New York: Penguin, 1988), 97-98.

The Coming of Islam

Outside sources have demonstrated an interest in the degree of Islamization in the coastal states. Generally, it appears that the role of Islam and the rapidity of its spread have been exaggerated, probably because the pre-tenth-century written sources were mostly in Arabic, and they ignore the pre-Islamic period. However, the *Kitab al Zanj*, corroborated by the chronicles of Lamu and Pate, confirmed that pre-Islamic Afro-Arab settlements existed along the coast. Called Kiswahili, a distributive coastal language began as a grammatically and syntactically Bantu language infused with numerous loan words from Kushitic languages. Arabic loan words were included after 1000 A.D. However, Arab cultural and linguistic influences in general remained quite circumscribed until 1600. Traditionalism predominated, with ancestral worship and totemic observances common among the indigenous population. Ibn Hawqal described Maliknajlu, the Zanj god, as the most widely worshiped.[15] Elaborate stone-pillar tombs, a dinstinctive feature of early coastal architecture, were not Arab in inspiration but rather of mixed Bantu-Kushitic origins.

The Islamization of the East African coast can be discussed in three time periods. In the first, Islam was a new religion, professed only by immigrant traders on the coast. For example, Rhapta was a pre-Islamic commercial city. In other cities, Islam did not influence the socio-cultural and religious life of the indigenous population. As indicated by Masao and Mutoro:

> For a long time Islam was professed only by the immigrants from Arabia or Persia who were settled in the coastal towns. It seems that these expatriate merchants had not developed any large-scale proselytizing activity, so that the number of native Muslims remained rather restricted. Gradually some people in the immediate entourage of the immigrants as well as those Africans who were interested in commercial intercourse with foreigners accepted Islam as their religion.[16]

This argument seems plausible. At its period of introduction to East Africa, Islam was a religion of the coast practiced only by the alien merchants that M. El Fasi and I. Hrbek referred to as "closed-class communities or insular settlements."[17] The Arab and Persian merchants at the coast were essentially traders, and not missionaries. At this time, Islam was not a strong factor for the growth of the region's commerce.

The second period began when Islam steadily penetrated into the indigenous population, developing a form of syncretism and divine monarchy. Traces of Islam were seen in Zanzibar and Pemba. One after the other, local rulers converted to Islam. Al-Masudi makes reference to Qanbalu an island, which was populated by Muslims and whose ruler adopted Islam. Similarly, al-Idrisi describes Zanzibar as a Muslim town with a great mosque. Commercial operations as noted by Ibn Battuta, especially in the large city-states attracted many Muslim

---

15. Mathew, "The East African Coast," 105-106.

16. F.F. Masao and H.W. Mutoro, "The East African Coast and the Comoro Islands," in M. El Fasi, ed., *Africa from the Seventh to the Eleventh Century*, UNESCO General History of Africa, vol. 4 (Berkeley: Heinemann, 1988), 605.

17. M. El Fasi and I. Hrbek, "Stages in the Development of Islam and Its Dissemination Africa," in El Fasi, *Africa from the Seventh to the Eleventh Century*, 88.

immigrants, who consequently established settlements at the trading posts along the coast.[18] The Shirazi dynasty of Kilwa was established during this time, but Islamization was slow to take hold among the people of the city-states. The earliest settlers had included non-Muslim Arabs and Persians, while later ones included members of various persecuted Islamic sects. They might all be Muslim but they were hardly compatible. As small settler communities they were forced to maintain a show of unity, but the easiest way to do this involved playing down religion and concentrating upon commerce. The former divided them, while the latter united the population of each state. However, competition for trade pitted one city-state against another. Thus, neither Islam nor commerce was conducive to the unity of the whole coastal region.

In the third period, which began in the sixteenth century, Africans who engaged in commercial relations with Islamized merchants were readily converted. The declaration for Islam constituted the economic diplomacy, that is, permitting better commercial relations with the foreign traders. During this phase Islam became an ideology for trade and a unifying factor among both indigenous and expatriate merchants. Nearly all sources mention Pemba as one of the earliest places where Islam predominated. As the Arabs increased in number they established large quarters in Pemba. Their influence, however, can be and often has been over-emphasized. The Swahili still offered sacrifices at the graves of their ancestors, and in 1505 the Portuguese reported that wealthy African Muslims did not practice circumcision. To counter Arab claims to religious superiority, Swahili Muslims began to emphasize or invent Shirazi/Persian ancestry as early as the thirteenth century.[19] Swahili women also enjoyed rights, privileges, and power even as rulers in the city-states. These are characteristics more typical of African than Arab Muslim society.[20] Developments in the southern region were no different from those in the north. On the Zambezi River at Tete and Sena, there were numerous Muslim traders.

The third phase ultimately produced complete Islamization of the coastal peoples. Islamic culture and literature dominated the history of the East African states from the seventh to the ninth centuries. However, Sutton describes ca. 1200-1500 as the greatest period of Islamic civilization of the East African coast. He attributes the development to the 'Shirazi colonization,' which was characterized by the building mosques, houses, palaces, and tombs.[21] Kiswahili became a literate language, the first written poem in it appearing in the seventeenth century and thereafter, the numerous chronicles of the city-states.[22]

---

18. Marc J. Swartz, *The Way the World Is: Cultural Processes and Social Relations among the Mombasa Swahili* (Berkeley: University of California Press, 1991), 28-30; Sutton, "The East African Coast," 9-10. Aside from the Indian Ocean, the Red Sea was also important to the growth of commerce in East African coast by the fifteenth century. R. Pouwells, *Horn and Cresecent: Cultural Change and Traditional Islam on the East African Coast, 800-1900* (Cambridge: Cambridge University Press, 1987), 38.

19. T.T. Spear, "The Shirazi in Swahili Traditions, Culture and History," *History in Africa*, 11 (1984).

20. Ann P. Caplan, "Gender, Ideology and Modes of Production on the Coast of East Africa," in J. de V. Allen and T.H. Wilson, eds., *From Zinj to Zanzibar: Studies in History, Trade and Society on the Eastern Coast of Africa* (Wiesbaden, Steiner Verlag, 1982), 29-40.

21. Sutton, "The East African Coast," 10-11.

22. Randall L. Pouwells, "Swahili Literature and History in the Post-Structuralist Era," *The International Journal of African Historical Studies*, 25, 2 (1992): 266-269.

Commercial Networks

The foreigners in East African coastal states focused primarily on the growth and conduct of commerce. An overall schema may be suggested. The East African states developed through their economic resources, which ultimately attracted merchants from the outside world. The local coastal peoples clearly saw the need for a balanced economic system. The interactions between the indigenous economic structure and the development of commerce through the Indian Ocean brought about the well-structured trading system which connected the coast to the outside world.

The chronicles and Arabic and Chinese sources show that the people lived on grains, especially millet and sorghum, fish, meat, and milk. The *Periplus* made reference to some alien food-crops such as bananas, coconuts, yams, and cocoyams, which probably came from Indonesia in the pre-Islamic and Islamic periods. Banana began to spread to the interior before the seventh century.[23] The assertion by J. E. G. Sutton that "East Africa has more varieties [of banana] than the rest of the world put together"[24] represents a direct consequence of the external linkage. This view is sturdily promoted by Roland Oliver on the basis that Indonesian seafarers, traders, and migrants had visited the East African coast by the early centuries A. D. He argues further that the food-plants spread inland principally through Lake Malawi up the valley of the Western Rift.[25] On this premise, it might be claimed that the articulation of the food-producing economy, hunting, and natural resources such as gold, iron, and copper with commerce only became elaborate when the expatriate merchants arrived. The foreign merchants revolutionized only the commercialization but not the production of commodities. As de Blij succinctly described it in *Mombasa: An African City*, "foreign trade was nothing new for East African settlements, and in this respect the Arabs and Persians provided a stimulus but not an innovation."[26]

Another group of foreign merchants was the Indonesians who arrived in Madagascar in the first century A.D. and were found along the coast of East Africa between the third and sixth century A. D. They used their well-built canoes to link East African commerce with Iraq, trading mostly in ambergris, gold, incense, iron, ivory, tortoiseshell, and slaves. When they began to transport slaves across the Indian Ocean to Iraq is not certain, how they got the slaves is also subject to speculation. But the number of slaves seems substantial given the series of slave revolts that took place in Iraq and other Islamic states in the ninth century A. D.

Roland Coupland also mentions the presence of the "Hindus" in the coast of East Africa. Like the Indonesians, they traded in ivory, gold, and slaves.[27] From the eighth to the twelfth centuries, the kingdom of Srivijaya in Sumatra experi-

---

23. Masao and Mutoro, "The East African Coast," 612-614.
24. J.E.G. Sutton, "The Settlement of East Africa," in B.A. Ogot, ed., *Zamani: A Survey of East African History* (Nairobi: Longman, 1968), 73.
25. Roland Oliver, "The Emergence of Bantu Africa," in Fage, *Cambridge History*, vol. 2, 402-403.
26. Harm de Blij, *Mombasa: An African City* (Evanston: Northwestern University Press, 1968), 16.
27. R. Coupland, *East Africa and Its Invaders: From the Earliest Times to the Death of Seyyid Said in 1856* (London: Oxford University Press, 1st edition 1938, reprinted 1968), 16.

enced such pronounced maritime development that it dominated the trade of the Indian Ocean. It was the terminal point for the ships that went to or arrived from China. Ultimately, Srivijaya brought together the Indonesians and Hindus. Through the growth of maritime trade Zanj slaves from Sofala were imported into Indonesia and China but according to Y. Talib evidence of the presence of Africans in India before the eighth century is scanty.[28]

The reference to slaves at this period is important. Slaves were procured from the East African interior as well as the coast and exported to Arabia, Persia, and India in exchange for glass, beads, clothes, spices, and cowries. Since the rise of the Abbasid dynasty in 750 A. D., Adu Muslim, a Mawla (Mallam) from Iraq had recruited slaves who were promised freedom if they joined the royal force. The volume of exports, however, cannot be accurately estimated. From the ninth century, considerable numbers of Black slaves were transported to the north and east "across the Red Sea and Indian Ocean to Arabia, Iraq, and Iran, down the Nile to Egypt, and across the Sahara to the slave markets of North and Northwest Africa."[29] The increasing number of slaves eventually created huge social problems that led to the outbreak of several revolts.

The East African Zanj are recalled in a number of place names in Iran such as Zanjibad ("village built by Africans") Deh-Zanjian ("village of Africans"), and Gala-Zanjian ("Castle of Africans") in Baluchistan near the Mount of the Blacks. In addition there exist African communities with a unique dialect at Jiruft, an interior entrepôt attended by merchants traveling from India to Egypt, from Ethiopia to Central Asia. There was another African community at the Iranian port of Bandar Abbas who originally worked on the nearby date plantations and as crewmen on the dhows which plied the waters of the Red Sea, the Persian Gulf, and the Indian Ocean.

While some of the black slaves were employed mainly for domestic or military purposes, others were engaged in mines, in the fleets, and in drainage of marshes.[30] Baghdad remained a slave-holding society for a long time. Numerous black slave revolts occurred in the ninth century with the longest one taking place in 868-883 A. D. The series of revolts seriously threatened the social and economic growth of the Baghdad Caliphate. Both Bernard Lewis and Ghada Talhami agree that the Zanj rebellion was not a direct attempt to eliminate the institution of slavery in Baghdad because that idea "would have been almost inconceivable at the time."[31] The revolts were, however, intended to fight the intolerable conditions, social injustice, and inequality in the society. The idea of rebellion did not originate from the slaves, neither was it solely organized by them. It was engineered by 'Ali bin Muhammad, a slave-descended Arab. To garner support and followers, Muhammad

> began to seek out black slaves working in the Basrah marshes and to inquire into their working conditions and nutritional standards. Once

28. Y. Talib, "The African Diaspora in Asia," in Elfasi, *Africa from the Seventh to the Eleventh Century*, 731-733.

29. Bernard Lewis, *Race and Slavery in the Middle East: An Historical Enquiry* (Oxford: Oxford University Press, 1990, reprint 1992), 51.

30. Bernard Lewis, *The Arabs in History* (Oxford: Oxford University Press, 1993), 112.

31. Ibid., 113; Ghada Hashem Talhami, "The Zanj Rebellion," *The International Journal of African Historical Studies* 10, 3 (1977): 454-455.

shown the economic and social deprivations under the troubled rule of the caliphs, the slaves quickly rallied behind 'Ali as a Kharijite leader bent on saving the caliphate from religious impurities and social abuses.[32]

When the rebellion broke out, other deprived groups joined to prove that it was a social revolution. However, the slaves were the core participants. At least half of those who participated in the rebellion were slave soldiers who fought religious wars. In spite of their failure to capture Basra, overall the Zanj were so successful that they built a city known as Al-Mukhtara, "the Chosen."[33] Since the Zanj revolt when the black slaves "displayed terrifying military prowess," Muslim rulers relied heavily upon them because they were loyal during wars.[34] Such warrior slaves converted to Islam and expanded its frontiers.

Another smaller group in Arab lands became sexual slaves as harem girls. Slave owners, however, required eunuchs to guard the harems. While Black and White female slaves were kept as harems, the White slaves were found mostly among the wealthy Turks. White female slaves were very expensive but Black slaves who possessed proficiency in singing were especially desired because of their capability to generate wealth for their masters.[35] Using slaves as palace guards and royal warriors became a widespread phenomenon.

Some sources give the impression that slaves were captured for sale only along the East African coast. This was not so, because reference is made to the merchants from the "Zanj Empire" traveling to the coast to sell ivory and slaves. The Yao of northern Mozambique, the Kamba, and the Nyamwezi were commercial peoples in the interior who established links with the merchants at the coast. Zanj slaves from the interior were exported to India, Arabia, and Persia. Researchers of the coastal regions have tended to assume there was little internal commerce except the gold trade of Sofala controlled from Zimbabwe. It seems clear, however, that thousands of Africans moved from the inland plateau and interlacustrine region, over the wastelands to trade at the coast with foreign merchants and slave dealers.

The Economic Rise and Fall of the States

By the tenth century A. D., the tempo of migrations and trade increased significantly, giving rise to the establishment of more towns. Motivated by the pursuit of commerce, there was north-south movement and inland migration by local coastal merchants. For example, movement from Mogadishu followed the developing gold trade in the south. Mogadishu witnessed its period of economic opulence between the tenth and twelfth centuries. Given its northern location on the Somalia coast and its dominance of overseas trade, it became a leading commer-

---

32. Muhammad had organized a series of unsuccessful revolts, including that of Basra in September 869 A.D. He appealed to the slaves by promising them a change in status, increase wealth, and provision dwellings as against the unbearable social injustice of the society. These conditions were attractive to the slaves who fought and recorded a number of victories. Talhami, "The Zanj Rebellion," 454-455; and Lewis, *The Arabs in History*, 113.

33. Lewis, *The Arabs in History*, 114-115.

34. Lewis, *Race and Slavery*, 56-57, 65.

35. Reference has been made to an Ethiopian slave girl who was worth 120,000 dinars because of her singing and attractiveness. Lewis, *Race and Slavery*, 56-57.

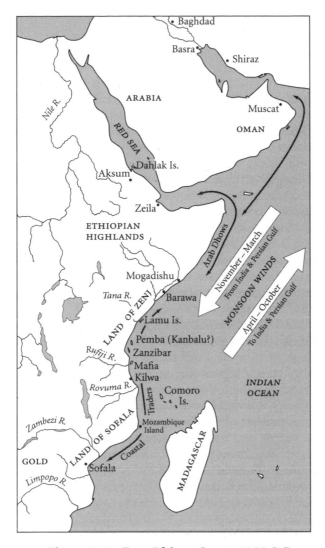

Figure 8-2. East African Coast, 1000 A.D.

cial town favored by the Arabs and Persians. The significant number of Arab settlers in the city was responsible for the rapidity with which the Arabic language and Islamic culture penetrated into Mogadishu and mixed with the indigenous languages.

Foreign merchants helped Mogadishu to develop to a position of prominence. As a symbol of its economic prosperity, Mogadishu minted its own coinage,[36] extended its network of trade to Madagascar and the Comoro Islands, and controlled the gold trade from Zimbabwe. The growth in commerce prodded merchants to move closer to Zimbabwe gold mines as from the eleventh century. The African merchants who traveled into the interior to purchase slaves, ivory, and gold dominated the major trade routes. From Sofala in the interior, gold was

---

36. G.S.P. Freeman-Grenville, "East African Coin Finds and Their Historical Significance," *Journal of African History,* 1, 1 (1960): 32.

1300s. Its trade, until the advent of the Portuguese, had been sea-rather than land oriented.[45]

Unaware of this situation, the Portuguese embarked upon the bombardment of Kilwa in order to monopolize its wealth. By the end of the fifteenth century, Kilwa had completely lost control over the Sofala trade.

The Swahili Culture

Swahili was derived from the Arabic word for coast. The rise of the Swahili culture was a product of the economic relationship between the East African peoples and foreign traders, especially the Arabs. Arab merchants began to intermarry with Africans beginning from about the twelfth century. Gradually, a new culture emerged. A. H. J. Prins subdivided the Swahili-speaking population into Arabs, Shirazi, and Swahili.[46] F. J. Berg also points out that 'a Swahili' is simply "any Muslim Swahili-speaker of African and Asian descent who regards himself as a Swahili and not as an Arab or member of some other coastal community." He goes further to say that some Swahili identify themselves as 'Shirazi' (somebody of a noble origin).[47] Both of them, however, agree that Swahili has assumed a lot of different interpretations that its usage depends on the context.

In the beginning, the Swahili people were not homogenous, nor was their culture very distinct. "The civilization established by the Swahili population," argues V. V. Matveiev, "was as heterogenous as Swahili society itself."[48] The society was stratified. The rich and politically influential elite class was at the upper level. Below them were individuals who were also wealthy, but possessed no political authority. The largest group was the commoners.

Agriculture and trade formed the bedrock of the economic life of the Swahili people. They cultivated food crops such as coconuts, oranges, bananas, and various vegetables. They grew cotton and raised animals. Because of the proximity of the Indian Ocean, they engaged in fishing and gathered seafood. They also practiced boat building. The maritime trade of the Indian Ocean continued to expand as participants profited from it. Archaeological excavations indicated that iron smelting was carried out, and in a few places, glass making was practiced.

The spread of the Swahili culture was accelerated by the shift of economic centers of power. The Swahili people made commercial contacts as dictated either by articles of trade or by changes in economic power. The changes helped the Swahili people to become more familiar with other cultures. They also adopted the Islamic religion to lure the people into their commercial and socio-cultural

---

45. A.I. Salim, "East Africa: The Coast," in B.A. Ogot, ed., *Africa from the Sixteenth to the Eighteenth Century*, UNESCO General History of Africa, vol. 5 (Berkeley: Heinemann, 1992), 750.

46. Merchant groups such as the Wa-Nyamwenzi, Wa-Hehe, Ba-Ganda, Wa-Sukuma, and Yao spoke the Swahili language. A.H.J. Prins, *The Swahili-speaking Peoples of Zanzibar and the East African Coast*, (London: International African Institute, 1967), 11.

47. F.J. Berg, "The Swahili Community of Mombasa, 1500-1900," *Journal of African History*, 9, 1 (1968), 35-56.

48. V.V. Matveiev, "The Development of Swahili Civilization," in D.T. Niane, ed., *Africa from the Twelfth to the Sixteenth Century*, UNESCO General History of Africa, vol. 4 (Berkeley: Heinemann, 1984), 456-480.

networks. Through their wealth, architecture developed with spectacular designs of mosques and personal houses. The Great Mosque of Kilwa is an excellent example.

In the twelfth and thirteenth centuries, the Swahili population grew steadily, especially in Kilwa and Mombasa. Here, Arab traders, missionaries, and architects converged. The Swahili language was spoken widely. There were three dialects—*Kiunguja,* (regarded as the standard one), *Kimvita,* and *Kiamu.* The Swahili language was essentially African (Bantu), with some borrowing from Arabic. It became widespread because it was used as a language of commerce in the thirteenth century displacing Arabic.

Conclusion

This chapter has discussed the growth of the commercial civilization of the early East African states before the arrival of the Portuguese. It has demonstrated that to better understand the early history of these states, heavy reliance has to be placed on certain primary and secondary sources. Evidently, without the sources, the history of East African coast before the arrival of the Portuguese cannot be put in correct and understandable perspective.

In spite of the commercial rivalries, which occurred over centuries of interaction, the early East African states illustrated the ingenuity of Africans and the strength of their economic structures. The establishment of long-distance trade, the diversity of articles of trade, and the diplomacy of Africans in dealing with alien merchants made the whole economic system a complex one. The pattern in East Africa was similar to that of other regions of Africa where powerful and effective trade networks were organized. The Indian Ocean facilitated trade because it linked the city-states to overseas market centers. In addition, the coast served as an important artery of economic growth for the interior. Both African and foreign merchants profited from the Indian Ocean trade.

Traditional religion withstood the penetration of Islam for a long time. It, however, collapsed when the numbers of Muslim merchants increased and Islam became a stimulant and an ideology for commerce. As a consequence, Islam was infused into the political and economic structures of the East African states. The growth of commerce in addition to the influx of foreign merchants ultimately led to the emergence of the Swahili civilization. The east African trade reached the highest thriving point in the fifteenth century, a period that can be described as the "Golden Age" of the Swahili culture. Although there was inter-city-state rivalry, major military conflicts with foreign merchants did not break out until the arrival of the Portuguese. Determined to control the trade along the coast, especially gold trade, the Portuguese disrupted the flow of commerce and destroyed some East African city-states.

Figure 9-1. Luba Seat

on the tracts of fertile land with virtually uninhabited land in between settlements. Politically, this lent itself to the formation of numerous chieftaincies with each settlement united under a single leader. While it is not known exactly when these chieftaincies emerged, they were founded by at least 1300 A.D. Some of these early chieftaincies included Kikondja, Katota, Kalundwe, Kasongo, Kaniok, Nsanga, and Mpimin. People subsisted primarily through farming and fishing, and occasionally hunted in the infertile tracts between settlements. The region's salt and metal resources provided local trading items, a means of providing tribute to central governments, and promoted linkages with other chieftaincies in the formation of a vast regional trade network.

As with most precolonial African kingdoms, locating the beginnings of the Luba kingdom is problematic due to conflicting Luba oral traditions. Some traditions assert that the beginnings of the kingdom can be found in a group of strangers who invaded the Lualaba River valley and asserted their control through military conquest. These foreigners could be local political leaders who acquired a religious aura—their power made them exceptional and distinct from the rest of the populace. Whether he was foreign or indigenous, oral traditions contend that a man by the name of Kongolo (Rainbow) established a capital near Kalongo, organizing the Luba east of the Lualaba River into a single polity in what would become the heartland of the Luba kingdom. It is estimated that this took place between 1300 and 1400 A.D. As with the earlier chieftaincies, this kingdom was formed by the fusion of several leaders under a single authority. Kongolo was slain by Kalala Ilunga, a foreigner from the east, who moved the capital to Munza. With this move, Luba became one of the few kingdoms that did not have its center in a river valley; instead it was located in the great plains of the Upemba Depression. From this vantage point it could control some of the surrounding chieftaincies such as Kalundwe and Kikondja and harness the resources from the nearby marshes, rivers, and lakes. Despite this, Luba remained a relatively small kingdom until the eighteenth century. [2]

The king was supposed to be without clan or lineage, although the office of the king was normally passed from father to brother to son. Luba had its share of succession disputes, but its history does not appear to be as rife with them as in many other kingdoms. Much of the authority of the Luba king was derived from the ideology of *bulopwe*, meaning sacredness or sacred kingship. It is this inherent sacredness of royal blood that gave the ruler the power to reign over the ruled. To this end, a number of rites, symbols, and taboos were used by the king to demonstrate his uniqueness and superiority. Kings were never seen eating and drinking so that their human qualities would not be exposed. Much as they are in many other parts of Central Africa, the snake and the rainbow were held to be royal symbols invested with power. It was well understood that the current king spoke with the authority of previous kings and much attention was paid to the ancestors and their shrine. The medium attached to the shrine of the royal ancestors was always a woman, who dictated the wishes of the ancestors to the king. The supernatural power of the king was an important source of legitimacy.

Politico-religious authority also rested in the institution of the *bambudye*. While the exact secrets of the *bambudye* have not been revealed, we do know it was a secret society which helped to unite the outlying districts with the central government. New district administrators were inducted into the *bambudye* to ensure their allegiance to the center, and they became subject to the society's rules and traditions. The *bambudye* maintained the sacred and secular traditions of the empire and promoted Lubahood and the state. The king was the head of the society, and the *bambudye* provided him with the means of cooperation and communication that cut across local allegiances and disputes, thus giving him direct contact with local administrators.

The Luba king ruled through a number of regional and local administrators. The *kibwindji*, or district, was ruled by a *kilolo* (regional chief) who gained his legitimacy from the king and his connection to a local *vidye*, or spirit. Below the district chief, the village households were linked through patrilineage and were often also ruled by a chief who also had supernatural powers. At every level of local government, the rulers gained their legitimacy and power from two sources: first, the king and the central government; and second, the supernatural world, local spirits, and the ancestors of each of the local chiefs. Because of the powerful nature of the local rulers, the centrifugal forces within the Luba kingdom were often strong. But the supernatural strength of the king, through *bulopwe*, and the

---

2. Nziem, 592.

normally built at least fifty to a hundred meters apart. Around each circle was cultivated land where the Gbaya grew their principal crop of yams, and later manioc. A number of circles allied themselves into a clan. A clan consisted of several circles scattered over a territory encompassing several square kilometers. Each clan also controlled the uninhabited surrounding land that was used for hunting and gathering and as excess farmland if necessary. This arrangement created a rather low population density. Each clan had a politically dominant group who claimed descent from the founders of the clan, and it was from this group that the clan's chief was drawn. But, as will be seen, the power of a Gbaya chief was nothing like that of the Luba king. Clans often identified with other clans based on dialect or shared custom, but no political institutions evolved at this level. Clan alliances were not unknown, but they were normally organized under duress, such as foreign invasion, and only lasted as long as the threat. Throughout Gbaya history, the clan was the largest institutionalized political organization.

The primary duty of the clan chief was that of war leader. He was expected to protect all the circles of the clan. His military prowess was believed to emanate from personal skill as well as supernatural power. Defeat in war often caused many of the people in the clan to move away and join a more successful clan. One's fidelity to the chief was not strong and lasted only as long as his protection did. Debate exists over how the precolonial Gbaya defined the institution of the chief. Some hold that the clan chieftainship was a strong institutionalized and ritualized office, but given the freedom that clan members had in relocating, it is very unlikely that the chief had much say in their lives. He served simply as the organizing mechanism and the figurehead for the clan's population. The chieftaincy was not a hereditary office, but instead, went to the most influential, powerful, and charismatic man in the dominant descent group. Competitors often left to form their own clans elsewhere, or migrated to another clan and allied with its chief. The centrifugal tendencies in Gbaya political structure were incredibly high, as anyone was free to migrate.

Trade was also conducted at the level of the clan. The chief organized armed trading expeditions to other clans, where they were entertained in the homes of their hosts, sometimes for weeks. Trading expeditions often created lasting trading relationships and were a means of creating minor alliances. Iron ore, iron implements, iron currency, camwood, and small livestock were common trade items.[5] Because people of the same clan were often related, men had to look for wives outside of the clan. Wives were drawn, then, from one's potential enemies. As such, the women were often treated as outsiders and foreigners within the clan. If war erupted between a woman's present clan and her natal clan, she was often called a spy and rarely trusted.

It is difficult to assess the role of religion in politics. Priests certainly existed throughout Gbaya history, but oral traditions offer contradictory accounts of how they related to the chiefs. It can probably be assumed that the priests played a role in strengthening and maintaining the supernatural power of the chief during wartime, and some chiefs were no doubt also powerful priests. But, for the most part, chieftainship does not appear to have been strongly connected to religion .

Our knowledge of the precolonial history of the Gbaya is limited. Archaeological and linguistic studies of the north central savanna remain in their infancy.

---

5. Burnham, 26.

Written references to the Gbaya are few because they did not directly border any of the Muslim states to the north. The key to understanding Gbaya precolonial history revolves around the theme of migration. Mobility was crucial to their political and social structure. As raiding expeditions for the trans-Saharan slave trade ventured into the region, the Gbaya often migrated to avoid becoming enslaved by raiders from Kanem-Borno, Wadai, and Darfur. Slave raiding brought greater violence to the region as well as aiding the spread of diseases such as smallpox, syphilis, and measles. Islamic culture began to filter southward as African customs flowed northward with the slaves.

The Gbaya were also affected by the introduction of the Atlantic slave trade. During the eighteenth and nineteenth centuries, the Atlantic trading system included the Zaire River, bringing the Gbaya ever closer to the network. Because of their late entry into the system, the Gbaya were not as harshly affected by the Atlantic slave system as many groups. But, on the other hand, they were also victims of predation by slavers for centuries having also endured the slavery of the trans-Saharan trade. Contact with the Atlantic system did bring new food products, however. Maize and cassava supplemented or replaced the indigenous millet and sorghum and increased caloric intake per capita. But entry into the Atlantic network also altered the region's distribution of wealth. Those involved in the slave trade, often the chiefs, continued to gain wealth at the expense of their neighbors and clanspeople. This affected the political structure because migration became more difficult as the power of the chiefs grew.

Islamic slave raiding did not end with the growth of the Atlantic system. On the contrary, much of the region's history in the late nineteenth century deals with the competition between the Muslim states and the growing encroachment of the European powers, especially France, Belgium, and Germany. With increased southward conquest by and the spread of influence from the Muslim states, many Gbaya clans began to adopt more centralized structures. In order to provide a larger fighting force against raiders, some clans began to live together in the same village, thus breaking centuries-old traditions. Each clan remained in its own quarter of the village, but the development forever altered the political structure and leadership of some Gbaya.

Nzinga Mbande of the Ndongo Kingdom (ca. 1582–1663 A.D.)

The sixteenth century was one of bitter conflicts for territory between the Portuguese, who had recently established numerous forts and settlements on the Angolan coast, and Kongo, the Jaga, Ndongo, the Imbangala, and Soyo, to name but a few African competitors. Into this landscape of political competition came Nzinga, a shrewd politician, brilliant strategist, and ingenious stateswoman who used tradition, religious conversion, and gender roles to her own ends. Some claim her brutality in ruling was excessive and unwarranted. Others claim that it is only present-day ethics that make Nzinga look ruthless; that in fact she was no more brutal than other leaders of the time. Whatever one may think of Nzinga, one can not deny her importance in African history and early African resistance to European incursions.

Nzinga was the daughter and sister of kings of the kingdoms of Ndongo and Matamba. Both kingdoms were located in Angola and were rivals of the Kongo kingdom. While she could make claims to the thrones of both, they were not as strong as those of others. It was evident that Nzinga would be unlikely to ever hold the throne of either, especially since neither kingdom had a tradition of female monarchs. She seized power during a succession dispute in 1624, but lost much of Ndongo's original territory to her rival and brother, Hari (1624-1626), to his successor (her sister) Ngola Hari (1626-1664), and also to the Portuguese. Nzinga attempted an alliance with the Portuguese that quickly crumbled. Nzinga then conquered the Matamba kingdom which was further from Portuguese control. From there, she launched guerilla-style attacks on Portuguese holdings. Nzinga refused to cede control of the Kindonga islands in the Kwanza River where the old Ndongo capital and ancestral burial grounds were located. She lost them twice, in 1626 and again in 1628, only to reconquer them a short time later. Nzinga's army included women warriors, who may be the origin of the myth of the Amazons, and her palace guard was composed entirely of trusted women.

Territorial struggles continued through the rest of Nzinga's reign between her, the Portuguese, and her sister. After the failed alliance with the Portuguese, she denounced Christianity, in which she had been baptized in 1622. In an effort to strengthen her army, Nzinga hired Imbangala warriors (the Imbangala were a neighboring people known for their military prowess) in 1624. However, two Imbangala bands switched sides in battle in 1628, almost costing Nzinga the battle. She modernized her army along Imbangala lines, but rejected other parts of Imbangala tradition because it called for the free election of monarchs, which would bring her own succession into question. She formed alliances with the Dutch and with neighboring groups and effectively took over the slave trade of the region. In the 1640s, Nzinga launched three successful military campaigns against the Portuguese. By 1656, she had forced the Portuguese into signing a peace treaty which included a share of the slave trade, but also allowed missionaries to enter her kingdom. Just before her death, Nzinga was said to have again converted to Christianity, perhaps with some sincerity. Nzinga died in December 1663, controlling an amalgamation of parts of the kingdoms of Ndongo, Matamba, and the surrounding area.

Nzinga manipulated gender roles to her own ends. In the 1640s, at the height of her state's expansion, she made several of her male slave concubines wear female clothing and sleep among her maids in waiting, thus strengthening her perceived virility and power. She led her troops into battle herself and was said to be quite skilled with weapons. Her reign established a precedent in the Ndongo kingdom, in which it was no longer unknown to have women rulers. In fact, women ruled for eighty of the 104 years after Nzinga's death.[6] Despite her achievements on behalf of the female aristocracy, Nzinga was often a ruthless and brutal ruler. In a meeting, the Portuguese colonial governor attempted to humble Nzinga by making her stand in his presence. Nzinga commanded a female slave to kneel and used her for a throne. Upon getting up, she had the slave executed in front of the governor. She was also said to have killed her concubines when they no longer pleased her.

Was Nzinga a heroine who resisted Europeans and advanced the position of women, or was she a merciless dictator who used her subjects as political pawns and cared nothing for human life? Historians will likely never agree. But whether

---

6. John Thornton, "Legitimacy and Political Power: Queen Njinga, 1624-1663," *Journal of African History,* 32,1 (1991): 40.

she is held to be benevolent or malevolent, one can not deny her importance in African history.

Answers to Good and Evil: Religious History in Central Africa[7]

Kongo

The BaKongo (hereafter Kongo) people inhabited the area around the mouth of the Congo River in a rough semicircle along the Atlantic coast. By 1400 a number of Kongo farming villages had united to form the Kongo kingdom with its capital at Mbanza Kongo. The Kongo were among the first peoples to establish diplomatic relations with Europeans. From the 1480s through the entire precolonial era, Portuguese influence on Kongo remained strong. When civil war erupted in 1506 between two factions, one wanting greater foreign contacts, the other fewer, the Portuguese sided with the former and helped a Christian convert, baptized Afonso I (1506-1543), to seize the throne. Following this, Portuguese influence infiltrated Kongo and its institutions, reordering much of Kongolese life, including religion. From the late 1480s onward, Kongolese indigenous religion existed side by side and in combination with Christianity. The Kongo are anomalous in Central Africa in terms of their lengthy contact with Christianity. Most peoples of the region did not become exposed to Christianity until well into the colonial period. Yet, despite Christianity's lengthy history among the Kongo, it is still possible to identify Kongo indigenous religion.

The basic tenet of Kongo religion can be expressed with a cosmogram, called "four moments of the sun" because it reflects the life cycle, divided into four segments. At the first point, one was born; at the second, one reached maturity. At the third point, one died and crossed the water mirror, entering the land of the ancestors. At the fourth point, some individuals moved on toward the first point again, to be reborn into the land of the living. In this sense, time was conceived of as spiral or circular because the souls of some people were reborn after passing through the land of the ancestors. The Kongo conception of time had linear qualities also, however, in that people conceived of a past, a present, and a future.

The universe, composed of the land of the living (associated with the color black) and the land of the dead (associated with the color white), was divided by an intermediary zone called the water mirror. This zone was associated with the color red and was an ambiguous region between the two worlds. While it was not thought that people could live in this zone, some individuals with uncommon physical characteristics such as twins, dwarfs, and albinos were believed to be able to see through the water mirror into the land of the dead. The organization

---

7. On Kongo religious history see Wyatt MacGaffey and Michael D. Harris, *Astonishment and Power: Kongo Minkisi & the Art of Renee Stout* (Washington: Smithsonian Institution Press, 1993): Robert Farris Thompson and Joseph Cornet, *The Four Moments of the Sun: Kongo Art in Two Worlds* (Washington: National Gallery of Art, 1981): and Wyatt MacGaffey, *Religion and Soceity in Central Africa: The BaKongo of Lower Zaire* (Chicago: University of Chicago Press, 1986).

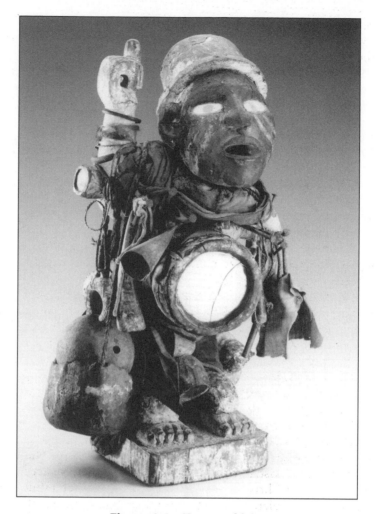

Figure 9-3. Kongo *nkisi*

of the universe into two lands and the associated colors of black, red, and white, were nearly universal characteristics of Central African religions.

Kongo religion was organized hierarchically with a number of intermediaries existing between the creator god, Nzambi, and the living. Nzambi was a distant being who created the universe but now had little interaction with it. Some scholars contend that Nzambi was identical to the Christian God. Since contact with Christians, the definitions of Nzambi and God have indeed become similar. But, it appears that this was primarily a result of cultural borrowing. Nzambi was not originally defined as God-like, but having a supreme being did make it easy for Portuguese missionaries to make analogies between Kongo religion and Christianity.

Ancestors lived lives in the land of the dead which were similar to the ones they had led while living. The recently dead could be reborn into another body. Those long dead could re-enter the land of the living as *bisimbi* . These were minor deities who had the power to control the natural and supernatural worlds. Their exact number was not known, and was not a point of theological inquiry for the Kongo.

Some were associated with natural phenomena such as rivers, trees, or rocks and in this way became territorial gods. Others were associated with particular powers, such as the ability to prevent a particular disease or provide fertility. Religious movements rose and fell as the power of particular *bisimbi* ebbed and flowed.

The power of the *bisimbi* was harnessed by the *banganga* (sing. *nganga*). The *banganga* constructed *minkisi* in which were placed the medicines or charms which would gather the power of the *bisimbi*. Many *minkisi* were human-like statues. For a fee, the *banganga* would pound a nail into the *minkisi* in order to alert the *bisimbi* of the wish of its worshipper. Some *banganga* gained a great deal of popularity and notoriety and were known over vast stretches of territory for the power of the *bisimbi* they could call upon. It was not uncommon to find *banganga* serving in political positions and as advisors to the chiefs and king.

Like many other societies, the Kongo also believed in witchcraft. Witches (*bandoki*) were defined as living beings who behaved in evil antisocial ways, and could be either male or female. They behaved as normal members of society by day, and practiced their craft at night. Unexplained and negative events were often attributed to witches, and great lengths were taken by the Kongo to protect themselves from their predations. Many *banganga* served this purpose. In addition, night time was day time for the land of the dead, so the ancestors were also active during the night. Mischievous ancestors could also cause trouble for the living. This was often interpreted by the living as a sign that they needed to offer a sacrifice to the ancestors and honor them. An unhonored ancestor could not enter the land of the dead and would cause trouble for its relatives until honored. As if witches and mischievous ancestors were not enough to worry the average Kongolese, ghosts (*min'kuyu*), the dead spirits of witches, could also cause them ill-fortune. So, for the Kongo, the world was full of supernatural beings and entities. This was the religious structure known to them before the 1480s.

Christianity came early to the Kongo kingdom and altered the religious landscape. Conversion to Christianity was a voluntary, not coercive act for most Kongo people. The strength of Christianity in the kingdom was often influenced by the religious identity of the ruler; it was stronger when the king was Christian. Some Kongolese certainly converted to gain economic or political advantages in the kingdom or with the Portuguese, but many converted for theological reasons as well. But, at all times, the Kongolese Church incorporated local elements into its beliefs. In fact, priests even called themselves *nganga*.[8] The amount of syncretization, or mixing, of beliefs varied widely and depended on the priest and converts in each local area. While European priests and missionaries were always present, the Church was distinctively Kongo, no doubt adding to its appeal. For the majority of Kongolese, there was little difference between Christianity and indigenous beliefs.

Mbuti

The Mbuti (or BaMbuti) live in numerous parts of Central Africa.[9] It was once thought that they were the descendents of Africa's original inhabitants who

---

8. John Thornton, "The Development of an African Catholic Church in the Kingdom of Kongo 1491-1750," *Journal of African History,* 25, 2 (1984): 156.
9. I have avoided the use of the term pygmy because of its derogatory connotations. While Mbuti only refers to the hunter-gatherer inhabitants of the Ituri forest in eastern Zaire,

been among them. How old is the idea of Mbuti religion? While data will likely never be found to answer that question, it is likely that it is quite ancient. What would have preceded a religious system where the forest is everything? If Mbuti religion could display such resilience in the face of colonialism, nationalism, and population encroachment, it likely survived the adversity of the precolonial period as well.

Answers to Livelihood: Economic History in Central Africa

Loango

The exact date of the founding of the Loango Empire is not known. Loango was one of a number of states in the region that exhibited Kongo-like characteristics. Yet, despite a number of political and religious similarities, Loango possessed a distinct and interesting economic structure. Most Loangoans were subsistence farmers. However, the coastal portion of Loango developed into a thriving center of trade and developed a large merchant and artisan class, especially in the capital city of Mbanza Loango.

Cloth was an important and fundamental part of the Loango economy. Raffia cloth, made from the fibers of the raffia, or wine palm, was the most common

Figure 9-5. Loango Nobleman

cloth produced and also formed the basis for Loango currency. Partly because they provided the basis for economic power, palm trees were highly valued in Loango culture (as they were in many parts of Central Africa) and great care was given to the cultivated trees, although wild ones were also utilized. The king even had his own palm trees that were used to create his own cloth. Often, palm fibers were not joined, so the length of the fibers limited the size of a piece of cloth. The most basic unit of cloth, called a *libongo* (*mbongo* in the plural) measured approximately fourteen inches square. Depending on the purpose for the cloth, *mbongo* could be joined together by raffia or pineapple threads to create larger pieces of cloth, especially in forming clothing or mats. A variety of colors could be achieved by exposing the fibers to differing amounts of sunlight or by dyeing them with redwood, charcoal, or chalk.

For the most part, weaving was a part-time occupation. However, there was a class of specialists who passed their skills from senior to junior family members. Some cloth was created on looms, while some was woven together by hand, much like basket-weaving. The amount of time it took to create the cloth depended on the technology involved and the quality of the cloth. Cloth intended for the king took upwards of two weeks to produce because it was of the highest quality. On the other hand, a weaver with a loom could produce several low quality *mbongo* daily.[10]

The quality of the cloth one owned was a symbol of status and wealth in Loango society. The best cloth was reserved for the king, and anyone attempting to wear royal cloth without the monarch's permission could be punished by execution. Nobles and the wealthy accumulated the highest-quality cloth they could, as a visible reminder to the rest of society that they were the elite. The more labor-intensive cloths were normally viewed as higher quality and more desirable. Raffia cloth had important ritual uses as well. Newborns were placed on it, and young people wore skirts of it at their initiation ceremonies. Raffia was also used as clothing for the dead. Just as cloth stood as a symbol of one's status in the land of the living, it also announced one's rank upon arrival in the land of the dead. The relatives of the deceased went to great lengths to acquire the best quality cloth they could afford in which to dress their loved one. Cloth was also often buried with the body as a display of wealth. The use of raffia cloth in these contexts suggests the importance and pervasiveness it played in Loango culture.

Raffia was fairly durable and portable, and as such, provided a useful means of currency. Its widespread acceptability and multiple uses ensured that it was in constant demand. It was exchanged for food and goods in marketplaces. It could be turned into clothing, decorations, mats, blankets, and even tents. Aside from practical uses, some raffia was simply stored and saved as an investment for a later time. Some *mbongo* were never used for anything but currency. So essential was raffia to the trade of the Loango Coast that the Portuguese issued a contract to a Portuguese trader to establish a factory at Loango in order to guarantee a supply. The raffia was in turn used to purchase slaves at Luanda on the Angolan coast.[11] The fact that Loango and Luanda are approximately 350 miles (500 km.) apart shows how important Loangoan raffia was to trade along a large portion of

---

10. Phyllis M. Martin, "Power, Cloth and Currency on the Loango Coast," *International Journal of African Historical Studies*, 19 (1986): 1-2.

11. Martin, 3-4.

Little is known of the Cameroon coast prior to the arrival of the Duala in approximately 1650 A.D. The area was not a large-scale trading center and the
trade that was conducted was done on the shores of the Rio del Rey. The Duala
moved from an inland home somewhere in the Sanga River valley and established
the city of Douala, displacing the Saa who lived there. The site was the best-situ-
ated one on the Cameroon coast for oceanic trade. The Duala destroyed their rivals on the Rio del Rey, and their trading town began to grow. After 1700, the
Duala began to absorb members of surrounding ethnic groups, increasing their
population. Trade was conducted by seasonal fleets of canoes that returned to
Douala when they had gathered sufficient cargo. Europeans came to Douala to
trade consumer wares, weapons, and semi-processed metals (which were used as
currency in many parts of this region) for local products, especially ivory. As trade
became more and more lucrative, dissension began to grow as trading houses
competed for the best position in trade.

Duala oral tradition holds that all Duala were descended from a single lineage
which later divided into sublineages. The Duala king was selected from among the
descendants of the original lineage, and the trading house of this lineage also enjoyed a dominant position. The economic structure of the Duala mirrored the political structure as the sublineages and their trading houses were held in a position
subservient to the original lineage. The history of the Duala is filled with tension
between the original lineage and the sublineages. As the seventeenth century progressed, social identity (the lineage) became less important, as economic identity
(the trading house one was identified with) became more important. The decline
of socially defined identity is evidence of the importance of trade to the society. So
important was trade that it began to form the basis for group identification.

Debate exists over the nature of the tension between the original lineage and
the sublineages and the degree to which the Duala can be considered a kingdom.
Some scholars claim that the amount of tension between the lineage and sublineages was so great and the power of the sublineages so large that the Duala can be
considered a kingdom in name only. Others claim that the Duala king enjoyed a
position of ascendancy for over 150 years and that Duala society can be considered a monarchy in the full sense of the word. The evidence examined below indicates that both groups are correct. The king did enjoy power for some time, but
decentralizing forces in the form of sublineages eventually won out.

From 1650-ca. 1800 the leadership of the king and the strongest trading house
was acknowledged by all. The ideology of common descent from a shared ancestor
and first occupancy of the royal office lent credibility to the regime. Leaders of
large trading houses who rivaled the king were forced from Duala and had to conduct their trade from Rio del Rey. Ivory, slaves, and local products such as salt,
yams, baskets and other woven goods, palm products, and boats were all produced in the hinterland and traded through Douala.[14] By 1700, and especially after
1750, Douala had become the hub of a thriving slave trade. Central Africa has historically been less densely populated than other regions of Africa, yet the slave
trade was no less demographically devastating in this region, despite the fact that
fewer people were exported from here than from centers like Luanda or Calabar.

---

14. Jan Vansina, *Paths in the Rainforest: Toward a History of Political Tradition in
Equatorial Africa* (Madison: University of Wisconsin Press, 1990), map 7.3, 212-214.

Figure 9-7. King Bell House

As elsewhere along the coast, trade was conducted through hierarchies. At the top stood the European traders. While they wanted African goods just as badly as the Africans wanted theirs, the Europeans had greater access to capital. It was Europeans who controlled oceanic shipping and had access to worldwide markets and goods, thereby giving them a superior economic position. Next in the hierarchy came the Duala. It was they who traded directly with Europeans and they who gathered African commodities from neighboring peoples into their trading towns. Middlemen came next in the hierarchy. Largely due to their geographic position, the middlemen did not have direct access to Europeans and were thus dependent on the Duala. Lowest in the hierarchy were the producers themselves. A lack of capital and of access to Europeans kept the producers at the bottom. They were paid little for their goods and charged highly for European imports. Except for the Europeans, few liked their position in the trading hierarchy; most were constantly looking for ways to improve their position.

Northwest Central African history is replete with stories of middlemen and producers attempting to gain direct access to the trade with Europeans. Most were trying to eliminate their dependency on groups like the Duala. This took the form of migration towards the coast. Some of this migration occurred at the level of individuals and families, most of whom became absorbed into the dominant ethnic group of the trading city. In some cases, however, migration of family groups or clans toward the coast was so steady that the entire settlement pattern of the ethnic group was altered, as with the Kribi or Fang. The process normally

took place over decades (and sometimes centuries) and affected the ethnic composition and distribution of the entire region.

Such were the conditions of trade until about 1800. By the beginning of the
nineteenth century, European power on the coast had grown to such a point that
Europeans were able to interfere in internal Duala matters. Europeans had gained
power through three means. First, Duala dependence on imported goods gave Europeans leverage in internal affairs. Second, Europeans established a military
presence at many trading towns and forced Africans to concede land and recognize false treaties. Third, after the establishment of a Baptist mission in 1845,
Christian missionaries were spreading Christianity and European values, which
created divisions in Duala society between traditionalists and those accepting the
European worldview. In 1792, a succession dispute arose and English traders favored the representative of a junior lineage known as Bell. In 1814 the representative of the senior lineage, Akwa, declared his independence of Bell. For most of
the nineteenth century the Duala were divided into two main groups, the Bell and
the Akwa, named for their respective leaders.

Another factor that aided European interference in this period was the abolition of the slave trade and the activities of slaves held internally. Largely through
British demand for "legitimate" trade items, such as palm oil and palm kernels,
the slave trade ended in this region about 1840. However, while the slave trade
ended, slavery as an institution did not. Slaves were held internally to work plantations and act as porters carrying the goods of the legitimate trade. As internal
dissension rose, slaves joined ranks and began forming secret societies of their
own. These societies were lent prestige by their connections to those of the
Bamileke Plateau in northwestern Cameroon, from which many of the slaves
came. Secret societies were used by slaves to resist increasing demands for labor,
thus creating another means of social strife.

In order to lessen the effects of the numerous divisions that were erupting in
Duala society, the Duala created the Ngondo around 1840. The Ngondo was a
council of notables comprising representatives of Duala villages and trading
houses. It has been said that the Ngondo was ineffectual until the mid-twentieth
century and did not serve as a ruling body until fairly recently. But even if the
Ngondo did not act as a ruling body, its very creation indicates some degree of co-
operation among the splintering Duala. Another means by which the Duala attempted to stem their disintegration was through secret societies. The most prestigious of these societies, *Jengu*, was based on the veneration of water spirits. This
was practiced by neighboring groups as well and proved to be a potent force in
the region's history. Divisions were even evident in secret societies, with *Mungi*
standing as the primary alternative to *Jengu*, mirroring the breach between Bell
and Akwa.

Duala society continued to deteriorate throughout the nineteenth century. By
the middle of the century both of the kings had lost most of their power to trading
firms. But dissension among the firms was so high that in 1856 they agreed to ar-
bitration by the British consul stationed at Clarence on the island of Bioko. As
dissension grew, trade on the Cameroon coast was declining in the 1860s and
1870s, while adding to the problems of the Duala. The chiefs of Douala, beginning in 1877 and continuing for a number of years, even petitioned Queen Victoria to extend British rule to their city. The feeling of social chaos must have been
high for the chiefs to have been voluntarily willing to concede their sovereignty. It

was amidst falling trade, increasing social strife, Christianization, and competition among the Germans, British, and French that the coast of Cameroon was annexed by Germany in July 1884. Resistance immediately broke out, especially when it became clear that the Germans intended to conquer the hinterland as well, thereby eliminating the position of the Duala entirely.

Bioko: A Case Study in Cultural and Institutional Transformation

The island of Bioko (also known as Fernando Po) has had an interesting history.[15] It is a small mountainous island with elevations reaching nine thousand feet. Despite its closeness to the mainland, it has been relatively isolated from developments on the African continent. Yet, it was not without connections to the continent either. Unlike the other islands off west central Africa, it has historically had a rather high population density with some areas of the island having eleven people per square mile.

Bioko was populated during the Bantu migrations, although it is not known precisely when. However, unlike all other Bantu-speakers, the Bubi (as the inhabitants of Bioko are called) never mined, smelted, or used metals until around 1800, largely due to a lack of ore in their volcanic soil. Pottery made its appearance on the island in the seventh century A.D. The pottery tradition was unique in Central Africa and remained consistent in its style through the nineteenth century. The original settlers landed on the northern coast of the island. They began moving inland around the eleventh century A.D. By the fourteenth century, large tracts of the rain forest were being cleared, as population densities rose and the interior became more intensively settled. The Bubi language contained a number of dialects. Only the speakers of the northern and southeastern dialects were incapable of understanding one another.

Bubi social structure was unlike that of the mainland. Society was organized around villages, as elsewhere, but the Bubi also spent the major farming seasons living in houses on their own land. Land was owned individually, not by the village as elsewhere in Africa. The village was ruled by a chief. Men were organized into two generational groups, the older married men forming one, the younger bachelors the other. Generational ties were more important than lines of descent. Thus, patrilinearity did not underlie chieftainship; rather it was the generational place among one's brethren. Chiefs often gained legitimacy from religious leaders who controlled local territorial spirits and conducted rituals and festivals in their name. Religiously, the Bubi shared many beliefs with other Bantu regarding witchcraft, spirits, and the power of nature. But they also held that each person had a guardian spirit, or *mmo* that remained with the individual throughout his or her lifetime. The *mmo* was held to be a male ancestor who belonged to the generation preceding that of the oldest living men. The *mmo* was always from the father's side of the family. It was also believed that it was the *mmo* who had purchased the baby's soul from the spirit who created embryos.

---

15. This section is based upon Vansina, *Paths*, 137-146, 192-195.

Immigrants arrived on Bioko in stages over a long period of time. Because they were absorbed into the indigenous population it is uncertain when they arrived or in how many phases. Bubi oral tradition holds that four great waves of immigrants came to the southern parts of the island from which they spread. Whether or not there were exactly four waves, oral tradition does demonstrate that the immigrants did not all arrive at once. There is little question that the immigrants conquered the original inhabitants. Their military formations of tightly massed spearmen with shields proved more than capable of defeating the more loosely organized phalanxes of the indigenes. Whenever the process may have begun, it is thought that this immigration was completed before 1400 A.D.

As these immigrants were moving across the island and mingling with the indigenous inhabitants, they were also transforming the political and social structure of Bioko. The victors developed into an aristocratic, hereditary class called *biota* while the remainder of the populace became a class of commoners, called *bobala*. The two classes did not live in the same houses, did not eat together, and rarely intermarried. Servants evolved into a third class and by the nineteenth century a caste system had emerged, even separating workers like fishermen and wine tappers. Social mobility was not entirely prohibited, as some common folks of outstanding wealth and reputation did move into the ruling class.

From within this new aristocratic class there emerged a new idea of chieftainship. Heritage through the chief's line began to take precedence over generational ties. Control over clients, as well as wealth and wisdom, came to be desired in the chief. Control over women became included in the idea of client control. While the indigenous culture had permitted polygyny, the new chiefs began to form large harems, the richest men having sixty to two hundred women each. Before the immigrants arrived, the inhabitants of Bioko had been relatively free in selecting their mates. After the immigrants came, the commoners were forced into greater reliance on the aristocrats for mates and social connections because many women were absorbed into harems. An assembly of councilors also emerged. With it, a set of military and civilian titles arose. This secured the position of the chief because all the holders of these positions were dependent on him for their existence. Transformations in society and politics were accompanied by alterations in religion. A new priesthood emerged which worshiped a creator god. The power of the chief was linked to that of this new creator god thus lending him spiritual legitimacy. A new set of rituals and ceremonies accompanied the emergence of the new priesthood, lending an aura of mystery to the institution of chief. It is not exactly certain when this transformation was begun or completed, but it was certainly in place by around 1400.

Despite all these changes, a number of aspects of Bubi culture survived. The belief in a personal *mmo* continued. Bubi handicrafts, best exemplified through pottery, still flourished. The Bubi language, while adopting many loan words from the immigrants, also survived. While generation sets lost some importance, they did not disappear entirely. Thus, despite being conquered and having a new political authority thrust upon them, the Bubi were able to not only maintain their culture, but also impress it upon the immigrants who also became culturally Bubi.

Because of Bioko's geographical position, it experienced European contact early on. The Portuguese were in the region by 1472. Yet the Bubi valued their independence and went to great lengths to keep foreigners off their island. With the emergence of the Atlantic slave trade, they even moved many of their settlements inland to escape raids from slavers. After 1750, African traders from the Niger Delta, Calabar, Douala, and the Rio del Rey began arriving on the northern coast and in the San Carlos Bay to trade for yams. Later, these traders also began to introduce iron which the Bubi learned to retool for their own purposes. By the early 1500s, the Bubi had already gained the reputation for being savage and warlike. But they did manage to keep European settlements off Bioko until 1827, when Clarence (Malebo) was established.

War between chieftaincies was endemic in Bubi history. A number of attempts at unifying the chieftaincies into a kingdom were attempted. One attempt was made in the densely settled area of San Carlos Bay, while another took place in the sparsely settled region around Ureka. Oral tradition from Lambe Lagoon states that a chief from the area toured the island attempting to get other chiefs to recognize him as paramount chief because he controlled a powerful spirit that dwelled in Lombe Lagoon. A successful attempt was finally made by the chief of Moka some time between 1835 and 1845. It appears that he succeeded not because he promised to rid the island of outsiders but because of his wealth, power, and superior spiritual backing.

It is ironic that the foundation of a unified Bubi kingdom coincided with the increasing encroachment of outsiders. After they founded Clarence in 1827, the British began using the settlement as a depot for freed slaves. The number of West African immigrants from the mainland increased dramatically after the 1840s. British and Spanish control, especially in the north, was also increasing and missionaries began to arrive at this time, challenging Bubi cosmology and culture. The influence of West Africans and Europeans chipped away at Bubi institutions and power and eventually led to the total collapse of the Bubi state by 1904.

While the tale of the Bubi and Bioko may seem trivial, it represents a phenomenon that was common in Africa. While Bubi history has a number of unique characteristics, it is a microcosm of the cultural and institutional transformations that occurred everywhere. Nowhere did culture remain static. Population movements, warfare, catastrophes, and new innovations led to reconstitutions and reformulations. Yet at the same time, parts of previous cultures were evident. How new and old traditions combined varied according to local circumstances, but dynamism was always evident. Europeans were not the only people to challenge and renew the traditions of Africans; however, their challenge was often the most profound.

Review Questions

1. What factors permitted the dynamic growth of the Luba state in the eighteenth and early nineteenth centuries?
2. What maintained the political stability and territorial cohesiveness of Luba?
3. What were the responsibilities of the Gbaya chief?
4. Why did the Gbaya and Luba develop such different political structures?
5. What was the role of the *nganga* in Kongo life? How did the Kongolese define evil?
6. What was the relationship between the Christian Church and traditional beliefs in Kongo?

7. In what ways did Mbuti religion differ from that of other African ethnic groups?
8. How was cloth used in precolonial Loango society? What changes did imported cloth bring?
9. In what ways were the Duala representative of the coastal area of northwest Central Africa?
10. What was the relationship between Duala economic, social, and political structures?
11. In what ways was Bubi history representative of that of other groups?
12. What makes Central Africa different from other parts of Africa? What does it have in common with the rest of Africa?
13. Does the equatorial forest environment of Central Africa appear to have greatly affected the history of the region?

Additional Reading

Birmingham, David. *Central Africa to 1870: Zambezia, Zaire, and the South Atlantic: Chapters from the Cambridge History of Africa*. Cambridge: Cambridge University Press, 1981.

Fernandez, James W. *Fang Architectonics*. Philadelphia: Institute for the Study of Human Issues, 1977.

MacGaffey, Wyatt. *Religion and Society in Central Africa: The BaKongo of Lower Zaire*. Chicago: University of Chicago Press, 1986.

Nowell, Charles E. *The Rose-Colored Map: Portugal's Attempt to Build an African Empire from the Atlantic to the Indian Ocean*. Lisboa: Junta de Investigacoes Cientificas do Ultramar, 1982.

Reefe, Thomas Q. *The Rainbow and the Kings: A History of the Luba Empire to 1891*. Berkeley: University of California Press, 1981.

Vansina, Jan. *Paths in the Rainforest: Toward a History of Political Tradition in Equatorial Africa*. Madison: University of Wisconsin Press, 1990.

Chapter 10

Ethiopia

Saheed A. Adejumobi

Introduction

Ethiopia is very significant in the history of the world in general and Africa in particular. The oldest state in Africa, the empire of Ethiopia occupies a unique position on the continent as the core of the empire has maintained itself almost continuously as an independent political entity for at least fifteen hundred years. Ethiopia also has a special historical role in world affairs. The failure of the League of Nations to heed its appeals for protection against Italian aggression in the 1930s has made the Ethiopian state, in the post World War Two era, an ardent champion of collective security through the United Nations. As a result of such political fortunes, Ethiopia was to cast aside an earlier isolationist policies and subsequently sought a larger role in international affairs.

The relevance of Ethiopia to historical and cultural studies lies in its place in the history and symbolism of global African religious and political development. Even the name Ethiopia is of international historical significance as the name "Ethiopia" was—as in the Biblical, Hellenistic and in Shakespearean literature — the broad and practically generic term for the whole universe of dark-skinned people. In spite of modern incredible travails to its traditional cultural and political institutions, Ethiopia has manifested an impressive capacity in trying to meet the fundamental challenges of the modern era.

The Setting

The Empire of Ethiopia is located in northeast Africa, with its center in highlands that overlook and dominate the littoral of the Horn of Africa, including modern Eritrea and Somaliland (now independent states.) The fragmented nature of the highlands in Ethiopia also played a major part in the country's political and cultural history. Isolated and mountainous plateau massifs have proven to be almost insurmountable obstacles to political leaders who have sought to unify the country; to the invaders who have desired to conquer it; and to those who have sporadically attempted to develop Ethiopian economic resources. Geographic isolation also influenced a spirit of relative independence in many areas where the pattern of life has remained relatively unchanged for hundreds of years, and where the central government still has only limited influence.

The core of the ancient empire of Ethiopia lies in the great plateau of the Amharas, and more especially the northern portion of that tableland. The plateau, with its wheat crops and Mediterranean trees and flowers ripening in a temperate climate, sets it apart from the rest of Africa. The northern wall of the Amharic plateau is formed by the mountains which divides the high country of Eritrea from the desert to the North. Ancient Ethiopia is unique in that while the desert people are mostly Moslems, the plateau was known as Christian land. The plateau, however, is the scene of all the central episodes of Abyssynian history. Beginning from the north, it contains within its frontiers Asmara in the Hamasien, then Aksum the spiritual capital, Adowa and Adigrat, Gondar, Debra Tabor and Magdala, successive fortress strongholds, Ankober and Addis Ababa.[1] Early contacts with the outside world was made with both northern and eastern world through tracks leading to the harbors on the Red Sea coast.

The Peopling of Ethiopia

Another name for Ethiopia, Abyssinnia, originates from the word Habesh, the name of an invading group, the Habashat. Ethiopia has been called an ethnic museum, and this is in many ways an apt description. An estimated total of seventy languages and over two hundred dialects are spoken in this state. The peoples of Ethiopia profess two major faiths: Islam and Christianity. There are in addition, a multitude of widely differing local religious systems. The peoples are also further distinguished by separate traditions of origin, political histories and organizations; by variations in physical appearance, dress, and customs; and by diverse sources of self-identification and loyalty. The ethnic groups that dominate the country-politically and culturally-are the Amharas and the closely related Tigrais, who together constitute about one-third of the population. The former speak Amharic (Amharinya), the latter, Tigrinya. The basic mixture of both the Tigrean and Amharic peoples is developed from a Semitic invasion out of Yemen in Arabia imposed upon a 'Hamitic group'. This group was in turn linked racially and through language use with the Danakil and Somali peoples of the desert plain. The Tigrais are concentrated in Northern Eritrea and Tegre, the Amharas in Begemder, Gojam, and Shoa. In essence, these two groups continue to occupy the highland provinces which are the core of historic Ethiopia. Both the Amharas and Tigrais are Ethiopian Orthodox Christians who, though often rivals in the past for political supremacy, have maintained awareness of their common religion and their descent from common Semitic forebears.[2]

The Galla peoples are the largest ethnic group in the country, comprising approximately 40 percent of the population. Formerly a nomadic people in southern Ethiopia, Somaliland and Northern Kenya, the Galla are bound by a common language (Galla) with mutually intelligible dialects. By the sixteenth century, the

---

1. David Mathew. *Ethiopia: The Study of a Polity 1540-1935* (London: Eyre & Spottswoode), 7.
2. Ibid., 34.

Gallas had imposed their political and cultural influence into the Ethiopian Plateau and areas south and west of it. Other remaining significant groups in the population are the Somalis (about 6 percent); the Sidamos (9 percent); the Danakil or Afar (4.5 percent); the Shankella peoples (6 percent) and the Gurages (2.5 percent).[3]

In the second century A.D., an historical document, *The Periplus of the Erythrean Sea*, was written by a Greek sailor living in Egypt. Included in the log of the journeys of his vessels are notes on trade and other items of interest such as the description of ancient Aksum's port of Adulis, a port "established by law." In addition, the writer of the *Periplus* refers to considerable imports into the territory, mentioning among other things sheets of soft copper, small axes, a little wine from Italy, gold and silver plates for the king, military cloaks, Indian iron, steel, and cotton cloth. In addition to serving as articles of trade, these articles reflected the global proportions of Ethiopia's contact with the outside world. Ceremonial images of lions alongside umbrellas were also mentioned as representing important political symbols of ancient Aksum. The emperor of Ethiopia's title "King of the Kings" appears to have first been used in Aksum. At its greatest extent Aksum was able to unify the principalities of north Tigre, and toward the end of the third century A.D., parts of western Arabia were included in the Aksumite Territory. The empire also controlled shipping in the Red Sea as the kingdom of Meroe to the west was destroyed in war. To further enhance the economic viability of the empire, coins were produced by the kings of Aksum in bronze, silver, and gold.

The Impact of Aksum on Modern Ethiopia

The Aksumite Empire which flourished in the northern part of Ethiopia for an extended period beginning in classical times is considered to be the lineal ancestor of Ethiopia. The Aksumites themselves comprised an amalgam of the Kushite inhabitants of northern Ethiopia and the Semite 'colonizers' who had crossed the Red Sea from southern Arabia to settle in this area. Christianity was introduced to Aksum during the fourth century A.D. Unlike other cultural imports which atrophied and disappeared with the demise of Aksumite civilization, this new religion was to take root and become the dominant cultural phenomenon in the Ethiopian highlands. This is the only place on the African continent where Christianity managed to survive largely as a truly indigenous creed.

Aksum rose to prominence in the first two or three centuries of the Christian era. During this era, the language of Ge'ez—a word derived from the Aguezat, or Agazian, peoples of the north—had developed from Sabaean. It became a new form of Semitic writing whereby the vowels were incorporated in the consonants as they are in Amharic, which is the first official language of Ethiopia today (English is the second). Amharic, a more recent language, has also drawn from what may be described as indigenous languages. Ge'ez, however, apart from being the liturgical language of the Church, is no longer used. Its relation to Amharic is rather like Latin's relation to the Romance languages.

---

3. George A. Lipsky & Wendell Blanchard, Abraham M. Hirsch & Bela C. Maday, *Ethiopia: Its People, Its Society, Its Culture* (New Haven: HRAF Press, 1962), 9.

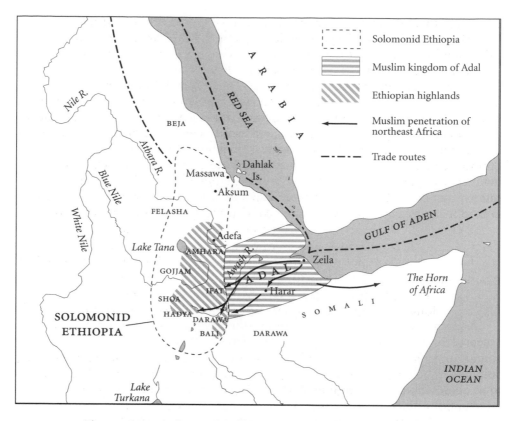

Figure 10-2. Solomonid Ethiopia in the Fifteenth Century

The Legend of Prester John and Other Foreign Influences On Ethiopia

Between the twelfth and the sixteenth centuries there had emerged a tale in Europe of a powerful Christian emperor who might aid the crusading powers against Islam. The legend of Prester John further encouraged the advent of European religious and commercial adventurers in the history of Ethiopia. The Portuguese in pressing their search for a route to India in the fifteenth century assumed that they might be assisted by Prester John, who was thought by them to be in the interior of Africa. The Prester John legend, diplomatic and religious correspondence, and the exchange of emissaries between Ethiopia and Europe, contributed to the construction of a national image of Ethiopia in the international arena. Only the successful assault by the Moslems in the Middle Period, which took place at the beginning of the sixteenth century, finally put an end to the legend.

The legend of Prester John was of great interest to the kings of Portugal from the time of Prince Henry the Navigator, and they soon established diplomatic relations with Ethiopia. Their ambassador, Peros da Covilha, reached Shewa in 1493. In 1509, the Empress Helena sent an Armenian, "Matthew," back to Portugal as her ambassador. The desire to encourage combined operations against

Islam was to give way to misconceptions in Lisbon and Rome that the Ethiopian Church was anxious to accept papal jurisdiction. This led to a disastrous phase in Ethiopian-European relations, a legacy of which was a lack of trust between Ethiopians and foreigners for a long period.

Nevertheless, among the many merchant visitors to Ethiopia in the fourteenth and fifteenth centuries were the Venetians who helped facilitate the availability in Europe of geographical information about the land. A popular early map known as *Fra Mauro's* map of 1457 and a succession of later works bear evidence to this international recognition of Ethiopia. The Papacy in Rome tried to establish contact through Ethiopian monks in Jerusalem. The Ethiopian Church however remained strongly attached to the Monophysite doctrine, the belief in there being one Person and one Nature in Christ, which while it linked them with the Egyptian Copts, served to separate them not only from Rome but from those other believed otherwise. A Spanish king wrote to the Emperor Zara Yakob (1434-1468), described as "a fanatical Christian" who encouraged the writing of books, the building of churches, and the instruction of the public through teaching. Yakob was also noted for reorganizing the government, suppressing a provincial rebellion, and forming an army of spies used to seek out those who were opposed to his convictions. His influence was felt even in the most distant and independent regions of Ethiopia. The chiefs and kings in the south and east were obliged to acknowledge him with tribute.

Missionary presence was felt in Ethiopia in the wake of European commercial exploitation. This combined with external attacks from Muslims and Portuguese to give an impulse to the central idea that was enshrined in the building of the Castles of Gondar as a permanent residence for the court.[5] It was not until the reign of Menelik II that the political center of the state was shifted to Addis Ababa.

By the 1770s the principal institutions of the ancient Ethiopian state had effectively collapsed. These institutions as earlier discussed, had owed their ultimate origins to a classical period associated with the Aksumite Empire in the early centuries of the Christian Era. They had evolved through an obscure period late in the 1st millennium and early in the 2nd millennium A.D., to emerge under the Solomonic dynasty in the late 13th century. The Solomonic kings subsequently presided over an expanding and flourishing empire into the 16th century, profoundly influencing the Ethiopian state and church.

Firearms played an important role in the development of both ancient and modern Ethiopian history. Materially, the struggle to reconstruct the Ethiopian empire was determined by military means: by generalship, the control of firearms, cavalry etc. For example, the ruler of Shoa, Sahle Sellassie was reported to have more than 1000 firearms including 300 muskets given to him by the British diplomatic mission of 1841-3. Sellassie also purchased about 140 muskets from the French representative Rochet d'Hericourt. In spite of the large arsenal, there was however a major problem of the lack of ammunition. At the social and political level, imperial reconstruction was determined by the manipulation of men along traditional lines which many observers have interpreted as feudal. The ideological and institutional level witnessed the struggle within the complex of ideas and traditions associated with the Ethiopian Orthodox Church.

---

5. David Mathew, *Ethiopia: The Study of a Polity*, 13.

equipped with arms procured through numerous agents, engaged in an extensive arms trade, and then began the conquest of Galla territories to the east, west, and south of Shoa. Yohannes was preoccupied with the appearance of new dangers on the borders of Ethiopia. Yohannes died on the battle field in 1888 and the throne passed on to the most powerful of the provincial rulers, Menelik II of Shoa. The period of Menelik's reign is a milestone in Ethiopian history. Menelik began to import arms fairly early in his career as the ruler of Shoa, and by the 1880s, the import reached even larger proportions. The sales of arms to Ethiopia, at that time the only independent state on the African continent other than Liberia, necessarily had important diplomatic repercussions in the era of the scramble for Africa. Carried on first by the Italians and later the French, the trade was for a number of reasons strongly opposed by the British. The latter power was unable to prevent arms trade with Ethiopia without the agreement of other powers dueling for influence in the entity. Nigra, the Italian Ambassador in London, reacted to the apprehension of the British by arguing that Menelik was "not a primitive tribesman" but an able and progressive ruler anxious to trade with Europe and to purchase arms like any independent power. The British, Italian and the French also could not agree on the suppression of arms trade to the Somali coast.

The result of a decade and a half of systematic arms purchase and acquisition was that Menelik was prepared for the final struggle against the Italians, being able to marshal a far larger number of modern weapons than any other African ruler; he could in fact bring into play greater firepower and several times as many rifles as the Italians who were reluctant to despatch large numbers of men on this venture. In February 27, 1893, Menelik informed the European powers of his decision on rejecting the Italian proclaim of a protectorate over Ethiopia. He declared "Ethiopia has need of no one; she stretches out her hands unto God." When war became imminent, Menelik issued a mobilization proclamation calculated to strengthen the religious solidarity of Ethiopian Orthodoxy in the face of Roman Catholicism:

> Enemies have now come upon us to ruin the country and to change our religion...Our enemies have begun the affair by advancing and digging into the country like moles. With the help of God I will not deliver up my country to them...Today, you who are strong, give me of your strength, and you who are weak, help me by prayer.[6]

In response to this call, every Tukul (hut) and village in every far-off glen of Ethiopia sent out their warriors. By March 1, 1896, at the battle of Adowa, the Ethiopians were to have at least 70, 000 rifles and 42 canons in the field. The Battle of Adowa, won by Ethiopia, besides giving Menelik great local and international prestige, underlined the ability of Ethiopia to resist anything less than a full-scale European invasion and thereby won it new allies. The event also rendered Ethiopia exempt from future 19th century-type colonial wars. Menelik's alliance with the French, a result of his enhanced diplomatic importance, was followed by larger arms gifts. After more than three centuries during which they have been a prey to attack by better-armed forces, nearly all the farmers of North-

---

6. H. G. Marcus, "The Black Men Who Turned White: European Attitudes Towards Ethiopians, 1850-1900," *Archiv Orientalni*, 39 (1971): 160.

ern Ethiopia had modern breach-loaders and plenty of cartridges, and could be mobilized very quickly if occasion should arise.

It has been suggested that Ethiopia's foreign policy under Menelik was dominated by an aggressive campaign of territorial acquisition all along the western frontier of Ethiopia. Others argue that rather than operate militarily with imperial motives within the ranks of European partition of Africa, Menelik simply tried to retain the confidence, and therefore the diplomatic support of France. Menelik, they argued, surbodinated his territorial aspirations in the Nile Valley to the promotion of good relations with the Khalifa; and that he frustrated rather than assisted the French missions to the Nile. Hence Ethiopia's "imperialism," they concluded, was more due to self-preservation and the need to prevent the British subjugation of Ethiopia.

It is also remarkable that in the signing of the Peace Treaty of Addis Ababa, whereby the Italians renounced the Treaty of Ucciali and recognized the absolute and complete independence of Ethiopia, Menelik did not consider himself in a position to insist on an Italian withdrawal from Eritrea though he had often expressed a desire of obtaining access to the sea. In the months which followed, the French and the British governments sent diplomatic missions to sign treaties of friendship with Menelik; other missions came from the Sudanese Mahdists, the Sultan of Ottoman Empire, and the Tsar of Russia. Addis Ababa thus emerged as a regular diplomatic center where several important foreign powers had legations.

Ethiopia witnessed the culmination and consolidation of the vast territorial expansion launched by Menelik while still the king of Shoa. The growth turned Ethiopia into an empire and gave it the reputation it enjoys in African history. In spite of such achievements, much socio-economic damage was done to civilians, loyal and rebel alike by the empire's military arm throughout the 19th century. The armies often times collected free provisions (*dirgo*), by decree and the imposition of taxes or the orderly levying of supplies for military campaigns. In addition, predatory soldiers in state's service and freelances, plundered many Ethiopian communities and confiscated lands and properties, leading to several peasant uprising. In spite of such shortcomings, military activities helped with the construction and fortification of a physical as well as geographical Ethiopia as different ethnic groups were politically unified. Military activities also allowed smaller ethnic group other than the Amhara and Tigreans opportunities in Christian armies. The Oromos, however, eventually became the emperor's preferred auxiliaries to suppress opposition from rebellious nobilities. Such military activities also added to the changing cultural and ethnographic terrain of Ethiopia. Military settlers in the lands of conquest became known to the local inhabitants as "Amhara" or "Sidama"(meaning Christian and alien). The intruders were neither so homogenous nor so distinct from the conquered as these misapplied ethnic terms suggest. Another important dynamic in this era was forced assimilation into new social groups as witnessed in the 'Amharization' of Oromo migrants to the native Amhara.

Conclusion

Beside Liberia, Ethiopia was the only African country to preserve its independence throughout the period of the European scramble. Its independence was maintained by her possession of arms and ammunitions and powerful religious and political institutions. In 19th century Ethiopia, as in other parts of Africa, religion played a major role in legitimating political reconstruction. Hence, Africans in general from the 19th century onwards proclaim Ethiopia as a liberator, a monument and living exponent and testimony of African political freedom.

Review Questions

1. Account for the significance of Ethiopia in the history of Africa.
2. Describe reasons behind the successes and failures of the Ethiopian political structure.
3. Explain the relevance of ethnicity and religion in Ethiopia.
4. Why is Ethiopia important in global African cultural history?

Additional Readings

Lepsius, Richard. *Letters from Egypt, Ethiopia, and to Peninsula of Sinai.* London: H.G. Bohn, 1853.

Markakis, John. *Ethiopia: Anatomy of a Traditional Polity.* Oxford: Clarendon Press, 1974.

Zewde, Bahru. *A History of Modern Ethiopia, 1855-1974.* Addis Ababa, Ethiopia: Addis Ababa University Press, 1991.

Chapter 11

North Africa: Peoples and States to circa 1880

Joel E. Tishken

Introduction

North Africa tends to be studied in conjunction with southwest Asia, but it can really only be fully understood if studied in the African context. While the history of the region does share many commonalities and common themes with southwest Asia, it is also distinctively African and has many connections with the rest of the continent as well. The region, as defined here, includes most of the area of present-day Morocco, Algeria, Tunisia, Libya, Egypt, Sudan, Western Sahara and Mauritania. This chapter provides an in-depth investigation of a number of peoples in a historical context. The cases selected were chosen for their historical importance, perceived readers' interest, and/or the amount of scholarship concerning them.[1]

Answers to Good and Evil: Religious History in North Africa

Carthage[2]

Carthage is most commonly known to history as the civilization that was crushed when it stood in the way of Roman expansion. Before its conquest by Rome, Carthage was a huge, vibrant civilization and a world power of the first order in the classical period. Because of its position as a vanquished culture, it is normally little discussed in history textbooks except as it relates to Rome. This

---

1. I wish to thank Anver Emon for comments on a draft of this chapter.
2. For Carthage's early religious history, see David Soren, *Carthage: Uncovering the Mysteries and Splendors of Ancient Tunisia* (New York : Simon and Schuster, 1990); and Serge Lancel,*Carthage: A History*, trans. Antonia Nevill (Oxford, UK; Cambridge, USA: Blackwell, 1995). For the later religious history of Carthage see J.B. Rives, *Religion and Authority in Roman Carthage: From Augustus to Constantine* (Oxford: Clarendon Press; New York: Oxford University Press, 1995).

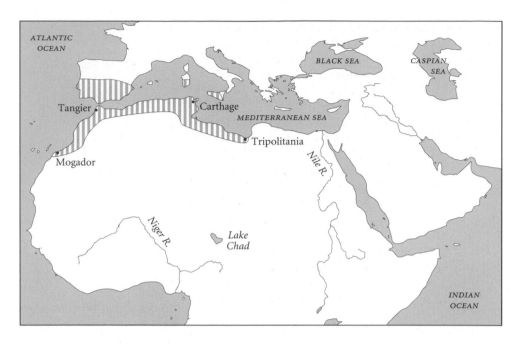

Figure 11-1. Carthaginian Empire

section will remedy that slightly, by addressing the role of religion in Carthaginian culture in order to gain a richer understanding of this powerful civilization.

Traditions of the civilizations of the Mediterranean basin all state that the city of Tyre in Phoenicia was responsible for the western Phoenician expeditions out of the region of present-day Lebanon. Tyre held a premier position among Phoenician cities in the thirteenth century B.C., and led the way in the search for sources of metals such as gold, silver, lead, tin, and copper. Tin was especially important as it was needed to turn copper into bronze, the primary war material of the period. The Phoenicians were by far the greatest supplier of metals in the Mediterranean world for most of the first millennium B.C. Their wealth in commerce made them prosperous, and their surplus population soon began to spread out and found colonies throughout the Mediterranean area. Phoenician trade depended on a large fleet of vessels that in turn depended on numerous depots. It was these depots which served as the foundation sites for Phoenician cities. The process of development of these cities was a gradual one, often occurring over decades.

The first Phoenician city founded in North Africa was Utica in 1101 B.C. and Cadiz, in southern Spain, had been founded in 1110 B.C. The founding date of Carthage is held to be 814 B.C., although this can not be corroborated by solid archaeological evidence. The city was initially no larger than a few hundred people. It grew rapidly, however, and became an important economic center. Carthage expanded its influence and established colonies in southern Sardinia, southern Spain and western Sicily, where it competed with the Greeks, as well as in other parts of North Africa. At its peak in about 380 B.C., the city of Carthage contained approximately four hundred thousand inhabitants, controlled the water-borne trade of most of the Mediterranean, and ruled part of Sicily and Sardinia, the Balearic Islands, a sizeable portion of Iberia, and the coastal strip of North Africa as far west as Mogador in Morocco.

A number of factors led to the collapse of the Carthaginian Empire. First, Alexander the Great captured the mother city, Tyre, in 332 B.C., along with the rest of Phoenicia, thus shutting Carthage off from the remainder of the Phoenician world. Second, the series of Punic Wars between Rome and Carthage drained Carthaginian resources and threatened its territorial integrity at a time when Rome was experiencing dynamic expansion. The First Punic War lasted from 264-241; the Second from 219-201; and the Third began in 149 and ended with the destruction of the city of Carthage in 146 B.C. It should be noted that Rome's conquest of Carthage did not happen overnight and was not easy by any means. Third, the Carthaginians were not known as benevolent colonizers. The Phoenicians did not settle an empty territory, but displaced the indigenous inhabitants of North Africa known as Berbers, whom classical sources refer to as Libyans. The Carthaginians conscripted Berbers into their army and navy, and charged a twenty-five percent tax on Berber agricultural produce. In bad times, the tax rose to as high as fifty percent. Many Libyans were not happy with Carthaginian rule and rose in revolt on several occasions, the most significant occurring around 380 B.C. Thus, the threat of internal revolt was often a danger to Carthaginian integrity. The Romans took advantage of this by forming an alliance with the Berber state of Massinissa in 205 B.C., forcing Carthage to fight a war on several fronts.

Carthaginian culture and religion, like those of other classical Mediterranean civilizations, were a blend of various cultural influences including those of ancient Mesopotamia including Babylon, Akkadia and Sumer, Semitic cultures such as Palestine and Canaan, Egypt, Greece, and in the case of Carthage, Berber culture as well. Since most Carthaginians were Phoenician émigrés, the Phoenician influence on them was the strongest.

The two most important gods in the Carthaginian pantheon were Ba'al Hammon and Tanit. Ba'al Hammon appears to be related to the Phoenician god El. El was the father of the gods and controller of the sun, who gradually relinquished power to his sons and retreated to a remote part of his heavenly home. Ba'al Hammon, on the other hand, was not a distant power but a very active god. The etymology of the word *hammon* is not known. It may derive from the root *hmn* (to heat or burn), and the god's name has been translated as Lord of the Incense-Burners (*hmmn*) or Lord of the Furnaces.[3] While images of Ba'al Hammon can be found, he was normally represented not through images but by symbols. His symbols pervaded Carthaginian architecture and art and were believed to possess magical powers. Common symbols included the horns of a ram, grapes and pomegranates, spears, or axes. The rule of the Carthaginian oligarchy, and the monarchy when it was in power, was often tied to the divine authority of Ba'al Hammon. Sacrifices were made to please him and ensure the success of Carthage's armies and the safety of its inhabitants. The importance of Ba'al Hammon can even be evidenced in names: Hasdrubal means "salvation in Ba'al"; and Hannibal means "favorite of Ba'al."

---

3. Gilbert C. Picard and Colette Picard, *The Life and Death of Carthage: A Survey of Punic History and Culture from its Birth to the Final Tragedy*, trans. Dominique Collon (New York: Taplinger Publishing Co., 1969), 45-46.

Figure 11-3. Stele from the Tophet of Carthage

tradition holds that general Hamilcar sacrificed to Ba'al Shamin before leaving for Spain, and that Hannibal swore hatred to Rome at a festival of the same god.

Melqart was the patron deity of Tyre and stood at the forefront of that city's pantheon. Melqart was also known in the Carthaginian Empire but was more popular in Lixus and Gades than in the city of Carthage itself . Tyrian refugees fleeing the conquest of Alexander the Great in 332 B.C., however, revived the worship of Melqart in Carthage. Roman accounts claim that priests of Melqart were required to be celibate and beardless with shaved heads, and women were not permitted in the precinct of Melqart. It is from Melqart that Hamilcar ("brother of Melqart") likely gained his name.

Resheph, god of fertility and the underworld, Eshmun, the god of vegetation who died and was reborn according to the seasons, and Shadrapa, the god of healing, were three other significant deities of Carthage based on Phoenician religion. Like other classical civilizations, Carthage also adopted the gods of their neighbors if the deities proved to be powerful. The Egyptian gods of Amun-Ra, Isis, Osiris, Set, Bast, Ptah, and Horus were all worshiped in the Carthaginian

Empire. In 396 B.C., the cult of the Greek goddess of agriculture, Demeter, was introduced. Demeter remained the most popular Greek god throughout the history of Carthage. Apollo, Artemis, Dionysis, Zeus, Hercules, Ares, and Hermes were also worshipped.

Carthaginian culture and religion did not die with the collapse of the Carthaginian state. A great deal of dialogue between the Roman and the Carthaginian religions was evident. For instance, Ba'al Hammon came to be identified with Saturn (Kronos to the Greeks). While worshipers referred to the deity as Saturn, he was defined with attributes of both Saturn and Ba'al Hammon. While he was rarely depicted in an image during earlier times, depictions of Ba'al Hammon/Saturn became common after Carthage's fall. The bull and ram were symbolic associations of this new hybrid deity. Melqart became identified with Hercules and Tanit with Juno (Hera). Thus, the religion of North Africa, even through intense Romanization, retained its Phoenician roots. Even two thousand years later, after Christianization from 100-700 A.D., and Islamization from 700 A.D. onward, North Africa continues to preserve some Carthaginian religious traditions. Blood sacrifices are still common in many rural areas of the Maghrib, the Phoenician curse of the "evil eye" still worries many, and hand and eye symbolism pervades Maghribian culture. The Carthaginian legacy makes North Africa a unique part of the African and Mediterranean world.

Answers to Livelihood: Economic History in North Africa

Trans-Saharan Trade in North Africa

If anything can be said to be an omnipresent part of North African history it is the trans-Saharan trade network. Until the growth of Carthage, however, trade among the peoples of the Sahara mainly consisted of goods passing from village to village and oasis to oasis, occasionally making their way across the desert. Most commonly, desert dwellers traded salt for food with peoples bordering the Sahara on both its north and south sides. From 800-500 B.C., the ascendancy of Carthage served as a magnet. The buying power of the markets of Carthage was large enough for trade routes to be established across the Sahara. Cave paintings which have been dated to this period show that trade was conducted with pack-oxen, mules, and horse-drawn chariots. While scholars do not know for certain which routes these early traders used, by "connecting the dots" between similar cave drawings researchers conjecture that there were two major routes. One began in Fezzan, passed through the Ahaggar Mountains, and connected with the Niger River. The second began in Morocco, passed through present-day Mauritania and ended in Akjouit and Tichitt. The trade was not conducted by the Carthaginians themselves but by the Berbers.

The trade goods in this period were luxury items, and the volume of the trade was quite small. The difficulties that oxen, donkeys, and horses had in getting across the desert ensured that these commodities retained a high value. The south-bound trade carried cloth, beads, metal objects, and most importantly salt. While it may now seem odd for salt to have a high value, the high-carbohydrate, high-

Trade grew steadily from the introduction of the camel until the close of the millennium. However, the height of the trans-Saharan trade was from 1000-1500 A.D. Salt, gold, and slaves were the most important items of trade during this period. West Africa was rich in gold and numerous tales exist of the lavishness and wealth of its rulers and kingdoms. Gold mines, largely if not exclusively operated by slave labor, existed throughout West Africa. Tales even existed of West Africans trading gold measure for measure for salt. It is likely that tales of this sort are merely myths but their very existence is evidence of the importance of salt to West Africans.

Salt mines existed throughout the Sahara. Some salt deposits were mined straight from the surface while others were extracted from tunnels in the earth. Some salt was strapped to camels in blocks and could maintain its integrity throughout the trip. Blocks of salt even served as a building materials in Taghaza where the fourteenth century traveler Ibn Battuta saw houses made of blocks of salt and roofed with camel skins. Lower-quality salts had to be placed in containers atop the camels. Each mine gained a particular reputation for quality and its prices were often set accordingly.

Slaves were another important commodity in the trans-Saharan trade system, although, unlike the Atlantic slave trade, gold for Mediterranean coinage, and not humans, remained the priority for Arab and Berber traders. Some traffic in Europeans and Asians was conducted southward, but the majority of the commerce in slaves consisted of Black Africans heading northward. Large numbers of people were enslaved through this system and sold in Europe, North Africa and Asia. The number of captives sold was much higher in times of war or jihad. Contemporary Saharan oral tradition states that slaves were sold for a block of salt equal to the length of their foot, illustrating yet again the importance of salt. When Europeans began to arrive on the West African coast beginning in the fifteenth century, they succeeded in diverting much of the traffic in slaves southwards and eastwards. The trans-Saharan traffic in slaves steadily decreased in the fifteenth-eighteenth centuries, but experienced a slight increase in the nineteenth century as the Europeans stopped the Atlantic trade in humans. For two millennia the trans-Saharan trade network was used to export human beings into servile labor.

Many cities grew fairly large to accommodate the volume of trade on the major routes. The exact location of some Saharan cities, such as Taghaza and Ijil, still remains a mystery for a number of reasons. One, some towns faded away centuries ago. Two, the written descriptions of travelers offer competing versions of the location of towns. Three, settlements shifted locations as mines became exhausted or as invaders forced them to relocate or suspend trading or mining. Four, given the climatic conditions of the Sahara, physical evidence deteriorates quickly. Despite this, the location of most extinct towns has been established with a fair degree of certainty. A number of towns, such as Agades, Ghat, and Murzuk remain important regional and trading centers to this day. Other towns, such as Walata and Tichitt, still exist but have lost their importance and wealth.[5]

---

5. Basil Davidson, with F.K. Buah and the advice of J.F.A. Ajayi, *A History of West Africa, 1000-1800*, 7th ed. (London: Longman, 1990), 31.

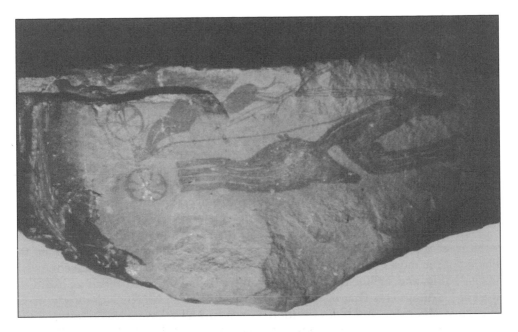

Figure 11-6. Prehistoric Rock Painting from Tassili n'Ajjer, Sahara

As one might imagine, the volume of trade depended on the political stability of North and West Africa. The greater the security of the caravans along the routes and in the "port" cities, the greater the volume of traffic. Some rulers went to great lengths to protect the trade routes. In the 1040s, the Almoravids (from al-Murabitun), a group of Sanhaja Berbers on jihad, conquered the region from Sijilmasa to Awdaghost, thus gaining control of the important trade routes of the western Sahara. Almoravid control over the region began to slip away in the 1080s. Almoravid hegemony did not last long as they themselves had a jihad declared against them by North African Berbers (Almohads) in the 1140s. The Almohads, however, while uniting a sizeable portion of the Maghrib (the region of present-day Morocco, Algeria and Tunisia), were not able to retain control over the trade routes.

In the late fifteenth and early sixteenth centuries, the West African kingdom of Songhai secured a major route as far north as Taghaza under the leadership of Askiya Mohammed the Great. A recently unified Morocco, which had successfully withstood Ottoman and Portuguese attacks, covetously eyed the trade routes and Songhai. An army largely composed of mercenaries and former Spanish and Portuguese prisoners set off from Morocco in 1590. Armed with arquebuses, the most up to date weapon of the time, and even a few canon, the army arrived in Songhai in 1591. The Moroccan force handily defeated Songhai and gained control of the western trade routes. As with the Almoravids, the Moroccan Empire was unable to maintain control of the routes. Military equipment and troops were spread too thinly to control such a vast amount of territory. Morocco lost its hold of its southern possessions by the mid-sixteenth century. The Almoravid and Moroccan cases are two successful instances of North African states conquering major trans-Saharan trade routes, but few were the leaders of North African

Salamiyya in Syria, their missionaries gained adherents in numerous parts of the Islamic world including southern Iraq, Bahrain, Persia, and Yemen. But their greatest success occurred in North Africa. The Kutama Berbers were among the earliest recruits, although it is not exactly clear why they converted to Ismailism so readily. The Kutama conquered the Aghlabid state, thus giving control of Ifrikiya to Fatimids and their current imam, Ubayd Allah, in 909. The Kutama remained an important part of the Fatimid military throughout the history of the Fatimid state, but were often prone to revolt if the conditions of their service did not suit them. Because of this, Sakaliba, as Slavonic peoples were called by Arabic speakers, were purchased from Venetian slavers and captured in raids to create a more loyal military. Most Sakaliba were of south Slavonic origin and many proved to be loyal fighters and skilled administrators, as they rose to prominence in North Africa. One in particular, Jawhar, was the eventual conqueror of Egypt and founder of Cairo and the al-Azhar Mosque and university.[7]

The foundation of a Shi'ite state in North Africa split the Islamic world into three hostile empires: the Abbasid Caliphate in southwest Asia, the Umayyad Emirate in Spain, and the Fatimid Caliphate in North Africa. The Fatimids viewed their early conquests merely as a means of preparing for further conquests to the east and the eventual conquest of the entire Islamic world in order to prepare the way for the Mahdi. To the west, scholars disagree as to the exact strategy of the Fatimids. Some argue that they wished to expand their empire all the way into southern Europe. Others argue that they were merely trying to gain access to the trans-Saharan trade in gold with their campaigns in the Maghrib. Whatever their intended strategy, the Fatimids met with very little success in the western Maghrib. The Abbasids and Umayyads were just as hostile to the Fatimids as the Fatimids were to them. The Umayyads and their Berber allies, especially the Zanata, succeeded in keeping the Fatimids from gaining a solid foothold in most of northwest Africa. However, the Umayyads never gained a solid footing either, and the region remained a collection of decentralized governments and Berber states.

With their conquest of the Aghlabids, the Fatimids obtained possession of Sicily which the Aghlabids had seized from Byzantium after a long struggle from 827-902. The advent of the new conquerors created a highly plural society that introduced Berbers and Arabic speakers from Spain, North Africa, and Arabia into the Byzantine society that had preceded it. The friction between the various parts of the Muslim population, as well as the tension between Muslims and Christians, meant that Sicily had a fairly volatile political structure often near civil war. Despite the tenuous grasp the Fatimids often had on Sicily, it was a vital part of their empire. From it they gained foodstuffs, grain, and lumber. The latter allowed the Fatimids to build a strong navy. Operating from Sicily, the Fatimids raided their Christian as well as Muslim neighbors, from Spain to the Balkans. The Fatimid fleet was especially active from 922-929 when it succeeded in capturing Genoa, scored several victories against the Byzantine navy, and landed troops on several parts of the Italian peninsula. For a time, the Fatimids were masters of the Mediterranean, controlling many of the main trading cities of the region.

---

7. I. Hrbek, "The Emergence of the Fatimids," in M. El Fasi, ed., *Africa from the Seventh to the Eleventh Century*, UNESCO General History of Africa, vol. 3 (London: Heinemann, 1988), 329.

From their base in central North Africa the Fatimids attempted to bring their vision of a totally Ismailian world to fruition. Expeditions were launched against Egypt in 913-915, 919-921 and in 925. It was not until the time of the fourth Fatimid caliph, al-Mu'izz, that Egypt was conquered in 969 by Jawhar. Jawhar founded Cairo (al-Qahira) that year and began construction of the al-Azhar Mosque a year later. Cairo was a well-planned and well-built city with a large efficient sewer system, some brick houses of five to six stories high, and some covered streets lit with lamps. In 973, four years after the conquest, al-Mu'izz moved the Fatimid capital from Ifrikiya to Cairo. This eastward shift of the Fatimid state was to have two important consequences.

First, it brought a Berber dynasty to power in the western Maghrib. In 972, al-Mu'izz appointed Bulukkin ibn Ziri, a loyal Berber leader, as his lieutenant over the western part of the Fatimid Empire. The Zirids were the first significant Berber dynasty since the arrival of the Muslims several centuries earlier. They established an important precedent and opened a period of Maghribian history that saw political power exclusively held by Berber dynasties (Almoravids, Almohads, Zayyanids, Marinids, and Hafsids).[8]

The Fatimid move to the east, however, lost them control over the rest of North Africa. With power primarily in the hands of the Zirids, divisions among the Berbers re-erupted. In addition, the transient influence of Ismailism on the generally Sunni population also became evident as the Sunni began to suppress the Shi'ites and remove the Ismaili influence. By the first half of the eleventh century, most of North Africa had reverted to a state in which Arabs were confined to urban coastal areas and Berbers were controlling most of the region through a number of states. In 1047, Zirid al-Mu'izz ibn Badis (not to be mistaken with the Fatimid imam al-Mu'izz) broke with the Fatimid state and recognized the suzerainty of the Abbasid Caliphate, thus making most of North Africa Sunni in name as well as fact.

The reaction of the Fatimids to the loss of their North African territory was not what one might have expected. The Fatimid caliph at the time, al-Mustansir, did not form an army to reconquer the territory and punish his recalcitrant vassal. Instead, following the advice of his vizier al-Yazuri, he encouraged two nomadic groups then living in Upper Egypt, the Banu Hilal and the Banu Sulaym, to migrate into what had been Fatimid North Africa. These groups had reputations for being undisciplined and independent, and al-Mustansir was glad to have them out of Egypt. As the migration offered booty and better grazing land, the chieftains of the nomads took al-Mustansir up on his offer and migrated into the region beginning in 1050-1051. The arrival of the nomads destabilized the region, causing many states to splinter and others to fall apart entirely. While the migration fulfilled al-Mustansir's plan to punish the Zirids, it also led to the partial collapse of the region's economy, created a more rural, nomadic-oriented society, and destabilized the eastern border of Egypt.

Second, the Fatimid move to the east furthered the solidification of the Fatimid presence in Egypt. Egypt prospered under Fatimid rule. Famine was rare, trade routes were extensive and lucrative, education flourished, and monumental architecture sprang up. The power and reputation of the Fatimid state spread far

8. Hrbek, "Emergence," 328-329.

from within Byzantium as well as modern Turkish military technology and techniques. The capital of Byzantium, Constantinople, fell to the Turks in 1453, effectively ending the Byzantine Empire. From their stronghold in Anatolia, the Turks began to conquer greater portions of Europe, Asia, and Africa under strong leadership and militarily adept troops.

The story of the Ottomans in Africa began with their conquest of Egypt. With the collapse of the Fatimids in 1171, Salah al-Din founded the Ayyubid dynasty which was to last until 1250. He imported Mamluk slave soldiers from Turkey, thus continuing the Islamic tradition of forming an army with foreign, servile, young men. Successful Mamluks were awarded freedom and tracts of land called *iqta*, and many grew to great power. In 1250, a group of Mamluk amirs killed the last Ayyubid sultan and established the first of two Mamluk dynasties that would rule Egypt until 1517.

The Mamluk state was quite successful militarily. The Mamluks even halted the advance of the Mongols in Palestine in 1260. The defeat of the Mongols helped preserve the culture and society of southwest Asia and North Africa. However, by the time the Ottomans threatened in the sixteenth century, the cavalry of the Mamluks, armed with bows and curved swords, was hopelessly out of date compared with the firearms and canons of the Ottomans. The Mamluks were able to offer little military resistance, and Egypt fell to the Ottomans in 1517.

The system of government that the Ottomans instituted in Egypt was one they would later implement in their other North African territories. A pasha, or viceroy, was appointed from Istanbul. Originally the pasha was always a Turk. But after 1700, as many Mamluk aristocrats began to regain power, many pashas were Mamluk. This was also a theme that would emerge in the rest of Ottoman North Africa, namely, the emergence of local leaders at the expense of Ottoman-appointed pashas.

After solidifying their power in Egypt, the Ottomans quickly embarked on further expansion in Africa. They extended the southern border of Egypt to the third cataract of the Nile in the 1550s and came into conflict with the Funj Sultanate. They succeeded in taking over the Red Sea port of Massawa, although they never achieved full control of the Red Sea trade network. Expansion to the west brought the Ottomans into conflict with the Spanish and Portuguese, both of whom had been attempting to establish footholds in North Africa. The local governments and their Berber allies had succeeded in keeping the Christians from conquering more than some coastal ports, but were neither powerful nor unified enough to repel them entirely. The first Turks to battle the Christians in the Maghrib were Ra'is, or corsairs, who, with the consent and aid of local governments, fought the Christians in the early sixteenth century. A particularly successful Ra'is, Khayruddin (also known as Khidhr) appealed to the Ottoman sultan for support after the death of his brother Arrudj (Urudj). Khayruddin recognized the suzerainty of the Ottoman sultan, who in turn provided slave troops known as Janissaries. Khayruddin and Arrudj were the famous "Barbarossa" brothers of literary and cinematic fame.

For about forty years (1534-1574), the region which was once the state of Ifrikiya witnessed a bitter struggle for control between Spain and the Ottomans. The rulers of Ifrikiya, the Hafsids, as well as other local rulers, battled the Spanish. The long conflict produced a number of Ra'is of great repute such as Torgut (Dragut) as well as a huge number of casualties. In the end, the Ottomans proved victorious, seizing Tripoli in 1551, central Tunisia in 1557, and Tunis in 1569 and again in 1574.

Thus began the Maghribian regencies or *iyala*. The Ottomans viewed their North African possessions as borderlands that they referred to as the "*odjaks* of the West" and they never put the same effort into integrating them into the empire as they did the Arabian heartland and the regions around Anatolia. Originally, a single leader was appointed to the three Maghribian regencies, headquartered in Algiers, who was referred to as the beylerbey. With the death of Beylerbey Killidj in 1587, however, the regencies broke into three: Algiers, Tunis and Tripoli. For most of the sixteenth century, the Ottomans were successful in appointing their own pashas to the three regencies. The Ottomans were not successful, though, in extracting regular tribute, in any direct administration, or in imposing European-style institutions which they had adopted themselves, such as fiefs and weaponry.[10]

A number of themes can be identified throughout the period of Ottoman rule in North Africa. The first was the tension between the Ottoman rulers and oligarchy and the indigenous elite. In all three regencies, local leaders eventually displaced the Ottoman-appointed pashas around 1700. The ascendancy of the indigenous elite coincided with a decline in Ottoman international power. It was in Algiers that the Turkish elite managed to hang onto power the longest, primarily due to the fact that the indigenous elite was weaker there than in Tunis and Tripoli. The pasha was left in place as a figurehead, but real power rested with the newly created office of the bey. The bey was the commander of the territorial forces who succeeded in solidifying his position through support from the local elite. Many Turks were integrated into Arab and Berber society, but the Turkish ruling class was continually viewed as foreign, thus aiding the rise of the local leaders.

A second theme during this period was a lack of unity both between and within the regencies. From 1600 to 1800, ten wars took place between Algiers and Tunis. It is difficult to call these two provinces of the same empire when they had enough autonomy to fight one another on a regular basis. They often sent troops to interfere in each other's civil wars and raided one another's shipping. Relations between Algiers and Tripoli and Tunis and Tripoli appear to have been more peaceful. That could be due to two factors. One, Ottoman control over Tripoli was tighter than in Tunis or Algiers, largely due to geographic proximity. Two, Tripoli was so internally unstable that Algiers and Tunis may have felt it was not worth expending energy on.

It was not just Tripoli that suffered from internal disunity and instability. Ethnically the regencies were divided into Berber, Arab, and Turkish enclaves. Geographically and socially they were divided into urban dwellers, suburban agriculturists, rural agriculturists, migratory peoples, camel herders deep in the desert, mountain dwellers, and sedentary oasis dwellers. The stability of the regency depended on the degree to which these ethnic and social differences could be overcome. The differences were usually overcome only in the face of a threat from Europeans. The mountainous areas, which housed a good number of the Berbers, were never integrated successfully at any point in post-Bedouin history. Yet, despite these divisions, the period of Ottoman regencies in the Maghrib provided greater stability than there had been seen since the rule of the Fatimids.

---

10. M.H. Cherif, "Algeria, Tunisia and Libya: the Ottomans and their heirs," in B.A. Ogot, ed., *Africa from the Sixteenth to the Eighteenth Century*, UNESCO General History of Africa, vol. 5 (London: Heinemann, 1992), 238-239.

by European shipping companies. This, in conjunction with Egypt's expenses in expansion, especially in the Sudan, led to massive foreign debt by the 1870s. In 1876, Isma'il was deposed by the British and French, and "Dual Control" of Egypt's finances was shared by the two European powers. In 1881, it looked as if an army coup might retake control of Egypt's budget into Egyptian hands. A number of riots occurred in Alexandria, and the British used this as an excuse for military intervention. On July 11, 1882, Alexandria was bombarded and the country was invaded. The British invasion was given the blessing of the French, whose own forces were occupied with the conquest of Tunisia. The French were content to look the other way while gaining territory of their own. In theory, Egypt was still ruled by the pasha and was still considered part of the Ottoman Empire until the collapse of the Ottoman state from 1918 to 1920. In practice however, Egypt was now a British colony.

Algiers

The story of the three North African Ottoman regencies, discussed earlier in this chapter, ends in the same way; with European occupation. How that occupation came about, though, differed. Like Egypt, these states suffered from foreign debt. Stabilizing their economies was a common excuse for European invasion. The Ottoman regencies and Morocco had also suffered major military setbacks in the 1820s with the destruction of their navies. Under the pretense of crushing privateering, ships from Britain, France, the Netherlands, the United States and Austria arrived on the North African coast in 1815-1816. Sanctions were imposed upon Tripoli and Tunis, and Algiers was bombarded with 34,000 shells on August 16, 1816. In 1819, an Anglo-French squadron reappeared off the North African coast and forced the regents of Algiers, Tripoli, and Tunis to declare an end to piracy. In 1825, the British again bombarded Algiers. At the Battle of Navarino on October 20, 1827, a united British-French-Russian fleet destroyed the already weakened navies of the North African powers. In 1829, Austrian ships succeeded in destroying most of the Moroccan navy. Thus, by 1829, the North African powers were virtually defenseless on the sea. There was little to prevent the European powers from bringing troops to North Africa where and when they wished.[11]

Algiers retained a higher degree of Turkishness in its government and society at the advent of the nineteenth century than Tunis and Tripoli did. That is, the Turkish oligarchy continued to hold much of the political and economic power throughout the regency. In part, this was due to Algiers's more rural nature; a middle class that could have ousted the Turkish oligarchy was slower in developing. However, this is not to say that important change did not take place. The Janissaries, as elsewhere, had been gradually edged from power and replaced by civilian Turks. Closer ties were established between the Turkish oligarchy and Arab and Berber notables in the outlying provinces. The primary reason that resistance to the French was so long and fierce in Algeria was due to these alliances. Algiers was able to rally more support from its general population than

---

11. N. Ivanov, "New Patterns of European Intervention in the Maghrib," in J.F. Ade Ajayi, ed., *Africa in the Nineteenth Century until the 1880s*, UNESCO General History of Africa, vol. 6 (London: Heinemann, 1989), 497-498.

Figure 11-9. Abd-al-Qadir

the other regencies could. In this sense, some have said Algeria was developing a sense of nationhood in the nineteenth century as the various ethnic communities and regions began to establish a common sense of identity and purpose. Nonetheless, some thought the process of integration in Algiers too slow and the power of the Turkish oligarchy unjust. Uprisings took place in 1803-1805 in the western part of the country and again in 1814-1815. Religious brotherhoods provided the leaders of the rebellions and seriously threatened the integrity of Algiers.

In the late eighteenth and early nineteenth century, relations between Algiers and France had been souring. Various issues led to a break in diplomatic relations in 1827 and a French invasion of Algiers in 1830. The French claimed they were interested in eliminating privateering in North Africa. But since privateering had ceased by 1825, it seems obvious that the invasion was largely an exercise of French nationalism. Thus began a brutal war that lasted from 1830 to 1879 costing tens of thousands of French lives and possibly hundreds of thousands of Algerian ones.

Algerian resistance was organized by Abd al-Qadir who proclaimed a jihad against the French, thus uniting the Algerian people against the "infidel." Abd al-Qadir kept the French from the interior of Algeria for decades, even gaining French recognition of his rule of the non-coastal areas. Despite his capture and exile in 1847, resistance continued utilizing his system of administrative districts. It was not until 1879 that the French had finally beaten most of the country into submission. It still took an occupying force of one hundred thousand French troops to keep the country "pacified."

Tunis

In the late eighteenth and early nineteenth centuries, a small middle class was growing in Tunis. This group was ethnically non-Turkish and developed many foreign trading contacts, especially with countries of the eastern Mediterranean, but also with European nations. This group also began to exert political influence and, as elsewhere in North Africa, the Janissaries and Turkish noble classes were eased out of many positions of power. To keep them pacified, however, some were left in positions of power. As the new, largely Arab, largely commercially oriented group expanded its influence, it laid the foundation for what many have called Tunisian nationalism.

Like its neighbors, Tunis had a large portion of its fleet destroyed by European powers interested in eradicating privateering in the 1810s and 1820s. This left Tunis devastated financially and bound by treaties which guaranteed the country would be opened up to European trading firms and enterprise. In the 1830s, the Ottoman Empire sent troops to Tripoli to gain greater control of that territory. The growing European control in Tunis and the reestablishment of Ottoman control to his east led the bey of Tunis, Ahmad Bey, to feel that drastic reforms were necessary. A new army (*nizami*) , largely composed of conscripts, was designed along Western lines using European techniques as well as weaponry. Factories were established to provide gunpowder, guns, cloth and footwear, to meet the needs of the modern army. The old tax system was overhauled and a new system of administration installed. The position of the Turks was weakened further when their privileges were reduced and they were forced to compete on an equal footing. In 1846, the bey declared the abolition of slavery, one year prior to the same decision by Turkey and two years before the French did the same in Algiers. Ahmad Bey also made an official visit to France in 1847.

Despite the ambitious reform measures, the pace of change did not conform to the bey's expectations. The *nizami* remained ill-equipped, poorly trained, and lacking in discipline. Some of the factories, built at great expense, never became operational. These expenditures quickly exhausted the treasury of Tunis and a large foreign debt developed. Perhaps most seriously, the bey's reforms were seen by many as a perversion of the traditions of Tunis. Some did not like the increasing Westernization of the regency while some groups, like the Turks, did not like the new alignments of power that left them on the outside. However, Tunis was not unlike its neighbors, Egypt, Turkey, and later Morocco, in that all these states saw their reform programs fail, by and large.

Muhammed Bey succeeded Ahmad Bey in 1855. Under threat of armed force, Muhammed Bey was forced to sign the Fundamental Pact, or 'ahd al-aman, with the British and French. The pact delineated rights and safeguards for non-Muslims, including the right for foreigners to own property. However, it was only the preamble to a constitution that came into effect on April 24, 1861. A constitutional system was outlined providing for the separation of the executive, legislative, and judicial branches of government as well as for centralized ministries and administration. Again, the regency's population, including most of the elite, resented the changes. However, Muhammed Bey had little choice but to adopt the measures. While little reform was actually brought about, the power of Europeans in Tunis continued to increase.

In 1864, the population of Tunis expressed its displeasure in the form of a revolt supported by nearly all ethnic segments of the population. For three to four months the insurgents displayed remarkable discipline and unity, but eventually the promises of the bey and political intrigues from the bey's court succeeded in undermining the unity of the rebels. As the unity was broken, the bey's government convinced groups, one by one, to lay down their weapons. But the position of the bey was far from secure. Poor harvests plagued Tunis from 1866 to 1870, with a particularly harsh famine and cholera epidemic occurring in 1867. The meager harvests only led Tunis into even greater debt. On July 5, 1869, various European powers, led by Britain and France, oversaw the establishment of the International Financial Commission to supervise the finances of the bey's government and ensure the payment of the foreign debt. A slight revitalization of Tunis occurred from 1873 to 1875 with a bountiful harvest and the oversight of Khayr al-din. Poor harvests again plagued Tunis after 1876, and the state was beset by political instability for the remainder of the decade. The fate of Tunis was sealed in May 1881, when France imposed a protectorate treaty on the Tunisian bey. French troops crossed into Tunis from Algeria.

Tripoli

Tripoli had always had a precarious history. Unlike its neighbors, many of the largest and most powerful cities of Tripolitania were deep in the Sahara. The trans-Saharan trade lasted longer in the Libyan region than anywhere else in North Africa, until about 1911. However, the importance of the desert cities also bred instability for Tripoli because power was divided between the coastal and inland peoples. In the early nineteenth century, the Karamanli dynasty was seriously threatened by two nomadic groups, the Mahamid and the Awlad Sulayman, who resented the extension of Tripoli's power into Tripolitania. Both groups managed to resist the Karamanli dynasty until its collapse in 1835. The dynasty collapsed because of the re-exertion of Ottoman rule over Tripoli. From 1830 to 1835, the

Figure 11-10. Print of Tripoli in the Late Seventeenth Century

Ottoman state gradually sent troops to Tripoli and re-established strict control. In an effort to win over the inhabitants, the Ottoman state granted tax relief and quickly won many Tripolitanians, especially the emerging middle class, to their side.

However, the Ottoman state still needed to deal with the perennial issue of Tripoli's history; how to deal with nomadic groups who wanted independence. An alliance was formed with another nomadic group headed by Tarhuna, who sowed discord between the leaders of the Mahamid and the Awlad Sulayman. The tactic eventually worked, as the Awlad Sulayman were defeated in 1842 and beaten back to the Chadian region. Weakened by famine and the death of their leader Ghuma, the Mahamids submitted in 1858. After the defeat of the Mahamids, the Ottoman presence over all of Tripoli was secured.

After 1860, the Ottoman state began to implement reforms similar to those being introduced in other provinces. The pace at which they were introduced, however, was very cautious. The Tuareg continually challenged the Ottoman state from Ghat and the Fezzan. The Ottomans were also careful not to alienate the middle class whom they depended upon for support. Some of the noteworthy reform measures included the judiciary (1865), local government (1872), administration (1864 and 1875), hospitals (1880), and food distribution centers for emergencies (1870). The middle class benefited from all the programs while the peasantry benefited only from the food distribution centers.

Tripoli, despite the increasing introduction of European goods, managed to maintain a healthy economy throughout the later part of the nineteenth century.

Tripoli's vibrancy began to change in about 1891 with massive food shortages that lasted until 1899. Exports declined while imports expanded, and Tripoli operated from a trade deficit from 1892 onwards. European firms and European influence grew while Ottoman power began to wane. The Sanusiyya brotherhood, which had managed to keep Cyrenaica largely stable, began to decline in power as well. The recently unified Italy had been covetously eyeing Tripoli in the 1880s and had even made plans for war in 1884-1885. A lack of support for Italy's claims from the other colonizing powers led Italy to delay its invasion of Tripoli until 1911. Even then, it was only able to gain control of the coastal areas of Tripoli and Cyrenaica, and not until the 1930s did it gain control of most of what became known as Libya.

Morocco

Morocco was able to hold off European conquest as long as Tripoli for two reasons. First, the European colonizing powers spent much time and energy attempting to outmaneuver each other in Morocco. Morocco's strategic importance in relation to the Straits of Gibraltar caused it to be coveted by all the colonizing powers. No state wished to see Morocco conquered by a rival. This worked in Morocco's favor, as European states were hesitant to conquer it outright and perhaps cause a war with their European rivals. Secondly, Morocco had been undergoing a revitalization program of its own. Under the reigns of Sultan 'Abd al-Rahman (1822-1859), Muhammed IV (1859-1873) and Hasan I (1873-1894), Morocco attempted to bring about greater territorial integrity as well as to thwart colonial conquest.

Part of the way in which the Moroccan government dealt with outside interference was to shut the country off from foreigners. In 1822, only five ports were open to Europeans and trade was carefully supervised. Morocco's relative isolation was to last for three decades until the signing of the 1856 Anglo-Moroccan Treaty, which forced Morocco to open the country to British goods and traders. British influence spread quickly. A recurrent theme of Moroccan history in the late nineteenth century was the constant wars with European powers as they sought to gain an effective sphere of influence that would be recognized by the other nations. Morocco lost a war to Spain in 1892 and was forced to pay a large indemnity. France fought many border wars with Morocco from Algeria and seized In Salah and Touat in 1900. Governmental and military reforms initiated by the Moroccan rulers were not enough to maintain the territorial integrity of Morocco. Europeans continued to conquer bits and pieces of Morocco, and European influence continued to infiltrate the nation. By 1912, the Treaty of Fez had established a French protectorate in Morocco with Spanish influence in the northern zone.

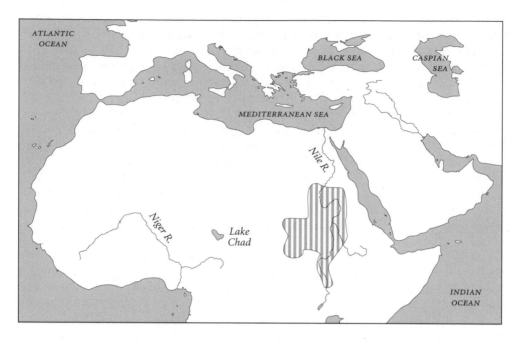

Figure 11-11. The Mahdist State

Answers to Good and Evil:
Religious History in North Africa

Mahdism in the Sudan[12]

Egypt had gained a new ruler in the early nineteenth century by the name of Mohammed Ali, who set Egypt on a course of expansion. Part of that expansion was to the south into the Sudan. Ali's army had been developing an increasing reliance on Sudanese slaves as a source of recruits for the military. The demand for slaves, in conjunction with the desire to stamp out the last of the Mamluk opposition, caused the Egyptians to invade the Funj Sultanate in 1820-1821. While the invading force was only four thousand people strong it was heavily armed with European weapons and artillery. It occupied Dongola and scattered the remainder of the Mamluk opposition. The force moved on to the Funj capital of Sennar, capturing it as well. The city of Khartoum was founded as an administrative capital at the confluence of the White and Blue Niles.

Throughout the nineteenth century, Egypt attempted to extend its control of the Sudan, first on its own accord and after 1882 in conjunction with the British. Their conquests and rule earned them the contempt of many Sudanese. Peoples of the southern Sudan resented the imposition of heavy taxes and the raiding of their people for army conscripts. Muslim traders disliked being ruled by the infidel

---

12. Byron Farwell, *Prisoners of the Mahdi* (New York, Harper & Row, 1967); and H.A. Ibrahim, with a contribution by B.A. Ogot, "The Sudan in the Nineteenth Century," in J.F. Ade Ajayi, ed., *Africa in the Nineteenth Century until the 1880s*, UNESCO General History of Africa, vol. 6 (London: Heinemann, 1989), 356-376.

British and resented British interference in the slave trade, an occupation from which many Muslim families had earned an income for centuries.

Such was the condition of the Sudan in the late nineteenth century. An amalgam of peoples with very little in common had been thrown together through foreign conquest. A foreign administration had been imposed which was part Ottoman, later part British, and resented by many. Into this confusion entered Muhammad Ahmed-ibn-el-Sayed-Abdullah. He was born on Darar, an island in the Nile near Dongola, in 1844, to a carpenter named Sayed Abdullah. However, Sayed Abdullah died before his son was born and the children and their mother were raised by Muhammad Ahmed's uncle, Ahmed Sharif, on the island of Abba, about 125 miles south of Khartoum. Muhammad Ahmed was interested in religion from an early age and attended a Qur'anic school. By the time Muhammad Ahmed reached his early twenties his knowledge of the Qur'an was so extensive and his piety and dedication so immense that he began to attract disciples and earn a reputation among the general populace.

Muhammad Ahmed's home on a Nile River island was a significant factor in his rise to power. At this time the Nile carried the Egyptian, Ottoman, and British boat traffic as well as being the venue for the local exchange of Arab and Sudanese traders. His preaching gained fame throughout the region and many travelers on the Nile stopped to hear him. His piety and asceticism increased as he fasted, fell into trances, and began to describe his visions. He preached a return to the true Islam, free of heresies and based on the teachings of the Qur'an and the Prophet. In order to reach the true Islam and rid it of heresies, many foreign elements, which had been added since the time of the Prophet, would have to be removed. Hence, many interpreted Muhammad Ahmed's message as anti-foreigner. After all, if he believed that foreign elements had polluted the true Islam and must be purged, than purging the foreigners would purify Islam. Muhammad Ahmed preached that the Turks (meaning both Egyptians and Ottomans) were not true believers. The Turk drank wine and oppressed other Muslims, therefore they were not following the true path. It is thought that Muhammad Ahmed was not certain of the political ramifications of this message and preached it purely out of religious devotion. Given the apolitical history of his life until this point, that is likely to be true. But whether he intended it or not, his message did have profound political consequences.

As Muhammad Ahmed's reputation grew, many began to question his legitimacy. After all, it was heretical to think one knew the mind of Allah. How was it that this man knew how to return to the proper Islam? His answer was that he was the Mahdi, the Missing One, the Expected Guide. Predictions said that one of the signs of the Mahdi was that the role would be accepted with reluctance. Since Muhammad Ahmed did not proclaim that he was the Mahdi until later in his life, many interpreted this as an indication that he was indeed the Mahdi. His charisma, asceticism, and knowledge of the Qur'an gave him further legitimacy in the eyes of the Sudanese. In addition, he had a birthmark on his right cheek and a v-shaped aperture between his front teeth. Both were said to be physical signs of the Mahdi. Through these proofs, he gained many disciples who began to spread his message far and wide, and word of his greatness soon began to spread throughout the region.

As the Mahdi's popularity grew, he soon gained the attention of the Egyptian administration in Khartoum. The Egyptian Governor-General, Rauf Pasha, sent his primary assistant, Abu Saud, to talk with Muhammad Ahmed. Not only did Muhammad Ahmed tell Abu Saud that he was the Mahdi, he also told him that he only recognized the authority of Islam and the precepts that had been revealed to him. Abu Said returned to Khartoum, raised an expeditionary force of 120 Egyptian soldiers to capture Muhammad Ahmed, and returned to Abba on August 12, 1881. The Egyptian troops went ashore on Abba straight into an ambush. They were routed and only a few survived. The Mahdi and his followers gathered the captured equipment and celebrated their victory. Word spread like wildfire that someone had successfully defied Egyptian authority.

Muhammad Ahmed had no intention of waiting for the next attack from the Egyptians. Much like the Prophet Muhammad before him, he fled his enemies by performing a *hijra*. Ill equipped and poorly armed, he and his followers traveled down the west bank of the Nile and took up refuge at Jebel Gedir, a mountain in southeastern Kordofan. The Mahdi's popularity continued to grow and many came to Jebel Gedir to join him. The Egyptians sent out several expeditions to crush the rebels. One force of 1400 approached Jebel Gedir in December 1881, but was itself crushed by Mahdist forces. A second force of about 3,500 approached the mountain and was also defeated on June 6, 1882. The Egyptian forces sent against the Mahdi continued to grow in number, but his own support grew at a far faster rate. Local rebellions broke out across the Sudan, many powerful enough to seize local garrisons. The Mahdi declared a jihad against the enemy.

While he was a great religious figure, the Mahdi knew little of administration. He looked to the Qur'an for guidance as to the organization of his followers. He gave them the name of *ansar* (supporters) which was the same name given by the Prophet Mohammed to his supporters in Medina. The *ansar* mimicked the attire of the Mahdi, wearing large white dervish-type shirts with black, red, and yellow patches sewn on. This became the uniform of the Mahdist army illustrating its orientation to the poor and common person. The Mahdi also appointed four khalifas (successors) who served as generals of the army. One of the khalifa was Abdullahi ibn Sayed Muhammad, a long-time follower from a pastoral ethnic group from southern Sudan. Each khalifa was given his own flag and color. In August 1882, the Mahdist army came down from Jebel Gedir and took the offensive. They laid siege to El Obeid, the capital of Kordofan. After a long and ugly siege, El Obeid surrendered on January 19, 1883. The city was looted and the Black Sudanese troops who had fought for the Egyptians were absorbed into the Mahdi's army. The Black Sudanese troops were often the only professional soldiers of the Mahdi's army and proved to be important assets.

The timing of the Mahdist revolt could not have been better. While the troops of the Mahdi were expanding across western Sudan, the British were extending their control of Egypt. British control of Egypt was solidified in 1882. British actions diverted resources from the Egyptians that they could have brought to bear on the Mahdi. In 1883, however, the British began to make plans for the Sudan. While they did not covet the Sudan in the same way as they did Egypt, controlling the Nile and stabilizing the region became appealing to the British. British-led Egyptian troops again began to hunt the Mahdi.

By 1883, few central and northern Sudanese questioned the fact that Muhammad Ahmed was indeed the Mahdi. His military victories, charisma, and religious convictions left little room in their minds for doubt. The Mahdist state continued to expand. Khartoum was captured and British General Charles Gordon killed after a long siege on January 26, 1885. But to the consternation of his followers, Muhammad Ahmed died in June 1885. By the time of the Mahdi's death, the state had been expanded from Darfur to the Red Sea, as far north as the third cataract and as far south as Fashoda. One would have expected such a movement to collapse with the death of its leader. However, Khalifa Abdullahi continued the message of the Mahdi and the policy of the jihad. Abdullahi unified the Mahdi's district administrators behind him, set up an efficient tax system, created a capital at Omdurman and maintained a communications network of camel-mounted couriers. Mahdist administration covered over two-thirds of the area of present-day state of Sudan. Abdullahi continued to fight a war on two fronts against the British/Egyptians in the north and against the Ethiopians in the east and south. Abdullahi's strict adherence to the tenets of Mahdism caused him to refuse an alliance between Ethiopia and the Mahdist state proposed by the Ethiopian emperor. The emperor had hoped a united Ethiopia and Sudan could successfully defeat the encroaching Europeans.

By 1896 the British had made a decision to crush the Mahdist state and conquer the Sudan. Between March and September 1896, Anglo-Egyptian forces under the command of General H.H. Kitchener, possessing superior technology, conquered most of Dongola province, surprising Abdullahi's army. At the battle of Atbara on April 8, 1898, three thousand Mahdist troops were killed and four thousand wounded. While the Mahdist army had been able to defeat the Egyptians when they were distracted by the British, they proved unable to defeat the Anglo-Egyptian forces sent against them, and Anglo-Egyptian victories began to accumulate. Superior military capability again proved decisive at the battle of Karari on September 2, 1898 when eleven thousand Mahdist troops were killed and sixteen thousand wounded. This battle was the deathblow to the Mahdist state and Anglo-Egyptian control of the Sudan was now fairly complete. Abdullahi continued to harass the administration for another year, but was finally defeated at the battle of Umm Diwaykrat. Following the battle, Khalifa Abdullahi was found dead on his prayer rug facing Mecca. Most other Mahdist leaders were either already dead or imprisoned.

A number of important ideas must be noted about Sudanese Mahdism. First, the influence of the Mahdi was never particularly strong in the southern Sudan. Where Islam was not particularly pervasive, Mahdism never gained enough popular support for the Mahdist state to gain official control. Many southern Sudanese joined the Mahdist army and proved to be a huge military asset, but they did it primarily for political reasons and not out of religious conviction. One must be careful not to equate the Mahdist state with that of today's Sudan, as their borders do not coincide. Second, despite the military defeat of the Mahdist state, neither the British nor Egyptians could defeat the idea of Mahdism. Mahdist revolts broke out nearly every year from 1900 to 1914. Even today the effects of Mahdism can be felt in the Sudan. The Mahdiyya brotherhood still exists and gains adherents. The Umma political party, founded by the Mahdi's son, Abd al-Rahman, after World War II, was based on the tenets of Mahdism. The party gained votes in the western Sudan as recently as the 1980s. It is clear that the influence the Mahdi has had on modern Sudanese history is strong, widespread, and very much alive.

Review Questions

1. Was Carthaginian religion a blending of the religions of the Mediterranean basin or a unique development of Carthage itself? Explain the reasons for your choice.
2. What effects did politics have on religion in Carthage? What effects did Rome have on Carthaginian religion?
3. What impact did the trans-Saharan trade have on North and West Africa? How did the introduction of the camel into Africa transform trade in the Sahara?
4. How did the Fatimids differ from other Muslims? What can Fatimid success be attributed to? What was the relationship between the Fatimids and the Berbers?
5. What was the relationship of the Ottoman Empire with its North African provinces?
6. What are the myth and the reality of privateering in the Mediterranean?
7. Why were the Europeans able to conquer North Africa in the nineteenth century?
8. How is Mahdism in the Sudan similar to the Fatimid state?
9. What contributed to the religious success of the Mahdi? What contributed to the military success of the Mahdists?
10. How does the Sudan differ from other parts of North Africa?
11. What was the role of slave troops in North African history? From which regions did the slaves derive?
12. To what degree is it accurate to say that North African history is the history of invaders? Explain the reasons for your response.
13. What was the historical relationship between the North African coastal strip and the inland regions?
14. In what ways has North African history been influenced by other parts of Africa? By Europe? By southwest Asia?

Additional Readings

Abun-Nasr, Jamil M. *A History of the Maghrib in the Islamic Period*. Cambridge: Cambridge University Press, 1987.

Cherry, David. *Frontier and Society in Roman North Africa*. Oxford: Clarendon Press, 1998.

Clancy-Smith, Julia Ann. *Rebel and Saint: Muslim Notable, Popular Protest, Colonial Encounters (Algeria and Tunisia, 1800-1904)*. Berkeley: University of California Press, 1997.

Halm, Heinz. *The Empire of the Mahdi: The Rise of the Fatimids*. Trans. Michael Bonner. New York: E.J. Brill, 1996.

Julien, Charles Andre. *History of North Africa: Tunisia, Algeria, Morocco, From the Arab Conquest to 1830*. London: Routledge,1970.

Lancel, Serge. *Carthage: A History*. Trans. Antonia Nevill. Oxford: Blackwell, 1995.

Morsy, Magali. *North Africa, 1800-1900: A Survey from the Nile Valley to the Atlantic*. London: Longman, 1984.

Chapter 12

Acephalous Societies

Ebere Nwaubani

To a considerable extent, the study of the history of Africa before 1885 is still the study of empires and kingdoms, their rulers and institutions. This has meant the neglect of the many other societies which were not organized in the form of kingdoms or empires. This chapter is intended to draw attention to the political systems of those other Africans. By "political system," I mean the machinery by which political decisions are reached. I begin with a conceptual clarification, to define the political systems I am dealing with here. Such a clarification should be helpful in making the distinction between the societies which were kingdoms and those which were not. I am using the Igbo, one of Nigeria's major ethnic groups, to illustrate the states in the latter category.

The Classification of African Political Systems: An Overview of the Literature

M. Fortes and E. E. Evans-Pritchard dichotomized precolonial African systems. Group A, they said, consisted of "those societies which have centralized authority, administrative machinery, and judicial institutions." Group B consisted of "those societies which lack centralized authority, administrative machinery, and constituted judicial institutions," and which were therefore characterized by "the absence of explicit forms of government." This latter group they also called "stateless societies." The political relevance of the lineage system provided Fortes and Evans-Pritchard with a major dividing line between the two groups. While acknowledging the importance of kinship ties in "the lives of individuals" in both Group A and B-type societies, Fortes and Evans-Pritchard emphasized that in Group-B societies, the segmentary lineage system "primarily regulates political relations between territorial segments."*

Not everyone welcomed the classification proposed by Fortes and Evans-Pritchard and the premise on which it was based. M. G. Smith challenged the restriction of the political relevance of the segmentary lineage to the so-called stateless societies. He pointed out that in any political system, policies were made through a process of competition between segments of the society and decisions

---

* M. Fortes and E.E. Evans-Pritchard, eds., *African Political Systems* (London: Oxford University Press, 1940), 5-6.

were implemented through a hierarchy of administrative roles. In this sense, all political systems, whether centralized or not, had their segmentary and hierarchical dimensions.[1] A more serious criticism centered on the inadequacy of the centralized state/stateless society dichotomy as an analytical tool for all African political systems. Aidan Southall, for example, held that there was another distinct political system, the "segmentary kingdom." This typology, he explained, was characterized by a centralized government with weak control of its constituent units; delegation of authority at the center; and the monopoly of the use of force by the center but not by the periphery.[2] In turn, Paula Brown contended that as far as West Africa was concerned, "finer distinctions are possible" since "not all these [West African] societies can be placed in one or other of these [the two originally proposed] categories." She then outlined four patterns of political authority, which she located in West Africa: one pattern in which authority lay in the kinship groups; a second in which it lay in a combination of kinship groups and associations; a third which combined authority in kinship groups, associations, and centralized state systems; and a fourth in which the centralized state system supplanted extant kinship groups and associations.[3]

Acephalous Political Systems: Definition and Typologies

Many have followed Fortes and Evans-Pritchard in referring to societies which did not have kingdoms as "stateless societies," while others refer to them as noncentralized (or uncentralized) states. According to Western political thought, a "state" means a community which "acquires, with a reasonable probability of permanence an organized government, a defined territory," its own citizenry, and "a reasonable degree of independence of control by any other state."[4] This definition certainly rules out the possibility of considering the political systems of African pastoral communities (for example, the Fulani, the Masai, and the Khoi) as "states," for these peoples hardly occupied a definite territory since they moved about, with their herds, in small bands. But, by the same token, no-one is sure of the precise political geography of many precolonial African empires or kingdoms. Many of these empires and kingdoms also lacked the slightest "probability of permanence," since it was in their nature to give way to stronger state-formations. If the western definition of a state hardly fits the precolonial kingdoms, "stateless" is also an awkward label for the non-centralized societies. And describing them as noncentralized or uncentralized is equally unsatisfactory because these are attempts to define the societies, not on the basis of their own intrinsic values, but in terms of their difference from the centralized political systems. All societies must have governments and governmental structures. Such mechanisms may vary from place to place (and over time as well), leading to vari-

---

1. M.G. Smith, "On Segmentary Lineage Systems," *Journal of the Royal Anthropological Institute*, 86, Part 2 (July-Dec. 1956): 39-80.

2. Aidan W. Southall, *Alur Society* (Cambridge: Cambridge University Press, 1956).

3. Paula Brown, "Patterns of Authority in West Africa," *Africa*, 21, 4 (October 1951): 261-278.

4. J.L. Brierly, *The Law of Nations* (New York: Oxford University Press, 1963), 137.

ations in the distribution of power. As John Middleton and David Tait have pointed out, the major factor which differentiated African political systems is not the relevance of lineages, but "the degree of specialization in roles that enter into political and administrative activities, the number of structural levels at which authority is exercised, and the principle of relationship between political functionary and subjects." They further contend that in the so-called stateless societies there was "no holder of political power at the center, and specialized roles with clearly defined political authority [were] less easy to find."[5] Against this background, a more appropriate descriptive label for such political systems would seem to be "acephalous," which, according to *The New Shorter Oxford English Dictionary*, means "having or recognizing no governing head or chief."

One result of the refinement of the Fortes/Evans-Pritchard classification has been to show that in some of the so-called stateless societies, other agencies, not lineages alone, also provided the basis for the allocation of political authority. Anthropologists have identified three distinct types of acephalous political systems in Africa: (i) those based on segmentary lineages (ii) those based on age-grades or age-classes, and (iii) those in which political authority was exercised by associations.[6] By implication, governing in both (ii) and (iii) was by "a council," which for now, I define as a formal group of people whose membership is limited.

The segmentary lineage system seemed to be the most common variant of the acephalous state category. S.N. Eisenstadt outlined five parameters for distinguishing between kinship-regulated and other patterns of social organization: (i) the extent to which lineages were organized in corporate units within and between which the political activities of the people were coordinated; (ii) the extent to which the lineage was a territorial unit; (iii) the extent to which there existed institutional machinery for the adjustment of inter-lineage quarrels and how far it was incorporated within the kin units; (iv) the extent to which the most important ritual, political, and prestige-bearing offices were vested in members of lineages and kin units; and (v) the extent to which social relations not confined to these corporate groups were, within the limits of the ethnic group, regulated by kinship criteria. Following these criteria, he identifies the Tallensi of Ghana as the "best recorded African example of a segmentary system in which descent units monopolize the social organization, in which the main social positions are allocated to these units or their representatives, and in which the most important social relations are regulated according to kinship criteria and obligations."[7]

Lineages are recruited on the basis of unilineal descent and are therefore defined as "groups of persons claiming genealogical relations unilineally; they may or may not be localized, and may or may not be exogamous units." Descent in this case may be either patrilineal or (as among the Igbo sub-groups of Ohafia and Abiriba) matrilineal; and in some societies (among the Yako, and among the Afikpo, a sub-Igbo group), both types of descent were present concurrently, providing two sets of lineages (patrilineages and matrilineages) to which all persons

---

5. John Middleton and David Tait, eds., *Tribes Without Rulers: Studies in African Segmentary Systems* (London: Routledge & Paul, 1958), 2.

6. Middleton and Tait, eds., *Tribes without Rules*, 2-3; M. Angulu Onwuejeogwu, *The Social Anthropology of Africa: An Introduction* (London, 1975), chap. 10.

7. S.N. Eisenstadt, "African Age Groups: A Comparative Study," *Africa*, 24, 2 (April 1954): 103.

belonged: in their patrilineages, descent and membership were traced through the father, while they were traced through the mother in matrilineages. Thus the phrase "segmentary lineage system" is "properly applied where a society is organized from top to bottom in terms of a single, embracing genealogical scheme, and where this scheme provides the sole or the dominant principle of social organization."[8] The Tiv, the Idoma, the Angas, the Birom, the Igbo, and the Ibibio/Efik, all in Nigeria; the Tallensi of Ghana; the Mandari, the Western Dinka, and the Nuer, all of the Sudan, the Lugbara of the Nile-Congo divide; the Tonga of Zambia, the Langi of Uganda, the pre-nineteenth-century Nguni of southern Africa, are just some of the best known examples of societies in this category.

Anthropologists usually make distinctions between "age-set," "age-class," and "age-grade," and they caution that "age" in this context refers to social rather than chronological or physical age: it was not uncommon for the former to coincide with the latter, but they could also vary widely. "Age-mates are thus not persons who are of the same biological age, but persons who are initiated together, or during the same period, into a social group or a certain type, and that is known in the literature as age-set, age-class or age-grade."[9] I will, however, use "age-grade" as a generic term for "a group of people who by reason of their falling within a limited age span are regarded as constituting a group, which is one of a series of such groups, each of which contains members of the same approximate age and is subordinate to all those of higher age and superordinate to all those of lower age."[10] Examples of acephalous political systems based on age-grades were found mainly in East Africa (as with the Kikuyu and the Nandi, both of Kenya), but I include the Afikpo in this category as well. In these societies, the age-grade system stratified the population according to seniority, and the individual's position within the system constituted an important index of social status. The system was organized in a series of sets conceived as unitary for the whole society. And since membership was universal, age-grades cut across the boundaries of kin groups. Entry into the system, through the formation of a new set (and its association with puberty rites) was based on the ascriptive criterion of age, and was incumbent on every member of the community who reached that stage. The passage of an individual from one status or grade to another was effected by a status change of his set as a whole and was both compulsory and automatic.

The third type of acephalous political system, those in which political authority is vested in associations, does not seem to have been as widespread. In this context, an association is defined as "an organized and corporate group, membership in which does not follow automatically from birth or adoption into a kin or territorial unit." Such an association could be a cult group with ritual sanctions

---

8. Robin Horton, "Stateless Societies in the History of West Africa," in J.F. Ade Ajayi and Michael Crowder, eds., *History of West Africa, Vol. I* (New York: Columbia University Press, 1972), 78.

9. For example, see Andriaan H.J. Prins, *East African Age-Class Systems: Galla-Kipsigis-Kikuyu* (Groningen: J.B. Wolters, 1953), 9-10; Simon Ottenberg, *Leadership and Authority in an African Society: The Afikpo Village-Group* (Seattle: University of Washington Press, 1971), 53.

10. G.I. Jones, "Ibo Age Organization, with Special Reference to the Cross River and North-Eastern Ibo," *Journal of the Royal Anthropological Institute*, 92, Parts 1 and 2 (Jan.-Dec. 1962): 193.

or a secular organization with its own sanctions; it might also combine both attributes. But the association must be able to exercise sanctions over persons and groups who are non-members. This typology has been identified only with the Yako of the Cameroons.

Given the space limitations here, it is not possible to treat these three types at great length. I have therefore chosen to concentrate on the Igbo, for two reasons. First, there is still much confusion about how the Igbo governed themselves in the precolonial period. More often than not, we have had simply generalizations. Many talk of the Igbo having been ruled by "councils of elders" which operated at the village level. And this has had a very serious implication: it has meant that anthropologists have habitually classified the Igbo under those acephalous political systems where political power was vested in village "councils." On the basis of those generalizations, Brown, for example, wrote that Igbo government "was exercised mainly by a loosely constituted *council* whose personnel included kin- group heads, elders, other notables and, in some places, members of title societies."[11] While some Igbo were certainly governed by one type of "council" or the other, most were not. As Simon Ottenberg has aptly observed, "One of the intriguing features of traditional Igbo society is its organizational complexity."[12] A major purpose here is to demonstrate and explain this complexity. And this leads to the second reason: given its complexity, Igbo political organization occurred in sufficient diverse forms to furnish us with examples of all three types of acephalous political system outlined above—that is: (i) those based on segmentary lineages, (ii) those based on age-grades, and (iii) those in which political authority was exercised by associations.

Igbo Political Systems

Like most others in the southern part of West Africa, the Igbo language was classified by Joseph Greenberg as a member of the Kwa sub-family of languages. Linguists have located the region of the Niger-Benue confluence as the original homeland of the ethnic groups in the sub-family. Using glottochronological evidence generated by Robert Armstrong which suggests that the members of the Kwa sub-family started separating from its ancestral stock between five and six thousand years ago, Adiele Afigbo posits that the "upper limit for the emergence of the Igbo as a distinct people with a characteristic language is about 6,000 years ago."[13] Today, the Igbo culture area is in southeastern Nigeria. M. A. Onwuejeogwu defines a culture area as "a geographical delimitation of areas that have the same dominant and significant culture traits, complexes and patterns." The Igbo culture area, according to him, thus encloses an area in which the people not

---

11. Brown, "Patterns of Authority in West Africa," 268. Also see, Middleton and Tait, eds., *Tribes without Rulers*, 3; Eisenstadt, "African Age Groups," 100; Audrey Richards and Adam Kuper, eds., *Councils in Action* (Cambridge: Cambridge University Press, 1971), especially the contribution by G.I. Jones, "Councils among the Central Ibo."

12. Ottenberg, *Leadership and Authority in an African Society*, xiii. (The emphasis is mine).

13. A.E. Afigbo, "Prolegomena to the Study of the Culture History of the Igbo-Speaking Peoples of Nigeria," in B.K. Swartz, Jr., and Raymond E. Dumett, eds., *West African Culture Dynamics: Archaeological and Historical Perspectives* (New York: Mouton, 1980), 311.

only speak the various dialects of the Igbo language but also share significant culture traits and patterns up to or above fifty percent.

In place of large political units, states or empires, precolonial Igbo society was organized around hundreds of villages and village-groups. Although they had some commercial and social interaction, each of the units had its own government and thus constituted a relatively independent social and political unit. There are qualifications to this generalization, for it is now accepted that the social diversities among the Igbo also translated into differing political systems. Afigbo has identified four systems, ranging from the Okigwe, Orlu, and Owerri regions where politics was based on kinship or lineage networks; to the Onitsha, Awka, and Nsukka regions where title-societies were the medium of political participation; to the Ohuhu (Umuahia) and Ngwa regions where government was shared by lineage-based structures and title-societies. In Afigbo's type four, found among

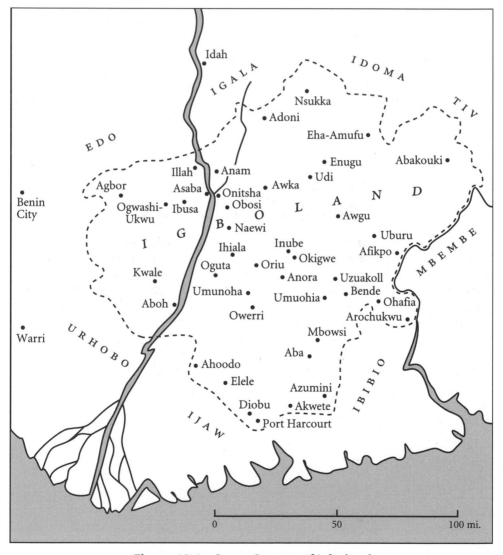

Figure 12-1. Some Centers of Igboland

the northeastern and Cross River Igbo, "the business of government was met largely by a combination of the kinship and age-set systems."[14] Similarly, Onwuejeogwu has identified nine sub-types of precolonial Igbo political organization: these, he fits into three broad categories, centralized democracies, middle range republics, and noncentralized democracies.[15] It is not necessary here to examine these categories, for they seem to differ from Afigbo's only in detail not substance. Both agree that "centralized democracies" obtained only among the Igbo west of the Niger and in the Onitsha-Awka areas, although Afigbo insists — correctly — that the "monarchies" in these areas "were in fact largely the highest titles in the communities."[16]

The Igbo had not one, but several political systems. But as I have already indicated, all the systems can be subsumed within the three distinct acephalous types, namely, those based on segmentary lineages, those based on age-grades, and those based on associations. Among the Igbo, one can identify three variants of the segmentary lineage system: (i) classical segmentary lineage system, (ii) segmentary monarchies (a terminology I am borrowing from Southall, but which I use differently), and (iii) segmentary council systems. In spite of their structural differences, these systems had a common denominator: lineage or kinship principles constituted a key feature in the recruitment of political participants. This explains my contention that all three types are variants of the segmentary lineage system. One obvious deduction arising from this is that the segmentary lineage system expressed itself in a number of sub-systems or variants.

The Segmentary Lineage System and Its Variants

The first step in understanding this system is to undertake a brief exploration of the Igbo lineage or kinship system. The boundaries of Igbo kinship relations were very fluid. As a result, a concept such as umunna ("children of the father") defined such relationships in the most restricted as well as in the widest sense, ranging from step-siblings, to the patrilineal circle within which there can be no intermarriage, to the entire village, depending on the circumstances. In spite of this vagueness, an umunna was a unilineal descent group in the sense that its members were agnatically related to each other and shared certain rights and responsibilities which could only be transmitted patrilineally. This meant that with the notable exception of the Ohafia-Abiriba matrineal communities, the Igbo kinship structure was a network of internally segmented descent groups or patrilineages, the lines of internal differentiation being genealogically determined. In this sense, an Igbo village was a big extended patrilineal family embracing all the agnatic descendants of a certain, initial nuclear family, usually the man who

---

14. A.E. Afigbo, "The Indigenous Political Systems of the Igbo," *Tarikh* 4, 2 (1973): 12-23.

15. M.A. Onwuejeogwu, "Evolutionary Trends in the History of the Development of the Igbo Civilization in the Culture Theatre of Igboland in Southern Nigeria," *Ahiajoku Lecture* (Owerri, 1987).

16. Afigbo, "Indigenous Political Systems of the Igbo."

founded the village, and whose sons, grandsons and great grandsons founded the constituent segments. Expressed according to the well-known order of segmentation in lineages, it can be said that the Igbo kinship network operated at four levels: (i) the minimal segment (the single, immediate extended family unit); (ii) the minor segment (a sub-lineage or the higher extended family unit) consisting of related minimal segments; (iii) the major segment (a lineage consisting of a combination of related minor segments); and (iv) the maximal segment (usually, the village, a combination of related major segments).

Each village was thus made up of lineages (major segments). A lineage (the major segment) was, in turn, made up of minor segments (sub-lineages), and a minor segment roughly consisted of the descendants of one man to the fourth or even the sixth generations. (Generally, the exogamous degree of the units was not standardized.) So essentially, each minor segment was composed of families, the heads of which were "brothers," that is, brothers, step- (or half) brothers and cousins. Each minimal segment consisted of a living patriarch (the head of the family), his wives, their children (and daughters-in-law and grandchildren); this may also have included the patriarch's mother, his step-mother(s), his brothers and half brothers and their own families.

In many parts of the Igbo culture area, the village was an exogamous unit. The north-eastern Igbo (Ezza, Ikwo, Izi, and Ngbo) lineage segments, including people of the same minimal segment, lived in dispersed settlements; but in other parts of the Igbo culture area, the village was a localized territorial unit. The constituent segments were, however, differentiated within this territory along the lines of lineage segmentation. Above all, the village was the highest and widest political unit, and therefore the jural community. Usually, too, each village recognized one lineage as the senior, by virtue of its founder being the eldest son of the village's founder. Thus lineages were ranked, with the last being the descendants of the most junior of the lineage founders.

With an increase in population, the minimal segment became a minor segment, and the minor segment became a major segment, but the strict adherence to descent ties ensured that, even with increasing consanguity, these new segments remained nonexogamous units. By the same process of fission, the maximal segment itself could also give rise to an entirely new maximal segment. But as Fortes has concluded following his study of the Tallensi, "A maximal lineage is fixed with reference to its founding ancestor."[17] Over a series of contiguous maximal segments, the widest local units which considered themselves roughly congruent, in the sense of sharing the same ancestor, were normally what anthropologists call the "village-group." Thus patrilineally-related villages (as in the Ngwa sub-group) federated and confederated to form village-groups.

Armed with this overview, I now explore how the Igbo kinship system found expression in the three variants of the segmentary lineage political system which I have identified.

---

17. M. Fortes, *Dynamics of Clanship among the Tallensi* (London, 1945), 33.

Classical Segmentary Lineage System

In this type of system, lineage segments provided the main basis for social organization, so the most important social relations were regulated according to kinship criteria and obligations. Age-grades and associations (such as title-societies), where they existed in these areas, were too weak for the purposes of any serious social and political organization. As a result, the political system here was characterized by deep-seated egalitarian and republican ideologies.

Each descent group (ranging from the minor segment to the maximal segment) operated as an internally autonomous unit. This statement has two implications: (i) at every level of segmentation, the resulting kinship group had a coordinate status with its equivalents in the wider group, and (ii) at every level of segmentation, each descent group had near-total authority over its own internal affairs. But the kinship groups combined with others in the wider group to regulate matters of mutual concern. Sovereignty was therefore pluralistic since it was located at several centers and in several (political) groups of coordinate status. This meant that these centers and groups were usually interlocked and functionally differentiated; integrated, yet not coordinated by an overall authority. The resulting political system lacked rulers, relying instead on a variety of leaders. Some of these held "offices" which were ascriptively filled, as with the heads of the minor and major segments, who were usually the oldest men in their social units. Otherwise, leadership was achieved by personal talent. Indeed, the Igbo placed a great premium on achieved status, for according to one of their proverbs, "if a child washes his hands clean, he eats with the elders." Thus some men attained leadership positions in their communities through their skill in oratory, as well as distinction in battle, wrestling, farming, and trading. In general, there was always the possibility of social mobility for the industrious. Perhaps this high degree of social mobility stemmed from the pronounced fluidity of the sociopolitical system: since there was no entrenched political class, the top was open to anyone who tried hard enough.

As in all societies, wealth certainly conferred power and influence. Thus, an individual of exceptional wealth and personality may have wielded some influence, or even authority, in the village. But, with each descent unit having a coordinate (and therefore politically equivalent) status, no-one was prepared to become a subordinate of the other. This meant that there was hardly room for an individual to claim executive authority outside his own minimal and minor segments. So, in the final analysis, the maximal segment was governed by the whole body of the people, through a participatory process. While political initiative may have resided with the elders and others of influence, the consensus of the opinion of everyone was paramount.

This type is the archetypal classical segmentary lineage political system. It was found in the southern and central sections of the Igbo culture area, from Oji River to parts of the Nsukka area, through the Agbaja (including Udi and Awgu) and the Ihiala-Uli-Oba-Ogidi areas, to the Orlu (including Ideato, Oru, and Ohaji-Egbema), Okigwe (including Etiti and Mbano), and Owerri (including Mbaise, Mbaitoli, Ikeduru, and Okpala) areas, as well as the Ikwere-Etche, Ukwa, Ngwa (Aba), Ohuhu-Ibeku, and Bende areas.

In those parts of the Igbo culture area categorized under this typology, the major segment was the principal social and administrative unit. Economically, it was also the basic unit for land ownership. The kinship network expressed itself conspicuously in the recognition of a "headship" position at the levels of the minor and major segments. This position fell to the senior male member of the descent group, who was succeeded, when he died, by the man of the same generation who was next in seniority, and when that generation was exhausted, by the oldest man of the next generation. Depending on the dialectical area, this headship position was known by various names: okpara, opara, okwara, or onye isi.

It seems that it was only at the level of the minimal segment that the patriarch could secure ready obedience from others (that is, the other members of the minimal segment). Beyond this, the headship of a segment therefore carried no special political weight distinct from that of the heads of the other minimal segments in the minor or major segment. Thus, no head of the minor or major segments could take any action in connection with the common welfare without the full support and consent of the adult males in all the lineages. Issues affecting a minor or major segment were discussed and decided at meetings of all adult (invariably) males (or married women in the descent group, if it was an issue in which the women had an interest). Such meetings of the men were usually held in the compound of the segment's head; although he presided, he had to argue his own point of view along with others until a decision was reached. At the end of the meeting, he served as the spokesman for the decisions reached.

At the level of the maximal lineage, two broad types of "office holders" can be discerned: the traditional or natural office holders and the nontraditional office holders. Those in the first category were ascribed (notably, the heads of the various segments); the other category consisted of those who had achieved fame and influence in the community. It seems that the most influential elements of these two groups convened meetings of the entire maximal lineage. The oldest male in the most senior major segment was, in some cases, the village's chief priest, the guardian of its worshiping grounds or sacred groves. But it was a position which conferred no special political leverage, especially if the man had no personal achievements to his credit.

As with the minor and major segments, decisions at the level of the maximal segment were derived from mass meetings of freeborn adult males: any of them who so desired was free to attend. And each person who so desired was also given ample opportunity to contribute to the discussions: useless contributions were jeered at with occasional and embarrassing shouts of "keep quiet," or "sit down"; useful contributions were welcomed with occasional claps, cheers, and shouts of "your speech is good." Such reactions helped to shape opinion and decide the issue. Political direction and initiative at such meetings was provided by the more assertive elderly men, the titled, the wealthy, and the orators: after a fairly exhaustive discussion of an issue, they retired into a caucus (igba izu), where a decision was taken. Victor Uchendu says "The right to participate in izuzu is a greatly cherished and respected one and is restricted to men of weight and prestige, men who have wisdom to understand and appreciate all schools of thought and achieve a compromise" which the assembly can accept.[18] On reaching an agreement, the caucus rejoined the rest of the assembly and its decision was put across by a spokesman chosen for his oratory, his persuasive talents, his abil-

---

18. Uchendu, *The Igbo of Southeast Nigeria*, 41.

ity to put issues in their proper perspective, and his ability to use captivating proverbs and idiomatic expressions. The decision was either accepted with general applause or rejected with jeers and protests. In the latter case, the caucus had to retire again, taking into account the grounds of protest against their earlier decision. In some cases, the village oracle might be consulted to ascertain the wishes of the metaphysical world.

Decisions reached at the meetings were sealed up and sanctified through ritual binders which involved the invocation of the ofo and Ala (Ani), the Earth Deity.[19] The binders took the form of invocations such as: "Anyone who violates this decision, may this ofo kill him, may the ancestors remove him, may Ala punish him." At each invocation, the ofo would be struck on the ground and everyone present would respond in affirmation.

It is thus clear that virtually all the adult males were involved in the political process. It is equally clear that although the opinion of the elders and the wealthy carried special weight in the deliberations, the collective will of the people, their consensus, was paramount. Among a people without any institutionalized coercive apparatus (police, courts, or prisons), the consensual approach was the only viable means of securing voluntary adherence to decisions.

The village assembly or meeting was not an elaborate, rigidly formalized instrument of government. True, the assembly appropriated all governmental roles, legislative, judicial (including powers of arrest, fines, seizure of property, and other sentences), executive and administrative, and was the highest forum for political action. But it was an ad hoc body which did not meet at regular intervals: meetings arose when demanded for a specific reason, usually issues which were of common concern to the entire village and so beyond the scope and capacity of any lineage; and it seems that such meetings were convened by those who had an interest in the matter at hand, with the support of men of influence in the village. Any freeborn adult male was free to attend or absent himself, so the village assembly was not a select body. Nor did sovereignty reside exclusively with the village assembly. As Uchendu has pointed out, "The village, whether its members are assembled after a funeral rite, a path clearing, or for some other purpose, is an all-purpose governmental machinery."[20] There were thus many organized centers of power and social action. These included, for example, meetings of the village and its constituent segments, including fraternities and guilds (such as those of titled men and medical practitioners), masquerades, and women's organizations, each of which gave different forms of political weight to different sections of the society. The married women in a segment had their own gatherings separate from those of the men, and these were primarily concerned with issues which affected women. Such issues included settling disputes between women as well as disputes between women and others, including their husbands. There were also the umuada (the married daughters of a minor, major or even maximal segment),

---

19. The most concrete representation of the ancestors is the *ofo*, a sacred stick. This stick is part of the *ofo* (Deterium *senegalence*) tree, which the Igbo believe was set aside by God as a symbol and guarantee of truth, and therefore justice. In Igbo cosmology, *Ala*, a female deity (also known as the "Earth Goddess") is in charge of all the land on which humans live, build, farm, and are buried. Apart from being the source of fertility in women, animals, and crops, she is also the guardian of morality and justice.

20. Uchendu, *The Igbo of Southeast Nigeria*, 42.

who acted as a strong pressure group in their segment. They were especially active as peacemakers, intervening to sort out issues which had become intractable, and their decisions were usually taken as final.

The emergence of the okonko, the ekpe, and the ozo title-societies in the southern and central sections of the Igbo area in the late eighteenth and early nineteenth centuries created a new dimension in the political system. These were wealthy men's clubs: membership was open to all freeborn adult males who could fund the elaborate and expensive initiation ceremonies. Membership of these societies certainly secured for an individual a privileged social and political status in the community. But the title-holders appear to have acted less toward creating alternative centers of authority; rather, they "generally acted to support established authority by restraining the fissiparous tendencies of lineage organization."[21] The okonko, for example, adjudicated over disputes, investigated crimes, and imposed punishments. But it never superseded the village assembly: cases involving murder and witchcraft, for example, were beyond its competence and handled only by the village assembly.

In this typology, one cannot talk of any meaningful governmental machinery beyond the village level. Generally, group solidarity beyond the village level was propped up by rituals and common history (common descent, migrations, and early settlement).

To sum up: in the classical segmentary lineage system, power was not vested in any one individual or group of individuals (or at least, any obviously perceptible group of individuals). At the same time, the wielding of authority as a specialized, full-time occupation was virtually unknown. Sovereignty was divisible, as there were many organized centers of power. Community decisions were made and disputes settled in a variety of ways and gatherings: at family, lineage and village assemblies, title-societies, and congregations at ceremonies, as well as by oracles and diviners. Politics was, therefore, diffusionary in nature, drawing into its network the masses of the people through formal and informal structures which allowed sufficient scope for the determination and expression of political opinion by the individual rather than a council of any sort.

Segmentary Monarchies

This type of system exhibited some of the basic features of a centralized political system: there was an easily identifiable head of the political system, some concentration and institutionalization of authority, and specialized roles in the exercise of political power. But in this system, the king was only one of several complementary, if not competing, sources of power, giving rise to a phenomenon captured by Richard Henderson's "the king in every man" label for the Onitsha system. After a close study of the Onitsha system, C. K. Meek remarked that its obi (monarch) "was not so much a king as the president of a bureaucratic society."[22] The other key feature of this system was the relevance of lineages in social organization. With reference to Onitsha, Henderson observed that "kinship values and norms pervade this society, and a procedure that systematically analyzes

---

21. Northrup, *Trade without Rulers*, 108.
22. C.K. Meek, *Law and Authority in a Nigerian Tribe* (Oxford University Press, 1937), 189.

Onitsha kinship will not fail very far short of encompassing the society as a whole."[23] According to Meek, the Onitsha monarchy is "confined" to two lineages, the Umuezearole and the Umudei.[24] I am borrowing Southall's terminology to describe the Igbo segmentary monarchies best represented by Onitsha, and perhaps also the more diffused Igbo monarchical states west of the Niger (such as Aboh and Agbor), as well as Oguta.

Onitsha

At the apex of the Onitsha political system was the obi (monarch) who was well-screened by elaborate rituals and taboos. For example, he lived secluded in his palace, from which he emerged on very rare occasions such as the annual ofala festival. But the king's palace was the hub of Onitsha political and social life; not only did the king himself handle cases involving murder and abominations, he also served as the appellate court of Onitsha; and the palace was also the venue for meetings which dealt with issues affecting the entire society. Beyond these functions, the obi depended on his chiefs, the ndichie, for the administration of the state. The ndichie consisted of three grades: an inner core, the ndichie ume, and two others, the ndichie okwa and the ndichie okwaraeze. The ume consisted of six chiefs, while the others consisted of thirty chiefs each. The ndichie ume functioned as the executive council: they were responsible for the formulation and execution of state policies as well as reacting to emergency situations; the ndichie okwaraeze served as a court of appeal for cases from the villages. The three ndichie grades combined, acted as the state working committee: they took decisions about war, concluded treaties and peace, fixed dates for the major festivals, and made the arrangements for such festivals. A general assembly of the representatives of all Onitsha patrilineages was the state's supreme policy-making organ; this assembly was usually convened when the obi and the ndichie felt that an issue required such a weighty attention.

One was nominated for an ndichie position by the obi, and the nomination had to be ratified by the incumbent ndichie chiefs. Like the monarchy itself, the ndichie offices were tied to the ascriptive base of specific descent group membership. This was of great significance because the use of lineages as units with hereditary rights to political positions constitutes a strong antidote for monarchical autocracy. And the fact that, once appointed, the ndichie could not be removed from office by the obi, further confirmed them as effective counterweights to the obi.

There was a female council of titled women, the otu ogene, which had the omu as its leader. This council was part of a wider organization which was open to all who were or had been married. Members of the otu ogene had title names which were identical to those of the ndichie. The obi had formal channels of communication with the women's council: one of his junior chiefs served as their representative to the king and his council, but they represented themselves in any matter which affected them directly.

The omu had to be the head daughter of her segment of the royal lineage, and her councillors had to be the head daughters of their village units as well. In addition, the positions of the omu and her councillors were wealthy women's titles; so

---

23. Richard N. Henderson, *The King in Every Man: Evolutionary Trends in Onitsha Ibo Society and Culture* (New Haven: Yale University Press, 1972), 105.

24. Meek, *Law and Authority in a Nigerian Tribe*, 185.

the omu for example, could only be "secured after a prodigious expenditure of money, hence but few could aspire to it."[25] The omu had so much influence that European traders who did business in Onitsha in the nineteenth century referred to her as the "queen of Onitsha." The extent of her authority was described by one missionary:

> It is not a merely honorary title, but carries with its own duties and responsibilities. The Omu is the Fountain of all honor to the women, as the Eze [Obi], or king, is the Fountain of honor to the men in the country. She has the absolute control of the trade in which the women are engaged, and can stop and open [the market] as occasion requires. No important law affecting the rights and liberties of her sex could be passed by the king and chiefs in council without being first communicated to her and her chief women... for their approval.[26]

In spite of her undoubted influence, the omu was not the female equivalent of the obi. Although she had precedence over the ndichie, the omu was subordinate to the obi. Her appointment followed the same procedure as with the ndichie, nominated by the obi and ratified by the ndichie. Like the ndichie, she held her position for life. On her installation, it was the obi who handed her ofo omu; and whenever she came before the obi, she had to bow down. Finally, the omu and her councillors each paid annual tributes to the obi.[27]

Oguta

In most other Igbo societies with "monarchical" systems, there was even less concentration of power than in Onitsha. In most cases, the king's role was limited by the actual structure of government: he could hardly take any independent action on any matter. Oguta is a very good example of this. The monarch in Oguta was known as the obi. Next in the hierarchy was the iyasara, and ten other titleholders who constituted the ndichie. In addition to these, there were two other colleges of titled men, the oririnzere and the ndi okpara. The latter were the heads of the lineages in Oguta. As in Onitsha, each ndichie title was invested in a specific lineage. Ikenna Nzimiro says, "The office of obi and of the kingly officials are acquired ones open to any person of wealth and influence with the right qualifications of ward [lineage] and agbanta membership."[28] Since any man of age who could pay the required fees and was eligible for the title could take it, a number of men were installed as obi at any investiture cycle. Usually, the oldest among the candidates was also the first to complete the installation ceremonies; with that he became the "first among equals," that is the true obi of Oguta, and the rest were ranked as oririnzere. When he died, and after his eldest son had served as regent for the three years the deceased's funeral ceremonies lasted, the obi next in seniority (in terms of age) acceded to the position. This succession pattern was

---

25. Elizabeth Isichei, *Igbo Worlds* (Macmillan, 1977), 139.

26. Johnson's Report 1884, *Church Missionary Intelligencer* (London: Seeley, Jackson, and Halliday, 1885).

27. Henderson, *The King in Every Man*, 294, 309-314.

28. Nzimiro, *Studies in Ibo Political Systems*, 67. Agbanta refers to membership of the ikwa muo society, see ibid., 56.

maintained until all the obi in the set had died. As soon as the eldest son of the last obi in the set completed his regency, a new college of obi was installed. This procedure also applied to the iyasara and the other ndichie. There could, at any time, be seven men with the title iyasara since there were seven minor segments with hereditary rights to the title.

The Oguta regarded their obi as "the highest being" on earth, hence he was also known as *eze igwe* ("king of heaven"). Except for the iyasara, any one who came before the obi bowed as a mark of respect. The obi's court was the appellate court for the courts of all other officials, and he had exclusive jurisdiction in cases of homicide. Beyond these responsibilities, there was hardly any room for independent political action by the obi. The military commander (the ndanike) could wage war on his own if he so desired. The *obieze*, analogous to the village assembly of the classical segmentary lineage system, was the highest legislative and policy-making body. Although the *obieze* was held in his palace, the obi "has no say in the deliberations. He is a silent on-looker." The *obieze* was usually directed by the ogana, one of the *ndichie*.[29] Indeed, the obi shared with the *ndichie* the prerogatives which set him apart from the rest of the society.

On the whole, Igbo monarchies lacked the political weight and latitude of the neighboring oba of Benin. In the nineteenth century, Bishop Samuel Adjai Crowther's contact with the Igbo was confined to those located along the Niger waterway, and therefore to areas such as Aboh, Agbor, and Onitsha which had the most pronounced representations of the monarchy in the Igbo culture area. Yet Crowther reached the conclusion that, "One common disadvantage which characterizes the Ibo country is, want of a king, who is supreme head of the nation...as in Yoruba, Benin, Nupe and Hausa."[30]

Segmentary Council Systems

I define a council as an exclusive club, a formal assembly or group of people whose membership was limited. More often than not, this limitation was because membership was based on unique and rigorous entry qualifications, followed by an elaborate (often ritualistic and expensive) initiation. In addition, the conduct of the members was governed by a series of rules and conventions. In this sense, a council was unlike a village assembly since the latter was an open mass meeting, without any elaborate membership requirements. Government by a council differed from the monarchical systems of Onitsha and Oguta because there was no one person who served as the constitutional symbol of communal authority. Government in the classical segmentary lineage system was by direct, participatory democracy; on the other hand, government by a council meant government by some people acting as a group, whether as an age-grade (as among some Cross River Igbo communities such as Edda, and some northeastern Igbo communities such as Izi, Ezza, Ikwo, and Ngbo, and in some western Igbo communities such as Asaba and Osomari) or a title-society/association (as among the Nri, Nsukka, and Nsugbe) or lineage heads (as in Arochukwu and Nnewi),

---

29. "Memorandum submitted by the Oguta Town Council."
30. Church Missionary Society (CMS) Archives, London: CA3/04(a), Charge at Onitsha, 13 October 1874; also CMS G3/A3/0, Crowther's Report of the Niger Mission, 1880.

Edda

As has earlier been pointed out, age-grades were structurally differentiated from descent groups on the ground that the former operated outside the framework of the latter. But in this system, the two were very closely aligned. Among the Edda, for example, the title eze ogo was used for the head of the village, who was the oldest man in the active senior age-grade of the most senior major segment. This was also applied at the village-group level. Ngusu was Edda's most senior village as it was their primary settlement point. Thus Ngusu's eze ogo was automatically Eze Edda. Matters of mutual interest to all Edda were decided by a council consisting of all the village heads, with Eze Edda presiding. Cases involving murder in any Edda village could only be decided by that council. Political authority in Izi lay with members of the most senior age-grade (ndi uke), who constituted themselves into a council. All the elders in each set of ndi uke were installed at the same ceremony. (One important qualification was that each of the elders must have made the title of isi nze before the installation.) Not until death had reduced their number to the point of political insignificance was a new set installed. At the installation ceremony, the head of each minimal segment was recognized as an "elder" (onye uke), and two of these became ndi isi uke ("heads of the council of elders"). Of the two, one became the secular head of the village, the other became the chief priest. These two positions were specifically reserved for two patrilineages.

Nsukka

By the eighteenth century, Igala had established its influence on parts of the northern Igbo community of Nsukka. Indeed, in August 1866, Samuel Crowther found that Igala still had considerable influence in the Nsukka area. The Nsukka villages which came under this influence were known as Igbo Omabe;[31] those which did not were known as Igbodo. The political system of the latter was of the classical segmentary lineage type. Among the Igbo Omabe, government was in the hands of titled men. Generally, titles in Nsukka were graded into greater (asogwa) and lesser (ndishi iwu) categories. The lesser titles were recognized only within the village. Each major segment in the village had a right to a particular asogwa title. Such a title carried with it the headship of the segment, and if the segment was the senior one, the headship of the village as well. A number of persons in the segment could make the title together, with the oldest among them being recognized as their head, and the others ranked after him according to age. This ensured that the oldest man in the major segment had the prior right to take the title; but if he could not, then it passed to the next oldest man who could afford it. It was usual for a segment to recognize its oldest man who could not take the title as its head for internal affairs, and its most senior titled man as its head or chief representative in external affairs. The title-holders in a village served as delegates of their respective descent groups at their meetings. The village assembly consisted of the lineage heads, titled men, and old men; it was presided over by the senior eze in the village (who would invariably be a lineage head himself).

In the Nsukka area, the word eze did not mean "king"; it was, instead, the highest title available, often, at the village-group level, and it was open to any

---

31. These are Orba, Opi, Eha Alumona, Obollo, Obukpa, and Edem Ani.

man who could afford it (provided he already belonged to his village's asogwa). There was thus more than one eze in the village-group at any given point in time. The eze title-holders constituted the oha, the ruling council of the village-group, with the senior eze from the senior village serving as the head of the village-group.

Arochukwu

Arochukwu was a village-group consisting of nineteen villages which were derived from nine patrilineages (otusi). Each of the villages had its own head (also known as otusi) who was the oldest man from the most senior major segment. He convened the village assembly which operated along the lines of similar assemblies in the classical segmentary lineage system. The operational units at the village-group level were the nine patrilineages. The oldest male tracing his patrilineal descent from Okenachi (the senior lineage in the senior village of Arochukwu) was (and still is) considered no matter his age to be senior otusi of all Arochukwu and therefore the Eze Aro (paramount head of Aro). Matters of common interest to all the Aro were discussed in an assembly in which all the villages were represented by their heads, with the Eze Aro presiding.

Government by Age-Grades

It seems that in all of the Igbo culture area, it was in Afikpo that the age-grade system was most highly developed. Afikpo was a village-group comprised of twenty-two villages. As among other Igbo, kinship principles maintained a strong presence in Afikpo According to Ottenberg, "Afikpo life cannot be understood without reference to the relationship of double descent which pervades the whole society...every person is a member of both patrilineal and matrilineal groupings."[32] But the kinship system was not a factor in the political system, certainly not at the village level. Government was the responsibility of those in the age-grade of the elders. Thus, although the elders' group was mainly composed of the senior members of the major patrilineages of the village, each person was there on his own merit: there was no system of representation for the descent groups (patrilineages and matrilineages) at the village level.

A man's position and duties in the village were determined by his status in the age-grade organization. Thus a thirty-five-year old man who did not participate in the initiation rites of his age-mates would still be subject to the more arduous village communal labor along with boys and young men whose sets had not yet formed. Once they reached about fifteen years of age, the boys in a village were constituted into an age-grade, which covered those born within a three-year span. Although they could seek the guidance of the elders on these matters, the age-grade itself ultimately determined its name, its internal organization, and its rules. Each age-grade kept its name and organization throughout the life of its members, but its status and duties in the village changed as its members grew older. From the time of its formation, the age-grade joined other age-grades in coopera-

---

34. Ottenberg, *Leadership and Authority in an African Society*, 8.

tive village activities; in such contexts, an age-grade acted as a unit within a larger village structure.

Authority within the descent groups below the village level was exercised by the elders of such groups. Otherwise, governmental authority was exercised by the age-grades of the elders: they had the final authority over village matters, including "the ultimate right to legislate and to administer the important rituals and feasts of the community." They also controlled the village property: farmlands, roads, streams, bridges, sacred grounds, and cemeteries. And if the village was beset by an epidemic, a crop failure, or any other natural disaster, it was the responsibility of the elders to seek appropriate remedies (first consulting a diviner). Their judicial functions included trying those who did not participate in communal work and those who had misused village property. Some meetings of these age-grades, especially those which had to do with village matters, were open to all adult men (and women, if a matter concerning them was to be discussed). Anyone in attendance could be invited to speak, but only the views of the members of the age-grades of the elders were taken into any serious account. This group was assisted by the age-grades of those in the thirty-five to forty-five-year-old age range; these saw to it that the decisions and orders of the elders' age-grades were implemented, and they also performed a number of other functions such as organizing labor for communal work and supervising the work of the age-grades of the younger men. For convenience, the elders were those who were at least fifty years old, but did not include the very elderly. In practice, however, the determination of who became a village elder was "based on the simultaneous joining together and upward movement of sets from the different villages in the village-group to form village-group grades." This arrangement ensured that the authority of the elders also covered the entire authority-group.[33]

Government By Associations

There were a few Igbo communities, of which Nri (with its highly developed ozo title- system) provides the best example, where political authority gradually shifted from institutions defined by age and kinship to those defined by wealth. The wealthy more or less monopolized political power through their membership of a title-society. Title-societies had other interests, but given that they counted as their members all the men of any serious standing in the community, the societies also achieved clear precedence over all other institutions. The result was that while the stress on wealth could be expressed in different ways, the starting-point was the purchase of a title.

It has been suggested that the ozo title-holders constituted the largest number of title- holders in the Igbo culture area. It was in Nri that the ozo title-society attained its clearest articulation. Indeed, it is believed that the society originated among Nri priests. From Nri, the society spread to the northern sections of the Igbo area, gaining some importance in the Onitsha-Awka axis. In Nri, the ozo society was organized as a series of eight hierarchical grades; consequently, member-

---

33. Ibid., especially 69, 89-90, 96-101, 71.

ship required an ascending order of rituals and fees. But it was only after one had made the sixth grade of the hierarchy that one was finally entitled to be called nze or ozo, and this marked the person's final transition to a status higher than that of other humans. A nze or ozo enjoyed many privileges such as exemption from assault; but at the same time, he was hemmed in by a maze of moral obligations which required him to live above the hustling of everyday life. Thus one could not be an ozo and continue to be a trader. Of greater importance, an ozo was expected to be honest; thus he had to wear a bell which jingled as he moved about, as an indication that he could not hide or do anything in secret.

Any freeborn male could take the ozo title, provided he had adult sons of his own, and his father (and elder brothers, if any) had taken the title themselves or were dead. The head of each lineage was its senior ozo titled man. This seniority was based not on age, but on the order of seniority in the membership of the society. The senior titled men of the lineages, assisted by other title-holders, constituted the government at the village level; political authority at the village-group level was exercised by the senior titled men of the constituent villages. Lineages played some role in political recruitment, but there was a close correlation between the individual acquisition of wealth and the exercise of political power, and this considerably muted the relevance of descent groups.

Conclusion

It is clear from the foregoing that the Igbo political culture was everywhere structurally opposed to the emergence of a real monarchy. Kinship units were of great importance in restraining the excesses of individualism in an ordinarily fluid social system. It should also be clear that Igbo political organization was far more nuanced than the picture projected by much of the relevant literature. As I have shown here, age, for example, had an almost all-purpose jural significance, which meant that the society was essentially gerontocratic in character. Yet, the Igbo, through one of their proverbs, have always recognized that "a traveler is wiser than the grey-haired." Indeed, old age on its own carried little social or political weight among the Igbo. The elders who were held in high regard were those who had made themselves known in the society: at a minimum, they had large families, had established themselves as successful farmers, and had taken any necessary titles. As a consequence, the pattern of authority which emerged, though outwardly fixed and therefore seeming stable, was competitive and elastic, so that achievement, for example, was widely acknowledged and rewarded through social recognition.

Review Questions

1. What do you understand by the concept "government by association"? How appropriate is it to classify the Edda, Nsukka, and Aro in this category?
2. Compare and contrast the monarchical systems in the Igbo culture area with those of any of the empires treated in this book.

Additional Reading

Afigbo, A.E. *The Warrant Chiefs*. London: Longman, 1972.

Forde, Daryll and G.I. Jones. *The Ibo and Ibibio-speaking Peoples of Southeast-ern Nigeria*. London: International African Institute, 1950.

Henderson, Richard N. *The King in Every Man: Evolutionary Trends in Onitsha Ibo Society and Culture*. New Haven: Yale University Press, 1972.

Lambert, H.E. *Kikuyu Social and Political Institutions*. London: Oxford University Press, 1956.

Northrup, David. *Trade without Rulers: Pre-colonial Economic Development in South-Eastern Nigeria*. Oxford: Clarendon Press, 1978.

Uchendu, V.C. *The Igbo of Southeast Nigeria*. New York: Holt, Rinehart, and Winston, 1965.

PART D

The Nineteenth Century

Section Overview

Africa entered the nineteenth century with an increasing role for Islam and European trade in its history. Many societies had to respond to the trade, many wanted to expand their territories, and some were bent on reforming their political systems. While some kingdoms collapsed, a few others were newly created. Many African states attempted to centralize political power and secure greater access to international trade.

As has been seen in chapter 11, the history of North Africa during the nineteenth century witnessed vigorous attempts by Europeans to colonize the region, the waning influence of the Ottoman empire, and the development of nationalism in many areas in resistance to local and foreign exploitation. In Egypt, Muhammad Ali embarked upon a program of modernization; he built a better army, set up factories, and created secular schools. European interest in Egypt led to British control in 1882. The history of Algeria was dominated by the French incursion after 1830, generating many protests. Tunisia retained its autonomy until 1881 when it was taken over by France. The Sultanate of Morocco survived as a sovereign state, and the Ottomans retained their control of Libya.

In West Africa, the jihad movements created new Islamic states and governments. Islam spread to many areas, becoming a mass religion. Further east, Islamic empires also emerged. The common theme in the savanna was that of political centralization and territorial expansion. Islam became a powerful ideological tool in attaining these goals, but whatever success was achieved was destroyed by the invading forces of Britain and France. In the rest of West Africa, states responded to increasing European incursions in several ways. In the area of the Niger Delta, some powerful city-states emerged. Elsewhere, coastal cities exploited commercial relations to enhance their political economies. The once powerful empire of Oyo disintegrated, and the Yoruba witnessed a period of chaos. States like Asante and Fante in the area of modern Ghana tried to consolidate and prevent collapse.

In East Africa, wars were fought to obtain greater participation in long-distance trade and consolidate political authorities. Sultan Seyyid Said (1806-1854) of the Omani used his navy to control the trade of the coast. Rwanda and Buganda enhanced their political stature in the region. In the Ethiopian Highlands, the emperors were able to establish strong confederacies.

Chapter 13

The Jihads in West Africa

Julius O. Adekunle

Introduction

In the eighteenth and nineteenth centuries, certain major political, economic, and religious occurrences transformed the course of West African history. One such revolutionary event was the emergence of Islamic reformist movements, which led to the outbreak of jihads in different parts of West Africa. There were numerous minor Islamic reformist movements in West Africa prior to the nineteenth century. Thus, the revolutionary events of the nineteenth century merely served as the cumulative results of a process that had begun long before. Localized attacks were carried out on non-Muslim or nominal Muslim communities in the name of the jihad. The inspiration derived from these early attacks found articulate expression in the major revolutionary movements of the nineteenth century.

This chapter will examine the three main jihads in West Africa, the Sokoto jihad, the Massina jihad, and the Tukulor jihad. The aims of these jihads were basically the same: the purification of the Islamic religion and the establishment of a theocratic form of government where the Sharia (Islamic law and principles) would be adopted. The sources of information available for the reconstruction of the jihads in West Africa will be analyzed. This chapter will consider the situations prevailing in West Africa, particularly in northern Nigeria before the outbreak of the Sokoto jihad. It will use available sources to explain the causes, course, and consequences of the jihads in West Africa.

The Main Sources of Information on the Jihads

There are numerous surviving sources on the jihads, falling into two broad categories. First, these were the written sources produced in the nineteenth century, including those by Arabic scholars and those by travelers who chronicled their impressions of religious conditions of West Africa, especially northern Nigeria. Eyewitness accounts, the writings of the leaders of the jihads, such as Usman dan Fodio, Seku Ahmadu Lobbo (Ahmadu ibn Hammadi), and Al-Hajj Umar

(Umar ibn Tall), and the correspondence of the viziers reveal a great deal of information about the events that preceded the outbreak of the jihads.

The second category of sources consists of materials from various colonial administrators, usually written versions of oral traditions collected in the first half of the twentieth century. Mostly anthropological and ethnographic notes, these documents preserve the traditions and history of the jihads. Piecing together the information from them helps us to understand the logistics and operation of the jihads.

Sheikh Usman dan Fodio (the leader of the Sokoto jihad) was himself a scholar and a prolific writer who produced several works in the Arabic language. Until the death of dan Fodio in 1817, most of the Arabic documents for the Sokoto jihad, were derived from his personal writings. For example, he wrote the *Kitab al-Farq*, which enunciated the characteristics of the old regime of the Habe rulers in Hausaland and the *Nur al-Albab* ("The Light of Consciousness") which emphasized the aims of purifying Islam from syncretic practices. He also wrote the *Withiqat ahl al-Sudan* that constituted the manifesto of the jihad; and the *Tanbih al-Ikhwan* in which he explained the origins of the jihad. Abdullah, dan Fodio's brother, also produced several works in Arabic, such as *Tazyin al-waraqat*, which detailed the history and chronology of the events leading to the Sokoto jihad. This vital document contains some poetic writings and intellectual commentaries on the jihad.[1] Abdullah also wrote the *Nasab*, which traces the genealogy of Usman dan Fodio.

Mohammed Bello, son of dan Fodio, wrote *Sard al-Kalam* and *Raudat al-Afkar*. In addition, he was the author of *Infaq al-maisur* in which he described the character of the sheikh and the correspondence between him and Al-Kanemi of Borno. Murray Last asserts that 598 letters were in the possession of al-haji Junaidu, 131 letters were retrieved from the Vizier's house (published by H. F. Backwell in *The Occupation of Hausaland* in 1927), and 227 letters were collected from Gombe. Most of these letters were found in the files of the Vizier Mohammed Bukhari (1886-1910).[2] Because the writers were insiders and participants in the jihad, the contents of the letters are reliable and useful sources for historians. The authenticity of other Arabic sources has been cross-checked with those of the sheikh and his lieutenants.

Some other leaders of the Sokoto jihad, such as Abd al-Qadir b. Al-Mustafa, Gidado dan Laima, and Umar b. Muhammad Bukhari, produced written works. The documents have been translated into English by various scholars and now constitute the bedrock of information on the Sokoto jihad. The *Kano Chronicle*, written in Arabic by an unknown author between 1883 and 1893, was discovered at Sabongari, near Katsina, and translated by H.R. Palmer.[3] The *Kano Chronicle* is comprised primarily of oral traditions, which provides considerable information on the origins and political development of Kano. References to the growth of Islam in the pre-jihad period in Kano have also been gathered from this historically important document.

European explorers to West Africa have left very useful accounts of their journeys. Leo Africanus, a Spanish born but raised in Morocco, visited West Africa

---

1. Thomas Hodgkin, *Nigerian Perspectives: An Historical Anthology* (London: Oxford University Press, 1975), 240-243; Constance B. Hilliard, *Intellectual Traditions of Pre-colonial Africa* (Boston: McGraw-Hill, 1998), 316-320.

2. Murray Last, *The Sokoto Caliphate* (New York: Humanities Press, 1967), xlv-xlvi.

3. H.R. Palmer, *Sudanese Memoirs* (London: Frank Cass, new impression 1967).

between 1510 and 1515. He was in Gobir, Kano, and Zaria. His record indicates the defeat of Kano by Zaria and Katsina, thus suggesting the political climate in Hausaland in the pre-jihad era. Friedrich Hornemann, a German explorer, described the socio-economic life of Hausaland where he died in 1801.[4] In the nineteenth century, Hugh Clapperton, a British explorer, visited Kano in 1824. As a political and economic hub of power in Hausaland, Clapperton described Kano as a well-populated city of between thirty and forty thousand people of whom "more than half are slaves."[5] Although his estimation of the number of slaves may appear exaggerated, it is not surprising because most of the captives of war may have been turned into slaves. He described Kano's vibrant economy, referring specifically to the shrewdness and significant role of the ubiquitous "dylala" [Dyula] merchants. Clapperton marveled at the size of the caravans and the variety of exotic goods he found in Kano market.[6] Surprisingly, Clapperton did not reveal much about the religious situation of Kano. Although the war had been over, the information would have enabled a historian to assess the success of the jihad in that part of Hausaland.

Richard and John Lander visited Yorubaland, Borgu, Nupe, and Kano between 1826 and 1827. Their report corroborated that of Clapperton that Kano was "one of the most important and considerable cities in Soudan, and is a general mart for all sorts of merchandize."[7] Dr. Henry (Henrich) Barth, a German scholar and explorer, visited several parts of Hausaland including Kano but stayed in Sokoto for two months in 1853. While in Kano, which he described as 'the emporium of Central Africa,' Barth discovered a copy of a very important document—*Tarikh as-Sudan*.[8] Information from these European travelers is important because it provides contemporary material, but historians are wary of employing them since the authors may exhibit biases, exaggeration, or give wrong impressions. Cultural practices that did not conform to the European norm might be described in negative terms. Aside from European travelers, there were also Arab and Hausa merchants in North Africa who recorded their observations before and during the Sokoto jihad. Meager as these sources may be, they remain vital for the reconstruction of the jihads in West Africa.

In the twentieth century, a major source for the history of the jihads has been provided by oral traditions documented by some British administrators. Among these were the oral traditions that form the basis of district notebooks, assessment reports, and provincial gazetteers. For example, J. A. Burdon, the first British Resident in Sokoto, made a collection of oral traditions, which was transliterated and later published. The oral traditions collected by the British administrators reflected their particular interests and needs, such as tax assessment. But no matter

---

4. David Robinson and Douglas Smith, *Sources of the African Past: Case Studies of Five Nineteenth-Century, African Societies* (New York: Africana Publishing, 1979), 126-128.

5. Ibid. Richard Lander estimated the population of Kano to be 4,000. He also mentioned that slave owners treated their slaves with kindness and temperance. Richard Lander, *Records of Captain Clapperton's Last Expedition to Africa*, vol. 1 (London: Henry Colburn and Richard Bentley, 1830), 200.

6. Clapperton, *Journal of a Second Expedition*, ch. 5; Robinson and Smith, *Sources of the African Past*, 127.

7. Lander, *Records of Captain Clapperton*, 200.

8. E.W. Bovill, *The Golden Trade of the Moors* (Princeton: Markus Weiner, first published 1958, reprinted 1995), 220-222.

how peripheral the information from these sources might be, it has been useful in filling gaps in the history of the jihads.

Hausaland Before the Sokoto Jihad

Hausaland is located in the West African Sudan. Human habitation in this region presumably dates back to the Stone Age period.[9] Agriculture and iron smelting flourished in Kano, with food and other crops such as cotton and peanuts enhancing the conduct of long-distance trade. Most of the Hausa states, however, derived their wealth and prosperity from the trans-Saharan trade with its structured network of routes and numerous articles of trade.

Hausa merchants were not restricted to the commercial orbit of Hausaland. They traveled to the west to participate in the gold trade, and the kola nut trade from Gonja in the Asante region. To the north they took part in the salt trade from Bilma, Taghaza, and Taodeni; the copper trade from Takedda; the natron trade from Borno; and they exported Kano cloth, leather, ostrich feathers, ivory, and gum. Hausa merchants developed very complex and diversified trade, which compared in range of articles and magnitude of operation with that of the ancient Phoenicians or the Wangara of the Western Sudan.

The inter-regional connections laid Hausaland open to political, economic, and socio-cultural influences. Arab and Berber merchants from North Africa played a vital role in the political and religious influences, which pervaded northern Nigeria. Ruled by the Habe kings who were traditional worshipers, Hausaland became a volatile region where religious reformation or violence could erupt. Since its introduction to the Western Sudan, the conspicuous and continuous influence of Islam cannot be disregarded.

Located on the northern fringe of Hausaland, Gobir was a prosperous state, like Kano and Katsina. Despite constant raids by the Tuareg, Gobir managed to maintain its economic and political stability. The aridity of Gobir's land made it impossible for agriculture to thrive, but it permitted pastoralism; hence the presence of numerous nomadic Fulani. Gobir embarked on a massive and aggressive process of shaking off the yoke of Borno early in the eighteenth century by organizing a formidable army. Although it successfully removed Borno's overlordship, Gobir experienced another period of domination when it suffered a crushing defeat by Katsina. Katsina rose against Gobir because it encroached on the territories of Zamfara and Kebbi. In Gobir, as in the rest of Hausaland, some Fulani were cattle-rearers, some were traders, and others were clerics and teachers of the Islamic religion in the employ of the Habe rulers.

In the history of the Sokoto jihad, Gobir became a focal point as the birthplace of Sheikh Usman dan Fodio, the leader of the Islamic reformers in Hausa-

---

9. The Bayajjida legend refers to an adventurous prince who once settled in Borno, got married to a Borno princess before leaving for Biram. He later went to Daura, where his wife gave birth to a son named Bawo. Bawo's children reputedly founded the ruling dynasties of the Hausa Bakwai. The states include Daura, Biram, Gobir, Kano, Katsina, Rano, and Zazzau (Zaria).

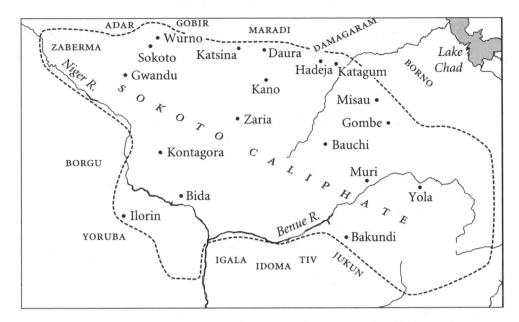

Figure 13-1. The Sokoto Caliphate and Borno Under Al-Kanemi

land. Born in 1754 at Maralta, dan Fodio belonged to the Toronkawa (Torodbe) Fulani group. His ancestors were said to have migrated from Futa Toro, the cradle of the Fulani people.

Dan Fodio was born into a highly educated and religious family. He thus received a sound Islamic education, and was well-versed in theology, the Sharia, the Arabic language, and mysticism. He belonged to the Qadiriyya Islamic mystic brotherhood.[10] He learnt about al-Maghili's religious activities and teachings in the Sudan. Abd al-Karim al-Maghili was a renowned Islamic scholar from the Maghrib. Before he died in 1503, he denounced the syncretic acts of rulers and called them *kaffir* (infidels). Against such unbelievers, the jihad was obligatory. The inspiration for the jihads in West Africa partly derived from him. Searching for more knowledge, dan Fodio and his brother Abdullah, moved from one Islamic teacher to another, ending at Agades under Jibril ibn Umar. Agades was a stronghold of the Tuareg who were extremely forceful in the purification of Islam. On his return to Hausaland in 1774, dan Fodio taught and preached the Islamic religion in places such as Gobir, Kebbi, and Zamfara. Because of his versatility, dan Fodio's fame spread so fast that he became known almost everywhere in Hausaland. He established communities of believers to whom he taught theology. Although Bawa Jangworzo, the fifty-fifth ruler of Gobir, did not adopt Islam and did not compel his people to convert, he nevertheless appointed dan Fodio as an Islamic teacher for the royal family in 1781.

Drawing his impetus from the Tuareg in Agades, there is little wonder that dan Fodio emerged as the leader of the Islamic revolutionary movement in Hausaland. Within a very short time, his fame constituted a threat to the political aristo-

---

10. Adu Boahen et al., *Topics in West African History* (Harlow: Longman, first published 1965, eight impression 1993), 44-45.

crats who were unequivocal in their drive to halt the spread of Islam and to clip the growing wings of its proselytes. The Habe rulers did not want to accommodate a religiously hostile community within their territories. The growth of the *jamaas* (community of Muslim reformers), with their unwillingness to interact with non-Muslims, was considered a strong proof of belligerence and an apparent indication of war.

Introduction of Islam in Northern Nigeria

While the Berbers were mostly responsible for the introduction of the Islamic religion into the Western Sudan from the north, its route into northern Nigeria has been debated. Some scholars argue that Islam penetrated from Borno while others support the information obtained from the *Kano Chronicle* that it came from Mali. In the *Kano Chronicle*, it is contended that forty learned Muslims brought Islam from Mali between 1349 and 1385. The Muslims supposedly converted Yaji, the ruler of Kano. There is a possibility that these Muslims were the Dyula (or Wangara), ubiquitous merchants in the Western Sudan, who were said to have arrived in Kano under the leadership of Abd al-Rahman Zaite between 1349 and 1385.[11] Both arguments are plausible. It could be suggested that Islam first made inroads into northern Nigeria through Mali, but the currents of Islamization from Borno reinforced the process. Since the Hausa merchants intermingled with the Wangara traders in their commercial enterprises, it is probable that the latter religiously influenced the former. But although Wangara economic and religious factors were very strong in Kano, effective Islamization does not seem to have penetrated the city until the reign of Muhammad Rumfa (1463-1499). The *Kano Chronicle* also suggests that the Fulani who migrated to Hausaland brought with them books on divinity and etymology.[12]

Some rulers and communities adopted Islam only in a nominal fashion and the Muslims continued to regard them as pagans. For some time, there was no open challenge to the moral conduct and political sovereignty of the Habe rulers. With increased awareness and accelerated proselytization, however, Islamic scholars began to openly confront their political overlords. Peaceful coexistence gave way to religious and ideological challenges, which triggered confrontations. Some of the formerly condoned actions of the Habe rulers were now condemned as sacrilegious, and therefore intolerable.

---

11. The Wangara people were identified by various names such as Mandingoes or Malinke by the early Arab writers. Utilizing evidence from Delafosse's traveler's accounts, Bovill mentions that they were also referred to as Gbangara, Gwangara, or Gangara. E.W. Bovill, *Caravans of the Old Sahara* (London: Oxford University Press, 1933), 60. See also Palmer, *Sudanese Memoirs*, 86-89.

12. Thomas Hodgkin, *Nigerian Perspectives: An Historical Anthology* (London: Oxford University Press, 1975), 113-114.

The Causes of the Sokoto Jihad

The presence of the militant Fulani Muslims living among non- Muslim or only nominally Muslim Hausa people was a potential cause for a holy war. With the Fulani presence, Hausa societies had become polarized. Many Fulani were not socially integrated and they remained religiously uncompromising. Their alienation was a result of the excessive taxes levied on their cattle by the Habe rulers. Others were embittered by their non-inclusion in the Hausa government. The Fulani strongly believed that justice would prevail if an Islamic system of government was instituted. Thus, the desire to reform Islam and institute socio-political justice according to Islamic principles served as part of the manifesto of the jihads in West Africa.

By the second half of the eighteenth century, there was growing militancy in Islamic education throughout the Western and Central Sudan. A number of scholars from North Africa had come to live in Hausaland. Mixing with those already established in Hausaland, they formed *jamaas* (Muslim communities). The scholars expressed themselves in pungent writings, against the religious practices of the Hausa people and against adulterated Islamic practices. Clearly, the books and pamphlets written and distributed by the scholars exposed many of the weaknesses of the Hausa rulers and raised peoples' consciousness of the shortcomings of the governments. The singleness of purpose and the cohesiveness of the scholars was energized by the fact that they spoke, and wrote in the Arabic language.

Their writings suggested that religious reformation could only be successful when devout Muslims assumed governance. The expanding aggression shifted the balance away from peaceful coexistence between the Hausa and Fulani on the one hand, and between Muslims and non-Muslims on the other. By the end of the eighteenth century, religious tension had risen so high throughout Hausaland that an outbreak of military violence became inevitable. The *jamaa*, in places such as Gobir, Gombe, Hadeija, Kano, Katsina, Kebbi, Zamfara, and Zaria, had become very militant.

The Fulani Muslim scholars accused the Hausa rulers and their people of syncretism and un-Islamic practices. Although some of the Hausa rulers professed to be Muslims, they blended Islam with traditional religion. Among the practices of the Hausa rulers were the marrying of many wives, the veneration of rocks and other natural phenomena, consultation of soothsayers, and participation in spirit dances. What seems to have been the most repugnant to the Muslims was the state of religious decadence with special reference to the practice of *shirk*-polytheism.[13] Since these were sinful acts, Muslims could not live under such conditions.

Other accusations included the abuse of power by the Hausa rulers. They were said to be corrupt, oppressive, and ostentatious. In addition, they taxed arbitrarily and collected excessive market dues. The Hausa rulers collected bribes such as the *kurdin sarauta*, money that was paid to the officer when taking up an office, and *gaisuma*, money that was paid for preaching. In other words, the Fulani nursed socio-economic grievances against the Habe rulers.

---

13. R.A. Adeleye, *Power and Diplomacy in Northern Nigeria 1804-1906* (London: Humanities Press, 1971), 18.

The Muslims argued that they lived under a government that was not only authoritarian but irreligious. Since Islam was the only acceptable religion, the Muslims prepared and propagated manifestoes, which stated the conditions under which they would like to live. To return Islam to its orthodox form, the Fulani had to be in political control. Against the background of a society perceived to be deeply involved in idolatry, highly oppressive, and gravely insensitive, dan Fodio and his cohorts planned to instill sanity and the only means was the jihad and the institution of an alternative government. Rather than a repressive bureaucracy, "the kind of state which the leaders of the revolution were pledged to establish was a state in which social justice, administered in the light of the *Sharia* by God-fearing rulers, took the place of the arbitrary decisions of irresponsible despots."[14] Thus, as the reformists increased in numerical strength, the movement became more revolutionary and assumed more political forms.

The events in Gobir provided the most immediate cause for the Sokoto jihad. A fairly large group of Hausa, Fulani, and Tuareg Muslims lived in Gobir and there was an uneasy coexistence between Muslims and non-Muslims. Nafata, the reigning king, enamored by the traditional religion and wishing to gratify his people, attempted to halt the spread of Islam. Usman dan Fodio had become the overall leader of the reformist Muslims. He became disgusted with the religious policies and proclamations of Nafata. When dan Fodio could no longer accommodate the king's religious attitude, he withdrew to Degel where he lived until after the death of Nafata. In Degel, dan Fodio's reforming impetus grew as his followers increased in number. When Yunfa became the ruler of Gobir in 1802, he paid a special visit to dan Fodio, his former teacher, presumably to curry his favor and solicit his political patronage. As a courtesy, Yunfa permitted the teaching and preaching of Islam. Encouraged by this positive gesture and believing that Yunfa was a Muslim, dan Fodio embarked on a massive and aggressive Islamization of the people. His teaching and preaching received widespread endorsement from the ordinary people, especially the Fulani. The Qadiriyya fraternity benefited as the number of its adherents increased remarkably.

The far-reaching spiritual impact of dan Fodio on the people, the swiftness of his accomplishments, and the rapidity of his rising popularity brought a great deal of concern to Yunfa, whose political power had begun to wane. His powerlessness, vis-à-vis the growing influence of dan Fodio, drastically shifted the direction of power in favor of the latter. To curtail the growth of the Islamic community and the threat it constituted, Yunfa revoked the right to teach, preach, and convert. He promulgated other laws such as banning the wearing of the turban. To the Muslims the laws were obnoxious, provocative, and excessive.

The crisis erupted when the new laws were tested in 1804 over the case of Abdul-Salam. A student of dan Fodio, Abdul-Salam, living in Gambana, a Muslim community, had incurred the displeasure of Yunfa. In retaliation, Yunfa attacked and captured Gambana, but dan Fodio's followers rescued the captives. Whether to avoid further clashes or having been expelled by Yunfa, as some scholars argue, dan Fodio embarked on the *hijra* or relocation from non-Muslim territory. This episode clearly indicated the total breakdown in the Yunfa-dan Fodio relationship on the one hand, and in Muslim-non-Muslim coexistence on

---

14. Hodgkin, *Nigerian Perspectives*, 53.

the other. The outcome was the declaration of the jihad. Following military en-counters, Yunfa lost control, lost power, and lost his territory to the Muslims. Ini-tially, the weapons of the jihadists' infantry consisted of poisoned bows and ar-rows with body armor while the cavalry possessed a few horses.[15] It would, however, seem that as the revolution progressed, the military technology of the Muslims became more advanced presumably, through the connection with the North African Berbers and Arabs who supplied firearms. It was primarily because of the added advantage of superior weaponry that they were able to swiftly over-run various areas. Most of the soldiers who fought against the jihadists were ei-ther lightly or ill-equipped, unorganized, and unprepared.

The promise of paradise to Muslim participants in the wars became a magnet of propaganda that attracted numerous people to Islam and provided willing war-riors for the jihads. Because of the propaganda, new converts or nominal Muslims joined the "holy warriors." They believed that the promise of paradise was enough reward for their service. The propaganda was effective not only among the Fulani and some Hausa in northern Nigeria, it also produced good fruits for Islam elsewhere.

Taking into consideration the remote and immediate causes of the Sokoto jihad, it would be misleading to describe it as a sudden outbreak of antagonism between the traditionalists and the Muslims. But, while the Muslims possessed a direct focus, were united in purpose, and were well organized under the leader-ship of a heroic religious figure, the traditionalists remained uncoordinated, merely struggling for survival. The Habe rulers fought to retain their political power rather than to sustain their traditional religion. But as many flag bearers lifted up the banner of Islam, the traditionalists crumbled one after the other. In addition, the kings received little military or political support from their subjects who were very distressed over losing their land, wealth, and possibly their fami-lies in the war.[16] To avoid such horrendous circumstances, some followers of the rulers chose to cross the line and join the jihadists.

Nature of the Jihad

Historians have held various views on the jihad. Its religious nature has been defended on the basis of the syncretist and polytheistic practices of the Hausa people and their rulers. These were obviously the reasons adduced by dan Fodio when he issued two manifestoes-*Wathiquat ahl al-Sudan* ("Dispatch to the Folk of the Sudan") and *Kitab-al-Farq*. Dan Fodio declared:

> To make war upon the king who is an apostate, and who has abandoned the religion of Islam for the religion of the heathendom is obligatory by assent, and that to make war against the king who is an apostate-who has not abandoned the religion of Islam as far as the profession of it is con-cerned, but who mingles the observances of Islam with the observances of heathendom, like the kings of Hausaland for the most-is also obligatory

15. Michael Crowder, *History of West Africa*, vol. 2 (London: Longman, 1974), 8.
16. Ibid., 10.

by assent, and that to take the government from him is obligatory by assent.[17]

This and other pronouncements clearly indicate that dan Fodio was unwilling to support anything un-Islamic. His purpose for the jihad, to redeem the lost purity of Islam and to establish a renewed form of Islamic worship and practices, was well expressed in this manifesto. He did not even agree that Muslims should live in *bilad al-harb* ("the territory of non-Muslims") because of the religious and social decadence of Hausa society. While dan Fodio's argument may have some validity, he painted a particularly gloomy picture of the Islamic religion and social relations in Hausaland in order to justify the jihad.

It is possible to argue that the jihad was imperialistic in nature. It was a war fought under the guise of religious reformation to overthrow Hausa hegemony and install Fulani authority. For example, Zamfara, which supported the Sokoto jihad, was later destroyed; and the Fulani leaders tactically alienated the Hausa in the military operations. This suggests that the Fulani planned to concentrate political power in their own hands. The scheme succeeded because thirteen of the fourteen flag bearers of the jihads were Fulani. There was also massive support for the jihad from the Fulani people because they were Muslims and because they were against the Hausa governments. Belonging to the established political order, many Hausa were either unwilling to wage war against their rulers or did not show much enthusiasm for fighting a holy war. As a result, they could not be rewarded with political offices after the jihad. This does not, however, mean that there were no Hausa who fought on the side of the jihadists.

While many Fulani people joined the jihad for religious reasons or to overthrow the Hausa governments, some joined to loot for reward or to be compensated with positions. The strong support of the Fulani was a crucial factor in the overall success of the jihad because they fought ferociously. Their zealousness could be understood considering that the Habe rulers imposed heavy cattle taxation *jangali*, market dues, and death duties on the Fulani. There was, therefore, a strong determination to overthrow a political order, which was oppressive and avaricious; to overthrow governments to which they paid heavy taxation without being given representation.

The Course of the Sokoto Jihad

After conquering several of the Hausa states, the Fulani turned against Borno during the reign of Mai Ahmed. They captured the capital, Birnin Gazargamu, in 1808. Following that, they established four emirates—Gombe, Hadejia, Katagum, and Misau—on Borno's western border. Borno could not ward off the Fulani menace because of military weakness until Al-Kanemi seized the throne. Al-Kanemi descended from a nomadic but scholarly family. Through his military skills, capable leadership, and assistance from the Shuwa Arabs, he successfully defended Borno against the Fulani on several occasions. He regained Birnin

---

17. Hodgkin, *Nigerian Perspectives*, 247-248.

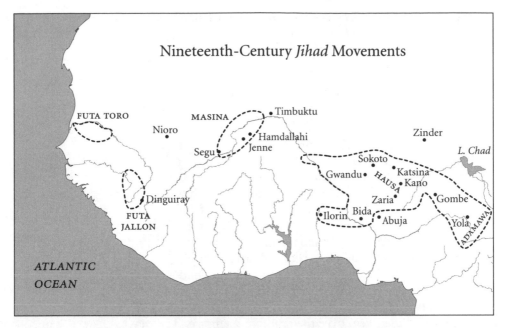

Figure 13-2. Nineteenth Century Jihad Movements

Gazargamu in 1809. In the same year, Zaria, Kano, and Katsina fell to the Fulani jihadists.

Borno had always been a Muslim state as evidenced by its rulers (Mais) who performed the pilgrimage to Mecca. The jihad was, however, extended to Borno because Mohammed Bello accused Borno of tolerating pagan practices and persecuting Muslims.[18] While to the Fulani these offenses-syncretism and apostasy-were convincing excuses for the jihad, they were refuted by Al-Kanemi. There was a great deal of correspondence between Mohammad Bello and Al-Kanemi concerning the jihad. The importance of the correspondence rests on the fact that it revealed the nature, which the Sokoto jihad assumed as the war progressed. Al-Kanemi wrote to Bello to ask why the jihad was carried to his territory, when it was a Muslim state and he himself was a reformist ruler. To Al-Kanemi, the extension of the jihad to Borno had no logical justification. He contended that his own faith was strong enough to bring about Islamic purity in his area of jurisdiction. Clearly, Al-Kanemi was of the opinion that the prevailing religious condition of Borno was the same as in the past, when the rulers were very strong Muslims. The jihad in Borno was therefore not religiously motivated, but had political motives. The development led Al-Kanemi to accuse the Fulani "of seizing political power in the guise of a religious revolt."[19] Apart from increasing our understanding of the rancor between Muslim leaders, the exchange of letters between Mohammed Bello and Al-Kanemi illustrates the high level of literary production in the first half of the nineteenth century in northern Nigeria.

---

18. Michael Crowder, *West Africa: An Introduction to Its History* (London: Longman, 1977), 81.

19. Michael Crowder, *The Story of Nigeria* (London: Faber and Faber, 1966), 97-98.

Modibo Adama, who was one of dan Fodio's flag bearers, led the jihad in the Nupe kingdom (south of Hausaland). After subduing his religious opponents, Adama established the Emirate of Fombina with Yola as the capital. In 1809 Yakub (the only non-Fulani flag bearer), founded the Bauchi Emirate. To the south of Fombina, Hammaruwa created Muri (mostly populated by the Jukun) as another emirate in 1833.[20] Mallam Dendo, a Fulani scholar, exploited the civil strife in the Nupe kingdom to seize political authority. He played one candidate against the other in the ongoing palace struggle. The Fulani continued to gain control until 1832 when they firmly established their hegemony.

South of the Nupe kingdom was the Oyo Empire. By the turn of the nineteenth century, Oyo was suffering military reverses and losses in the hands of its Nupe and Borgu northern neighbors. This circumstance, in addition to internal political problems, contributed to the gradual disintegration of the empire during the second decade of the nineteenth century. A major setback for Oyo occurred in 1817 when Afonja, the Are Ona Kakanfo (commander in chief), intending to carve out Ilorin as an independent state under his control, invited Alimi, a Fulani scholar, for assistance. Alimi seized the opportunity to spread the jihad to Oyo. Afonja was solidly supported by Solagberu a powerful Muslim Yoruba leader in Ilorin. Thus, the internal disunity and rivalry within the Oyo Empire served as an opportunity for the Fulani to assert their grip over the crumbling empire. The massive backing in soldiers and weapons that Oyo received from Borgu, another anti-Muslim state, could not prevent its capital from falling to the jihadists. The victory of the jihadists prompted the relocation of the Oyo capital to the south. Since Ilorin, the gateway to the heartland of Oyo, had fallen to the Muslims, the jihadists, thereafter, felt confident to advance southward until they were halted in 1840 at Osogbo.

The Main Consequences
of the Sokoto Jihad

The creation of the Sokoto Caliphate was one of the immediate and most conspicuous consequences of the jihad. It was an imposition of political power over a wide region formerly controlled by several independent Hausa states. Henceforth, "emirates" replaced the "Hausa states." Consisting of fifteen emirates with an area of about 180,000 square miles, the caliphate assumed an Islamic administrative structure with the Sultan of Sokoto at its head. The emirates, controlled by the sultan's officers, became subordinate to the sultan with the obligation of tribute payment and military levies. While the caliphate served as a unifying political structure, Islam served as a common religious bond, thus providing a reasonable degree of internal security in a region formerly riven with political and economic rivalries. The Sokoto Caliphate evolved the same pattern of administration in the emirates thereby ending the previous inter-state competition. The jihad brought about political peace and order, which consequently restored the economic prosperity of northern Nigeria. Industries, commerce, and agriculture flourished when the jihad wars were over.

---

20. Crowder, *West Africa*, 81.

The irretrievable loss of political power meant much to the Hausa people who were the unquestionable majority. If the Hausa had willingly relinquished power, it would not have been as painful a loss. With the forfeiture of political authority, the dignity of the old Habe rulers was lost, their social status was reduced, and they no longer wielded any influence. The erstwhile rulers may have confessed the Islamic faith in order not to be overthrown. Thus the overthrow of the Habe rulers had pervasive effects on the entire Hausa society. In Borno, the jihad brought about an end to the long-established Safuwa dynasty and a new one emerged.[21]

During and after the war, demographic movements altered the pre-existing population in Hausaland. Survivors who remained unconverted migrated from the Muslim-dominated areas to places in which they could more comfortably practice their religious beliefs. Although Islam had spread widely, traditionalism persisted for many years following the conclusion of the jihad. Aside from that, people who wanted to escape death or enslavement at the hands of the conquering armies of the jihad moved to safer regions.

The jihad provided a new stimulus to Islamic learning and literacy because dan Fodio, his brother Abdullah, and his son Mohammed Bello were leading scholars as well as political leaders. Their scholarly works and those of their associates arose out of the necessity to explain and justify the jihad and the political reformation that accompanied it. They were also compelled to preserve the records of the jihad. In accomplishing this, there was a revival and spread of Islamic learning. Subsequent rulers used the numerous writings as a detailed plan of governance. Islamic intellectualism thus spread beyond the confines of the Fulani Muslim territories in Hausaland to several parts of West Africa. Along with Islamic education came the development of Arabic, which emerged as the official language of literacy and correspondence. Although Hausa remained the lingua franca in northern Nigeria, Arabic gradually spread among the Muslims. Arabic schools were instituted to promote Islamic religion and education. From those schools, scholars proceeded to Borno or North Africa for further studies.

The Sokoto jihad served as a springboard for others, which occurred in several parts of West Africa such as Massina and Segu. These other jihads will now be examined.

The Jihad of Seku Ahmadu in Massina

Massina was located between Djenne and Lake Debo in the Niger bend. As in the Futa Djallon region and Hausaland, the Fulani, although in the minority, comprised one of the influential groups in Massina. They lived among the Berbers, the Muslim Soninke, and Mande-speaking people. The Bambara and Bozo, the dominant group, were traditional worshipers and strictly anti-Muslim. Because of its multi-ethnic composition, Massina ranked among the most cosmopolitan centers of nineteenth century West Africa. Like Djenne and Timbuktu, Massina emerged as an important center of Islamic learning.

---

21. Boahen, *Topics in West African History*, 49.

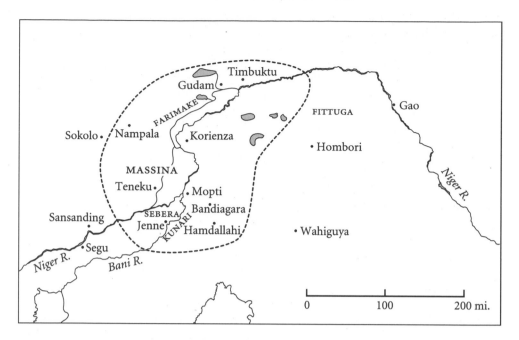

Figure 13-3. Massina at Its Apogee

The Fulani arrived in the Massina area under the leadership of an Ardo from the Djalo group, who was a non-Muslim. Within a short time, the Fulani grew in numbers and influence. Indeed, "the eastern confines of Massina from the 15th century onwards became a focal point of Fulbe [Fulani] settlement and rediffussion."[22]

The jihad in Massina was led by Seku Ahmadu Lobbo, born in 1775 into the Bar (Bari) clan of the Sangare Fulani group.[23] As a youth, he tended cattle, traveled extensively, studied Islamic education, and was initiated into the Qadiriyya Islamic fraternity. He not only drew inspiration from dan Fodio and read his scholarly work, he even participated in the jihad in Gobir. This experience aroused his interest in the purification of Islam and helped to spur his declaration of a jihad on his return to Massina. His writings and teachings focused on interpretations and application of Islamic dogma. Seku Ahmadu displayed a high degree of piety as measured by his disciplined life and strict adherence to Islamic principles. Like other jihad leaders, he attracted to himself a great number of adherents and students at his base in Djenne. The more his popularity increased the larger his community of followers and the higher the likelihood of the outbreak of a jihad. The ardo's political post and power were endangered by the speedy growth of the Muslims. His fears increased because the Dyalo and Sangare Fulani groups had been arch-rivals.

In time, the presence and activities of Seku and his reformist group created uneasiness and constituted a political risk for the ardo who promptly solicited the assistance of the ruler of Segu. Both the ardo and the ruler of Segu were anti-Muslim, and therefore they allied to fight against a common enemy-the Muslim re-

---

22. Elizabeth Isichei, *History of West Africa* (London: Longman, 1978), 29.
23. Some scholars refer to him as Ahmad Bari, after his clan.

formers-for political survival. The alliance was also formed to take revenge on Seku Ahmadu, who was accused of killing the ardo's son. The ardo was also preventing the seizure of rule by the Sangare group.

From Seku Ahmadu's perspective, the practice of traditionalism and the persecution of his disciples formed a strong basis for a possible attack. Nothing was more abhorrent to the Muslims than paganism and apostasy and, since these were allegedly prevalent in Massina, the most practicable solution was to relocate. Thus, following the pattern of Prophet Mohammed and dan Fodio, Seku performed the *hijra* from Djenne to Noukouma.

The ardo received considerable assistance from Segu, but that neither lowered the morale of the reformers nor put their plan of a jihad to rest. The reformers optimistically believed that the forces of traditionalism would not overpower the military machine of Allah. Fortunately, the support for the jihadists came partly from the propaganda that soldiers who died during the holy war would enter paradise and partly from the impressive support of the Qadiriyya members in and outside Massina. No sooner had the war broken out than Seku Ahmadu captured Djenne in 1817, and by 1827, he had established a centralized Islamic monarchy extending from Djenne to Timbuktu.

Both dan Fodio and Seku Ahmadu "drew considerable moral inspiration for their revivalist movements from al-Muhkta, whose "preaching and the extent of his literary output gave impetus to a renewed interest in mystical studies and restored dignity to Islamic piety."[24] Before declaring the jihad, Seku Ahmadu sought the permission of dan Fodio as a flag bearer. The impact of the Sokoto jihad had been so great that it transcended Hausaland. Wherever strict, learned, and zealous Fulani adherents of Islam converged, there was often the unquenchable desire to declare a holy war.

Surprisingly, before the approval was granted, Seku Ahmadu had already declared war. Because he acted on his own volition, Ahmadu "refused to accept Sokoto's authority, or send tribute, and he established his own independent caliphate, with his capital at Hamdallahi."[25] To strengthen his position as both the political and the spiritual leader of Massina, Ahmadu assumed the Amir al-Muminin (leader of the faithful) in 1819. With the conquest of Timbuktu in 1826, Ahmadu strengthened his political control over Muslim dominated areas.

Although smaller than the Sokoto Caliphate, Massina was outstanding for its high level of spiritual purity, which proved the sincerity of purpose of the jihadists. The Muslims were in the minority but they dramatically transformed Massina society through their piety and then imposition of a theocratic form of government. The success of the reform of Islam in Massina far exceeded that in other places where the jihad was fought. The Islamic state of Massina was "probably the most purely religious in inspiration, and it was undoubtedly the one where the original ideals were adhered to most closely in later practice."[26]

The Islamic state of Massina encompassed Islamic centers such as Djenne and Timbuktu. In both places, the Kunta Berbers, renowned for their devotion to

---

24. John Ralph Willis, "The Western Sudan from the Moroccan Invasion (1591) to the Death of Al-Mukhtar Al-Kunti (1811)," in J.F. Ade Ajayi and Crowder Michael, eds., *History of West Africa*, vol. 1, 542-543.

25. Isichei, *History*, 29.

26. Ibid.

Islam and strict practice of the doctrines of the Qadiriyya sect, dominated religious life. The strategic location at the bend of the River Niger made Massina's economy a vibrant one. It controlled the trans-Niger trade and enjoyed thriving agriculture. Water transportation facilitated external commerce. Until his death in 1845, Seku Ahmadu remained in firm. After him, his son Ahmadu II ascended the throne, but in 1862 when Al-Hajj Umar of the Tukulor Empire sacked Hamdallahi.

The Jihad of Alhajj Umar Tall (1794–1863)

Al-Hajj Umar was a Tukulor from the south of Futa Toro on the lower Senegal. The Tukulor were emigrants to Futa Toro. Born in 1794, Umar was initiated into the Tijaniyya mystic brotherhood. He became a learned scholar whose intellectualism and personality immensely appealed to numerous people and attracted them to the *zawiya* (Islamic school) which he established.

One school of thought argues that the beliefs of the Tijaniyya were fundamentally and theologically different from those of the Qadiriyya. While the Qadiriyya (founded in Persia in the twelfth century) was older and more elitist, the Tijaniyya (which spread to West Africa from Algeria) presented the Islamic faith in a simple way that attracted new converts and permitted Muslims to comprehend the basic teachings and requirements of the religion. Members of the Tijaniyya claimed that they had been specially chosen to spread divine grace

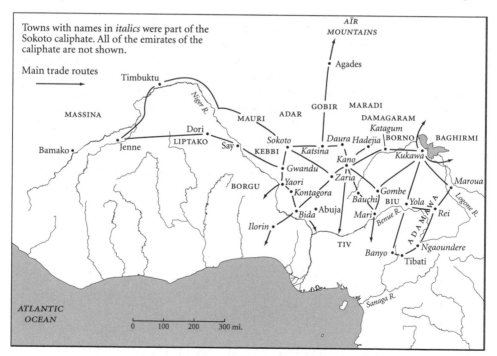

Figure 13-4. The Sokoto Caliphate and Borno

through the jihad. The Qadiriyya emphasized the purity of Islam while the Ti-janiyya elaborated on the distribution of divine grace to all people.

The Tijaniyya regarded other Muslims and non-Muslims as inferior people upon whom grace had to be imposed. In particular, Al-Hajj Umar "found it intolerable to live side by side not only with pagans but also with other Muslims whom he regarded as misdirected and unequal to members of the Tijaniyya."[27] Umar's conviction was congruent to that of dan Fodio, who instructed Muslims to move away from non-Muslims and live in separate quarters as indicated in the manifesto for the jihad.

While fulfilling one of the Islamic obligations by performing the pilgrimage to Mecca in about 1825-1826, Umar was appointed the Khalifa, that is, the supreme head of the Tijaniyya brotherhood for the Western Sudan. Strengthened by this appointment and the Tijaniyya brotherhood's doctrine of egalitarianism, Umar and his associates presumed that the jihad would make available the spiritual privileges and needs of all Muslims.

When returning from Mecca, he sojourned in Borno and Sokoto for a long time. His political and religious ambitions led him to establish diplomatic relationships with Al-Kanemi and Mohammed Bello, rulers of Borno and Sokoto respectively. He married their daughters to confirm the affiliation. While in Sokoto, he assisted Mohammed Bello in some military campaigns for which he received numerous slaves as his reward. Umar availed himself the opportunity of benefiting from the scholarship of dan Fodio and others. His readings and personal discussions with Mohammed Bello indisputably influenced him by increasing his spirituality and zeal. In 1838 he visited Seku Ahmadu of Massina where the jihad had been declared. His travels apparently had a far-reaching impact on him. He acquired administrative skills, religious knowledge, and skill in military tactics. His book entitled *Rimah*, in which he "attacked the devil and illegal practices and condemned 'mixed Islam'" proved his erudition.[28] He was, however, unpopular among other Muslims simply because he belonged to a brotherhood that challenged the Qadiriyya, which dan Fodio supported. To many Fulani Muslims, belonging to a different Islamic fraternity was tantamount to directly opposing dan Fodio. But since Umar was a Muslim he possessed the same right as dan Fodio to wage a jihad on the "unbelievers." Belonging to a different brotherhood should be no hindrance to the declaration of a holy war. Clearly, Mohammed Bello did not regard Umar as a religious opponent; that is why he allowed him to stay for a period of time.

In preparation for the jihad, Umar built up his *tabala* (army of disciples), relocated in Dinguiray, and obtained weapons from the Atlantic coast. His relocation was presumably spurred by the fact that Dinguiray was economically important for the procurement of firearms, gold, and agricultural products. The profits from Umar's economic enterprises were expended on the acquisition of weapons.

The intensity of his arrangements for the jihad, combined with his continued conversion of Qadiriyya members to Tijaniyya, threatened the political and spiritual authority of the almami, the ruler of Futa Djallon. It will be recalled that dan Fodio's increasing fame also became a threat to the ruling authorities of Gobir,

---

27. T.A. Osae and A.T. Odunsi, *A Short History of West Africa: A.D. 1800 to the Present Day* (London: Hodder and Stoughton, first published 1973, reprinted 1977), 22.

28. Adu Boahen, et al., *Topics in West African History*, 52.

hence his *hijra*. Umar deliberately modelled his actions and movements on those of the Prophet Mohammad and those of dan Fodio. For example, his move from Futa Djallon to Dinguiray has been considered a *hijra*. Following the name muhajirin, given to the advocates of Prophet Mohammad during his *hijra* from Mecca to Medina, Umar called his followers muhadyiriina, while he was referred to as Myaddid. In addition, his new supporters in Dinguiray were named lansaaru, similar to the al-ansar name given to Prophet Muhammad's followers in Medina.

As his popularity grew, the strength of his military force also expanded and his political ambition increased. To accomplish his political ambitions he proposed collaboration with the French who were already stationed in Senegal. Through the French, Umar intended to diplomatically secure arms and the endorsement to become the ruler of Futa Djallon. To strengthen the arrangement, Umar promised to guarantee law and order within his territory, but he was not submitting to French protection. He would permit the French to engage in commerce on the payment of custom duties. Regrettably, the French turned down these proposals in 1847.

Why the French declined is of interest. First, they were opposed to the growing power and political ambition of Umar. Realizing that a unified administration of Senegal under Umar would create both political and religious difficulties, the French refused to endorse the plans. Second, since the French were Christians, they would rather spread their own religion than assist Umar in propagating Islam. A powerful Umar was likely to persecute the Christians. The vigorous and obvious preparations for a jihad sufficiently proved that Umar would attack the Christians. Furthermore, it was perceived that Umar was unwilling to tolerate anyone who was not a Muslim in his territory. Third, the French were skeptical of creating a powerful African state in which the concept of egalitarianism would heighten racial crises and political disturbances. Given the reins of authority, Umar would create political, religious, and racial problems. Fourth, the self-interested imperialism of the French cannot be ignored. Their prevention of Umar's expansion southward was clearly evidence of their own imperialistic designs, and marked a desire to consolidate their hold on that region.

Umar, however, remained resolute. His failure with the French did not hinder his plans for the jihad. In 1852, after forty days of isolation and meditation, he proclaimed that he had received a special call to purify the country. He thereafter declared a jihad. He attacked Futa Toro but was driven back. He proceeded to subjugate Nioro. In 1855 he blockaded Fort Medina, but the French, under Governor Faidherbe, prevented him from overrunning it. He solicited the support of the large Muslim population in St. Louis. He appealed to traders, artisans, and other professionals. He conquered one town after another in pursuit of his ambition to create a Tukulor empire. In all the places he conquered, strict Islamic laws and principles were enforced. For instance, women were to wear the veil and be segregated during prayers, men should marry a maximum of four wives, and no liquor was to be consumed.

The rapid conquest and occupation of new territories by Umar alarmed the French, and it became an issue with which they had to deal. It would have been possible for the French to halt Umar's military triumph and advancement into core areas with relatively little effort, considering their superiority in weapons and strategies. But they were cautious in engaging in military encounters with him. For instance, Governor Faidherbe was not totally opposed to the purification of Islam and he was amenable to co-operation, but he was averse to permitting Umar's expansion to the coast.[29] In 1859, Umar made a proposal to recognize boundaries of operation between himself and the French. Although the French were willing to consent as long as the arrangement favored their own imperialistic plan, they continued to be suspicious of Umar's ambitions. Eventually, the French counter-attacked and captured Guemou, one of Umar's military outposts.

Umar extended the jihad to Segu in 1861, where he captured the capital. To justify his attack, he accused the Muslims of hypocrisy. With a similar claim of hypocrisy, Umar launched the jihad against the Muslims of the Fulani controlled state of Massina in 1862. He argued that Ahmad III had allied himself with the pagan ruler of Segu, and since Islam should not be permitted to coexist with paganism, there was the compelling need for a jihad. This argument is analogous to that which dan Fodio used when he attacked Borno.

The conquest of Massina and Segu inspired the French to suggest the construction of a line of demarcation to fortify the coast. The action became necessary to guarantee continued firm control of the coast by the French, who perceived Umar's ambition of a large theocratic empire. As would be expected, Umar vehemently opposed the proposal, observing that the line went beyond the provisional frontiers agreed to in 1859. Considering it an encroachment upon his own area of operation, Umar not only declined, he increased his efforts to establish a formidable theocratic state. This was made possible through certain strategies. First, there was direct conversion or submission of conquered chiefs. Second, Umar exploited the already existing fear and tension, which he had created in neighboring states in order to defeat them. Third, after conquering a place, Umar installed his own approved candidates who acted officially as spiritual leaders, but more practically as political flag bearers for the newly created Tukulor Empire. The purpose was to guard against dissension and rebellion. To achieve this, he ensured that members of his family, and religious or military leaders, who were close and loyal to him, ruled the conquered states. Throughout the conquered territories, taxation was levied on the people and the governors were forced to pay regular tribute.

What brought about the downfall of Umar was the imposition of the doctrines of the Tijaniyya brotherhood on the entire conquered population who were predominantly Qadiriyya members. The idea of Islamic revivalism stretched to doctrinal imposition over the Qadiriyya. Umar intended to suppress the Qadiriyya, but this scheme produced religious and political upheavals. Ultimately, he became estranged from the Toronkawa Fulani. Confrontations ensued between the two Islamic sects, with the Qadiriyya receiving considerable military assistance from the Kunta Arabs who were widely spread throughout West Africa. The conflicts weakened Umar's army and allowed vassal states to revolt. It was during this period of turmoil and skirmishes with political and religious opponents that Umar met his death in 1863.

Umar's son, Ahmadu Seku, succeeded to the throne at a difficult time in the history of the Tukulor Empire. On account of the religious and political climate of the time, the empire became very volatile. Seku inherited huge problems with po-

---

29. J.B. Webster et al., *The Revolutionary Years of West Africa Since 1800* (London: Longman, fifth impression 1989), 21.

litical opponents such as the French, religious rivals such as the Qadiriyya members, and from conquered areas such as Segu and Massina. Revolts arose among Umar's trusted army officers who were appointed as governors. After they had garnered enough military support and weapons, most of these governors detached themselves from Seku. As a result, Seku faced very grave internal political upheavals and economic weakness.[30] Only a charismatic leader could restore the lost glory of the empire. Another major problem was that Seku's candidacy was vigorously challenged by two of his half brothers. For the rest of his reign, Ahmadu Seku was immersed in fighting with the Qadiriyya brotherhood on the one hand, and the French on the other.

The success of the jihad in the Tukulor Empire is difficult to assess. Umar does not appear to have accomplished his objective of purifying Islam. He did not succeed in distributing divine grace or imposing the Tijaniyya on the populace. Rather, he created further alienation between the two brotherhoods. Unlike the Sokoto jihad, Umar's theocratic state did not last, partly because of Umar's own uncompromising character, partly because of conflict between the two brotherhoods, and partly because of the French who were desperate to dismantle an empire which would threatened their economic and political ambitions. Umar's army officers and associates were more anxious to acquire political office rather than purify Islam or distribute divine grace. For these reasons, Umar's empire was short-lived, but its revolutionary impact cannot be forgotten in West African history.

Conclusion

It is necessary to assess the religious, political, and social success of the jihads in West Africa. A revolutionary trend of that magnitude should have left multifarious imprints. The creation of Muslim theocratic states has been one of the most enduring effects. Throughout West Africa, Islam remained not only an instrument for socio-cultural engineering, but also an important factor in the process of nation building.[31] In all the Muslim states of West Africa, Islam continues to serve as an identity, a status symbol, and a rallying point for believers.

In terms of literary production, the leaders of the jihads did extensive and impressive work. Their Arabic documents are strong proof of their versatility and high level of intellectualism. Without the written works of the reformist leaders, it might have been difficult to unravel some of the mysteries, which surrounded the jihads.

The purification rationale behind the jihads seems credible in view of the fact that there are other major religions, which do not condone syncretism. But there was absolutely no means of completely eradicating syncretism among the generality of the people. Individuals chose to indulge in certain practices, which indirectly were considered impure. What may be criticized is the forceful enforcement

30. J.D. Fage, *A History of Africa* (London: Routledge, first published 1978, third edition 1995), 210-211.

31. J.F.A. Ajayi, "West African States in the Beginning of the Nineteenth Century" in J.F.A. Ajayi and Ian Espie, *A Thousand Years of West African History* (Ibadan: Ibadan University Press, first published 1965, reprinted 1970), 265.

and the political coloring which the jihads assumed in the course of the reforming exercise. As the jihad spread from Sokoto to other parts of West Africa, it gradually drifted from its original purpose. The jihads appear to have been used to accomplish political ends. Even if the religious objectives were realized, the jihads created more ethnic bitterness and disunity in some places. Islam benefited immensely from the jihads: more people were converted and a vigorous attempt was made to reform the religion according to the standards of the age.

Review Questions

1. What were the main objectives of the jihads in West Africa? How far were they achieved?
2. Identify the common characteristics of the jihad leaders in West Africa.
3. Who were the Fulani? What provided a sense of unity for them?
4. Discuss the major consequences of the jihads in West Africa.

Additional Reading

Boahen, Adu, with Jacob F. Ade Ajayi and Michael Tidy. *Topics in West African History*. 2nd ed. Harlow: Longman, 1993.

Brooks, Geraldine. *Nine Parts of Desire: The Hidden World of Islamic Women*. New York: Anchor Books, 1995.

Clarke, P.B. *West Africa and Islam: A Study of Religious Development from the 8th to the 20th Century*. London: Edward Arnold, 1982.

Clarke, Peter B. *Mahdism in West Africa: The Ijebu Mahdiyya Movement*. Weather Hill: Luzac Oriental, UK, 1996.

Davidson, Basil. *West Africa: Before the Colonial Era*. London: Longman, 1998.

Hanson, John H. *Migration, Jihad, and Muslim Authority in West Africa: The Futanke Colonies in Karta*. Bloomington: Indiana University Press, 1996.

Hiskett, M. *The Development of Islam in West Africa*. London: Longman, 1984.

Hiskett, Mervyn. *The Sword of Truth: The Life and Times of the Shehu Usuman Dan Fodio*. Series in Islam and Society in Africa. Evanston, IL: Northwestern University Press, 1994.

Loimeier, Roman. *Islamic Reform and Political Change in Northern Nigeria*. Series in Islam and Society in Africa. Evanston, IL: Northwestern University Press, 1997.

Mason, Michael. "The *JIHAD* in the South: An Outline of the Nineteenth Century Nupe Hegemony in North-Eastern Yorubaland and Afenmai," *Journal of Historical Society of Nigeria*, vol. 5, no. 2 (1970): 193-210.

Stride G.T. and Ifeka Carolina. *Peoples and Empires of West Africa*. New York: Africana Publishing Corporation, 1971.

Trimingham, Spencer J. *Islam in West Africa*. Oxford: Clarendon Press, 1964.

Waldman, Marlilyn Robinson. "The Fulani Jihad: A Reassessment," *Journal of African History*, vol. 5, no. 3 (1965): 333-355.

Webster, J.B. et al., *The Revolutionary Years of West Africa since 1800*. 5th impression. London: Longman, 1989.

Chapter 14

The Omani Empire

Jacqueline Woodfork

Introduction

As has been seen, the coast of East Africa enjoyed lively and extensive relations with other peoples of the Indian Ocean in the precolonial era. Sailors crossed the Indian Ocean and mercantile activities connected lands stretching from Africa's eastern coast to the Middle and Far East. One of the most important contacts was between the Omani and the peoples of coastal East Africa. This chapter will examine how this meeting of people resulted in colonization, the use of existing trading networks, the introduction of a new religion, new governmental and economic structures, and the creation of a new culture and language.

Early Coastal East Africa

The area that would become part of the Omani Empire in East Africa stretched over more than three thousand kilometers of coastline between Mogadishu, in present-day Somalia, and Sofala, in present-day Mozambique. This area had numerous inlets, harbors, and islands, which allowed water-borne commerce and regular, reliable transportation and communications. Although the distance from Oman to Zanzibar was over three thousand kilometers by water, it was not an obstacle to those who sailed the Indian Ocean for commerce and conquest.

The fusion of fragments is a way in which to view the composition of the physical area and the people. Just as the coast was comprised of separate entities, the Swahili language and culture was produced by various sources. The indigenous people of the coast labored in various occupations as farmers, fishermen, and traders. As early as 247 B.C., Greek sailors made their way to the coast of East Africa in search of ivory. Greek, Roman, and Arab traders were present in areas of the Horn of Africa and Southern Somalia by 110 A.D.

Swahili is today one of the African languages most commonly recognized outside the African continent, and it is one of the most commonly spoken languages in Africa, stretching from the coast to the Democratic Republic of Congo as the lingua franca. The word "Swahili" is derived from an Arabic word meaning "coast." Currently there is a debate as to the origins of the Swahili language and

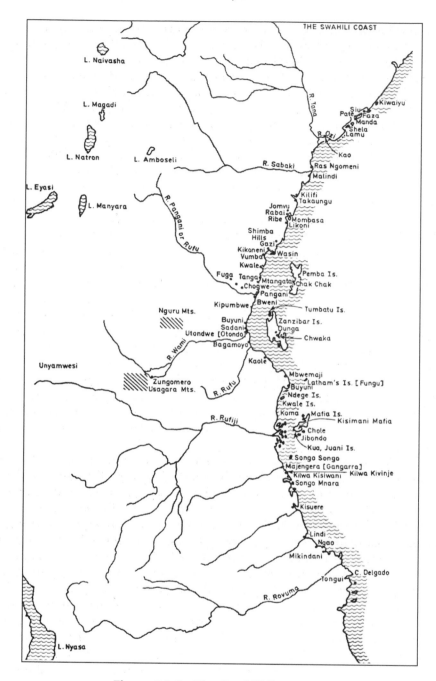

Figure 14-1. The Swahili Coast

culture. The orthodox interpretation of the rise of the Swahili culture and language holds that Arabic speakers encountered Bantu speaking people who had probably displaced indigenous hunter/gatherer groups. Archeological evidence indicates that these Bantu-speakers migrated from the west. Another school of thought is that the language, often called Kiswahili, was created from the synthesis of Bantu languages and Arabic to form a unique tongue when traders arrived from the Persian Gulf. Yet another school holds that the language and culture of the Swahili people were established prior to the arrival of non-Bantu-speaking people and that Persian words were "borrowed" and adapted by the indigenous population.[1] Nonetheless, Bantu, Persians, Arabs, and other Asians all contributed to this culture. The Swahili developed their own solar calendar and rejected the lunar calendar introduced by Arabs as inappropriate. The Swahili were strongly patrilineal, but in practice they were not as strict as the Arabs. The Swahili could be divided into two groups: the Shirazi were the nobility and in the minority, and the Swahili made up the rest of the society. These two groups were united by their religious affiliation; almost all were Sunni Muslims.

The Swahili language and culture developed over centuries continuously enriched by travel and trade. When Arabs and Persians arrived on the shores of East Africa, they called the area "the land of Zanj" or "the land of the Black people." By 1000 A.D. there were many Arab settlers; these settlers intermarried with the indigenous African populations and learned local languages. The Swahili Coast's physical location facilitated the region's cultural development. The annual monsoon winds of the Indian Ocean assisted those who engaged in ocean-borne commerce. From December through February the winds came from the north-northeast, from April through September they came from the south-southwest; thus, a trip that began in December in Mombasa would progress to India and return to the East Coast of Africa in September. This annual pattern provided a few months of time during which sea-borne transportation was unavailable due to unfavorable or absent winds, and many of those Asians who sailed the Indian Ocean stayed on the coast of East Africa, bringing with them their cultural and linguistic traits, which became part of the Swahili tradition. Instead of assimilation, the meeting of these civilizations gave rise to a new culture, that of the Swahili.

The Arabs and Persians took up temporary or permanent residence in the trading cities that developed along the coast. The Swahili Coast had developed into a distinctive entity due to the contacts with the various trading interests of the Indian Ocean, all of whom left their mark on Swahili society. These contacts extended as far as China. Early Chinese sources make reference to Africa, mentioning items of trade such as ivory, gold, and sandalwood; they also provide physical descriptions of the inhabitants of the East African Coast. Commercial interests in the area were not confined to the peoples of the Indian Ocean, and the trading goals of the West had a profound impact upon this area.

At the end of the fifteenth century, a new route to India had been discovered by European sailors who hoped to bypass the overland route and the commercial agents of the Middle East. In 1497, Vasco de Gama rounded the Cape of Good Hope at the tip of Southern Africa and ventured into the Indian Ocean. He was swiftly followed by his compatriots. The Portuguese arrived on the shores of East Africa at the time that the power of the Swahili city-states was waning. These city-states were politically independent and rivals in trade, and the lack of unity

---

1. The debate about the origin of the Swahili language—and culture—reflects a wider debate in African history concerning origins of culture and agents of change. Historians such as Roland Oliver and Sir Reginald Coupland have emphasized the contributions of Arabs made to African cultures, while historians such as Cheikh Anta Diop and V.V. Matviev have insisted upon the primacy of the African aspects.

among these cities facilitated Portuguese conquest. The subjection of the Swahili Coast took less than ten years; by 1508 the Portuguese had taken control of the major towns of the coast of East Africa. They then concentrated their attention on the areas at the southern end of the series of the city-states.

The Portuguese occupied the area to facilitate their mercantile interests, yet trade and politics were intertwined; thus, the Portuguese became entangled in the politics of the indigenous population. The fiscal benefits anticipated by Portugal were not realized, as Portuguese activities did not build upon the foundations laid by the Swahili. The ancient connections with India were severed and trade decreased when the extensive caravan system faded from use. For more than a century and a half, the Portuguese were the dominant political and commercial power on the East African Coast, yet they were neither able to take full advantage of the pre-existing trading systems, nor to sustain their own dominance in the region. As Portuguese power crumbled, the Omani were there to pick up the pieces, but a stronger hold on the former Portuguese possessions in the Indian Ocean proved difficult and often elusive.

The Emergence of the Omani Empire on the East Coast of Africa

When the people of Mombasa looked for a way to escape the domination of the Portuguese, who were acting solely in their crown's interests in the Indian Ocean, they turned to a well-known person, the Imam of Oman, Sultan ibn Saif[2]. In the Omani, Mombasa saw allies who were well-known through long-established trading contacts, who had the same religious beliefs, and who were an integral part of Swahili society. The Omani had already successfully driven the Portuguese out of the capital, Muscat, in 1650 and expelled them from the empire. Not content to rest with the eviction of the Portuguese, the Omani set their sights upon taking control of other Portuguese dominions, including those on the East Coast of Africa.

In 1652, the sultan sent ships to attack Portuguese settlements at Pate and Zanzibar. The capture of these two islands signaled the beginning of the end of Portuguese influence on the Swahili Coast. The East Coast of Africa was an Omani versus Portuguese battleground during the later half of the seventeenth century. The struggle between the two powers culminated when Saif ibn Sultan sailed to Mombasa in 1696 with more than three thousand men, and, after a three-year struggle, the Omani captured Fort Jesus (at Mombasa) in 1698. Though the physical presence of the Portuguese was gone, traces of their culture would still be found in Kiswahili and in the architecture of the coastal cities.

The Omani believed that they needed to keep a firm hand in the running of the Swahili Coast while trying to contain the continuous political unrest in Oman itself: control was tenuous. Initially, the Omani feared that the Portuguese would try to exact revenge against the Omani homeland by launching retaliatory attacks

---

2. An *imam* is a Muslim leader of prayer; the title is also used by Islamic leaders who serve in the capacity of religious and government leaders.

Figure 14-2. Fort Jesus, Mombasa, Kenya

at the East Coast of Africa. The Omani were great mercantilists with a long tradition of ocean-borne commerce, and they realized that other Europeans wanted to supplant Portugal in the Indian Ocean trade. The Omani strove to maintain control in the motherland and simultaneously to prevent a possible erosion of the empire from both internal and external sources on the Swahili Coast.

Political Unrest

The inhabitants of the Swahili Coast were content to be rid of the Portuguese, expecting that they would at last be allowed to administer their own affairs. Imperialism was not an exclusively European phenomenon, however, and one set of foreign rulers was exchanged for another as Omani hegemony progressed. The inhabitants showed their displeasure through limited rebellion and the refusal to pay taxes. The period from the 1710s to the 1740s was one of great upheaval and reversal of fortunes. For example, Kilwa was liberated from Omani rule briefly in 1724 with the aid of Europeans in Mozambique. The Mazrui family in Mombasa bristled under the constraints of the Omani and attempted to act as independent rulers, not as subjects of the sultan or the imam. The Mazrui were an Omani clan who were not very prominent in Oman, but were very important in coastal East Africa as rulers of city-states. The Mazrui often rebelled against Omani rule in the attempt to wield greater power in their city and looked for any weaknesses to exploit. Mazrui attempts to gain control over the areas which they governed were constant throughout the period of Omani rule.

As Oman's sea-borne commerce increased, so did the need to control the Swahili city-states. The capital was moved from the interior of Oman to Muscat in 1749. At its peak, the empire stretched its control from the Swahili Coast into parts of what are now Pakistan and India. The empire was over-extended and many clashes resulted. East Africa was the most profitable part of the empire and the area that was guarded most jealously.

The Swahili Coast was not the only site of political unrest in the empire. Problems surfaced domestically as political leaders were in the process of attempting to consolidate their power in Oman. In spite of East Africa's importance, the internal political power struggles in Oman itself meant that full attention could not be devoted to the area. Upon the death of Ahmad ibn al-Busadi, the founder of the Omani Busadi dynasty, in 1784, Oman tried to exert direct political control over the Swahili Coast. At this time, a rivalry developed between the Busadi brothers, and a power struggle, which was played out in East Africa, ensued. The rivalry of the two aspirants to the seat of power divided the islands and resulted in a protracted series of battles and intrigues that included assassinations and the seizure of forts. Again, Swahili resistance to Omani rule played a role in the drama as the Omani took advantage of the sentiments of the islands' populations in their political machinations, with Ahmad emerging as the winner.

In 1799 Seyyid Sultan ibn Ahmad signed a treaty with the British, agreeing to keep the French out of East Africa. The demise of Portuguese power in the sub-region drew the interest of European powers who recognized that the Omani were reaping financial benefits from their East African possessions and wanted either to become involved in these activities or at least to prevent their European rivals from doing so. East Africa was also important on the geo-political level because of its proximity to the Middle East and because of its long-established trading links with the Far East. When Seyyid Sultan ibn Ahmad came to power, only Zanzibar was under the control of Oman. His son, Seyyid Said, changed that situation.

Seyyid Said

"I am nothing but a merchant," Seyyid Said remarked to a French traveler shortly before his death. This seriously understates his position. Seyyid Said was one of the most important rulers of the Omani Empire. Although his interests were mostly mercantile, commerce was not the only area that he affected, and his presence in Zanzibar and the policies he introduced would have a profound impact upon the Swahili Coast. Born in 1791, he took control of Oman when he killed his eldest brother and rival in 1806. He then proceeded to bring the other city-states within the confines of his political control. In 1817, Seyyid had sent 4,000 men to Pate, which was eventually captured. The Mazrui governor of Pate was replaced by a hand-picked representative of Seyyid who was supported by a number of soldiers. After 1817, Seyyid issued a decree that none of Oman's East African subjects were to trade with Mombasa, whose Mazrui rulers were still not loyal to Oman. This year also saw the "liberation" of Pemba and Brava from Mazrui rule by Zanzibar. One way in which Seyyid recognized the importance of the East African possessions was by eventually moving his capital from Muscat to Zanzibar, where he built himself a modest palace. The predominance of Zanzibar

Figure 14-3. Seyyid Said

can also be seen in the declaration that no foreign commercial agents were to interact with mainland traders; all commercial activity was to be carried out in conjunction with Zanzibar. Seyyid's extension of power was not done easily, however,
or without meeting resistance.

The Mazrui of Mombasa

Although Seyyid made remarkable progress in the consolidation of his East
African empire, there was constant turmoil in Oman and on the Swahili Coast,
and his activities in East Africa met with continued resistance. The Mazrui family of Mombasa, whose presence on the Swahili Coast antedated that of Seyyid
Said, tried to attain sovereignty of the island. The first Mazrui became governor
of Mombassa in 1727, and his rule was so fierce that the citizens revolted, but
the family persisted in its desire to rule. The Mazrui tried continuously to regain

the power they had held before the Omani tightened their control of the coast of East Africa and took advantage of any weaknesses they could exploit. The Mazrui acted upon tenuous Omani control by attempting to act as independent rulers and by frequently revolting against Oman, even calling upon the Portuguese who were eager to take action against those who had ousted them from East Africa. Between 1810 and 1812, Mombasa attacked Lamu in an attempt to remove one governor and to install a pro-Mazrui governor in his place. Lamu appealed to Seyyid Said for assistance against the encroachment of its neighbor, and Said sent his own governor and a garrison of soldiers in 1813. In 1814, a new Mazrui ruler, Abdullah ibn Ahmad, came to power in Mombasa. Instead of sending the tribute expected of a governor to the sultan, he sent only paltry gifts in defiance of Omani domination. At the time, Seyyid was too preoccupied with political events in Oman to respond to the slight, but it was neither forgotten nor forgiven.

The Mazrui refused to relinquish power to Seyyid and divisive family quarrels played a part in the takeover by Oman. Seyyid unsuccessfully attacked Mombasa in 1829. He sent a second large contingent against the city-state later in the same year. Upon hearing that the expedition had been sent, the Mazrui had the throat of one of Seyyid's most trusted advisors slit. The two attempts at landings in Mombasa were blocked and resulted only in heavy causalities and the renewal of an old treaty, the only new provision of which was the removal of Seyyid's troops from Fort Jesus. Temporarily thwarted, Seyyid pursued the matter at a later date. Trying to increase Omani power on the coast of East Africa in 1837, members of the Mombasa Mazrui family were lured into a fortress where they were seized and bound, then taken by their captors to a ship bound for Oman. Some were thrown overboard; others languished in a prison on the Persian Gulf before succumbing to starvation. Seyyid was very serious about the consolidation and maintenance of his power in East Africa. Revealing the importance of the Swahili Coast through the deployment of military personnel, Seyyid committed an army of 6,500 men and a navy of fifteen ships to maintain his domination of the area. Finally, Seyyid made Zanzibar the capital of the Omani Empire in 1840.

The strength of Omani control of its East African empire varied greatly; in some areas traditional rulers continued to direct governmental affairs with the Omani governor as a titular head; some areas had traditional leaders who served on governmental advisory boards. Omani hegemony was strongest in Zanzibar, Mombasa and Kilwa. The most important concerns for the Omani were maritime trade, the collection of revenue, and diplomacy. Seyyid Said instituted a government that was theocratic, yet tolerant. Based on a form of patriarchal absolutism, Seyyid's government had neither departments nor ministers. Other than his own, the only important office in the administration was the city governorship, and that position was under his scrutinizing eye. The government blended religion and secular concerns. Non-religious people were appointed to positions of authority. In the legal system, all cases were judged by a *qadhis* (a judge of Islamic law) who was almost always a scholar, but offenders were not punished strictly according to *sharia* (Islamic law) and were most often fined, jailed, or whipped. European visitors reported only the rarest incidents of harsher corporal punishment. Zanzibaris were relatively content with their situation because of the great economic prosperity that the island enjoyed. They were also very aware of the looming threat of the Europeans whose boats plied the waters surrounding their island.

Cloves, Slaves, and Society

The benefit of the East African possessions to the Omani was financial. The greatest source of income was through customs duties, and there was also an annual poll tax. The Chief Customs Collector was also the Chief Treasurer. The position entailed the direction of most economic affairs. Seyyid appointed an Indian as the Chief Customs Collector of Zanzibar and encouraged the settlement of Indian immigrants to stimulate the economy. Many of these immigrants became customs agents, middlemen, moneylenders, and wholesale traders, effectively dominating the state's economic affairs. Zanzibar was attractive to merchants because it maintained low and predictable duties. The island's revenues increased steadily from the beginning of the nineteenth century. Much of the economic activity concerned the re-exportation of imports, both people and materials, to India, Persia, Egypt, and inner Arabia. The revenues of Zanzibar increased to equal those of Muscat. There was increased caravan trade into the interior, and many inland-trading settlements grew to support these commercial activities. The interior trade will be examined in chapter 15.

Perhaps the most significant contribution that Seyyid Said made to East Africa was the introduction of cloves to the Swahili Coast.[3] Cloves were also grown in the Dutch East Indies, but production there could not meet the demand. Prior to the introduction of this cash crop, coconuts, palm oil, and grains were the most frequently produced agricultural items. Indian cloth, rice and other foodstuffs, beads, and guns were imported. The region's export trade items also included ivory and slaves. Cloves arrived from Mauritius in 1828, and Seyyid tested the product before having seeds distributed throughout Zanzibar and Pemba. These two islands came to dominate the clove market.

Although cloves were a financial boon to the Omani owners of clove plantations, their production brought great changes to the Swahili Coast where they were grown. In Zanzibar, Omani appropriated the most fertile lands to the north and east of Zanzibar City from the indigenous population. It is unclear what happened to the Swahili land-owning elite when the Omani governors were appointed, but almost certainly some of them worked for these officials. Small-scale, indigenous farmers were alienated from the land, and their property was appropriated first by the Swahili and then by the Omani. Clove production is a delicate and time-consuming process; thus, more and more slaves were needed to manage the plantations as production increased. The switch to cloves meant that traditional foodstuffs were produced at greatly reduced levels. The dependence upon a specialized product was both a boon and a bane to the plantation owner. It neither aided a general expansion of agriculture nor did it create great upheavals in

---

3. Although many scholars focus on the role of the clove in the market economy of coastal East Africa, historian Steven Feierman emphasizes the role of the trade in ivory. See Philip Curtain, Steven Feierman, Leonard Thompson, and Jan Vansina, *African History* (London: Longman, 1985), 396-397.

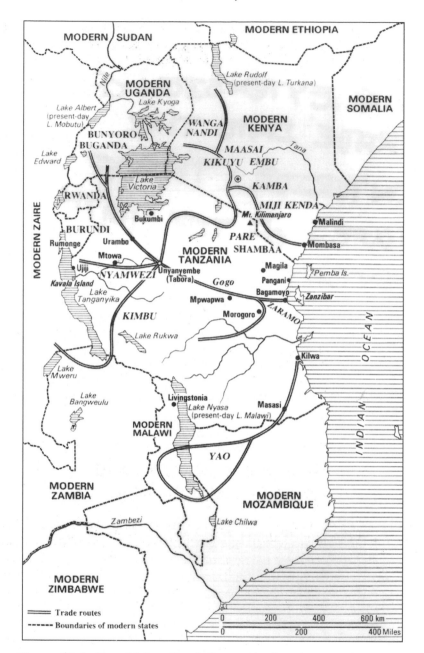

Figure 14-4. East African Trade Routes in the Nineteenth Century

the society. After a long history of slave trading, the elite shifted their emphasis from trading slaves to owning them.[4]

There was a great increase in the slave trade in the middle of the nineteenth century to meet the demands of clove production. Islam and the cultural incorpo-

---

4. For a fuller discussion of slavery in Zanzibar, see Frederick Cooper, *Plantation Slavery on the East Coast of Africa* (New Haven: Yale University Press, 1977).

ration of the slave into society were major factors in the development of plantation systems on the coast of East Africa, and a particular relationship between the master and slave was forged. The plantation owners were Muslims who usually lived by the Qur'anic teachings of the obligations of the master to the slave (and certainly of the slave to the master), including the indoctrination of the slave into Islamic culture. Islam was one of the methods by which the slaves were brought into the social structure and given a position in their new situation. Some slaves held positions as artisans and caravan leaders. These slaves came to identify themselves as coastal people and Muslims, as did other Africans in the sub-region.

Slaves on the Swahili Coast were to be treated in the manner prescribed by the Qur'an and were incorporated into the dominant society. This was done through conversion to Islam and because the offspring of a master and a slave woman was not only free, but a part of the family of the master. Concubinage was a method of fostering greater cultural interchange and cohesion, which brought cultural blending to the level of the Omani ruling elite and to the sultan's palace.

It is in the production of cloves and their importance in trade that the irony of Britain's abolitionist stance can be seen. Africans were also culpable in this system, the procurers and sellers of slaves, and did not want to see their source of livelihood eradicated. The trade continued. While fewer slaves were in the international market, the domestic use of slaves increased. The government actively sought the end of the slave trade, but the production of cloves, an already expensive commodity, depended upon slave labor. Thus, "legitimate trade," or commerce involving items other than humans, relied upon slave labor.

The Decline of Oman and the Advent of the West

Seyyid died on 19 October 1856 at the age of sixty-five while returning to Zanzibar from Muscat. His second son, Seyyid Majid, succeeded him in Zanzibar. The empire was then split into two entities, Oman and the East African Coast. Majid ruled in Zanzibar and Seyyid Thuwaini controlled Oman. Zanzibar was the more lucrative of the two areas, and Majid had to compensate his brother for the superior richness of Zanzibar by paying an annual sum of forty thousand dollars to Muscat. Majid, however, did not do so until the British intervened at his brother's request and the sum was paid until Thuwaini's death. Majid established the city of Dar es Salaam (Haven of Peace) on the mainland in present-day Tanzania, hoping to strengthen his control over the interior trade. The city was not completed at the time of his death in 1870. This cleavage in the empire and the subsequent erosion of power was the beginning of the demise of the Omani, as European powers took advantage of the political intrigues and destabilized empire to begin moving onto the Swahili Coast.

Disaffected people in the Swahili city-states continuously used contacts with European powers to try to strengthen their position against the ruling Omani. Earlier appeals for help went to the Portuguese, but as the British achieved dominance in the Indian Ocean, a switch was made. Mombasa sought British protec-

Figure 14-5. View of Zanzibar, c.1857

tion in 1824 to resist the encroachment of Seyyid Said. The Omani were paying close attention to their East African possessions, which limited the power of the Mazrui. Captain W.F. Owen of Britain was assisted by the Mazrui in declaring Mombasa a British protectorate. Owen envisioned Mombasa as a center from which to wage war against the slave trade. Said wanted neither a strengthened Mazrui family nor anti-slavery activities in his realm. The British found themselves in a difficult diplomatic situation and Mombasa's protectorate status was hastily rescinded in 1826 when the British realized that it was more economically advantageous for them to support Seyyid than the Mazrui. As circumstances on the East Coast of Africa changed, so did its relationship with Britain.

Britain, seeing that the Omani had reaped economic benefits from the Swahili Coast, was interested in establishing its effective navy in the area to engage in sea-borne mercantile activities. One of the major items of trade caused numerous problems between the encroaching British, the Swahili and the Omani. Britain banned the slave trade in 1807 and put pressure on its allies to do the same. That the French displayed an interest in the slave trade in Kilwa also encouraged the British to establish themselves in the areas of the Swahili Coast. The British government declared that the slave trade had officially ended and set about policing international waters themselves in search of illegally-obtained humans for sale. It stopped ships carrying slaves. Seyyid realized that slavery was the basis of clove production on Zanzibar and the island of Pemba, and declined to follow suit. It was not until 1873 that the then sultan of Zanzibar bowed to pressure and banned all trade in slaves by sea. Slavery was still legal on the mainland, and slaves were still smuggled to the clove producing islands.

New England sailors, primarily from Boston and Salem, Massachusetts, were very much involved in Indian Ocean commerce, and, at the apex, they made as many calls to the port of Zanzibar as did the British. The New Englanders' interests included slaves and, because of the agreeable climate, consideration of founding settlements along the coast. Seyyid Said encouraged U.S. business by imposing a minimal tariff on in-coming American goods and not requiring U.S. merchants to pay any duties on East African goods that they purchased. Cotton cloth was one of the principal American imports—slavery was important on both sides of the exchange. U.S. trade overshadowed that of Britain, which encouraged the latter to become further enmeshed in the political affairs of the Swahili Coast in order to, gain a stronger foothold in trade. The British encouraged fear of the French in Seyyid who needed British military support in Oman. Germans, too, made their commercial interests felt.

In the following years between the establishment of the first treaty between Oman and Britain in 1839, a number of interdependent factors increased the interests and presence of the British on the coast of East Africa. Britain was interested in the economic benefits to be gained through its presence in the Omani Empire, and the position of the sultan of Zanzibar was strengthened to abet trade. In 1841 Britain sent its first consul to Zanzibar. The persistence of the slave trade turned the attention of British abolitionists to the Swahili Coast, and Christian missionaries and explorers swiftly moved into the area. These factors were separate, yet interconnected. Christianity was often the organizing principal around which abolitionist movements were founded, and some Europeans believed that Africans needed saving from slavery as well as their traditional lifestyles, which the Europeans deemed uncivilized. Some missionaries, such as David Livingstone, were also explorers. This region was not the only area in which competing European powers had varied interests. The Omani empire in East Africa was but one of the areas where Occidental people and their governments were trying to establish, maintain, or change control of political, economic, and cultural systems for their own benefit.

During the "Scramble for Africa," the Germans became a factor on the Swahili Coast. The Anglo-German Agreement of 1886 left Zanzibar, Pemba, Mafia, Lamu, Kismayu, Brava, Merca, Mogadishu, and Warsheikh defined as dominions of the Sultan of Zanzibar. Two years later, however, Zanzibar was declared a British protectorate. This formal measure was undertaken to secure Britain's interests on the island and to exclude it from German control. Events close to the Swahili Coast, such civil unrest in Buganda, also encouraged European powers to tighten their grip on the coast of East Africa.[5] Britain and Germany came to control the Swahili Coast and much of the interior of East Africa by the close of the nineteenth century.

Conclusion

The East Coast of Africa was an area of great economic activity that drew together various groups of people. The Swahili combined elements of African,

---

5. Buganda is the southern part of present-day Buganda. In 1888, the king, Mwanga, put into motion a xenophobic plan. To rid his country of all foreigners and their religions, he planned to entice them to an island in the Lake Victoria and leave them there to starve. News of the scheme was leaked to the missionaries, which led to a rare convergence of Protestant, Catholic, and Muslim efforts. Mwanga was deposed in favor of a younger brother.

Arab, Indian and, to a lesser extent, Portuguese culture to create a unique and vibrant culture that was made possible by the geography of the East Coast of Africa. The increasing economic importance of the Swahili Coast led to an influx of labor, which contributed to the commercial activity of the area. Urbanization led to a population that was more ethnically varied as more people came from the East African hinterland as domestic and plantation slaves, and from various parts of Asia as merchants. This dynamic society drew the attention of a number of foreign powers that sought to dominate the coast in order to reap the economic benefits.

Review Questions

1. How did the geography of the East Coast of Africa affect its history?
2. How was Omani imperialism in East Africa different from that of the Europeans?
3. What role did the coast of East Africa play in the battle between European powers in the nineteenth century?
4. How did the Omani imperial project change from the time of the demise of Portuguese power in East Africa to the coming of Europeans in the nineteenth century?

Chapter 15

East and Central Africa in the Nineteenth Century

Patrick U. Mbajekwe

The nineteenth century was a period of traumatic and momentous transformations in East and Central Africa. The changes were brought about mainly by the growing integration of the area into the world economy and the ways in which Africans responded to the new opportunities. However, the enormous external influences were only some of the experiences that impacted the region in the nineteenth century. There were many internally induced changes as well. In other words, the impact of the external and internal forces combined to shape the nineteenth century history of East Central Africa.

In this chapter, I shall discuss first East and then Central Africa. Under East Africa, I shall discuss: (a) the penetration of the international trade through the Indian Ocean into the interior; (b) the impact of the Ngoni invaders from southern Africa; (c) the political dynamics in the Great Lakes region and the northeastern interior; and (d) the European advances. Under Central Africa, I shall discuss: (a) the developments in the Atlantic trade; (b) the political transformations among the peoples and kingdoms of the savanna; and (c) the invaders from southern and eastern Africa.

East Africa

International Trade

Until the beginning of the nineteenth century, contacts between the coast and the interior of East Africa had been limited. They were mostly along the southern trade routes running from Kilwa on the coast to Lake Nyasa (now Lake Malawi), controlled by the Yao traders of northern Mozambique. Thus, although international trading had been going on the coast of East Africa for centuries, it took until the nineteenth century for many areas, especially in present-day Kenya, Uganda, and Tanzania to be extensively drawn into and influenced by the commerce. Trade brought with it great transformations, offered new opportunities for state-building in some areas, and at the same time, threatened existing polities.

The southern coastal port of Mozambique which had been under the control of the Portuguese since the fifteenth century had been exporting gold and ivory

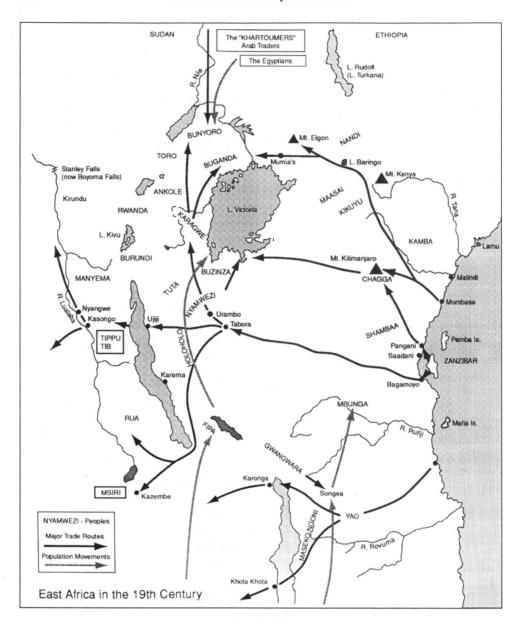

Figure 15-1. East Africa in the Nineteenth Century

for several centuries. But in the eighteenth century, decline in the gold trade and a shift of the ivory trade beyond the area of Portuguese control made Mozambique increasingly turn to the trade in humans. The growth in the slave trade was stimulated by the development of the sugar plantation economy on the Mascarene Islands, including Mauritius and Réunion (east of Madagascar) by the French. The plantations demanded African slave labor. Further stimulus was given to the Mozambican slave trade by New World demands, particularly from Brazil. Cuban-bound Spanish vessels, and even a few United States vessels bought slaves from Mozambique. It was estimated that between the 1820s and 1830s, about fifteen thousand slaves were exported each year from the port of Mozambique Island alone.[1]

Further north, trade in slaves and ivory had been growing in the port of Kilwa since the eighteenth century. Mozambique had considered Kilwa a stiff competitor, and Portuguese attempts to control the port were checked by the Omani Arabs. The Portuguese position was made even more difficult by two other factors. First, the insatiable demand for slaves in the rapidly expanding French plantations in the Mascarene Islands made the French look for more slaves from Kilwa. Second, the Yao traders who used to supply Mozambique with ivory shifted their attention to Kilwa at the beginning of the nineteenth century in search of better deals. Indeed, by this time the demand for ivory was rising dramatically in the world market, and so was Kilwa's commerce. It was to be the foundation of Zanzibar's commercial empire.

From the beginning of the nineteenth century, the foundation for the future development of Zanzibar as a major trading center had been laid. The Omani Arabs under Sayyid Said bin Sultan established a more effective administration on the island which was to be the center of their economic imperialism in East Africa in the nineteenth century. Sayyid Said had come to power in Oman in 1806. For the next decade he was principally concerned with consolidating his power in Oman. He cleverly allied with Britain, which not only helped him strengthen his position against his adversaries, but also won British approval of his objectives in East Africa. With stability at home, Said embarked on overseas adventures. He began to assert Oman's claims to the overlordship of what he regarded as the "Arab" areas of East Africa. He encouraged increasing numbers of Omani Arabs to settle on the East African coast. Making skillful use of local quarrels and rivalries, he conquered a number of the coastal towns and imposed his protégés on them. He paid his first visit to the East African coast in 1828, and transferred his capital from Muscat to Zanzibar in 1832. This was to have considerable impact on the economic fortunes and politics of the coast as well as the hinterland.

Strategically located, and blessed with an excellent harbor, an attractive climate and fertile soil, Zanzibar was nurtured by Said to a position of paramountcy, making it the "greatest single emporium on the western shore of the Indian Ocean."[2] Within a short time Zanzibar became the most important market on the East African coast for ivory, slaves, cloves, and gum copal, and the greatest importer of Indian, American, and European goods.

Ivory was by far the greatest export, and its value rose continuously throughout the century. The price of ivory rose uninterruptedly from $22 per *frasila* (1 *frasila* equals 35lb. or 16 kg.) in 1823 to $89 per *frasila* in 1873.[3] Ivory was the cornerstone of the Zanzibari economy, and indeed dominated the entire East African long-distance trade in the nineteenth century. Cloves, which were introduced in Zanzibar in the early nineteenth century from the French island of Réunion, were another major export. Sultan Said, realizing the high profitability of the crop, exploited the fertility of Zanzibar and Pemba Islands to embark on

---

1. Philip Curtin, et al., *African History from Earliest Times to Independence*, 2nd ed. (London: Longman, 1995), 354.

2. A.I. Salim, *The Swahili-Speaking Peoples of Kenya's Coast, 1895-1965* (Nairobi: East African Publishing House, 1973), 15.

3. Curtin, 375.

large-scale plantation production of cloves. By the time of his death, the plantations were producing about four-fifths of the world's supply of cloves, and the revenue from it was next only to ivory and slaves.

The clove plantations, however, raised new demands for slaves since the cultivation of cloves was labor-intensive. There was, consequently, a big demand for slaves in both Zanzibar and Pemba by the Arab plantation owners. Zanzibar became a major slave mart, mostly for internal use. It is interesting to note that the increase in the slave trade was happening at a time when Zanzibar was signing treaties with England to end the trade. What happened was that the treaties suppressed the export slave trade, and lowered the prices of slaves, so the Arab plantation owners filled their plantations with cheap slaves. In fact, the total number of slaves captured each year in East Africa continued to increase by mid-century.

Besides encouraging production for export, Said initiated commercial policies that greatly enhanced international trade. He unified and regularized the multiple and irregular customs duties on the coast to import duties of five percent flat; and levied no duty at all on exports from his domain. He signed commercial treaties with the United States (1833), Britain (1839), and France (1844). These nations established consulates in Zanzibar. Similar encouragement was given to Germany, although no treaty was signed until after Said's death. Zanzibar imported sugar, beads, brassware, firearms, and cotton cloth from Europe and the United States, and exported ivory, slaves, cloves, rhinoceros horns, gum copal, and other goods.

The ever-growing volume of trade on the coast meant an increasing demand for trade goods, particularly ivory and slaves, from the hinterland. As the ivory-producing regions near the coast became denuded of elephants, the impetus to move deeper inland increased. It is important to note that the initiative for this inward movement came from the Africans of the interior, especially the Yao, Nyamwezi, and Kamba, who developed all the major caravan routes. However, the Arab-Swahili caravaneers competed very effectively with the Africans, their advantages being force of arms, access to credit (from Indian financiers based in Zanzibar), influence over Zanzibari trade policies, and their ability to build alliances with local leaders. It is not clear when the Arab-Swahili led their first caravans into the interior, but it is probable that by the 1820s they had gone beyond Lake Tanganyika into present-day Zaire. Although they went along many trading routes, their activities were strongest on the Pangani-Bagamoyo route that ran through the Nyamwezi country. They established trading settlements inland, the most important being Tabora and Ujiji. These settlements were not only depots for storage and supplies, but sometimes bases from which they organized attacks and raids. As subjects of the sultan of Zanzibar, they carried his flag to impress those they met, but that did not mean that they always acted in his name.

One of the greatest Arab-Swahili traders of the East African interior was Hamed bin Mohammed, otherwise known as Tippu Tib. He was born in 1830, and his father had been a trader in Tabora. After a period of apprenticeship working for his father in the caravan trade, he launched his own business and, in 1865, reached Ruemba on the eastern shore of Lake Tanganyika. He continued to move deeper into Zaire in search of ivory. Through intrigues and conquests of the scattered chiefdoms, he established himself around Stanley Falls (now Boyoma Falls), controlling much of the Manyema area, with his capital at Kasongo. He established plantations and imposed a monopoly on the ivory business in the area. To

Figure 15-2. Tippu Tib's Captives Being Sold into Slavery

secure safe passage for his caravans to the coast, he entered into agreements with
Mirambo of the Nyamwezi and Rumaliza of Ujiji. When the explorer Stanley
came in 1876, Tippu Tib welcomed him and accompanied him downriver deep
into the rainforests. Later, when King Leopold of Belgium gained control of the
Congo Free State, Tippu Tib accepted the post of governor of Stanley Falls (now
Boyoma Falls), hoping to preserve his position in the face of the encroaching Europeans. But he could not, and in 1890 he returned to Zanzibar, never to return
to the interior. He died in 1905. With the death of Tippu Tib ended an era in East
African history—the era of the Arab-Swahili trading adventures in the interior.

The career of Tippu Tib tells us many things about the activities of the Arab-
Swahili caravaneers in the interior. First, it shows how they used intrigue, diplomacy, some of which was sealed by marriages, and force to gain influence among
the Africans. It demonstrated how independent of the direct control of the sultan
of Zanzibar most of them were in the interior. They survived for the most part on
their own. And the way Tippu Tib was easily cut out by the Europeans and fled to
the coast was indicative of the shallowness of the political hegemony they had
built in the interior. As Norman R. Bennett puts it: "The Arabs had built a domination that outwardly appeared powerful to nineteenth-century observers, but
there were no germs for successful development within it."[4] Their interest was
primarily commercial, which was immensely beneficial to them as well as to the
Africans who cooperated with them. Perhaps one of the greatest contributions of
the Arabs in the interior of East Africa was the wide spread of the Swahili lan-

4. N.R. Bennett, "The Arab Impact," in B.A. Ogot and J.A. Kieran, eds., *Zamani: A Survey of East African History* (Nairobi: East African Publishing House, 1968), 236.

guage. The language spread through the trade routes, and later became the national language of some modern East African countries. Finally, we should not forget the devastation that the Arabs and their African allies wrought on the many communities who were raided for slaves.

As noted earlier, there were a number of African peoples who were involved in the development and organization of coastal-hinterland trading activities. Indeed, the initiative for the opening up of the trade routes was that of Africans. The peoples that played the most prominent roles were the Yao, the Nyamwezi and the Kamba.

The Yao are known to have been the earliest group involved in the coastal-hinterland trade. They controlled the southern trade route that ran from Kilwa into their territories in the whole region of Lake Nyasa (Lake Malawi). They used to supply slaves and ivory to the Mozambican port before they diverted their attentions to Kilwa for better deals. Even during the peak period of this trade in the nineteenth century, the Yao were almost exclusively in control of this route. The Yao had previously been loosely organized in small groups, but a combination of factors, the long-distance trading activities and the invasion of the Nguni from the south, plus the reactions of the local peoples to these forces, made them form larger polities in the nineteenth century. Powerful chiefs emerged, like Mpanda, Mataka, Machemba, and Mtalika, who not only controlled the trade, but effectively kept the Arabs out of this control, except in isolated places like Khota-Khota and Karonga in present-day Malawi. The political and commercial base of the Yao rulers was simply too strong for the Arabs to challenge. The Arabs who carried on business in these areas did so only as clients of these rulers.

The Nyamwezi were the most prominent people in the central route that ran from the port of Bagamoyo into the areas of Lake Tanganyika, eastern Zaire, and the Buganda territories. By 1800 Nyamwezi caravans had started to arrive at the coast. Unlike the Yao, the Nyamwezi were successfully challenged by the Arabs for control of the trade in their territory. In 1839, Sayyid Said had signed a treaty with one of the Nyamwezi chiefs to grant Arab traders passage through Unyanyembe without paying taxes. This was the beginning of the establishment of Arab settlements among the Nyamwezi, the most important of which was Tabora. In order to ensure their objective, which was the free flow of trade, the Arabs sometimes meddled with Nyamwezi local politics, although the overall effect was small.[5] Some African chiefs also used the Arabs to enhance their position over their rivals. As trade grew, competition between the Arabs and the Nyamwezi increased. The Arabs made efforts to undercut the Nyamwezi, using their access to credit and discriminatory tariff structures at Zanzibar. For example, in 1864 while the Arab traders paid $9 per *frasila* of ivory as duty to Zanzibar, the Nyamwezi were charged $15. Indeed, that the Nyamwezi traders survived under these conditions was a clear testimony to their competitive capabilities. The combination of Arab and Nyamwezi trading activities made the central route the busiest and largest of the major trading routes, and certainly the one best known by European travelers and missionaries in the nineteenth century.

On the northern route that ran from Mombasa through the Ukambani country and moved towards the Kenya highlands and beyond Lake Victoria, the

---

5. See Bennett, 219-226.

Kamba were the prominent African traders. Having dominated the regional trading network in the eighteenth century, the Kamba moved into the international trading network in the early nineteenth century. By the 1840s, Kamba caravans were sending about three to four hundred *frasilas* of ivory to the coast every week. In the interior, their trading parties were visiting not only their Kikuyu neighbors, but also places as far away as Mau, Gusii, Lake Baringo, and Samburu country.[6] By the later part of the nineteenth century, however, Arab-Swahili traders edged out the Kamba from control of this route. But, although the Arabs did gain control of the use of the routes, they were not known to have established major Arab centers as they did among the Nyamwezi.

The nineteenth century long-distance trade had a variety of impacts on the people of East Africa. In discussing these impacts, however, it is vital to bear a number of issues in mind. First, we should realize that not all East African societies came in direct contact with the trading networks. There were many peoples who continued to live their lives almost unconnected with the commerce. Second, some of the transformations brought about by the trade were not isolated from other historical forces at this time in the region, such as the invasion of the Ngoni from the south (which I shall discuss shortly). Third, whatever transformations did take place were primarily directed by the African peoples and their leaders, given the opportunities and choices available to them.

The impacts were as diverse as the reactions of the peoples of East Africa. Many political relationships were realigned. Some polities broke up, new ones arose, while other older ones were strengthened. Some people seized the new opportunities and, with increasing access to firearms and a stronger material base, were able to build larger political organizations. But at the same time, this meant tragedy for others, who fell prey to the slave raids. One person's nation-builder sometimes became another's nation-destroyer. In some cases, insecurity caused by incessant raiding forced some weak groups to run to their stronger neighbors for protection. Military organization was revolutionized in East Africa during the nineteenth century. The impetus for this came from both the need for security and the frequent armed conflicts associated with the struggle for control of trade. This was exacerbated by the increasing access to guns and firearms from the coast. However, military revolution in some parts of East Africa was a process that was first started by the invading Ngoni, who brought along with them Shaka's military strategies. Firearms from the coast thus accelerated a condition that was already in process. The use of standing professional armies and mercenary armies (known as *ruga-ruga* in western Tanzania) spread in East Africa.

To illustrate these changing political relationships, let me briefly examine the fortunes of the Nyamwezi, who were able to build large "empires" for themselves during this era, and those of the people of the Pangani valley, who had their states devastated by the trade. Among the Nyamwezi, Mirambo, a powerful man, seized on the new opportunities to build one of the largest states during this era. Mirambo started as a ruler of the small state of Uyowa. He was believed to have been captured when he was young by the Ngoni, who taught him their military art. By the 1860s he had started to raid the neighbors of Uyowa using his army.

---

6. I.N. Kimambo, "The East Africa Coast and Hinterland," in J.F. Ade Ajayi, ed., *Africa in the Nineteenth Century until the 1880s*, UNESCO General History of Africa, vol. 6 (Paris: UNESCO, 1989), 243.

By his death in 1884, he had created a vast empire that extended from Buha and Burundi, to the Vinza and Tongwe in the west, to the Pimbwe and Konongo in the south, to the Nyaturu, Iramba, and Sukuma in the east, and to the Sumbwa in the north.[7] He stoutly challenged the Arabs for control of the Tabora-Ujiji trade route and the Buganda route. He also recognized potential sources of power and welcomed missionaries to his capital, especially the London Mission Society, hoping to use them to his advantage. Unfortunately, however, Mirambo's empire had no real foundation. Lacking a unifying organizational machinery, his empire disintegrated as soon as he died in 1884. Mirambo's case is a good example of the tenuousness of the political gains of the nineteenth century international trade in the East African interior. Many of the states that were built during that era lacked a secure foundation and many collapsed by the end of the century.

In the Pangani valley, the experience of the international trade for the Shambaa kingdom and the Pare states was mostly destructive. These states had been established before the trade invasion and were orderly, peaceful, and prosperous. By the middle of the nineteenth century, however, all that had changed. The trade route that passed through their territories brought wealth and power to a number of subordinate chiefs. This weakened the center. The subordinate chiefs, supported by their trade and raiding allies, not only broke away, but engaged in a series of mutual raids and wars. The big states were dismembered and, from the 1870s till the colonial invasion in the 1890s, the area was engulfed in constant violence.

Analysts have often used the impressive trade statistics of Omani Zanzibar to generalize about the economic prosperity of all East African peoples from the nineteenth century international trade. If Zanzibar and the coastal trading islands profited from the trade, for many hinterland people the era was a disaster. Even the profits from the coast did not go to Africans, they went to the Arabs, Indians, Europeans, and Americans. Many hinterland people recall this period as an era of turmoil and destruction—caused by the slave raiders and the armies of the nation builder/destroyers. Prosperity in the interior was deceptive. To get ivory, Africans had to kill elephants. To get slaves, they engaged in destructive wars and raids. They sold ivory and slaves and received guns which caused more destruction. Since elephants and human beings could not be easily reproduced, there was no basis for economic growth; Africans were only depleting their limited resources. By the end of the century, the supposed prosperity was gone.

The Ngoni Invasion of Southern Tanzania

As noted above, historical changes in nineteenth-century East Africa were not shaped by the international trade alone. The Ngoni, who invaded southern Tanzania from the 1830s, clearly caused fundamental transformations in the region. The Ngoni were one of the Nguni-speaking peoples of northern Zululand that were displaced during the rule of Shaka. Led by their great chief Zwangendaba, the Ngoni fled their homeland in about 1820, moving northwards into the area of southern Mozambique. After wandering for about fifteen years in this region,

---

7. Jan Vansina, *Kingdoms of the Savanna* (Madison: University of Wisconsin Press, 1969), 75.

they crossed the River Zambezi in November 1835, and continued their relentless march northwards through Malawi and Zambia until they arrived at the Fipa plateau in the early 1840s. Here, Zwangendaba established his capital. In the process of this migration the Ngoni incorporated a number of peoples, including members of the Thonga of Mozambique, the Shona of Zimbabwe, and the Senga, Chewa, and Tumbuka from the region north of the Zambezi river in Zambia and Malawi. They were able to do this using a combination of revolutionary military tactics and a dynamic social system which they originally copied from Shaka, and which they improved on as they moved along. Shaka's military innovations included the replacement of the traditional long throwing spear by the short stabbing spear and the organization of soldiers into highly disciplined age-regiments. The social system was organized in such a way that the conquered peoples were easily assimilated into the society, with an emphasis on a strong centralized political system.

In 1848, Zwangendaba died, and succession disputes led to the splitting of the nation into five groups. Three moved south and established their kingdoms in Zambia and Malawi, while two, the Tuta and Gwangara, remained in East Africa. The Tuta moved towards the eastern shores of Lake Tanganyika, raiding as they went along. They encountered the Holoholo, who successfully repelled them in the 1850s. The Holoholo had earlier suffered defeat at the hands of the Ngoni, and many of them had fled across the lake. There, they adopted the Ngoni military tactics, and successfully used them to defend themselves from the invading Tuta. The Holoholo experience is indeed one of many examples of East African peoples who adopted the new military techniques of the Ngoni and used them to defend themselves against the invaders.[8] Recovering from this setback, the Tuta turned toward the Nyamwezi, where they upset the Arab trade route between Tabora and Ujiji. They eventually settled northwest of Tabora and raided as far as the southern shores of Lake Victoria. One of the Nyamwezi captured by the Tuta was Mirambo, who learned military techniques from the Ngoni (strengthened by firearms) to build his nation.

The Gwangara, on the other hand, moved southeast into the Songea area, east of Lake Nyasa (Lake Malawi), where they encountered another established Ngoni kingdom, Maseko. The Ngoni-Maseko had broken away before the Ngoni reached the Zambezi and moved eastwards, crossing the Zambezi closer to the River Shire, and eventually settled east of Lake Nyasa. Under their leader, Maputo, the Maseko were stronger than the Gwangara, who accepted their overlordship. But this was only for a short period. In about 1860 when war broke out between the Maseko and the Gwangara, Maseko superiority had been greatly weakened. The Gwangara defeated and drove them south across the Ruvuma River, to eventually settle in southwestern Malawi. The Gwangara themselves, however, split into two kingdoms: the Mshope kingdom under Chipeta, and the Njelu kingdom led by Chabruma. These two held sway in the Songea area, raiding extensively throughout the area between Lake Nyasa and the coast until the imposition of German colonial rule.

---

8. E.A. Alpers, "The Nineteenth Century: Prelude to Colonialism," in Ogot and Kieran, eds., *Zamani*, 241.

While the impact of the Ngoni invasion in the development of East African history is unquestionable, historians have debated whether it was primarily destructive or constructive. On the one hand, the Ngoni invasion led to nation-building and the consolidation of other existing states. The kingdoms created by the Ngoni in East Africa continued to flourish as strong nations well into the period of European colonial rule. Some existing states adopted the Ngoni military techniques to unify, strengthen, and expand their territories and to protect themselves not only from the Ngoni, but from other slave raiders. Such were the cases of Mirambo, the Holoholo, the Sangu, and the Hehe. On the other hand, life became increasingly insecure for many weak and defenseless peoples. They became prey not only to the expanding states, but to bands of renegades and mercenaries that arose in the process of the Ngoni migrations and roamed about raiding and plundering at will. This era was, for a number of communities, a period of insecurity, lawlessness, devastation, and misery.

Political Dynamics in the Great Lakes Region and the Northeastern Interior

The states and peoples of the Great Lakes region and the northeastern interior underwent great transformations in the nineteenth century. They were unaffected by the Ngoni invasion, but a number of them were affected by the coastal trade to varying degrees. The nineteenth-century history of the kingdoms of the Great Lakes region is an extraordinarily rich and complex one. It is a history of great dynamics in which the old order matched up with the new to produce unique political orders. It is a history of extensive political transformations in which intelligent, innovative, and courageous leaders were able to use both the old system and the emerging opportunities to build stronger, centralized, cohesive political structures with elaborate bureaucracies. In the nineteenth century, Bunyoro, Buganda, Burundi, and Rwanda emerged as the most powerful of these kingdoms. Developments in these kingdoms had the most demonstrable effect in the shaping of the region. Other less powerful states included Busoga, Toro, Karagwe, Buzinza, and the Buhaya states. Generally, the stronger states raided the smaller ones.

In the closing years of the eighteenth century and into the early nineteenth, the ancient kingdom of Bunyoro was on the verge of disintegration. Its provinces were breaking away, some being taken over by neighboring Buganda and others asserting their independence. For instance, Toro province, led by Prince Kaboyo, successfully seceded early in the nineteenth century. However, by the second half of the century, traders from Khartoum and Zanzibar had reached Bunyoro and a powerful ruler, Kabalega, was rising to power. With increasing access to firearms and his fortune from the trade, Kabalega built a strong army, and began to unite the feuding provincial chiefs and kingdoms. With the army he was able to repel external invasions. In 1872 at the battle of Baligota Isansa for example, Kabalega defeated Sir Samuel Baker's Egyptian forces. Baker had gone to establish a protectorate in northern Uganda on behalf of Khedive Ishmael of Egypt. For seven years Kabalega was able to engage the British in guerrilla warfare. By the end of the nineteenth century, however, the Bunyoro kingdom declined. The difficulty of keeping the kingdom together was exacerbated by provincial feuds, the steady rise of Buganda, and the persistent advance of the European invaders.

By the nineteenth century, Buganda had been established as a powerful kingdom with centralized government and a disciplined bureaucracy. Coastal traders reached Buganda by the mid-nineteenth century. Immediately, the intelligent Kabaka Mutesa (1856-1884) saw the immense potential of using the various foreign forces both for territorial expansion and for internal consolidation. He seized absolute personal control of the commercial traffic in his territory, particularly the guns. He embraced both Islam and Christian religious missionaries and used both effectively to his advantage, playing one against the other, and using both to offset the adherents of indigenous religion. When Mutesa died in 1884, however, these forces turned into a nemesis for Buganda, escalating the factional conflicts. In 1888, his successor Mwanga, who had earlier executed some forty-two of his Christian pages, was deposed by the feuding factions. When invading British troops reached Buganda in 1890, they found four armies controlled by the Catholics, Protestants, Muslims, and traditionalists, each in charge of different parts of the empire. The experiences of Bunyoro and Buganda show clearly that the great states had their positions strengthened in the nineteenth century by their effective manipulations of the opportunities offered by the new external forces, even if they could not always hold on to their gains.

However, not all the powerful states had their rise or consolidation tied to the external forces. The experiences of Rwanda and Burundi are indicative of transformations that were more internally oriented. Both states successfully kept the coastal traders out of their region and developed effective tactics for coping with the guns of their enemies. By the nineteenth century, both states had developed centralized polities based on Tutsi dynasties, although Rwanda later emerged as the stronger and more dynamic of the two kingdoms. The Tutsi exploited their links with the semi-divine Chwezi kings to establish a strong political hegemony over the Batwa and the Hutu. What eventually developed was an ethno-class division, with the land- and cattle-owning Tutsi aristocracy on the one hand, and the Hutu and Batwa peasants and serfs on the other. This was a relationship, exacerbated by colonial influences, that was to have devastating consequences in the twentieth century.

In the region of the northeastern interior, the most important peoples were the Kikuyu, Maasai, Nandi, Wanga, and Chagga. The Kikuyu had, in the eighteenth century, due to a population increase, moved into the areas of the Nyandarua in the west and Kiambu in the south. Expansion and consolidation continued in the nineteenth century as population continued to increase. They traded with the Kamba on the fringes of the forest, but refused to allow the Arabs into their territory.

The Maasai were the lords of the plains in the rift valley between central Tanzania and central Kenya, up to the foot of Mount Kilimanjaro in the south and the Kenya Highlands in the north. By the nineteenth century, they had reached the peak of their territorial expansion, and struggles over the control of resources—cattle and pasture land—led to a series of civil wars with important consequences for the entire region. There was strife in all parts of Maasailand. A number of groups were displaced and they fled into neighboring territories. Among the Nandi, the orkoiyot ritual office (known as oloiboni among the Maasai) was said to have been introduced by one of these fleeing Maasai groups. This ritual office initiated the rise of Nandi power in the nineteenth century. The Wanga used another Maasai refugee group, the Uasin Gishu, to strengthen their kingdom. As a

sent Richard Burton and John Hanning Speke on an expedition to trace the source of the Nile. With the assistance of two experienced Yao guides, Sidi Bombay and Mwinyi Mabruki, they travelled from Bagamoyo and reached Lake Tanganyika in 1858. Speke moved on alone to Mwanza and saw the big lake there which he named after his queen, Victoria. He thought that was the source of the Nile. Burton and Speke went back to England. In 1860, Speke led a second Royal Geographical Society expedition, this time accompanied by James Grant. They traveled along the west side of Lake Victoria and came to Buganda, where they were welcomed by Mutesa. They kept on until they reached the town of Jinja where the Nile leaves the lake, and traveled back to England down the great river.

There were also other explorers of note. Samuel Baker, who came up the Nile from Egypt, saw Lake Albert. Journalist Henry Stanley surveyed Lakes Victoria, Albert, and Tanganyika, and traveled along the Congo River to the Atlantic in 1877. Hungarian Count Teleki saw and named Lake Rudolf (now called Lake Turkana) in 1888. The Scottish geologist Joseph Thomson did extensive exploration of Kenya between 1882 and 1884, collecting geological and biological information.

Geographical and scientific interests, yes; but they certainly were not the only driving forces that brought these men to the interior of East Africa. The European governments and traders needed the information too. By the 1880s, the Europeans had overcome their ignorance of the interior of East Africa. They knew the physical outline of the land, the climate, and the people. Most importantly, they had discovered that white people could survive for years in good health in East Africa. Their urge to grab and rule East Africa became unstoppable.

The commercial activities of Livingstonian-inspired missions in the East African interior have been noted above. Earlier, the establishment of a British Consulate in Zanzibar had increased British trading interests there. In 1872, a member of the Scottish Free Church, William Mackinnon, opened the operations of his British India Steam Navigation Company in Zanzibar. Shortly after, he convinced Sultan Bargash, with the influence of the British consul John Kirk, to grant him a concession to construct roads and a railway from the coast to Lakes Nyasa and Victoria. A lack of funds stalled the project, but Mackinnon's dreams were to mature in the imperialistic organization known as the British East Africa Company. By 1882, the stage had been set for the European takeover of East Africa. The high "tides of imperialism" were already flowing. King Leopold had earlier established his empire in the Congo, Britain occupied Egypt in 1882, the Germans had grabbed South West Africa and Cameroon in 1884, and Karl Peters, the treaty-collecting wizard of the German Colonization Society, had arrived in East Africa.

Central Africa

The Atlantic Trade and Central Africa

While the impetus for the international trade of East Africa came from the Indian Ocean, that of Central Africa came from the Atlantic, although some traders from the East African coast did penetrate into the territory known as Central Africa. The Central African Atlantic trade in the nineteenth century can be di-

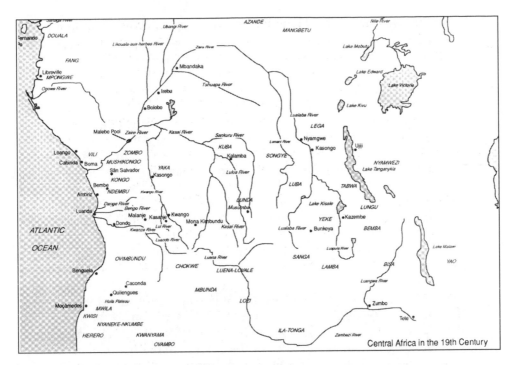

Figure 15-3. Central Africa in the Nineteenth Century

vided into two sectors: the coastal sector and the inland sector. The coastal sector stretched from the ports of Benguela and Luanda in the south to the Cameroon estuary in the north. By the second half of the nineteenth century, the Atlantic trade had expanded right into the heart of Central Africa with far reaching consequences.

In the opening decades of the nineteenth century, the slave trade remained the dominant business in the southern segment of the Central African coastal trade, particularly at the ports of Luanda and Benguela. The Portuguese and Brazilian shipping interests and the Luso-African merchants were in control. Indeed, by 1820, slaves accounted for eighty-five percent of all government revenue and ninety percent of all exports. In 1836, Portugal abolished the slave trade, but a major decline in the trade did not start until the 1840s. Then, in 1850 when Brazil abolished the trade, it finally collapsed. But an illegal traffic in slaves still continued alongside non-slave ("legitimate") products. Slave exports finally stopped in the 1860s, only to be replaced by the export of bonded laborers or *libertos*. The slave trade however continued in the interior as the political and commercial systems that were based on slaving continued to generate captives.[12] With the ending of the export slave trade, the African lords began to put slaves to new use inside Africa. There was a growing internal demand for servile labor in the hinterland.

The abolition of the export slave trade encouraged the expansion of trade in ivory, wax, palm oil, sugar, coffee, groundnuts, and cotton. Luanda's (the princi-

---

12. Joseph C. Miller, "The Paradoxes of Impoverishment in the Atlantic Zone," in David Birmingham and Phyllis M. Martin, eds., *History of Central Africa*, vol. 1 (London: Longman, 1983), 15.

pal port of the Portuguese colony of Angola) trade in ivory grew rapidly in the 1840s and 1850s to become the major source of income for the government of the colony. Many coffee, cotton, and sugar plantations also sprang up in the colony. Cotton prices, in particular, experienced a boom in the 1860s because of the civil war in the United States, which led to the further expansion of plantations.

The shift from the slave trade to "legitimate" trade had more impact in Angola. Many European slave dealers, unable to adapt to the changing trade pattern, left the country in the 1840s and 1850s. This caused a temporary decline in the overall fortunes of the region and, at the same time, a shift in political and economic control from Europeans to the Luso-Africans. Indeed, the period between the 1830s and the 1870s was the most prosperous for the Luso-Africans in Angola. Many of them profited from the boom in the illegal slave trade that followed abolition and invested their profits in the establishment of plantations in the nearer hinterland, capitalizing on the very cheap slave labor. The metropolitan authorities in Portugal almost lost control of the colony to the Luso-Africans.

By the mid-1870s, however, there was a resurgence of metropolitan control. From 1822, when Brazil, an important Portuguese colony, became independent, there had been an increasing marginalization of Portuguese businessmen in Brazil. These businessmen, therefore, began to divert their attention to the Portuguese Central African markets. The renewed interest in the Central African market was given a boost at the beginning of the 1870s by a boom in the Angolan rubber and coffee trade. This attracted new credit from Europe, along with a new wave of immigrants from Portugal, who began to establish plantations. At first, the Luso-Africans vigorously resisted this challenge to their hegemony, but Lisbon effectively backed the immigrants from Europe. New laws, particularly on labor and tariffs, were introduced to undermine the Luso-Africans' control. By the 1890s, the Luso-Africans had been reduced to impotent political agitators.

The northern segment of the Central African coastal trade from the Cameroon estuary to the point where the River Zaire (formerly known as the Lower Congo) joins the Atlantic ocean, with the most important centers being Douala, Libreville, Loango, and the Cabinda-Boma axis. The Napoleonic Wars had disrupted trade in this zone but by 1815, trade was picking up, with firms from Britain, Holland, France, Brazil, Spain, Germany, and Portugal competing effectively. The Europeans bought ivory, palm nuts and oil, timber, dyes, wax, honey, copper ore and, of course, slaves. They sold textiles, guns, liquor, metalware, beads, and sundry other goods. Between 1815 and 1880, the volume of trade is estimated to have increased fifty-fold.[13]

In the far north, along the southern shores of the Bight of Biafra, is Cameroon, with its principal port of Douala. The African merchants of Douala were in effective control of the trade in this region. They had a flourishing trade in ivory. By 1800, 1,000 kg. of ivory was worth £240, this being made up of "fifteen thousand kilograms of salt, seventeen kegs of powder, fifty 'Tower' proof guns, ten pieces of Indian 'baft', ten pieces of Indian 'romal', forty cheap Manchester prints, twenty good-quality prints, two kegs of brandy, thirty copper pots-and-pans, and a residual sum in beads, ironmongery, crockery and cutlery."[14] Trade in

---

13. Curtin, 378.
14. David Birmingham, *Central Africa to 1870* (Cambridge: Cambridge University Press, 1981), 142.

slaves and other products also flourished, so much that as many as twenty-five ships at a time were sometimes reported in the Cameroon estuary. But from the 1820s, the attention of the British anti-slave trade squadron was attracted to Cameroon. In 1827, Britain established a naval base at Fernando Po (the island also known as Bioko), and opened a small settlement of freed slaves, similar to that of Freetown, in Port Clarence. In 1843, the Baptist Missionary Society came to minister to the freed slaves in Port Clarence, and from there began to penetrate on to the mainland. As was the case in many parts of Africa, abolition did not stop the slave trade immediately. As late as 1861, a ship destined for South America was caught with four hundred slaves. Gradually, however, the export slave trade died and was replaced by the export of palm oil. The reallocation of resources brought about by the transition from the slave trade to "legitimate" trade created political crises among the Duala people. Contestations among the trading princes became so fierce that even the secret society whose function it was to maintain a negotiated public order could not contain them. The crises became an opportunity for British consuls to meddle in Douala politics. It was Germany, however, that finally annexed Douala in 1885.

South of Cameroon, the coast of Gabon also witnessed considerable trade in the nineteenth century. The French, not the British, were responsible for the suppression of the slave trade in this region. In 1839, they established a naval base which later became Libreville (French "Freetown"). That was the beginning of the French imperial campaign in Gabon. The Mpongwe merchants were in control of the trade here earlier in the century. Rival trade Houses fought among themselves for control of the trade as middlemen. Their position was soon to be challenged from two sides: from the interior by the Fang expansion to the coast, and from the coast by the European penetration into the interior.

The expansion of the Fang was one of the most dramatic features of nineteenth-century Cameroon and Gabon. The Fang, who originally lived in the Sanaga region of eastern Cameroon, were under constant pressure from raiders from the north, particularly the Bamum, the Chamba, and the Fulani of Adamawa. The raids forced them to begin to move south towards the Cameroon and Gabon forests. By the 1840s, they had started to participate in the Gabon trade, exchanging ivory for guns. Access to firearms and increasing prosperity from the ivory trade accelerated the Fang migration towards the Gabon estuary and the Ogowe River, thereby impinging on the Mpongwe hegemony.

The Cabinda-Boma axis was pre-eminent at the mouth of the River Zaire in the nineteenth-century Atlantic trade. While Cabinda embraced "legitimate" trade earlier, Boma continued as the hub of the illegal slave trade until the 1860s. Economic transformations in the nineteenth century led to the rise of powerful merchants in Cabinda, the most prominent of whom was Chico Franque. Son of a wealthy slave dealer, Franque was educated in Brazil (a practice that was not unusual then). On his return, he established an enormous business organization, effectively using his networks through marriage alliances at the local level, and his connections in Brazil and Portugal (where he sent two of his sons to study). He built ships, and organized coastal shipping between Luanda and Cape Lopez. In the 1860s, he sent a couple of ships directly to Brazil. He held sway till his death in 1875. In 1885, it was his family who signed the treaty that delivered Cabinda to Portugal. Boma also had powerful entrepreneurs, the foremost of whom was Nemlao, but none was as successful as Franque. Between 1875 and 1880, the

Boma market was exporting a hundred tons of groundnuts, sesame, and palm products daily. It was later to come under the rule of King Leopold of Belgium.

The immense growth of the trade on the coast led to expansion inland. Traders went further and further in search of trade goods. This brought about enormous transformations in the interior. It brought wealth to some Africans who seized on the new opportunities. Some of the *nouveaux riches* used their newly acquired wealth to challenge the old nobility. The trade also brought turmoil and misery to many people. In the northern sector, penetration into the hinterland centered on the mighty River Zaire and spread along its many tributaries, developing into a great trading network. Its major inland market was at the Malebo Pool, where modern Kinshasa is located. The markets were controlled by the Tio middlemen, who were stoutly challenged by the Bobangi. Further north, trading centers were established along the banks of the river at Bolobo, Irebu, and Mbandaka, dominated by the Bobangi. Minor traders relayed goods to them from the tributary rivers of Tshuapa, Ubangi, Likouala-aux-herbes, and Kasai.

The trade affected political and cultural organization in the region. Political organization revolved around trading firms known as Houses. A House was a large trading organization, usually with several hundred members. The Houses strategically located themselves for commerce on the banks of the River Zaire and the tributary rivers. The leaders of the various Houses competed and cooperated among themselves for trade. Succession to leadership in the Houses was not hereditary. Anyone with talent and organizational skills, including former slaves, could compete. For example, Ngaliema, who was the leader of the most prosperous House at the Malebo Pool in the 1870s, had been acquired as a slave. Culturally, the trading activities created almost a single common culture over a huge area of Equatorial Africa. A language, now called Lingala, developed and spread all over the area as a trade language. Leaders built social links over great distances through marriages and blood alliances. Religious cults and beliefs, like the belief in the underwater spirit guardian, spread widely. Furthermore, architectural features and fishing and agricultural techniques also spread along the trade routes. The process was so much that the early European visitors concluded that it was one single "tribe," the "Bangala," who spoke the Lingala language and occupied the whole area.

In the southern sector, the Ovimbundu, who occupied the Benguela highlands, controlled the hinterland trade from the port of Benguela. Some of their chiefs allied with Luso-African merchants on the coast. By the end of the eighteenth century, they had begun to organize large, well-armed caravans into the interior, known as "Mambari." By the 1840s, they had broken the Imbangala monopoly in the Lunda capital. They then advanced northwards to the Luba and Kuba states in the heart of Zaire, where they met with the Nyamwezi.

Perhaps, one of the most spectacular transformations brought about by the nineteenth-century Atlantic trade in Central Africa was the creation of an entirely new trading empire by the Chokwe. The Chokwe, who occupied a small territory near the headwaters of the Kasai and Kwango rivers, had sent small quantities of ivory and wax to the Angolan coast in the eighteenth century, but it was not until the mid-nineteenth century that the rapid expansion of the Chokwe started. The impetus for the Chokwe rise was created by the expanding "legitimate" trade, particularly the increasing demand for wax and ivory at the coast. Chokwe wax was highly esteemed and was collected from carefully prepared log hives. Chokwe men were reputed hunters and their woodland was rich in elephants. They were also expert gunsmiths, and skillfully maintained the guns they acquired through the wax trade. More prosperity came from ivory sales. They used their wealth to buy female slaves whom they married and absorbed into their households. Soon the population began to explode. At the same time, the elephant population in their immediate territory began to diminish. Thus, a combination of the need for more farmland and richer hunting grounds stimulated the expansion of their frontiers. In the 1860s, the base of the Chokwe economy moved from wax and ivory to rubber. This also accelerated the expansion further up the Kasai basin into Lunda country. When they had exhausted the ivory and rubber along the upper Kasai River, the Chokwe transformed themselves from producers and suppliers to middlemen. They established their own long-distance caravans. Controlling the middle Kasai River, they eventually reached the Luba country. Within the short space of fifty years, the Chokwe had risen from being a small, remote, forest people to being one of the most dominant and dynamic forces in Central Africa.[15] With their formidable military force, the Chokwe were constantly raiding their neighbors from the 1880s, inflicting serious injuries on the Lunda Empire. Their raids went unchecked until the late 1890s when local African leaders allied with the Congo Independent State to contain them.

The Peoples and Kingdoms of the Savanna: Lunda, Luba, Lozi

The nineteenth-century history of Central Africa was not only a period of upstarts and transformations, it was also an era of ancient tradition and continuity. A number of ancient kingdoms survived. The old states rallied their traditional structures of power, like ritual and mysticism, and meshed them with the emerging material opportunities to revitalize themselves and survive. In the savanna region, the most important of these states was the Lunda Empire. This was an amalgam of colonized peoples, with its roots in the seventeenth century, which came to dominate the upper Kasai basin. The empire reached its peak in the nineteenth century. The factors that led to its success and stability were the strong tradition of unity that dated back to the early period of Lunda migrations; a strong administrative structure that evolved over generations; and a strong economic base that combined internal prosperity with external trade and a two-way tradition of tribute.

In their nascent years, the Lunda had developed the systems of positional succession and perpetual kinship by which the successor to the throne acquired the identity, social roles, responsibilities and kinship ties of his predecessor.[16] This enhanced continuity and stability. In the dynamic years of the nineteenth century, the political structure evolved into a system in which the mwanta yav (king) ruled with a complex combination of two sets of supporters. On the one hand were traditional elders, descendants of early Lunda clan leaders, and religious leaders,

---

15. Birmingham, 124; see also Joseph C. Miller, "Cokwe Trade and Conquest in the Nineteenth Century," in Richard Gray and David Birmingham, *Pre-colonial African Trade* (London: Oxford University Press, 1970).

16. Thomas Q. Reefe, "The Societies of the Eastern Savanna," in Birmingham and Martin, eds., *History*, 189.

some of whom held hereditary posts associated with leading figures of Lunda "creation". One of these was the lukonkeshia (the mother of the nation), who ruled an independent court where she received state visitors and tributary taxes of her own. On the other hand, there were bureaucratic office-holders appointed by the king, who were responsible for the daily administration of the kingdom. In addition to this effective system, Lunda was blessed in the nineteenth century with three great long-reigning rulers—Yavo ya Mbanyi (early ninteenth century), Naweji ya Ditende (ca. 1820-1852), and Muteba ya Chikombe (ca. 1857-1873). Their long reigns helped to ensure the stability of the kingdom. The reign of Naweji saw the massive involvement of the Lunda in international trade.

The economic structure of the state was based on internal and external prosperity. Agriculture and copper mines were the basis of the internal prosperity. Earlier phases of long-distance trade had introduced into the region cassava on which the Lunda people capitalized to revolutionize their agricultural system. Cassava became the staple diet as well as the food of the long-distance trade. Lunda kings and nobles established cassava plantations that were maintained by serf labor. In fact, cassava became so popular among the people that one Lunda community, Mutombo Mukulu, referred to themselves as "The Cassava People."[17] Copper was mined in the southeastern part of the empire, some was exported and some was made into trade wire used as currency. In addition to internal prosperity, the empire derived considerable wealth from external trade. The slave trade flourished in the empire. The mwata yav obtained his slaves through raids as well as from his tributary states. Long-distance caravans from the Chokwe, the Imbangala, the Ovimbundu, and the Luso-African traders of Angola became regular visitors to the *mussumba* (the state capital) in the nineteenth century. The king not only participated directly in the trade, he also collected taxes from the caravans. During the reign of Muteba, Angolan traders and travelers began to establish themselves in the *mussumba*. They introduced a new agricultural system and cultivated crops imported from Brazil and Portugal such as rice, maize, and tobacco, as well as African staple crops. They traded alongside Lunda families. They intermarried with the Lunda and became involved with Lunda politics. One of their leaders, Lourenço Bezerra, popularly known among the Lunda as Lufuma, became a titled Lunda dignitary. He was so important that he was the person who organized the funeral of the lukonkeshia during Muteba's reign.

After the death of Muteba in 1873, Lunda started a process of decline. Chokwe expansion had started to inflict heavy casualties on the Lunda, particularly in the region between the Tshikapa and Kasai Rivers, breaking up and scattering the Lunda villages there. A power struggle over the control of trade in the capital flared out of control. One of the contenders, Shanam, allied himself with the Chokwe and seized power. His reign, until his death in 1883, was a period of violence and disintegration.

Luba was another savanna state with an impressive history in the nineteenth century. With a high degree of technical ability in metallurgy, the Luba Empire dated as far back as the fourteenth or fifteenth century. When international trade reached Luba in the late eighteenth century, the rulers appropriated it and became monopolist entrepreneurs which greatly enhanced their economic as well as polit-

---

17. Ibid., 190.

ical power. The empire rose to its peak in the nineteenth century. Between 1800 and the 1860s, the number of Luba's tributary states doubled.[18] As in the case of Lunda, three powerful, long-reigning kings supervised the rapid expansion of the empire in the nineteenth century. Ilunga Sungu (ca. 1780-1810) expanded the empire eastward over the region between the Lualaba and Lake Tanganyika. His son and successor, Kumwimba (ca. 1810-1840), completed the conquest and annexation of the Lualaba lakes and took over the rich fishing and palm oil industries. He then moved southwards to take over the copper industries of the Samba, and consolidated Luba control of the northeastern province of Manyema. Perhaps the most successful nineteenth century emperor was Ilunga Kalala (ca. 1840-1870). During his reign Luba came to be at the center of a wide-ranging and diverse international commercial system: in the east and southeast the empire traded with Ujiji and the Bisa ivory traders; in the southwest with the Ovimbumdu caravaneers; in the west with Lunda through the Luba Kanyiok kingdom; and in the northwest with the Songye and the Kuba.

In the 1870s, Luba began to decline. An important factor in its decline was the weakening of its economic base, particularly the depletion of its ivory supplies. At the same time, the trading states of Yeke-Nyamwezi in the south and the Arab-Swahili of Ujiji in the north began to exert more pressure on the empire. These upstart neighbors not only put an effective stop to Luba's expansion, but they began to chip away at the frontier territories of the empire as well. Political dissension within the empire aggravated the situation. By the 1880s, the empire had broken into warring factions.

The Lozi (Barotse) occupied the upper Zambezi flood plain. In this rich plain, the Lozi developed a strong farming and pastoral economy. They shunned the early traders who came to their land from the Lovale territory in the west. In the seventeenth and eighteenth centuries, the kingdom was said to be very rich and dynamic and ruled by an arrogant aristocracy. In 1840, the kingdom was conquered by the Kololo, led by Sebetwane. The Kololo were one of the peoples of southern Africa who were thrown out of their homelands by the Mfecane. A succession dispute among the Lozi, after the death of their king Malumbwa in 1830, had facilitated their defeat by the Kololo, who effectively took over the control of their economy. Sebetwane established a flourishing state, using intermarriage to foster unity. He even co-opted some Lozi chiefs into his administration. The Kololo opened the Lozi kingdom to international trade. They welcomed the "Mambari" traders from Angola, and even sent a few caravans of their own to the coast. Sebetwane ruled with firmness, but great generosity to the Lozi, declaring that "all were children of the king." His policy seems to have enjoyed considerable success, ensuring stability at least during his reign. David Livingstone, who met him shortly before his death in 1851, considered him one of the greatest African rulers he had known.[19]

However, Kololo overlordship did not last long. The heterogeneous group Sebetwane forged became unstable soon after his death. His son and successor, Sekeletu, did not help matters. Sekeletu reversed his father's policy of accommodation and became dictatorial and ruthless towards the Lozi. He dismissed the

---

18. Anne Wilson, "Long Distance Trade and the Luba Lomami Empire," *Journal of African History*, 13, 4 (1972), 577-579.

19. David Livingstone, *Missionary Travels and Researches* (New York: Harper and Brothers, 1858), 59.

Lozi from the administration and terminated the marriage alliances with them.
When Sebetwane conquered Lozi, a few Lozi nobles had fled the state. They
maintained a kind of government in exile and kept alive the embers of Lozi nationalism. By the 1860s, this group had grown strong enough to challenge the
Kololo for their fatherland. Sekeletu's anti-Lozi regime helped to inflame Lozi nationalism, both within the kingdom and among the exiles. After the death of
Sekeletu, one of the Lozi exiles led an army into the capital, defeated the Kololo,
and restored the Lozi dynasty. The liberated Lozi kingdom under the rule of
Lewanika rose in the 1870s to be stronger and even better-organized than it had
been in the pre-Kololo era. This time, it was with a new economic base, the ivory
trade, which was also to help cause its downfall. Shortly after the restoration of
Lozi independence, Lewanika came under the attack of ivory hunters from southern Africa who eventually brought colonial conquest in their wake.

The Invaders

The discussion of the Kololo in Lozi sets the stage for further discussions of
external invasions of Central Africa in the nineteenth century, a process that was
eventually completed by the loss of sovereignty to the Europeans at the end of the
century. In the nineteenth century, Central Africa was invaded from all corners:
from the south by the Ngoni and the Kololo; in the far northeast by the Egyptian-
Sudanese; from the east by the Arab-Swahili traders; and finally from all sides by
the Europeans. Although the Ngoni, led by Zwangendaba, marched through Central Africa before establishing themselves in southern Tanzania, the Kololo were
the southern African group that had the greatest impact on Central Africa. I have
shown above how they overran and ruled the Lozi from 1840 to the 1860s. Sebetwane's incorporative policy left an indelible mark on the Lozi. The Lozi adopted
the Kololo language and a number of their governmental institutions. It was at
this time that they were said to have changed their ethnic name to Lozi, which
was what the Kololo called them.[20]

The defeat of the Kololo by the Lozi did not totally eliminate Kololo influence
in south Central Africa. When David Livingstone was traveling to Angola and
down the Zambezi, he had recruited some Kololo porters. After they were discharged, some sixteen of them decided to settle in the Shire valley. They took wives
among the local Manganja people. These young men possessed guns and had acquired experience of the Kololo military and political systems. They defended the
Manganja against the Ngoni and Yao slave raiders. They later organized the Manganja into two kingdoms led by Molokwa and Kasisi, the strongest of the Kololo
men. They welcomed and cooperated with the Livingstonia mission. The powers
of the Kololo in the Shire valley endured till colonial rule in the 1890s.

In the far northeastern sector of Central Africa, traders from Cairo, the Red
Sea, and Khartoum scoured the Bahr al-Ghazal and the area south of the Vela.
This network developed as a result of the commercial and military expeditions of
Mohammad Ali of Egypt into the Sudan and Darfur.[21] Their ruthless slave raiding

---

20. A.J. Wills, *An Introduction to the History of Central Africa* (London: Oxford University Press, 1985), 62.

21. J.L. Vellut, "The Congo Basin and Angola," in Ajayi, ed., *Africa in the Nineteenth
Century*, 305.

displaced most of the Banda-speaking peoples, who migrated westwards and exerted great pressure on the inhabitants of the present-day Central African Republic. The raiders continued southwards until they met a formidable force, the Azande, who routed them temporarily in the 1860s. In the 1870s, however, many Azande principalities lost their independence to the North African invaders. When the Mahdi rose, the Azande recovered their independence, only to lose it again in the 1890s to the European colonial forces.

From the east coast, the Arab-Swahili traders started to penetrate Central Africa from the 1830s. At the same time, the Nyamwezi long-distance traders were also approaching. They were all searching for ivory and slaves. They were also armed with guns. At this time the Kazembe state (under Lunda colonization) of Luapula was at the height of its power. The Kazembe state was in control of the trade, collecting taxes from the traders. At first, the Arab-Swahili came as peaceful traders and established small trading posts in which to organize their caravans. By the 1870s, however, they had become so powerful that they began to meddle in the local politics of the region, supporting one faction against the other. I have discussed above the activities of one of these Arab-Swahili merchants, Tippu Tib, who established his raiding state on the fringe of the rainforest with his capital at Kasongo. Around the same time, a Nyamwezi warlord and trader, Msiri, was also establishing his own base of operations in the copperbelt.

The Nyamwezi, like the Arab-Swahili, had been penetrating and trading peacefully in the Luapula territory with the Kazembe. By the 1850s, however, they began to bypass the Kazembe, to trade directly with the copper-producing area of Katanga. The Sumbwa Nyamwezi, who became known as the Yeke in Katanga, were particularly successful at this. Msiri, the son of a Sumbwa trader, arrived in the area around 1860, settled in Shaba, and gradually became involved in local politics. He organized people from western Tanzania around him and, with the help of guns, imposed himself on the local chiefs. By the 1870s, he had gained sufficient power to challenge the overlordship of the Kazembe. His success led to the incorporation of many peoples from all parts of Katanga, and they broke away from the control of the Kazembe. With the weakening of the Lunda empire, Msiri's kingdom of Yeke came to dominate the copperbelt. In fact, it is considered to have been one of the most successful upstart conquest states of nineteenth-century Central Africa. Msiri's political power was based on aggressive militarism, effective and coercive administration oiled by political marriages, and a strong economy. His kingdom was rich in ivory, copper, and salt, and with his strong army, he was regularly raiding his neighbors for slaves. He sent caravans to both Benguela on the Atlantic and Zanzibar on the Indian Ocean. His capital, Bunkeya, was one of the largest cities in nineteenth-century Central Africa. He welcomed European missionaries to his domain. At the beginning of the partition, both the Congo Independent State and the British South Africa Company offered him protectorate status, but he refused. In 1891, he was murdered by an official of the Congo State.

Conclusion

The nineteenth century was a period of great change for the peoples of East and Central Africa. A combination of external and internal factors contributed to

these changes. It was a period of great population movements; and a period of nation-building and consolidation for some, as well as devastation, disintegration,
and insecurity for others. Change in itself, it is important to note, was not new to
these people in the nineteenth century. In previous centuries, as seen in preceding
chapters of this book, social, economic, political, and personal forces had been al-
tering the societies. What was unique about the nineteenth century was the intensified and accelerated nature of these transformations. By the end of the century,
the nations and peoples of East and Central Africa had lost their sovereignty to
the invaders from Portugal, Belgium, Germany, France, and Britain. At face value,
it would seem as if all the gains Africans had made in the nineteenth and preceding centuries were lost to the imposition of European colonial rule. But that is not
correct. Africans readapted to the new circumstances and converted the miseries
of colonial domination into strength for survival, resistance, cooperation, and ultimately, independence.

Review Questions

1. Examine the roles of Africans in the development of long-distance trade in
   East Africa during the nineteenth century.
2. Explain how international trade affected the peoples of East and Central
   Africa in the nineteenth century.
3. What were the effects of the Mfecane on East and Central Africa?
4. Describe and explain the political transformation that took place among the
   states and people of the Great Lakes region of East Africa in the nineteenth
   century.

Additional Reading

Alpers, Edward A. *Ivory and Slaves: Changing Patterns of International Trade in
    East and Central Africa to the Later Nineteenth Century*. Berkeley: Univer-
    sity of California Press, 1975.
Cooper, Frederick. *Plantation Slavery on the East Coast of Africa*. New Haven:
    Yale University Press, 1977.
Martin, Phyllis M. *The External Trade of the Loango Coast, 1576-1870*. Lon-
    don: Oxford University Press, 1972.
Mworoha, Emile. *Peuples et rois de l'Afrique des lacs: le Burundi et les royaumes
    voisins au XIXe siècle*. Dakar: Nouvelles Editions Africaines, 1977.
Vellut, Jean-Luc. "Notes sur le Lunda et la frontiere luso-africaine (1700-1900)."
    Etudes d'histoire africaine. 3 (1972), 61-166.

Chapter 16

The *Mfecane* and South Africa

Funso Afolayan

The nineteenth century was a time of revolutionary changes in African history. In the southern half of the continent, two closely inter-related, ultimately interlocking, and conflicting movements dominated the century. The first of these was the *Mfecane*, a revolutionary process of state formation, which began at the beginning of the nineteenth century among the Nguni-speaking peoples but soon engulfed the whole of the southern Africa in warfare and cataclysmic socio-political transformations. Concurrent with this movement was the expansion and intensification of White settlement, which by the end of the century was to bring the whole of the southern Africa under effective European domination and colonization. This chapter examines the nature and the consequences of these developments.

The Mfecane

Causes and Explanations

Many explanations have been offered for the origin, nature, and consequences of the *Mfecane*. Some of these explanations border on the mythical. One approach has been to seek external explanations. This approach associates the beginning of the *Mfecane* with the career of Dingiswayo, a prince of the Mthethwa group. Dingiswayo was said to have been involved in a palace coup that failed. Thereafter, still suffering from a major wound, he fled the wrath of the ruling monarch, his father. In the course of his flight, he was said to have come across a European doctor, named Cowan, who was having difficulties finding his way to the Portuguese base at Delagoa Bay. Dingiswayo became Cowan's guide and companion. On the way, however, Dr. Cowan ran into a hostile reception among the Qwabe, whose chief ordered the trespassing stranger to be put to death to forestall whatever evil his presence might bring. Dingiswayo, however, managed to escape, taking with him Cowan's horse as well as his gun. Returning to his people, he found that his father was dead and one of his brothers was already installed on the throne. Dingiswayo, with his recently acquired prestigious equipment and the knowledge of state building he had supposedly acquired from Cowan, successfully seized the throne. Interesting as this story is, it is very problematic. Henry

Fynn was the first European visitor to narrate the story of Dr. Cowan.[1] It is not corroborated by any other source and we have no other record of any European by the name of Cowan traveling through southern Africa during this period. May be the story arose out of the general tendency of early European writers to seek external explanations for any major, significant achievements and innovations in Africa. Since Africans were believed to have been incapable of conceiving high-order ideas in the area of state formation, major revolutionary developments like the *Mfecane* could only have occurred through the intervention of superior European or other external intelligence and ideas.

Closely related to the Dingiswayo myth are attempts to connect the *Mfecane* with the expanding and colonizing activities of White settlers from the Cape.[2] It is argued that this northeastward push of the Boer pastoralists blocked the Bantu-Nguni and arrested them in their own southward push. This is said to have created land hunger and pressure on available resources among the Nguni, who thus, balked in their natural expansion and constricted in their territorial fission and economic expansion turned on each other. The problem with this argument is that it is not supported by available evidence. We have no evidence, for instance, that the Zulu *Mfecane*, under Shaka, was in any way provoked by or connected to the gradual but purposeful push of the Trekboers from the Cape. Besides, this explanation does not explain why the Trekboer pressure should have been more decisive in provoking revolutions among the northern Nguni than among the southern Nguni or the Xhosa, who were more directly affected by the Trekboer migrations. And in any case, available evidence indicates that displaced groups splitting off and migrating southward to settle among and even beyond the Xhosa-speaking Nguni communities to the south often solved the problem of overcrowding among the northern Nguni.[3]

Connected with the Trekboer stimulus is the attempt to explain the *Mfecane* through reference to the impact of trade with the Europeans on the coast.[4] This argument states that the desire of the larger Nguni states to control or profit from the ivory and other trades with the Portuguese at Delagoa Bay on the east coast was instrumental in the outbreak of the *Mfecane* and the transformation of smaller polities into larger states. There is evidence to support the view that many of the Nguni states, like the Hlubi Ndwandwe and the Ngwane and Mthethwa participated and benefited from trade with the Portuguese, especially through Tsonga middlemen. We also know that rulers such as Dingiswayo and others, like Zwide of the Ndwandwe and Sobhuza of the Ngwane, were very keen on extending their imperial control to the coast in order to open up access to the Indian Ocean trade. But while the trade factor as an incentive for socio-political transfor-

---

1. H.F. Fynn, *The Diary of Henry Francis Fynn*, eds., J. Stuart and D. M. Malcolm (Pietermaritzburg: Shuter and Schooter, 1950), 4-8; and J. Bird, ed., *The Annals of Natal 1495-1845*, vol. 1 (Pietermaritzburg: Davis, 1888), 62-3.

2. R. Oliver and J.D. Fage, *A Short History of Africa* (Harmondsworth: Penguin, 1962), 163.

3. J.D. Omer-Cooper, "Aspects of Political Change in the Nineteenth Century Mfecane," in L. Thompson, ed., *African Societies in Southern Africa* (London: Heinemann, 1969), 207-229.

4. M. Wilson, "The Early History of the Transkei and Ciskei," *African Studies* 18, 4 (1958): 172; and A. Smith, "The trade of Delagoa Bay as a Factor in Nguni Politics 1750-1835," in Thompson, ed., *African Societies*, 171-189.

mation can not be entirely discounted, it must not be pushed too far. The evidence in support of it is still largely tenuous. It is mainly from accounts left by contemporary European observers who had reasons to present these rulers and their states as trade lovers in the age of European commercial expansion. There is no evidence to show that external trade with the Europeans on the coast was decisive in the processes that culminated in the *Mfecane*.

More radical but obviously more controversial have been attempts to explain away the *Mfecane* as a mere alibi for slave raiding. Absolving the Zulu from culpability for inter-group conflicts in the region, these scholars argued that the image of Shaka-as-monster was a deliberate and calculated invention of the Europeans, traders and missionaries, to mask their slave raiding activities. A myth of an internally induced process of Black-on-Black violence is said to have been created by racist historians and propagandists to legitimize the policy of apartheid and unequal land division in twentieth century South Africa. As the leading proponent of this position says, "African societies did not generate the regional violence on their own. Rather, caught within the European net, they were transformed over a lengthy period in reaction to the attention of external plunderers."[5] Two points can be made in support of this position. It is true that history was systematically distorted in apartheid South Africa to legitimize White domination. However, the image of Shaka as a monster and the memory of his atrocities were not solely the creation of his White enemies, but were also drawn from contemporary oral traditions in African societies, especially those who had suffered from Shaka's depredations and "tyranny." Secondly, it is also true that European-sponsored slave raiding was a factor contributing to the generation of violence in parts of southern Africa during the *Mfecane*. These points notwithstanding, there are many problems with this position. The evidence implicating the missionaries in the *Mfecane* is tenuous and inconclusive. Similarly, there is little evidence to support the claim that the slave trade existed on a large scale in the Delagoa Bay area before the third decade of the nineteenth century. Whatever role slavery and the slave trade may have played in the *Mfecane*, there is no evidence to show that they were decisive in the socio-political transformations that occurred. Dingiswayo, Shaka, and Moshoeshoe were not slavers. The wars and raids no doubt produced captives who were disposed off as slaves, and the need for European goods may have made slaves and captives of war valuable commodities of exchange. Nevertheless, the available evidence will not support the thesis that the wars and raids associated with the *Mfecane* were inspired by the slave trade or the desire to trade with the Europeans on the coast.[6]

Attempts to find explanations for the *Mfecane* in the characters and personal qualities of the principal leaders of the revolution, most especially its personification, Shaka, have been equally problematic but ultimately fruitless and unhelpful. The Zulu revolution has been put forward by some scholars as a typical example

---

5. Julian Cobbing, "The *Mfecane* as Alibi," *Journal of African History (JAH)* 29 (1988): 519.

6. For critiques of Cobbing's revisionist position see E. Eldredge, "Sources of Conflict in Southern Africa, ca.1800-30: The '*Mfecane*' Reconsidered," *JAH*, 33 (1992): 1-36; C.A. Hamilton, "The Character and Objects of Chaka: A Reconsideration of the Making of Shaka as '*Mfecane* Motor,'" *JAH*, 33 (1992): 37-63; and Omer-Cooper, "Has the *Mfecane* a Future? A response to the Cobbing Critique," *Journal of Southern African Studies*, 19 (1993).

of the negative repercussions of terroristic controls and despotism, a by-product of the capricious nature and cruel whims of Shaka. Writers competed with one another to psychoanalyze Shaka and root the *Mfecane* in his illegitimate birth, unhappy childhood, and pitiless nature. He was denounced as "an insatiable and exterminating savage," a "despotic and cruel monster," a "horrible and detestable" tyrant and the "most ruthless conqueror the world has ever known."[7] While the personalities and personal experiences of the leading historical figures can not be dismissed as insignificant in influencing the nature and specific character of the various manifestations of the *Mfecane*, the psychoanalytical explanation for the *Mfecane* is fraught with problems. It is difficult to see how the birth, childhood, and idiosyncrasies of these men alone can explain the entire history of socio-political transformation in Bantu Africa during the nineteenth century. More importantly, however, this explanation fails to explain why all these leaders arose at about the same time and why all these converging events coalesced to produce the *Mfecane*. No explanation that fails to take cognizance of the socio-economic environment and cultural-historical contexts of the Nguni will suffice to unravel the enigma of the *Mfecane*.

Emergence of Centralized Polities

Whatever the circumstances surrounding Dingiswayo's accession, after consolidating himself on the throne, Dingiswayo embarked on a program of imperial expansion, which brought several neighboring groups under his imperial control. His was the first deliberate and successful and deliberate attempt to forge larger political formations among the largely decentralized Nguni-speaking groups of southern Africa. Convinced, as a contemporary account noted, "that it was not the intention of those who first came into the world that there should be several kings equal in power, but that there should be one great king to exercise control over the little ones,"[8] Dingiswayo incorporated the conquered groups into his kingdom. While this was going on among the Mthethwa, a similar process of political centralization was occurring among the Ndwandwe ruled by Zwide and the Ngwane ruled by Sobhuza. The emergence of these centralized states marked a new departure in the history of the Nguni-speaking peoples and ultimately in the history of the region. The process of socio-political centralization that they set in motion reached its climax with the emergence of Shaka and his Zulu nation and had far reaching consequences for the region.

Understanding the *Mfecane* requires an examination of the nature of socio-political formations in pre-*Mfecane* southern Africa and especially among the Nguni. Beginning in their original homeland in the areas bordering on the Benue River and the Cameroon highlands, the vanguard of the Bantu reached the coastal area of Southern Africa by the beginning of the seventeenth century. Here they came in contact with the indigenous Khoisan groups, many of whom they conquered, displaced, or assimilated. The high rainfall and the fertility of the soil in the areas between the Drakensberg Mountains and the sea ensured that this region received the largest concentration of Bantu settlers. The more arid region

---

7. For a fuller discussion of these stereotypes, see David Chanaiwa, "The Zulu Revolution: State Formation in a Pastoralist Society," *African Studies Review*, 23, 3 (1980): 1-20.

8. Omer-Cooper, *The Zulu Aftermath* (London: Longman, 1966).

further west, including the Kalahari Desert, received only a sparse population. The surviving remnants of the displaced Khoisan groups remained in this region, which also came to be dominated by other Bantu groups, some of who soon consolidated themselves into the Ambo and Herero of Namibia. By the beginning of the eighteenth century, the Bantu of southern Africa had been differentiated into two major linguistic and cultural groups. In the east, lying between the Drakensberg and the sea, were the Nguni-speakers. Beyond this area and in the interior plateau to the west were the Sotho/Tswana-speaking peoples.

Despite their linguistic and cultural differences, the Nguni and the Sotho/Tswana peoples shared many common characteristics. Both groups were pastoralists with highly developed skills in cattle herding. Both also practiced agriculture, planting crops such as millet, sorghum, pumpkins, calabashes, melons, beans, and roots. Both groups were organized into patrilineal family systems. While they were settled in fairly distinct regions, their territorial distinctiveness was not absolute. Over the years, considerable overlapping in settlements and intensive interactions were major features of the relations between the two groups. By the beginning of the eighteenth century, ecological and economic adaptations and innovations, as well as socio-political experimentation, had resulted in the emergence of many sub-chiefdoms in the region. This process of state formation reached a climax towards the end of the eighteenth century, setting the stage for the *Mfecane* revolution of the late eighteenth and nineteenth centuries. This movement, which took a dramatic and decisive turn among the Zulu during the second decade of the nineteenth century, had far-reaching and cataclysmic consequences in the history of southern and Central Africa. It fundamentally altered the geo-political character and history of the region. Scholars are still debating the factors responsible for the *Mfecane*. Some have argued that there was no such thing as a *Mfecane* and that the term should be abandoned entirely.[9] Others have denounced the attempts to explain away the *Mfecane* as a figment of the imagination of some fertile or perfidious minds. Such scholars have insisted that, no matter the romanticism of the storytellers and the zeal of the political and racist pundits, the evidence shows that the *Mfecane* was a historical fact.

One explanation that has received increased support among scholars is the ecological factor.[10] The scholars who put forward this explanation see the *Mfecane* as the culmination of the processes of ecological and economic adaptation that had been going on in the region for decades. The fact that this process exploded into a crisis at the end of the eighteenth century has been explained by reference to many intervening variables. One of these was the growth in population. In the early years of Bantu settlement in southern Africa, population expansion was accommodated through expansion into new and largely unoccupied areas. Ambitious or disaffected individuals and groups could always chart new courses for themselves by simply breaking away from old chiefdoms to establish independent chiefdoms. Constant political fission and proliferation of settlements became the hallmark of cultural adaptation during this period. As long as the rate of population increase remained relatively small and stable, pockets of unclaimed land existed to absorb the new increase, and there was no major demographic influx

---

9. Cobbing, "The *Mfecane* as Alibi," 519.

10. M. Gluckman, *Analysis of a Social Situation in Modern Zululand*, (Manchester: Manchester University Press, 1958), 30; and Omer-Cooper, *The Zulu Aftermath*, 3, 170.

into the region, the situation did not portend any crisis. In the area of the Drakensberg and the sea, this delicate balance began to be upset by the middle of the eighteenth century.

This destabilization was a consequence of three interlocking factors. One of these was the advent of White settlers from the Cape, whose relentless land-colonizing progress inland and northeastward was rapidly reducing the land available for secessionist scions of Bantu chiefdoms and other separating migrant groups to settle. In the meantime, among the Nguni especially, improved agricultural techniques, more intense exploitation of the resources of their fertile environment, coupled with the introduction of the staple diet crop, maize, some time during the seventeenth century, appear to have combined to bring about a major population increase in the region. As if to compound an already worsening situation, the northern Nguni area was struck by a series of devastating famines, known as Madlathule, in the last decades of the eighteenth and early decades of the nineteenth centuries. Similar cases of severe famines are recollected for this period in the traditions of the Basotho people. The combination of increased population and drought, unrelieved by the availability of new lands or other resources, increased the pressure on the dwindling resources. The resultant competition produced the restlessness and the violence that became leading features of interpersonal and inter-group relations in this region in the eighteenth and early nineteenth centuries.

The Importance of Cattle

The importance of competition over land in provoking the *Mfecane* must not, however, be overemphasized. In the case of the Zulu, as with many of the other groups involved, land seizure and occupation did not feature prominently in military and imperial policies. In almost every case, cattle seizure and other material expropriations loomed larger than any other objectives. It would appear that more than anything else the *Mfecane* was a revolutionary movement of state formation in a pastoralist society.

Pastoralism was the major economic occupation among the Nguni. Their staple diet was meat and milk, supplemented by grain and vegetables. Cattle were the measure of wealth and the symbol of status. It separated the rich from the poor and determined the class and power of the individual. It was also the most important medium of exchange. The products of cattle, such as meat, milk, hides, and butter, were exchanged by those who had them for other valuable commodities like clothes, foods, and weapons of war such as shields, swords, spears, and bows and arrows. Cattle were also used for the payment of bride price, *lobola*, without which a young man would have no hope of obtaining a wife. Cattle provided the beef consumed on important occasions such as marriages and funerals, as well as during family and state religious and political rituals and festivals. The Nguni lavished much care on their cattle, training them as pack animals, riding and racing, giving them personalized names, composing poems to celebrate them, and boasting of and displaying them at public dances. To show the centrality of cattle, they were kept in the center of the kraal or compound. Herding, milking, and hunting were exclusively men's occupations, and were considered more honorable than farming which was relegated to women. Only men driven by necessity, such as lack of wives or loss or lack of cattle, turned to farming, a more arduous and time-consuming occupation, for subsistence. Contemporary European observers, who visited the Nguni, in the course of the nineteenth century, time and again spoke of their excessive fondness for cattle. Some of them noted the fact that the desire for cattle, the longing for cattle ownership was at the center of many of the wars fought by them and the *leit motif* of their state formation outbursts during the nineteenth century.[11]

Pastoralism and Class Formation

The intensification of this capitalist mode of pastoralist production among the Nguni was to result in class formation. Those who were in a position to accumulate cattle, either by inheritance or hard work, became richer. Powerful chiefs were able to increase their wealth through tributes, presents, booty, court and death fines, and expropriation of cattle from newcomers, conquered groups, and miscreants in the community. Recalcitrant and disloyal individuals could also be punished or brought into line through acts of economic deprivation or threats of isolation and expulsion. Before long, such chiefs and other rich individuals were able to free themselves altogether from menial jobs, by engaging the services of poor and cattleless individuals in the society. A system of client-patron relationships developed, in which the poor and cattleless Nguni were given cattle on loan by the rich in return for milk and occasional gifts, which could sometimes include a share of the offspring of the loaned cattle. Through such services and rewards, an enterprising client could begin to build up his own stock, while rich, astute, and generous chiefs, through judicious deployment of their herds, could enhance their status in society by attracting and building up a retinue of followers, clients, and dependents.

The sharpening of the discrepancies between the rich and the poor, occasioned by the capitalization and intensification of pastoral production, created tension in the society. The existence of cattleless client-herdsmen and other deprived and impoverished commoners created an army of disenchanted individuals who began to perceive the existing socio-economic system as one characterized by inequality, injustice, and oppression. Driven to submit themselves to often unattractive conditions of fealty and dependency, disadvantaged in the perennial contest for women and cattle, and constantly suffering from indebtedness, which increasingly became the lot of many of them, this deprived and disgruntled class was anything but committed to the preservation of the status quo. They became ready followers of revolutionary leaders among the Nguni who, through systematic politicization and exploitation of the state of economic deprivation of the cattleless peasants, were able to rally them to their causes. Materialistic incentives, especially the prospect of cattle redistribution promised by the nascent revolution, were sufficiently attractive to enlist the support of the Nguni peasants in the warfare and state formation which dominated the life of the Nguni and their neighbors from the closing decades of the eighteenth century onwards.

---

11. For a fuller discussion of the importance of cattle among the Nguni and its connection with the Mfecane, see the incisive article by Chanaiwa, "The Zulu Revolution," 6-11, from which much of this section derives.

Nguni Traditional Socio-political System

To understand the significance of the emergence of revolutionary leaders among the Nguni during the last decades of the eighteenth century, it is necessary to examine the nature of traditional Nguni society. It was a lineage-based society, in which the chiefdom, organized around one or two lineages, constituted the major political unit. The society was highly decentralized, organized into numerous and largely autonomous chiefdoms. This was due largely to the fissile nature of Nguni pastoralist homesteads and the ever-present possibilities of chiefdoms fragmenting. The chief was considered to be the lawgiver, the chief judge, the chief priest, and the health of the chiefdom, but he was not all-powerful and could hardly be authoritarian. His real power depended on the size of his chiefdom and the number of his cattle and other resources, and thus his ability to dispense favors and patronage to his followers and clients. He was also dependent on the advice and support of his councilors, who could fine or even dethrone him, and who constituted the balancing force in the perpetual contest for supremacy among the princely elite.

In a society where land had no mystical or ritual connotation, people were considered more valuable than landed property. An oppressive and unpopular chief could find the basis of his authority eroded by the emigration of his disgruntled subjects from his domain. Ambitious princes and rival claimants to the throne and neighboring chiefs often exploited a chief's unpopularity or political oppression to detach his followers from him, build up their own strength, and eventually supplant the unpopular chief. A powerful chief might command the respect and service of weaker and subordinate chiefs, who would be expected to be present at major public meetings and ceremonies, pay nominal tribute, and contribute contingents in times of war. For all practical purposes, however, the subordinate chiefs remained largely autonomous. They armed, maintained, and led their own local armies as independent detachments in times of war.

With political authority so widely dispersed spatially and with no central authority available to regulate and mediate relations between the chiefdoms, the situation remained politically volatile and inherently unstable. The competition for cattle, grazing land, and followership, the basic ingredients of power and influence, often resulted in considerable tension and conflicts among ambitious princes, while also straining relations between subordinate and superior chiefs. The absence of any pan-Nguni nationalism and corporate leadership promoted a spirit of individualism and a corresponding weakening of kinship and ethnic loyalties. The political atmosphere thus provided room for individual freedom, mobility, creativity, and initiative. The constant political and territorial fission that resulted created problems of unity and integration.

The instability was further compounded by the Nguni's inheritance principle of primogeniture. Under this system, princes born to a chief before his accession were excluded both from succession as well as from inheritance to cattle. Only princes born to wives the chief married after his enthronement had recognized claims to royal inheritance. As a rule, the first son of the official queen mother usually succeeded to his father's throne and inherited all the cattle. Other princes, born before and after accession as well as to other wives, were thus technically without inheritance. Deprived and sidelined, many of them became, naturally, resentful and dissatisfied. Some attempted to remedy the situation by conspiring to seize the throne and supplant the rightful heir. Others redirected their frustration and energy by migrating to establish new chiefdoms for themselves, supported by their initiation or age grade mates, their mothers and other followers, and other equally disgruntled or adventurous individuals. The incessant intra-elite competition and conflict resulted in constant segmentation and the fissiparous multiplication of chiefly polities.

By the late eighteenth century, as the alienated and frustrated political elite turned to the equally deprived and powerless masses, the situation became volatile. Visibly hostile or indifferent to the status quo that had failed them, the political elite provided the leadership, while the masses provided the followers for a revolutionary upheaval that promised a transformation of the unequal and unjust socio-political order. It is against this background that the emergence of revolutionary leaders like Dingiswayo, Shaka, Mzilikazi, Moshoeshoe, and others as spokesmen of the masses and as catalysts of change can be understood.

Institutional Reforms

The struggle for power and the intensification of warfare and unrest necessitated the modification of traditional practices and systems to cope with the exigencies of the time. The disturbed conditions soon led to the abandonment, in many places, of the time-honored practice of cattle herding on a loan basis. More consequential was the transformation that occurred in the system of manhood initiation. The institution of initiation, usually involving circumcision, was of major social significance among the Nguni people. Initiation into manhood and organization into age grades fulfilled important cultural, educational, and psychological functions. Members of the same age grade were initiated and educated together. They usually fought together in time of war and could be called upon to perform specific duties for the community. However, the disturbed conditions of the late eighteenth century called into question the continuing adherence to some features of the rites. The traditional initiation rites, which required ritual seclusion for several days, and the act of circumcision which could render the initiates physically incapacitated, could render a community vulnerable to external attack, should a wily enemy decide to launch an assault at a time when a sizable number of its fighting men were recovering from circumcision and its attendant festivities.

In the war-ridden circumstances of the late eighteenth century, military strategy and reasons of survival dictated the abandonment of many aspects of the initiation rites by many Nguni groups. Instead of the circumcision and initiation rites, service in age-regiments and participation in actual warfare became the rite of passage of young men into adulthood. The Nguni and others adopted the Sotho-Tswana practice of coordinating and controlling initiation rites on a communal rather than an individual family basis. The age-regiment became a more effective system of military organization. In its new formation, its membership cut across communal and ethnic origins. Young men of the same age but from different backgrounds were brought together as members of the same national regiment. They were quartered together, lived together, and fought together as brothers for the duration of their service. All these promoted the development of a sense of loyalty and common identity, transcending ethnic and communal differences. The age-regiment thus became a powerful instrument for the integration of subordinate and conquered groups into the general political framework.

The Rise of Shaka

As noted earlier, one major feature of political change among the Nguni towards the end of the eighteenth century was the emergence of large-scale kingdoms. Three of these became notable. These were the kingdoms of the Ndwandwe led by Zwide, the Ngwane led by Sobhuza, and the Mthethwa led by Dingiswayo. These states were built through the centralization of political power, the conquest and incorporation of other chiefdoms, the collection of tribute from subordinate polities, the use of an army based on national age-regiments, cattle raiding and control of trade and trade goods. Continued warfare and the exacerbation of rivalries between these three soon led to conflicts and collisions. The struggle for the control of farmland along the Phongola River valley brought Zwide and Sobhuza to blows. Sobhuza was defeated. He fled with the remnants of his followers southward, eventually establishing the state that developed into the modern Swazi kingdom. The stage was thus left for Zwide and Dingiswayo, who squared off in a series of engagements in which Dingiswayo had the upper hand. However, in an engagement that took place in 1818, Dingiswayo was surprised by a Ndwandwe ambush. Separated from the bulk of his army, he was captured and killed. With the death of their leader, and because of the personal character of Dingiswayo's rule, a power vacuum was created in the Mthethwa state. It never recovered.

Into the vacuum now stepped a new force, Shaka, the new ruler of the Zulu, a small Nguni chiefdom, hitherto subordinate to the Mthethwa. Shaka was born to one of the junior wives of Senzangakhona, the ruler of the Zulu. The violent temper of his mother led to her and his expulsion from the palace. He grew up among his mother's people. His fierce determination and reckless courage soon brought him to the attention of Dingiswayo, who made him a commander in his army. With the death of Senzangakhona, and with the assistance of his mentor, Dingiswayo, Shaka was able to easily dispose of the legitimate heir, Mfokazana, establishing himself firmly on the Zulu throne while maintaining his nominal loyalty to Dingiswayo.[12]

Having established himself on the throne, Shaka took steps to strengthen his power and consolidate his position. His first major effort was directed to revolutionizing the Zulu army. He did this in a number of ways. In the area of weaponry, he introduced the *assegai*, a short-handled, broad-bladed hand-stabbing spear, as the main weapon of war, in addition to the traditional long throwing spears or javelins, axes, and clubs. Shaka's experience in Dingiswayo's army had convinced him of the ineffectiveness of traditional methods of warfare. In place of these he initiated a system whereby his army could disarm the adversary by placing themselves at a great distance and allowing the enemy to exhaust their arrows, deflecting both arrows and long spears with cowhide shields, before closing in to devastate the enemy in hand-to-hand combat with the stabbing spears. Each soldier was given his stabbing spear on enlistment. This he was not to replace or lose on pain of death. Shaka also adopted longer and broader shields for his army and made them discard other encumbrances like sandals, so that they fought barefoot for improved endurance and greater speed and mobility.

---

12. On Shaka see E.A. Ritta, *Shaka Zulu: The Rise of the Zulu Empire*, (London: Longman, 1968); Omer-Cooper, *The Zulu Aftermath*, 24-48; and the historical novel, T. Mofolo, *Chaka*, (Portsmouth: Heinemann, 1981).

In his early military engagements, Shaka limited himself to harrying the few settlements around Zululand. He carefully avoided any open rupture with either Zwide or Dingiswayo. In the charged atmosphere of the period, however, confrontation could not be postponed indefinitely. Shaka could not pretend to be neutral in the conflict between Zwide and Dingiswayo, and in the final showdown between the two warlords, Dingiswayo summoned his protégé, Shaka, to match his regiments against Zwide. Shaka did not participate in the fighting. Either he arrived late or he deliberately slowed his movement in order to betray Dingiswayo into the hands of the enemy and thus pave the way for his dominance of what was left of the Mthethwa confederacy. This was precisely what happened. With the elimination of its paramount chief, the Mthethwa confederacy crumbled. Exploiting the succession dispute that followed, Shaka killed the heir, Mondisa. Thereafter, he installed a claimant loyal to himself and in the process incorporated what was left of the Mthethwa State into his fledgling Zulu kingdom. Not long after this, the inevitable clash with Zwide occurred. The initial advantage went to the more numerous troops of the more experienced Ndwandwe. Outnumbered by the new force mustered against him, Shaka avoided open battle with his adversaries, wearing them out and exposing them to starvation. What he lacked in number, he compensated for in superior military acumen and resourcefulness. After tracking the exhausted and withdrawing Ndwandwe army to the bank of the Mhlatuze River, he suddenly pounced on them with the full force of his army, routing them, turning their apparent victory into a colossal disaster and forever eliminating the Ndwandwe as a major force in the region. The attempt made by Zwide's successor, Sikhunyana, in 1826 to revive Ndwandwe power and avenge the defeats of 1819 and 1820 similarly ended in a debacle. The Ndwandwe lost sixty thousand cattle and their power was completely broken. They never recovered, and they disappeared as a major, distinct group.

Military and Political Innovations

Shaka's victory had been made possible by his well-developed military strategy and the superior discipline of his army. He adopted the cow-horn formation method of fighting, in which his force was usually organized into four units. The center unit, made up of the bulk of the army and known as the "chest," was made to directly engage the full force of the enemy, while the reserve regiments waited in the rear. At the crucial moment in the battle, the remaining left and right units formed horns which radiated from the two sides of the "chest," gradually encircling, outflanking, and trapping the enemy in the center before closing in on them. Shaka also preferred surprise attack on his enemies at dawn. The Zulu army became noted for its rigorous discipline. The introduction of new techniques entailed prolonged drilling, exercises, and ceremonies. The practice of adhoc mobilization was discarded for permanent regimentation. Men under the age of forty were constituted into age-regiments. These were quartered together in special military settlements where they remained and fought together on a continuous basis until the expiration of their term, or when they reached the age of forty. Each regiment was made up of between two thousand and five thousand soldiers. While engaged in active service, the soldiers were excluded from normal civilian pursuits such as pastoralism, farming, and family life. There were also female regiments corresponding to the male regiments. They took part together with their male

Figure 16-1. Zulu Chief, c.1880-1905

counterparts in national festivals. The two sexes did not live together and were expected to remain strictly celibate until the dissolution of the regiments, when they could get married. Ingenious use was also made of spies, psychological warfare, and witch doctors to keep Shaka informed, instill courage in the soldiers, and ensure their loyalty and commitment. Desertion, cowardice, and treachery were punished by death.

The consequences of these innovations were revolutionary. The age-regiment system became an effective instrument of national integration. With members drawn from different backgrounds, but organized into one single unit and exposed to similar ideas and values, the age-regiments facilitated the inculcation of feelings of common loyalty and common identity among heterogeneous groups. The new directions in the organization of age-regiments also radically altered the balance of power in the society. With the bulk of the young men, the fighting force, stationed in the regiments and at the command of the supreme ruler, the power and freedom of action of the segmental rulers were impaired. Left only with old men and discharged soldiers, provincial rulers could no longer easily pursue independent policies, or seriously threaten, or check the paramountcy of the central monarch. The soldiers were furnished with their spears, shields, meat, and milk from the royal stores and herds. In addition, only the king could authorize them to wear the head ring, the insignia of manhood, and it was from him that they received their brides at the completion of their years of military service. This made them personally dependent on the king, while giving them a direct stake in the success of the king's wars. The result of this was to focus their loyalty and commitment on the king instead of on the heads of their separate communities.

In the place of the territorial chiefs, a new class of appointed officials came to the fore. Known as *indunas*, they were appointed by the king to command the regiments and administer the royal homesteads. While ignoring the territorial chiefs, Shaka was careful to regularly consult the council of *indunas*, both to ensure their support, but also to give an appearance of accessibility and public legitimacy. The *indunas* were, however, weak. Their advice was not binding on the king. Since they were appointed by the king, they owed their position directly to his favor. And since they were usually of commoner origin, and had no royal legitimacy, they were severely limited in their ability to challenge, restrain, or replace the ruler. Thus, in the perilous circumstances of the time, the traditional socio-political system was radically transformed. The problem of unity and integration was solved through new political experimentation accompanied by military despotism. The decentralized, segmentary political system became, under Shaka, a highly centralized militarist state. The new system was centered on a nearly absolute ruler, possessed of considerable power which was exercised through a bureaucracy of officials appointed by and responsible to him. The concept of kingship was further elaborated and legitimized in the royal family, with the king becoming the embodiment of his people and the personification of the state in his power and office.

"The Zulu Aftermath" in Southern and Central Africa

The *Mfecane* was a revolutionary movement of state formation in nineteenth century southern Africa. It led to the creation of many new states in the region. These states were organized, with varying degrees of difference and similarity, after the example of the Zulu State. Many of the states and societies that eventually became dominant in much of southern and Central Africa had their roots and assumed their present shape and character during this period. A few of these will be described, to illustrate the consequences of the *Mfecane* on state formation in precolonial Africa.

Emergence of New States: Swazi and Gaza

After his defeat by Zwide, Sobhuza, the ruler of the Ngwane, fled southward with the remnants of his people. He settled in present day Swaziland. He succeeded in imposing political control over many of the smaller clans in the region,

dominated by the Sotho-speaking people. Sobhuza retained the chiefs of the conquered clans in their positions after assuring himself of their loyalty. The chiefs
were given considerable local autonomy, and through intermarriage they were
gradually integrated into the new society. The Sotho already had a well-developed
age-regiment system, which Sobhuza now incorporated into his own military system. Sotho youths were recruited in large numbers into the army and made to
fight for and along with their conquerors. As part of his attempt to consolidate his
position and ensure his survival, Sobhuza maintained cordial relations with his
neighbors. After his defeat by Zwide, he concluded peace with him by marrying
one of his daughters, making her his *nkosikati*, or senior wife. Following the rise
of Shaka, he sought friendly relations by giving him regular presents of beautiful
young girls, princesses, and presents. This cordial gesture saved Sobhuza's kingdom from the devastating depredations of Shaka's regiments. While Sobhuza's
successors were not as competent, they carried on his policy of political consolidation through intermarriage and peaceful relations with neighbors. The combi-
nations of these policies and efforts had, by the end of the century, welded a
largely amorphous group of peoples into the highly centralized and politically homogenous and stable state of Swaziland.[13]

Following their two successive defeats by Shaka in 1819 and 1820, the Ndwandwe confederacy fragmented. One of the beneficiaries of this dissolution was
Soshangane, formerly a general in Zwide's army. Breaking away with a small following, he was able to establish control over several small groups such as the
Manyika, Ndau, and Chopi in the Tsonga country and in the neighborhood of
Delagoa Bay. His control of the trade between the Portuguese at Delagoa Bay and
the interior kingdoms of the Nyaka, the Thembu, and the Maputo gave him enormous wealth. With the aid of his regiments he was able to conquer new areas, in-
corporating their young men and women into his service and appropriating their
grain and cattle. The process of integration was, however, not complete. The society was divided into two, with the original Nguni group from the south, known
as "ba-Nguni," occupying a higher status, while the conquered and semi-assimi-
lated Tsonga and others were referred to as "ba-Tshangene." While the new state,
Gaza, adopted many of the military techniques of the Zulu, the age-regiment system was not used as an instrument for the integration of diverse communities. Instead the conquered groups were organized into distinct age regiments of their
own, though led by "ba-Nguni" officers.[14]

Mzilikazi and the Ndebele Kingdom

Another state that came into being during this period was associated with one
of Zwide's leading generals, Mzilikazi.[15] Mzilikazi's rise shows the consequences

13. H. Kuper, *An African Aristocracy: Rank Among the Swazi of Bechuanaland* (London: Oxford University Press, 1947), 14-20; J.S.M. Matsebula, *A History of Swaziland*
(Cape Town: Longman, 1972), 15-20; and P. Bonnar, *Kings, Commoners and Concessionar-
ies: The Evolution and Dissolution of the Nineteenth-Century Swazi State* (Cambridge: Cambridge University Press, 1983).

14. Smith, "The Trade," 169-177; and Omer-Cooper, *The Zulu Aftermath*, 57-63.

15. On Mzilikazi and the Ndebele state he founded see R. Moffat, *The Matabele Journals*, J.P.R. Wallis, ed., vol. 1 (London: Chato and Windus, 1945); and R.K. Rasmussen, *Mzilikazi of the Ndebele* (London: Heinemann, 1977).

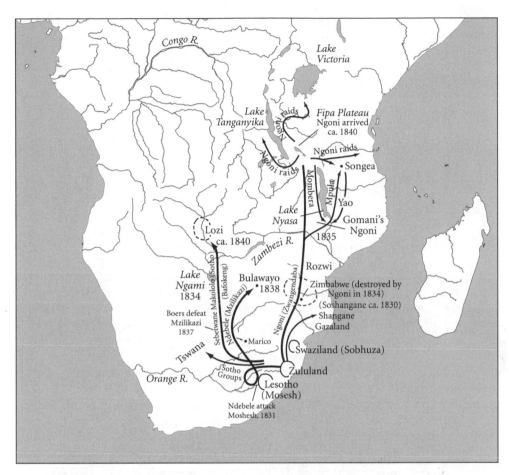

Figure 16-2. Sotho and Nguni Movements in the Nineteenth Century

of the limitations of Shaka's centralization policies. Outside the central area of the empire, and beyond the militarization of the society, the traditional segmentary system of political authority was left largely unchanged. The rule of conquered territories was, as much as possible, left to indigenous rulers. Those removed were usually replaced by others from the same royal families. Even the age-regiment did not entirely alienate the soldiers from their origin. Soldiers could look forward to getting married at the end of their period of active duty and returning to their places of origins, though imbued with new common loyalties that were often at odds with the particular values of local groups. In some cases, trusted territorial chiefs were allowed to command regiments made up essentially of their own peoples.

After the defeat of Zwide, Mzilikazi had transferred his allegiance to Shaka, who confirmed him in his position as the chief of the Khumalo, making him one of his generals and allowing him to command the military regiments made up of his own people. However, in 1822, Mzilikazi fell out with his overlord, when he refused to hand over the booty of cattle he had captured from a neighboring Sotho group. After repulsing the first Zulu contingent sent to dislodge him from his Ntumbane mountain fortress, he fled with about two hundred of his warriors.

Evading his Zulu pursuers, he marched northward with his foot soldiers, subduing the smaller groups he encountered along his path, and swelling his fighting force in the process. His military adventures and political career lasted for another forty-seven years. He traversed a distance of about 1500 miles that took him through the territories of several ethnic groups, most of whom felt the brunt of his military conquest and economic depredations. His march brought him into conflict with many Sotho-Tswana groups, the Kwena, the Kgatha, the Koranna, and the Griqua. Successively attacked by many of these groups, still dreading another Zulu attack, and continuously harassed by the Boers, who by now had become a player in the fray, Mzilikazi veered northward. He eventually established his capital at Bulawayo in the heartland of the Shona country, many of whose chieftaincies, like those of the neighboring Kalanga, he subdued and incorporated into his new Ndebele kingdom.

The new state was an expansionist and militarist one. To ensure the regular supply of much needed materials, regular predatory expeditions were sent out from the capital, year after year, harrying groups near and far and expropriating their stocks of cattle, grain, and iron tools, and requisitioning their members for service in the army. Following the Zulu tradition, Mzilikazi adopted the age-regiment system. As with the Zulu, the regiments were quartered in newly established regimental towns. Unlike the Zulu, the regimental towns were not usually dissolved at the end of service, but became permanent. In addition, married men were allowed to live with their wives in their regiment, where they constituted a reserve force that could be called upon for service in times of emergency. Membership of regiments also became hereditary, as sons were allowed to enroll in the regiments of their parents. The militarization of society notwithstanding, the ordinary villagers continued to live in their traditional ways, with each village, for the purpose of military service and tribute gathering, attached to a regimental town.

The new Ndebele society that emerged was divided into three strata. At the top were the *Zansi*, made up of the families of Mzilikazi's original followers and others who had joined him south of the Vaal. The second group, known as *E-Nha*, consisted essentially of Sotho-Tswana peoples who were incorporated into the fledgling Ndebele group in the course of their migrations north of the Vaal. The last group was the *Hole*, made up of the people conquered and incorporated north of the Limpopo River. The prestige, social distinctions, political influence, and economic privileges of the *Zansi*, as well as the centralizing tendencies of the military formation, ensured the spread of Ndebele customs and the Sindebele language, and the inculcation of a spirit of loyalty to the state and to its supreme ruler.

Unlike Shaka, Mzilikazi was neither capricious nor tyrannical. Contemporary observers described him as a man possessed of a genial and pleasant nature, a tactical politician and diplomat who preferred negotiation and compromise to confrontation. He was receptive to new ideas. He opened his country to Christian missionaries and permitted and even encouraged Europeans to trade and settle in his state. Mzilikazi's strong personality, his long reign, his impressive military achievements, and his political sagacity made him the personification of the state. The position of the king as the pivotal center of the polity was ritually commemorated during the annual *incwala*, or harvest festival. This festival, observed at the capital and attended by all his people, became an occasion to celebrate the authority of the king and an opportunity for the people to affirm their loyalty to him.

Moshoeshoe and the Lesotho Nation

Another kingdom born out of the turbulence of this era was Lesotho.[16] The *Mfecane* wars had thrown much of the area north and west of the Drakensberg Mountains into a period of unrest and instability. Several of the small Sotho chiefdoms in the region disintegrated in the face of incessant attacks and the depredations of their more powerful neighbors. Exploiting the state of confusion and chaos in the region, Moshoeshoe, the son of the insignificant chieftain of the small Mokoteli clan of the Kwena, established himself as a major force. Recognizing the defensive potential of flat-topped mountains, Moshoeshoe secured himself, his family, and members of his age-grade on top of the Butha-Buthe Mountain. His leadership abilities, his talent for organization, and his success in defense against attackers attracted many frightened peoples and displaced groups to his mountain fortress. Following his defeat of the Tlokwa, he moved his people southward, establishing his headquarters on top of the well-nigh impregnable Thaba Bosiu mountain, whose location on the Little Caledon River with an extensive flat topped grazing summit made it an ideal nucleus of a new nation. After militarily subduing the pre-existing Bamantsane group, he secured the allegiance of several Sotho and Nguni groups whose need for security drove them to his protection. Larger groups, such as the Baphuthi, the Bataung, and the Barolong, all of who were smarting or fleeing from the disturbances of the *Mfecane* were forced to acknowledge his sovereignty or seek his protection.

Towards groups that were too powerful for him, Moshoeshoe adopted the policy of conciliation, courting their friendship by sending presents. To defend his state from their attacks, he sent regular tribute to Matiwane of the Ama-Ngwane and blue crane feathers to Shaka. Even his defeated enemies were given cattle to save them from starvation and assuage their desire for revenge. Moshoeshoe's success in beating off the much-dreaded Ngwane and in frustrating the redoubtable Ndebele, while checking the depredations of the Thembu and the harassment of the Tlokwa, brought him tremendous respect and prestige among his allies as well as among his enemies.

Ultimately, however, the most serious threat to the new Basotho State came from groups of musket-firing Griqua and Korama mounted raiders and their Trekboer allies. Moshoeshoe's frantic attempts to stem off Boer encroachment by welcoming missionary activities and playing the British against the Boers could not prevent the Boers' eventual expropriation of much of the Sotho country. After two devastating wars with the Boers of the Orange Free State in 1858 and 1865, Lesotho, at the prompting of its ruler and founder, was annexed by the British Government. Virtually outliving all his contemporary nation builders, Moshoeshoe, at the time of his death in March 1870, had succeeded in preserving the core of his kingdom from Boer annexation and laying the foundation of what eventually became the modern nation state of Lesotho.

---

16. G. Tylden, *Rise of the Basuto* (Cape Town: Juta and Co., 1950); L. Thompson, *Survival in Two Worlds: Moshoeshoe of Lesotho, 1786-1870* (Oxford: 1975); and E.A. Eldredge, *A South African Kingdom* (Cambridge: Cambridge University Press, 1993).

New States, Revolutionary Leaders

Thus, the *Mfecane* had far reaching effects on the peoples and societies of Central and southern Africa during the nineteenth century. It led to the disappearance of many polities that had been significant in the region before the nineteenth century. Notable among these were the states of the Hlubi, Ngwane, Mthethwa, Ndwandwe, Zizi Bhele, and others. Those that did not cease to exist, like most of the Tswana states, were broken into fragments, and virtually eliminated as major factors in the region. Some pre-existing states, such as those of the Pedi, Tlhaping, and Tlharo appear to have been strengthened by the turbulence of this period. More significant, however, for the subsequent history of the region was the emergence of new states. Some of these, like the Zulu Empire, grew out of pre-existing small chiefdoms. Others, like Lesotho and Gaza, resulted from new conglomerations of groups and polities.

Concurrent with the development of new states was the rise of new and outstanding leaders whose skill, military valor, political acumen, and leadership and organizational abilities made them founders and builders of states. Notable among these was Shaka of the Zulu and his brother, Dingane, who assassinated and succeeded him. Others who left lasting legacies were Moshoeshoe who established Lesotho, Mzilikazi who established the Ndebele State, and Sebetwane who built the Kololo State and imposed its authority over several conquered groups. Another was Zwangendaba, who, after effecting the unity of his Jere Ngoni people, destroyed the Changamire Empire of the Shona, routed the Rozwi army, and eliminated its monarchy.

Militarism and Nationalism

The turmoil of this period also resulted in the militarization of society. The pervasive state of warfare and the need for security demanded constant military mobilization and preparedness. The age-regiment system became a common feature of the military machines of both the new and old states in the region. Some of these states, like the Zulu, the Ndebele, and Gaza, were aggressive militarist states. As expansionist and imperialistic states, they established professional standing armies quartered in regimental towns. Others, like Lesotho and Swazi, were defensive states. They were not essentially imperialistic or expansionist in nature, except as dictated by the need for security and the acquisition of wealth such as cattle and grain and the control of trade routes. This explains why some of the founders of such states placed a premium on defensive locations. Examples of these were Moshoeshoe, who built his headquarters on the naturally fortified Butha-Buthe flat topped mountain, Sobhuza in his inaccessible mountain capital and Sebetwane on the treacherous islands of the Kafue River flood plain. Unlike the expansionist states, the defensive states did not establish permanent standing armies, and the age-regiments served as military units only in time of war. The defensive states also allowed more freedom of action and more local autonomy for their component parts, who were welded together more by political consensus, mutual interests, and intermarriage than by the charisma of the rulers and by military force.

The *Mfecane* generated a new sense of nationalism in the region. Most of the new states that came into being were multi-ethnic states. In many of them, the age-regiment became an instrument for the unification of diverse and disparate groups. Made up of people from several different ethno-cultural backgrounds, the age-regiment became a multi-functional institution. In its mission of preparing youths for service and adulthood, it facilitated the inculcation of common ideas, values, and norms, and the fostering of feelings of common identity and loyalty to the state. The institution of practices such as regular war dance ceremonies and annual first fruit festivals contributed to the emergence of an enduring sense of corporate identity. In some places, as among the Kololo, the language of the conqueror became the lingua franca for the state. In others, as among the Ndebele, the prestigious position and influence associated with the ruling group facilitated the easy acculturation of subordinate groups into mainstream culture. This process was further accentuated by the emergence of new distinct sub-cultures and the creation of new heroic traditions derived from the epic achievements and stirring events of the period.

All over the region, new opportunities were created for social mobility, political participation, and economic self-improvement. In places where kinship, birth, and ethnic ties had previously been paramount, the emphasis was now placed on talents, competition, valor, promotion, service, and territoriality. These changes also had repercussions in the political sphere. In many places, and to varying degrees, the *Mfecane* resulted in the transformation of the social order. Power became highly centralized, while the institution of kingship gained in power and prestige. The king, known as inkosi among the Ngoni, became the commander in chief, the Chief Justice, and the Chief Priest. He had absolute power, sacralized and ritualized in his office, and was theoretically the owner of all cattle and dispenser of booty. The king also became the symbol of nationhood, and the focus of service, loyalty, and patriotism.

Paying the Price: Violence, Devastation, and the Long Memory

All these developments were, however, not without cost. The *Mfecane* exacted a heavy toll on its victims. In its militaristic expression, it was violent and destructive. Militarism and violence became veritable ways of life and means of self-actualization and achievement. Continuous cattle raids and political violence became instruments of nationalism. Wars provoked wars and violence generated more violence. As soldiers sallied back and forth in search of new loot, destroying settlements and annihilating states, the process became a vicious circle. Defeated and displaced groups descended on their even more helpless neighbors, who in turn pounced on other yet more hapless groups with the chain reactions reverberating far and wide. The perennial warfare occasioned much suffering for everyone involved. For the ordinary soldiers, the demands of militarism were exacting, tiring, and exhausting. The situation was not helped by the capricious and unpredictable nature of some of the rulers. Shaka's violent and sadistic tendencies, his sense of insecurity, and his fear of death drove him to pernicious extremes. A failed assassination attempt on him in 1824 and the sudden death of his mother, Nandi, and grandmother in 1827 produced massacres that alienated the loyalty of his people and provoked his eventual assassination in 1828. He was only forty-one years old, still single and without an heir.

Figure 16-3. Zulu Temple at Maryloa

Economically, the *Mfecane* was self-destructive and ruinous. Based on the seizure of cattle and the expropriation of grains and other commodities, not on production, it was bound to be counter-productive. Every year as the regiments raided far and wide for cattle, they had to penetrate further and further for readily available loot. The frequent fighting and the state of unrest it occasioned hampered agricultural production and other peaceful pursuits. Relentless and ruinous raids and migrations reduced the population of many areas to misery, desolation, and starvation, well attested to by many contemporary observers. Finally, the *Mfecane* produced profound demographic upheavals in Central and southern Africa. It created a major distortion in the population of the region. In places like Natal and the Orange Free State, it resulted in a drastic demographic hemorrhage, which led to the myth of the "open spaces" that later became a powerful rationalization for White settlers' colonizing incursion into the region. Similarly, it weakened many African states and groups and rendered them particularly vulnerable to a second and more effective *Mfecane*, the gradual but effective encroachment and colonization of the White Trekboers from the coast. That the memory and the traditions of the *Mfecane* have remained a powerful force and inspiration in African history is a function of the fact that the achievements of the men and groups associated with it demonstrated, in the word of a leading *Mfecane* historian,

> not only courage, powers of leadership and military skill but the capacity
> for original thought and action; the ability to devise or adopt new institu-

tions and new techniques to solve new problems; the statesmanship to rise above a narrow tribal point of view. [Their traditions] underlie moral values and character, as well as attitudes to authority in general and to relations between groups within, as well as across, the race barrier.... the victories and defeats, heroes and villains of the period, survive in memory as a potent force moulding moral, social and political attitudes in the contemporary world.[17]

The White Invaders

A Refreshment Station: The Dutch Arrival and Settlement

The *Mfecane*, as we have noted, prepared much of southern and East-Central Africa for eventual European conquest and domination. The European advent and activities in the region, however, antedated the nineteenth century. Beginning in the early decades of the fifteenth century, Portuguese mariners had, by slow but definite progress, reached the South African Cape peninsula by 1487. In 1497, five years after Christopher Columbus opened the Americas to Europe, Vasco da Gama rounded the Cape, and with the aid of an accomplished Arab sailor, ibn Majid, crossed the Indian Ocean, reaching Calicut in India, before returning to Portugal, with two of his ships loaded with gold, ivory, and other exotic goods from Africa and the Orient. With Africa thus opened up, a period of intense trading interaction with Europe was inaugurated. Early in this period, contact was established with the indigenous African peoples of southern Africa, especially the Khoikhoi. They began to supply passing European trading ships with meat, vegetables, and fresh water, in exchange for iron goods and copper.

Early in the seventeenth century, the Portuguese monopoly gave way to Dutch dominance in the African and Indian Ocean trades. As trade increased, so did the demand for cattle. The attempt of the Khoikhoi to control the quantity of cattle supplied without jeopardizing their holdings made the merchants to take to cattle seizure, which in turn provoked retaliation from the Khoikhoi. In an attempt to secure a more effective foothold and guarantee a more regular supply of provisions, the Dutch East India Company sent Jan van Riebeeck with eighty company employees to establish a refreshment station at the Cape in 1652. There is no evidence to show that this was meant to be anything more than a convenient victualising and stopping post for trading ships, allowing their sailors to rest, take on fruits, vegetables, and meat and for their sick to recuperate. Before long, however, the situation began to change.

As the population of the Dutch settlement increased, they began to annex more land, to accommodate their growing needs. They did this in three ways. First they made use of free burghers (citizens). These were company employees who

---

17. Omer-Cooper, *The Zulu Aftermath*, 180-182. On the enduring mythical, ideological, political, and historiographical significance of the Shaka story see Hamilton, *Terrific Majesty: The Powers of Shaka Zulu and the Limits of Historical Invention* (Harvard: Harvard University Press, 1998).

were released to colonize new land and establish farms to service the settlement and supply trading ships with food. Soon, the role of the free burghers was taken over by the Trekboers (farmers). These were semi-migrant White pastoralist farmers who became the chief instruments of White expansionism. Second, from about 1657, they began to make use of slave labor. Under Dutch supervision, the slaves were employed in construction as well as in farming. The first two methods led to the third, the gradual but certain displacement of the local pastoralists. The indigenous Khoikhoi, who had granted the settlers initial permission to settle, began to perceive the potential threat posed to their independence and land ownership by the newcomers. In the meantime, more immigrants began to arrive from Europe. These were made up of adventurers, opportunists, outcasts, the persecuted, the poor, and the unsuccessful as well as other enterprising and resourceful individuals.

The Khoisan and the New Society at the Cape

These developments had far-reaching consequences. The most immediate was the ascendancy of the Dutch and the Dutch language in Cape society. Then there was the expansion and consolidation of the institution of slavery. Indeed, for a time during the seventeenth and eighteenth centuries, the slave population exceeded that of the free born in the society, with the company holding the largest share of slaves. For the indigenous Khoisan groups, the Dutch advent was a major catastrophe. It had an eight-fold impact. They lost their pastures and land. Their livestock was decimated by Trekboer seizures and by new and lethal strains of cattle diseases brought from Europe. Their fragile socio-political system disintegrated as they came under Dutch political control and had to live under Dutch laws. European settlers also introduced smallpox, which within a short period wrought demographic havoc on the helpless Khoisan groups. Denuded of their livestock and their independence, and forced by reasons of survival to labor for

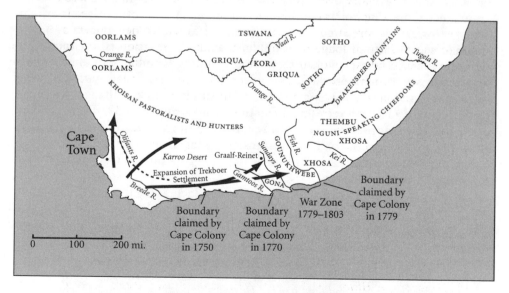

Figure 16-4. Boer Expansion in South Africa, 1750-1803

the new invaders, they experienced cultural and economic devastation that ultimately set the stage for their near extinction as a distinct cultural group.[18]

The new society that emerged at the Cape was an alien one and a combination of different influences. Foreign influences were marked in seven major areas: trade, religion, language, art, settlement patterns, building styles and fashion. It was a self-sufficient society, producing all its basic necessities. It disregarded formal education, which remained meager, and was indifferent to religion. It was noted for its moral laxity and its corruption, which became a way of life as rules were routinely ignored and subverted. The new society was rife with fissures. Divisions of class resulted in gradations of status and wealth, masters and slaves. While the governor earned about two hundred guilders a month, a common sailor on the average earned about nine. Mutual suspicion and rivalries marked relations between company officials and settler farmers. Intermarriage and other forms of conjugal interaction, mainly between White men and Black women mediated the division between the races. As sexual liaisons and genetic intermingling intensified, a new class of mixed-race people came into being. Over time, the African population of the Cape became progressively lighter in complexion, while the Dutch became darker.[19]

European Expansion and African Resistance

African resistance to the White invaders was constant and relentless. It took many forms. The White settlers created and co-opted willing collaborators among the indigenous population. Referred to as "Coree," these individuals became beachrangers, mediating settlers' relations with their peoples. In some cases the practice backfired, with the beachrangers fomenting protest and leading revolts against the foreigners. Generally the African populations reacted in one or more of three different ways. One was open or covert resistance. Tension and conflict developed because of rivalry over trade, cattle raids and counter-raids, encroachment on pasture and grazing land, coerced labor recruitment, and enforced enslavement. Those who were not prepared to accommodate or serve the newcomers and were unable to successfully dislodge or resist them took to desertion from service and migration to inaccessible regions. For the majority, however, the path of accommodation and cooperation appeared more promising. They became involved with the newcomers through trade, intermarriage, and provision of services. The Khoisan, with their loosely knit socio-political organization, became noted for their propensity for acculturation, a tendency that appears to have turned out to be culturally disastrous, as they gradually and virtually acculturated themselves out of existence.

By the middle of the eighteenth century, demographic pressure and land hunger had brought the Trekboers to the bank of the Great Fish River. Their at-

---

18. For a fuller discussion of the consequences of Dutch advent and colonization as well as African dispossession in South Africa, see the authoritative study by Leonard Thompson, *A History of South Africa* (New Haven: Yale University Press, 1995), from which much of this section derives; and A.T. Moleah, *South Africa, Colonialism, Apartheid and African Dispossession* (Wilmington: Disa Press, 1993).

19. Thompson, *A History*, 31-52. On slavery see R. Ross, *Cape of Torments: Slavery and Resistance in South Africa* (London: 1983).

tempt to cross the river and push eastward into the fertile and well-watered land on the other side brought them into direct confrontation with the southernmost vanguard of the Bantu migrants, the Xhosa, who were already domiciled in this region. The Trekboers found in the Xhosa a much more formidable opponent, one they could not easily subdue. The first major clash occurred in 1779. This marked the beginning of a series of nine inconclusive "Frontier Wars," which lasted with varying vicissitudes and fatalities for the next one hundred years. The most notable of these wars occurred in 1793, 1811-1812, 1818-1819, 1834, 1846, and 1850. The Trekboers were also caught up in the encircling vortex of the *Mfecane* revolution, fighting, among others, Mzilikazi's Ndebele in 1837 and Dingane's Zulu in 1838. In the meantime, a new factor had been introduced into the picture; this was British imperialism.[20]

British Imperialism and the Consolidation of African Dispossession

Responding to pressures from its agents and traders at the Cape and recognizing the strategic importance of the Cape especially in the light of the Napoleonic Wars going on in Europe, Britain seized control of the Cape Colony from the Dutch East India Company in 1799. This was a pre-emptive annexation meant to prevent the Cape from falling into the hands of the French, who had by 1799 established their imperial rule over Holland, the Dutch homeland in Europe. Thereafter, from the Cape, Britain kept a constant watch on the Trekboers, intervening in their affairs, forestalling their imperial designs and checking their excesses. The British abolition of slavery in 1833 and the earlier abolition of the slave trade gave a decidedly humanitarian tone to British imperial policy. The Trekboers were resentful of British taxation, control over land and labor, and constant administrative interference. Even more galling was the fact that the British determination to abolish slavery in Cape society threatened the already ingrained racial assumptions and practices at the Cape. Equally important was the attraction of so-called "vacant" or "empty" fertile lands in the interior left by the unraveling *Mfecane*. Added to this was the gradual replacement of locally- elected Boer officials by British-appointed magistrates, the Anglicization of the colony, and the failure or inability of the British administration to seize more land from the Xhosa for Trekboer farmers. All these factors combined to inspire the celebrated Boer Trek of the 1830s and 1840s, which resulted in the gradual but effective extension of permanent White settlement into the interior of southern Africa.

Led by daring and rich group leaders, taking advantage of the chaos and upheavals created by the *Mfecane*, and undeterred by relentless African resistance and continuous British interference, the Voortrekkers ("Front trekkers") had by the 1860s established themselves firmly in Natal and the Orange Free State. In their new settlements, the settlers faced many problems. With their limited numbers and frail polities, surrounded by many hostile and restive African groups and ever suspicious of British intentions, they became self-conscious and defensive. To

---

20. Shula Marks, "Khoisan resistance to the Dutch in the Seventeenth and Eighteenth Centuries," *JAH,* 13, 1 (1972): 55-80; on the Xhosa see J. Peirs, *The House of Phalo: A History of the Xhosa People in the Days of Their Independence* (Berkeley: University of California Press, 1982); and Thompson, *A History,* 70-109.

preserve their distinct identity in the face of Anglicization and other corrosive assaults, they developed a strong race consciousness, patriotism, and ethnic nationalism as Afrikaners.

The success of the Boers or Afrikaners in holding out their own against the British, in colonizing African land, and in laying the foundation of an exclusive racialist and apartheid society should not lead to the conclusion that African societies were disintegrating. Indeed, unlike the Khoisan, the Bantu African societies that came into contact and conflict with the Boers succeeded in preserving their socio-political institutions largely unaffected by the new invaders. There are many reasons for the survival and resilience of these societies. They had already developed immunities to deadly European diseases like the smallpox and measles that had decimated American Indians and the Khoisan. Unlike the Khoisan, these Bantu communities were more populous and were settled farming communities. Their economy was more varied and more complex, their social networks more resilient, and their political system better-organized. Thus they were able to maintain their cohesion as organized communities, while pragmatically adapting their socio-political system to the new order. In addition, and in spite of the turmoil, these groups continued to increase in population, while remaining vitally important to meeting white labor and economic needs. The discovery of the largest diamond field anywhere in the world in Kimberley in 1867, and of a similar concentration of gold in the Witwatersrand in 1886 further accelerated the process of European immigration, land alienation, African dispossession, and White colonization and domination in southern Africa.

Review Questions

1. "A mere random expression of marginal frustrations, savagery and heathenism." How accurate is this description of the *Mfecane*?
2. With reference to the historiography of the *Mfecane*, critically examine the nature and the context of the contest over historical interpretation in African history.
3. Assess the significance of ecological factors in the outbreak and development of the *Mfecane*.
4. Acount for the major achievements and failures of Shaka the Zulu.
5. What were the main features and the major consequences of the *Mfecane* in the history of Central and Southern Africa?
6. Examine the nature and the major consequences of resistance to European conquests in southern Africa before the twentieth century.

Additional Reading

Elphick E. and H. Giliomee, eds. *The Shaping of South African Society, 1652-1840*. Middletown: Wesleyan University Press, 1989.
Omer-Cooper, J.D. *The Zulu Aftermath*. London: Longman, 1966.
Ngcongco, L.D. "The *Mfecane* and the Rise of New African States," in J.F. Ade Ajayi, ed., *Africa in the Nineteenth Century*, UNESCO General History of Africa, Vol. 6. Paris: UNESCO, 1989, 90-123.

Thompson, Leonard. *A History of South Africa*. New Haven: Yale University Press, 1996.

PART E

Africa and Europe

Section Overview

From the fifteenth century onward, the Europeans began to encounter the states located along the African coast. The search for slaves by the Portuguese led to the fall of the Kongo kingdom in the late sixteenth century. In West Africa, Euro-African relations revolved lagely around the slave trade from the sixteenth to the early nineteenth centuries. The Portuguese, English, Dutch, Danes, Swedes, and French participated in the trade which linked Africa with Europe and the Americas. This trade caused enormous population loss, triggered warfare to make war captives to sell into slavery, ruined many families, and destroyed productive economies.

Euro-African relations during the nineteenth century underwent a transformation. This century opened with the continuation of the slave trade. However, the slave trade was then abolished. This meant profound adjustments for states and society that had participated in it. The alternative was to produce raw materials for external markets. The use of slaves for domestic production intensified, as exports increased. European firms came in large numbers to compete for trade, and Africans became mainly middlemen. Traders were joined by explorers who wanted to know more about Africa, and also by missionaries who wanted to evangelize and initiate their own economic changes. Both explorers and missionaries did so much to pave the way for imperial control.

In the last quarter of the century, the partition and conquest of Africa were under way. While Europeans were mainly confined to the coastal areas at the beginning of the century, they had penetrated the hinterland and imposed control in many areas by the end of it. While the majority of African states were independent in 1880, virtually all became European colonies within the next twenty years. Previous European enclaves were quickly converted into areas from which to move inland, as the flag followed trade. The Berlin conference of 1884-1885 tried to minimize conflicts by recognizing the spheres of influence of competing powers and laying down the conditions for annexation and effective occupation. African resistance, whether bold or feeble, was crushed. By 1900, a new map of Africa, representing areas that each European nation was able to take, had been drawn.

Chapter 17

Africa and the Trans-Atlantic Slave Trade

Joseph E. Inikori

From the late fifteenth to the mid-nineteenth century, there was a trade in captives, which forced Africans into employment as slaves in European- and American-held plantations and mines in the Western Hemisphere and elsewhere. This chapter attempts to shed some light on a number of questions concerning the trade. Why did the Europeans of the period seek slave labor rather than free wage labor? If they had to procure slave labor, why did they not do so in Europe or Asia instead of Africa? How did the European trade in African slaves compare with the one in European and Asian slaves that preceded it? How many Africans did the European traders ship from Africa during the trade? What long-term effects did the procurement and sale of such numbers have on the process of socio-economic development in western and Central Africa?

These are some of the main issues addressed by the chapter. There are two major sections. In section one, the emphasis is on demonstrating the impact of the trade on the long-term process of socio-economic development in Africa, drawing mainly from the West African experience. For this purpose, a clear distinction is drawn between the short-term private gains of a few individuals and groups, and the long-term developmental consequences for economies and societies as a whole. In the second section, students are introduced to the major controversies surrounding the trade.

The Atlantic and Previous Slave Trades

From biblical evidence, we know that a large number of Hebrew slaves were employed by African rulers in ancient Egypt. The Greeks employed slaves procured from Europe and Asia. Then came the most elaborate slave system of the ancient world, Roman slavery. The slave population in Rome was built up initially with captives taken in the imperial wars. Subsequently, the slave markets in Rome were supplied with slaves from the British Isles and continental Europe. The rise of Islam from the seventh century A.D., and the socio-economic and political system to which it gave rise in the Middle East and North Africa, occasioned the development of yet another major slave system that supported an important international trade in slaves. Again, the main supply sources for the Middle East and North African slave markets were, for many centuries, in Europe, especially central and Eastern Europe. Italian slave traders were in charge. When the Roman Church decreed that European Christians must not be sold as slaves to Muslims in North Africa and the Middle East, the traders ignored the Papal injunctions.

The early centuries of the last millennium witnessed the consolidation of politically and militarily strong state systems all over Europe. The weakly organized communities in Europe were now incorporated into empires and other state systems sufficiently strong to defend their territorial integrity and their subjects. With this development, the taking of captives became very costly to captors. The increased costs lowered the economic incentives for captive-taking. As the European supply of captives to the Middle East and North African markets dwindled and became more expensive, North African and Arab merchants trading across the Sahara to West Africa began to take more interest in procuring captives from that region. By the middle centuries of the last millennium, a regular trade in West African captives across the Sahara had been well established. Arab merchants trading to the East African coast also brought back slaves. The main difference between Europe and sub-Saharan Africa, in terms of captive-taking at this time, was the continuing existence of political fragmentation in the latter area. Sub-Saharan Africa was still characterized by a multiplicity of small-scale political systems co-existing with a smaller number of larger and stronger political organizations. This political contour facilitated the taking of captives from the weakly organized communities by the stronger polities at very little cost to themselves.

European colonization of the Atlantic islands and the Americas, following the fifteenth century explorations, became the source of a hitherto unprecedented demand for slave labor. Commercial exploitation of the vast resources of the Americas demanded a large number of workers separated from their means of production and the products of their labor, and under the effective control of profit-seeking entrepreneurs. Such workers could be free wage-laborers, indentured servants, or slaves. The Europeans experimented with the enslavement of the American Indians with disastrous results. Humiliated, overworked, and infected with European diseases, the American Indian populations were almost wiped out in a few decades. The experiment with European indentured servants was no more successful; with vast unoccupied lands available in the Americas, the few European migrants to the New World at this time preferred independent employment. Large-scale commercial exploitation of the American resources thus had to depend on slavery, if it was to take place at all.

But where would the slaves come from? Supplies within the Americas had already dried up. The taking of captives in Europe had become so costly that even the limited demand in the Middle East and North Africa could not be met as in previous centuries. This left sub-Saharan Africa and East Asia as possible sources. That East Asia was a potential source of supply is evidenced by the use of Asian slaves by European entrepreneurs who operated in East Asia in the centuries that followed the arrival of the Portuguese in 1498. But, relative to Western Africa, the cost of transporting Asian slaves to the Americas would be prohibitive, given the rudimentary ocean transportation technology of the time. Thus, for as long as the politico-military situation in sub-Saharan Africa in the middle centuries of the present millennium prevailed, cost considerations ensured that the supply of slaves to the Americas would concentrate on that region. The same cost considerations virtually ruled out eastern Africa until the British anti-slave trade naval patrols significantly raised the cost of procuring slaves from several sub-regions in Western Africa in the nineteenth century.

What made the European slave trade from Africa different from preceding trades in captives was its scale and character. For the first time in human history, the demand for slave labor was based on the employment of slaves to produce commodities on a very large scale for a growing capitalist market that embraced all the shores of a vast ocean. It has been estimated that in the last decades of the eighteenth century the value of commerce conducted across that ocean was over £100 million (sterling) per annum, and over three-quarters of the New World produce that formed the basis of this commerce came from the labor of African slaves: The use of African slave labor to exploit the vast natural resources of the Americas was big business; the trade that supplied the slave labor was big business; distributing the slave-produced commodities was big business; and supplying in Europe the resources that supported the entire enterprise was very big business that was highly profitable, privately and socially. This was a new phenomenon in world history.

Consequently, European slave traders were able to pay on the African coast slave prices that made captive-taking privately rewarding for some political and economic entrepreneurs in the short run. In the second half of the eighteenth century, European traders carried to West Africa alone various manufactures worth more than £2 million (sterling) annually, over ninety percent of which were exchanged for slaves. This amount of manufactures looks ridiculously small in light of the value of commerce based on the products of the labor of those slaves as stated earlier. This in itself is an indication of the low cost of captive taking in Western Africa. Nevertheless, the amount of manufactures involved was sufficiently large to encourage a sustained supply of large numbers of captives by a few individuals and some ruling elites, since initially the short-term costs were borne by one group and the short-term benefits went to another until all were ravaged in the long run by the cumulative effects. It must be stressed that people on the continent during the period did not see themselves as Africans. They only identified with their local polities and communities. Ruling elites were, therefore, not constrained by ideological considerations in taking captives from other polities and selling them to European traders in exchange for imported manufactures.

Impact on Africa's Population

An important aspect of the consequences of the European slave trade for western Africa is its effects on the region's population. Although the total numbers shipped from Africa are still being debated by historians, archival researches conducted by specialists in the last two decades have demonstrated that the available evidence can support an export estimate of at least 13 million slaves. How much allowance to make for missing records is a difficult task. In my view, 15.4 million may be closer to the actual total numbers shipped from Africa during the European trade. However, the 13 million, based narrowly on currently known records — or even the now discredited 11 million employed by some historians in the past — is still adequate for assessing the demographic effects.

While the trade lasted from the 1440s to the 1860s, the exports were concentrated in the two hundred years from 1650 to 1850, particularly from 1700 to 1850. Between 1700 and 1809, about two-thirds of the total exports were from West Africa (Senegal through Cameroon), and virtually all the rest from West-

Figure 17-1. Capture and Sale of a Slave

Central Africa (Congo-Angola); exports from East Africa at this time went mostly to French islands in the Indian Ocean. From 1811 to 1867, West Africa's contribution declined to about 38 percent, that of West-Central Africa rose to 48 percent, and Southeast Africa now contributed about 14 percent, excluding exports to French plantations in the Indian Ocean. On the average, 36 percent of the exports were female and 64 percent male. The very young and the very old were rarely included; the bulk of the exports being aged 15 to 30. These export characteristics were determined primarily by the preferences of the European employers of slave labor in the Americas.

Because the slaves were procured largely through violence—state-organized military operations, raids by organized groups, and kidnapping by individuals or small groups—the demographic effects went far beyond the numbers actually exported. The socio-economic disruptions arising from the wars caused by the trade, and the attendant demographic consequences, have been elaborately documented by recent research, especially for West-Central Africa, the Slave Coast (from the Volta in Ghana to Lagos in Nigeria), the Gold Coast, and the Middle Niger Valley. While many regions shared the impact, two were most hard hit: West-Central Africa and what geographers call the West African Middle Belt. The extremely low population densities of both regions in the late nineteenth century are historically explained in terms of the slave trade's effects rather than in terms of rainfall and the physical environment both of which are broadly similar to those of the more densely populated regions of western Africa.

Some historians treat the introduction of American food plants into Western Africa as a benefit associated with the slave trade. This is a misconception. The American crops were introduced at a time when European trade with Western Africa was predominantly in African products, such as gold, copper, ivory, cotton cloth, wood, and pepper. The introduction of American crops to sub-Saharan Africa, like their introduction in Europe at about the same time, and the earlier introduction of Asian crops, was independent of the slave trade. On the other hand, those crops were not adopted on a significant scale in West Africa until the late nineteenth century, even the twentieth century in some areas. In West-Central Africa where they seem to have been adopted much earlier, they still could not prevent the devastating effects of the trade, which attacked the region's populations at a time when the societies of Bantu migrants were still going through the process of diffusing new techniques of production and socio-political organization.

Political and Socio-economic Consequences

As stated earlier, the European demand for captives to be shipped as slaves began at a time when the political scene in western Africa was still characterized by a multiplicity of small-scale autonomous political units. Growing population and expanding internal and external trade provided the main driving force for the incorporation of these independent units into larger political organizations by economic and political entrepreneurs. Some remarkable advances had already been made in this regard. In the Western Sudan, a succession of large and complex political organizations developed from the last centuries of the first millennium A.D.; Mali and Songhai were the climax of that process. Other early complex political organizations included the Kingdom of Kongo and a host of city-states. Most of these polities were still going through their early stages of formation and enlargement when the Europeans arrived. All over western Africa at this time, the foundations were being laid for the competitive process of building large and complex state systems.

Initially, the European demand for African products, such as gold, copper, pepper, and cotton cloth tended to encourage the emergence of state systems and ruling elites with vested interests in peaceful relations and trade with their neighbors. A good example here is the Akan trading empire ruled by merchant corporations in what is now Ghana. The combination of European and trans-Saharan demands for gold in the region stimulated general production and trade, which gave rise to the Akan socio-political system dominated by merchants. The early Portuguese demand for copper also tended to reinforce the central elements in the Kongo system based originally on the production and distribution of copper and shell money.

As European demand shifted increasingly from products to captives, a fundamental change occurred in the political process. At the beginning, the Europeans arranged with the rulers of the more strongly organized states, such as Benin and Kongo, for them to supply captives from their weaker neighbors. But the European demand for more and more captives soon gave rise to the formation of groups of bandits all over western Africa. In places where the foundations already laid had not yet given rise to firmly established large political organizations, the process was hijacked by these bandits, who became successful political entrepre-

tives — including the political dominance of warriors, limited size of states, and recurrent hostility with neighbors — induced state policies that secured the short-term interests of ruling elites at the expense of long-term development.

Controversial Issues

Several areas of controversy remain in the historiography of the trans-Atlantic slave trade. How many Africans were enslaved? How did the trade affect long-term processes of socio-economic development in Africa? The study of the Atlantic slave trade and its impact on African societies was pioneered by John Fage from the 1950s.[2] Walter Rodney's critique of Fage in the mid-1960s and early 1970s improved the quality of discourse.[3] Philip Curtin's quantitative study of the slave trade touched on several aspects of the literature and thus further fueled the debate.[4] I will start this section with a summary of the broad hypotheses of John Fage. The critique of Walter Rodney is then examined, followed by the reaction of both scholars to the quantitative study by Curtin.

Fage's original approach was designed to solve two related historical problems: (i) to explain why African societies were willing and able to supply large numbers of people for sale to European slave traders; and (ii) to show how this trade in people affected African economies and societies. For the first problem, two factors were presented as critical. One was the desire for European goods by consumers in the coastal societies of western Africa; the other was the presence of a slave class in those societies before their first contacts with the Europeans. At the beginning, Fage held, trade with the Europeans was primarily in African products, such as gold, ivory, pepper, copper, and cotton cloth. This early trade in African products helped to establish a taste for European manufactures among coastal peoples of western Africa. Then came a switch in European demand, from products to slaves, due to the labor needs of mining and plantation agriculture in the Americas. As this change in demand occurred, Fage argued, the presence of a slave class in the coastal societies made possible the transition from a trade in products to one in people. As he expressed it:

> When Europeans first began to ask for slaves in return for the goods they brought to West Africa, they were not repulsed. There was already an established demand for European goods among the Africans, and there was already an African merchant class on the coast accustomed to buying such goods and supplying the European traders in exchange with the commodities they wanted. If the Europeans wanted slaves as well as or

---

2. John D. Fage, *An Introduction to the History of West Africa* (Cambridge: C.U.P., 1955).

3. Walter Rodney, "African slavery and other forms of social oppression on the Upper Guinea Coast in the context of the Atlantic slave trade," *Journal of African History*, vol. 7, no. 3 (1966): 431-443; Walter Rodney, *A History of the Upper Guinea Coast, 1545-1800* (Oxford University Press, 1970); Walter Rodney, *How Europe Underdeveloped Africa* (London and Dar es Salaam, 1972).

4. Philip D. Curtin, *The Atlantic Slave Trade: A Census* (Madison: University of Wisconsin Press, 1969).

instead of, gold, ivory, pepper, and gum, then the merchants were willing to provide slaves. The presence of a slave class among the coastal peoples meant that there was already a class of human beings who could be sold to Europeans if there was an incentive to do so, and an economic incentive already existed in the form of the growing African demand for European imports.[5]

Continuing, Fage argued that the coastal African traders began by selling the slaves already present in their own communities; but as the growing American demand exhausted the previously accumulated stock of slaves, merchants and chiefs in these communities increased the enslavement of their people through the judicial system or debt. Subsequently, the profitability of selling people to the Europeans encouraged the procurement of captives from other communities through kidnapping, organized raids, and war.[6]

With respect to the problem of how this trade in people affected African economies and societies, Fage started with the demographic impact. Based on what he considered to be the "best figures" available at the time, he calculated that, between 1530 A.D. and the final abolition of the trade in the third quarter of the nineteenth century, a total of 14,650,000 Africans were landed alive in the Americas.[7] Assuming a middle-passage mortality of 16.7 percent, and including various additional mortalities from the point of capture to the final sale to the Europeans, Fage guessed that "between thirty and forty million souls must have been lost to West Africa" as a result of the Atlantic slave trade.[8] By extrapolation backward from the known population of West Africa in the 1950s, he estimated that the population of the region during the slave trade period was about twenty million, and computed the average annual rate of population loss during the roughly three hundred years of the slave trade to be less than one percent. The conclusion was that: "Such a rate of loss need not necessarily have been a crippling one for a healthy society." Fage argued further:

> Even if in general the slave trade tended to reduce the population of West Africa in an unhealthy manner, we still cannot say with any certainty that, had there been no slave trade, the population of West Africa today [1955?] would have been larger, or even that it would have been of a higher physical standard.[9]

Fage was, however, categorical on the devastating impact of the slave trade on African economies. "We can, however, be quite certain," Fage wrote,

> that the slave trade acted generally as a factor retarding orderly progress and development in West Africa. The dominant economic activity for many peoples became trade, and a peculiar kind of trade which discouraged rather than stimulated agricultural and industrial production, which indeed discouraged productive work of any kind. It became cheaper and easier for West Africans to buy tools and clothing and all sorts of manu-

---

5. John D. Fage, *An Introduction to the History of West Africa*, 3rd ed. (1962), 78.
6. Fage, *An Introduction to the History of West Africa* (1962), pp. 78-79.
7. Fage, *An Introduction to the History of West Africa* (1962), pp. 59 and 83.
8. Fage, *An Introduction to the History of West Africa* (1962), 84.
9. Fage, *An Introduction to the History of West Africa* (1962), 85-86.

factures from the Europeans rather than make them for themselves. Many arts and skills, which they possessed, such as iron-making, the making of pottery, of cloth, of brass and copper ware, deteriorated or even died out. And the West Africans paid for the European-made substitutes, not by any productive endeavor in other fields, but by the economically negative and destructive work of waging wars and capturing and selling men, the labourers whom they needed for the achievement of sound prosperity.[10]

Unquestioned for many years, Fage's arguments became the received wisdom, although no empirical research was conducted. The first major challenge to them came from Walter Rodney in the mid-1960s. On the basis of his detailed empirical study of the Upper Guinea coast of West Africa in the years 1545 to 1800, Rodney questioned the validity of Fage's hypothesis that the prior existence of a slave class in the coastal societies of western Africa made possible the establishment and growth of the Atlantic slave trade. On the contrary, Rodney argued that on the Upper Guinea coast no slave class existed before the arrival of the Europeans in the fifteenth century. What existed were political clients, servants, and other similar dependents. Rodney then demonstrated that the response of the political and economic entrepreneurs on the Upper Guinea coast to the conditions created by the European demand for captives subsequently gave rise to the growth and development of chattel slavery in the region. From this empirical study, Walter Rodney proposed an alternative perspective for the whole of western Africa. He argued that, with the exception of regions where limited slavery had developed earlier in response to conditions associated with the trans-Saharan slave trade, the growth and development of chattel slavery in western Africa was a function of the Atlantic slave trade.[11]

There was very little open disagreement expressed in Rodney's early writings concerning the rest of Fage's arguments. On the total number of Africans imported into the Americas, he accepted the same figure of roughly fifteen million that Fage had proposed.[12] Because Rodney was primarily concerned in his early work with the distortion of African social structures wrought by the slave trade, he did not pay much attention to the demographic impact of the trade. This changed after the publication of Curtin's quantitative study of the slave trade in 1969.

Based on his examination of the published data, Curtin concluded that all existing estimates of the volume of the Atlantic slave trade were too high. He therefore reduced the global total of Africans imported into Europe and European-held territories in the Atlantic and the Americas to 9,566,000. The findings were presented in the form of a hypothesis to be tested against empirical evidence and confirmed or modified. But Curtin made it clear that the margin of error for the global figure of 9.6 million would certainly be within +9.8 percent and -16.4 percent. As he put it: "it is extremely unlikely that the ultimate total will turn out to be less than 8,000,000 [16.4 percent reduction] or more than 10,500,000 [9.8

10. Fage, *An Introduction to the History of West Africa* (1962), 86.

11. For details, see Rodney, *A History of the Upper Guinea Coast, 1545-1800.*

12. Walter Rodney, *West Africa and the Atlantic Slave-Trade,* Historical Association of Tanzania, Paper No. 2 (Dar-es-Salaam: East African Publishing House, 1967), 4.

percent increase]."[13] He further stressed that while it was "doubtful that the re-vised estimates...are too low, it is easily possible that they will be too high."[14]

Fage probably had serious difficulties in the 1950s trying to convince his readers that the pre-industrial societies of West Africa, with a total population of twenty million, sustained an average loss of between 100,000 and 133,000 people per year for three hundred years without a serious negative effect, especially since the loss was through the socio-economically disruptive process of raids and wars. Curtin's thirty-six percent reduction of the fifteen million figure earlier employed by Fage would thus appear to be helpful in making the latter's earlier argument easier to defend. The confidence with which the new figure was presented, and the insistence that in all likelihood the figure would be reduced further as empirical research was conducted, could only have helped to convince Fage that the earlier demographic argument was correct after all. Apparently believing that a reduc-tion of the estimated numbers exported meant a proportionate reduction of the negative impact on African societies, he restated his earlier arguments on demog-raphy and on the pre-existence of a slave class in the coastal societies more boldly. On the issue of African slavery, he conceded that Rodney might be right in the case of the Upper Guinea coast; but he was wrong, Fage held, in generalizing about Africa. What is more, Fage now thought it necessary to abandon his earlier categorical statement that the Atlantic slave trade had had a devastating impact on the process of economic development in West Africa. Fage began to present the Atlantic slave trade as "part of a sustained process of economic and political de-velopment" in West Africa.[15]

Rodney responded in 1972, in a book that soon became one of the best known publications in African history. His argument about the historical devel-opment of slavery in Africa was now neatly contextualized in a systematically for-mulated hypothesis on the transformation of transitional social formations of pre-contact Africa. He argued that African societies were changing from communal to quasi feudal formations when the Europeans first arrived on the African coast. There were serf-like slaves in those regions affected by the trans-Saharan slave trade, but in the rest of western Africa slavery developed after the arrival of the Europeans, in response to conditions created by the Atlantic slave trade. Taking a general view, Rodney lamented that many things remained uncertain about the slave trade and its effects on African societies, one of which was the question of how many Africans were exported. Continuing, he wrote:

A recent study has suggested a figure of about ten million Africans landed alive in the Americas, the Atlantic islands, and Europe. Because it is a low figure, it is already being used by European scholars who are apologists for the capitalist system and its long record of brutality in Europe and abroad. In order to whitewash the European slave trade, they find it con-venient to start by minimizing the numbers concerned. The truth is that

---

13. Curtin, Census, 86-87.

14. Ibid., 86.

15. In particular, see his *A History of Africa* (London and New York, 1978); "Slaves and Society in Western Africa, c. 1445-1700," *Journal of African History*, 21 (1980): 289-310; and "African Societies and the Atlantic Slave Trade," *Past and Present*, no. 125 (November, 1989): 97-115.

any figure of Africans imported into the Americas which is narrowly based on the surviving records is bound to be low, because there were so many people who had a vested interest in smuggling slaves (and with-holding data).[16]

Rodney continued to place emphasis on the impact of the trade on African socio-economic structures. But his reformulated hypothesis also stressed the demographic impact as a factor that retarded the process of economic development in Africa, although the logical details were not worked out. With Curtin's quantitative data, and the more sharply reformulated competing perspectives of Fage and Rodney, the stage was set in the 1970s for empirical research that has continued to the present.

What Was the Relationship Between the Atlantic Slave Trade and Slavery in Africa?

There are two positions on this: (i) pre-existing institutions of slavery in the coastal societies made it easy for Africans to supply slaves and participate actively; (ii) chattel slavery developed in Africa under circumstances created by the Atlantic slave trade and the trans-Saharan trade. I will demonstrate that the second position is the correct one by reviewing the details of recent research on the historical development of the slave trade.

Walter Rodney's argument provoked an impressive amount of research on African slavery in the 1970s and later. Papers and monographs devoted to the general history of African micro-regions, or more specifically to the overall impact of the Atlantic slave trade on such regions, contain useful empirical evidence on the timing and circumstances of the growth and development of slavery in western Africa. In the context of Rodney's formulation of the problem, the extensive empirical study of Central Africa, especially the early Kingdom of Kongo, is particularly important.

Now, how do these empirical studies relate to the competing arguments of Fage and Rodney on the connection between the Atlantic slave trade and slavery in coastal African societies? Since West-Central Africa was not affected by the trans-Saharan slave trade, which preceded the European slave trade from Africa, evidence on the relationship between the Atlantic slave trade and slavery in this region may be seen as critical to the validity of both hypotheses, as Fage recognized. The Kongo Kingdom was one of the early major polities in sub-Saharan Africa, and certainly the first large-scale state system in West-Central Africa. It was also one of the first major supplying states for the European slave traders. If the Atlantic slave trade developed and grew on the basis of a pre-existing slave class in coastal African societies, the Kongo Kingdom should be a good place to find the evidence of it.

The most balanced and detailed study of the early Kongo Kingdom is that of Anne Hilton.[17] Her evidence shows that the development of the kingdom from the early fifteenth century was associated with the production and trading of copper and copper products. The political economy of the pre-European kingdom rested on the collection and redistribution of tribute products from different ecological regions of the state. As the kingdom expanded geographically, the range of tribute

---

16. Walter Rodney, *How Europe Underdeveloped Africa*, 95-96.
17. Anne Hilton, *The Kingdom of Kongo*.

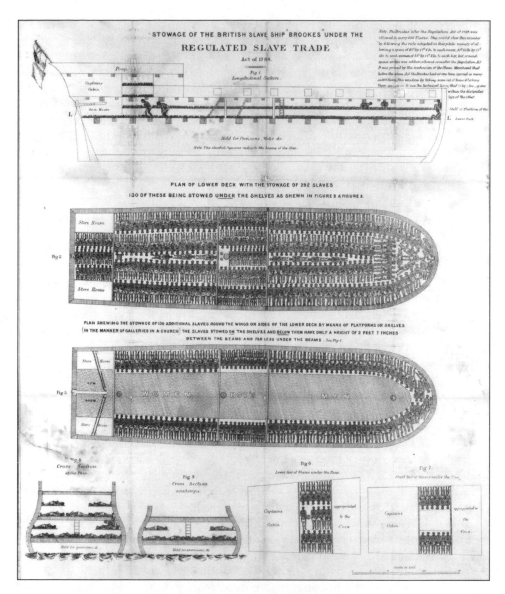

Figure 17-2. Stowage of a British Slave Ship, c.1788

products increased and the income of the ruling elites came to depend on the tributes.[18] This early tribute system apparently eliminated the need for slave production to support the rulers. There were political clients, servants, and prisoners of war or captives, but no slave class; there was no trade in people of any type before the coming of the Portuguese. Hence, there was no word for slave or slavery among the pre-contact Kongo people. In the course of the sixteenth century, Kongo words that originally meant servants, prisoners, or captives took on new meanings, which included slaves and slavery, as the words were applied to describe new social phenomena. As Hilton points out, even as late as the seven-

18. Ibid., 32-35.

teenth century, "[t]he only term which referred to purchase [that is, purchased people], *muntu a kusumbira,* was a compound construction suggesting that the phrase had been devised to express a new condition."[19]

A more elaborate linguistic study of Central Africa by Jan Vansina confirms the non-existence of a slave class and trade in people in the region before the arrival of the Portuguese. Vansina shows that the various words for "slave" in the region are "loanwords" which evolved as the European slave trade spread from the coast into the interior. In particular, Vansina studied in detail the etymology of the term, *-pika, which in Kongo meant "servant" before 1500, but later came to mean the traded slave in the major communities of Central Africa that were involved in the Atlantic slave trade.[20]

The main initial Kongo trade with the Portuguese had been in copper. Thirty years after their arrival, the Portuguese shifted their emphasis from copper to slaves. Even by this time, the King of Kongo had no immediately available "disposable people" to sell when the King of Portugal sent a trade mission specifically to prepare the way for large-scale slave exports. As Hilton narrates, while the Kongo ruler accepted the new trading arrangement and the gifts from the King of Portugal, he had no slaves to send even as return gifts.[21]

Thus, during the early years (up to the second decade of the sixteenth century) when the slave trade remained marginal, while copper and cloth were dominant, not even the Kongo king "had a large retinue of slaves,"[22] let alone the title-holders and provincial governors under him. At this time, the kingdom did not even have a standing army.[23] In the course of the sixteenth century, however, the socio-political and military conditions associated with the Atlantic slave trade led to the accumulation of slaves in Kongo. In the first place, the state was forced to establish a standing army made up predominantly of slaves. Alvaro II (1587-1614) had 16,000-20,000 Tio slave guards. The office-holders and merchants in the capital city and other trading centers employed many slaves in agriculture to meet their subsistence needs. In the course of the seventeenth century, slave-holding in the central region of the kingdom became so widespread that almost every ·aggrieved person demanded slaves as compensation.[24]

Robert Harms's study of the central Zaire basin shows a similar pattern in the development of slavery. The fishing villages in the region had no slave class before their involvement in the supply of slaves to the Atlantic trade. But by the nineteenth century the region had many slaves. Significantly, the dominant slaveholders in the region were the Bobangi who moved from fishing to slave trading, and

---

19. Ibid., fn. 86, p. 233.
20. Jan Vansina, *Paths in the Rainforests: Toward a History of Political Tradition in Equatorial Africa* (London: James Currey, 1990), 278; Jan Vansina, "Deep-Down Time: Political Tradition in Central Africa," *History in Africa,* vol. 16 (1989), 352. Map 3 on p. 353 of the latter work shows the spread of the term from the slave trading coastal communities to the interior, along the main trade routes.
21. Hilton, *The Kingdom of Kongo,* 57.
22. Ibid., 78.
23. Ibid., 58.
24. Hilton, *The Kingdom of Kongo,* 78, 85, 122-123. See also John K. Thornton, *The Kingdom of Kongo: Civil War and Transition, 1641-1718* (Madison: University of Wisconsin Press, 1983), 15-27, which describes the urban setting for slave employment, but does not trace the historical development of slavery in Kongo.

later to ivory trading. The Moye who remained fishermen in the same region had no slave system.[25] The historical development of slavery in the early fishing villages of the eastern Niger Delta of Nigeria may well have been similar. That the process must have been similar is further suggested by the pattern of development of slavery in nearby coastal Cameroon.[26]

Regional studies of Central Africa, especially the early Kingdom of Kongo, thus fail to support Fage's hypothesis on the relationship between the Atlantic slave trade and the pre-existence of a slave class in the coastal societies of western Africa. The Kongo evidence shows clearly that Atlantic slave exports developed without the prior existence of a slave class. It also shows unambiguously that by law, the political clients, servants, and other dependents in pre-contact Kongo could not be sold, and no trade in people existed in Kongo before the arrival of the Europeans in the late fifteenth century. What is more, there is no indication in the Kongo evidence that the rulers had a pathological drive for the accumulation of people as an end in itself, as Fage and some other historians have repeatedly suggested. On the contrary, these rulers saw people as potential producers and subjects, like rulers in all pre-capitalist societies. Their attitudes were influenced by political expediency and the relative value of all production factors as determined by market opportunities. No one who knows the response of African political and economic entrepreneurs to the European demand for agricultural and other products in the nineteenth and twentieth centuries will be surprised by this. Western Africans never produced and traded cocoa and rubber before the coming of the Europeans. But when the latter demanded those products and were willing to pay prices that made their production relatively more materially rewarding than other activities at the time, they were produced in rapidly growing quantities, although there was no previous experience to fall back on. Given the circumstances of the Kongo and Benin kingdoms in the late fifteenth century, Portuguese trade missions, like the one sent to Afonso I of Kongo in 1512, must have found it quite easy to persuade the rulers of those kingdoms to sell slaves, since they could procure the captives from outside their own polities.

While the empirical evidence from Central Africa invalidates Fage's perspective on slavery in the coastal societies of western Africa, it unmistakably confirms that of Rodney. The evidence is clear that the slavery observed in Central Africa in the nineteenth and twentieth centuries by the agents of European colonial powers was a phenomenon that evolved in response to conditions created by European activities in the region. It did not antedate the arrival of the Europeans.

The Central African data are further buttressed by evidence from studies of the Gold Coast, Senegambia, and the Western Sudan. The fact that some Akan people, in the fifteenth and sixteenth centuries, bought from the Portuguese traders captives imported from Benin and Kongo was interpreted by some historians as evidence of the pre-existence of a slave class on the Gold Coast and elsewhere in Western Africa. The Gold Coast case was not contested by Rodney. He

---

25. Robert W. Harms, *River of Wealth, River of Sorrow: The Central Zaire Basin in the Era of the Slave and Ivory Trade, 1500-1891* (New Haven and London: Yale University Press, 1981).

26. Ralph Austen, "Slavery Among Coastal Middlemen: The Duala of Cameroon," in S. Miers and I. Kopytoff, eds., *Slavery in Africa: Historical and Anthropological Perspectives* (Madison: University of Wisconsin Press, 1977).

simply accepted it as part of the response to conditions created by the trans-Saha-ran slave trade. However, Ivor Wilks has now shown that the purchase of people by the Asante in the fifteenth and sixteenth centuries did not produce a slave class at that time. The wealthy Asante, who bought people to clear the primordial for-est for agriculture in these early years, took pains to avoid the creation of a slave class. The matriclan institution was invented at this time for this particular pur-pose.[27]

By the late sixteenth or early seventeenth century, the new social order in As-ante was firmly established. The empire was to be built on that foundation from the late seventeenth to the eighteent century. So, again, the chattel slavery that existed in nineteenth-century Asante developed under circumstances very different from those of the fifteenth and sixteenth centuries. The early Asante evidence agrees with the point made frequently by Meillassoux that the existence of captured or pur-chased people in a society does not necessarily make it a slave system.[28]

The empirical studies of the Senegambia and Western Sudan have also gener-ally confirmed Rodney's argument, by linking the development of slavery in these regions to the trans-Saharan slave trade, while demonstrating at the same time that the growth of the Atlantic slave trade from the sixteenth century stimulated the expansion of slavery and the worsening of slave conditions in them, especially in Senegambia. Searing's account of sixteenth-century Portuguese reports on Senegambia offers a glimpse:

> Portuguese sources give only a rudimentary description of slavery, but they emphasize the use of slaves in agriculture and the links between slave holding and the existence of a slave-raiding, slave-trading nexus linking Senegambia with North Africa and Portuguese Atlantic trade.[29]

If Valentim Fernandes's early sixteenth-century account of the Senegambian coast is correct, then there is clear evidence that chattel slavery, akin to the Amer-ican type, had already developed in Senegambia by the sixteenth century: "The slaves of this country work and earn for their master during six days and the sev-enth day they earn what they need to live the other six."[30] This is a totally differ-ent labor system from the one described by Cissoko for Songhai from the twelfth to the sixteenth century. In Songhai at this period, according to Cissoko's evi-dence, dependent producers were settled in villages held by the ruling elites, in-cluding the askiyas and the Islamic scholars in the towns. These dependent work-ers produced for themselves and paid rents to their lords, rent which Cissoko says "was never crushing."[31] Cissoko calls these producers slaves, but D. T. Niane more appropriately calls them serfs:

---

27. Ivor Wilks, "Land, Labour, Capital and the Forest Kingdom of Asante: A Model of Early Change," in J. Friedman and M. J. Rowlands, eds., *The Evolution of Social Systems* (London: Duckworth, 1977), 523-524.

28. Claude Meillassoux, "Female Slavery," in C. Robertson and M. Klein, eds., *Women and Slavery in Africa* (Madison: University of Wisconsin Press, 1983), 50.

29. James F. Searing, *West African Slavery and Atlantic Commerce: The Senegal River Valley, 1700-1860* (Cambridge: C.U.P., 1993), 22.

30. Quoted by Searing, *West African Slavery and Atlantic Commerce*, 22.

31. S.M. Cissoko, "The Songhay from the 12th to the 16th Century," in D.T. Niane, ed., *Africa from the Twelfth to the Sixteenth Century*, UNESCO General History of Africa, vol. 4 (Berkeley: UNESCO, University of California Press, 1984), 202-203, 205.

Up to the present time in black Africa, before the monetary economy developed, land was considered to be the indivisible property of the community. The kings and emperors had "human estates"; that is, lands worked by subjugated communities; but closer examination shows that this was a system of serfdom rather than slavery.[32]

This is a pointer to the general confusion in the literature on slavery in Africa, a confusion arising from terminological inexactitude. Lack of terminological precision has led to the lumping together of labor systems approximating to serfdom with those that can properly be described as slavery. Meillassoux has rightly commented that

One approach to African slavery, which stresses its benevolent character by comparison to American or West Indian slavery, tends to play down the differences between slaves and other dependent or dominated social categories, such as pawns, serfs, or even married women.[33]

It is this terminological looseness that has clouded the debate on the historical development of slavery in Africa. It is often argued that African societies had the same capacity as other major regions of the world to develop slavery. But the same point is not made about serfdom, which terminological imprecision has eliminated from African history. The evidence indicates that when the term slavery is more precisely applied, the timing of its existence in Africa moves into the much more recent past and the huge numbers mentioned repeatedly in the literature, even for the late nineteenth century, appear to be a gross exaggeration. From Cissoko's evidence it even appears that slavery, properly so called, did not exist in the Western Sudan at the time historians have suggested.

How Many People Were Taken from Africa?

Much empirical research has focused on the impact of the Atlantic slave trade on African populations. In the first place, a reasonable estimate of the total numbers of people actually exported from Africa during the roughly four hundred years of the trade had to be established. Empirical research on this question has been conducted around the figures published in 1969 by Philip Curtin. Curtin's estimate, presented as a grand quantitative hypothesis, gave a global import figure of 9,566,000, with an overall average Atlantic-crossing mortality of fifteen percent, meaning an export figure of approximately eleven million. Curtin thought that it was "extremely unlikely" that subsequent archival research would produce global import figures lower than eight million or greater than 10.5 million. Applying the Atlantic-crossing average mortality of fifteen percent, this translates into an export range of approximately nine million to twelve million.[34]

Since then there has been much activity in archival research. The eighteenth and nineteenth centuries have been reasonably well covered, although the coverage of the Portuguese trade remains somewhat unsatisfactory, due mainly to the

---

32. D.T. Niane, "Conclusion," in Niane, ed., *Africa from the Twelfth to the Sixteenth Century*, 682.

33. Meillassoux, "Female Slavery," 50.

34. Curtin, *Census*.

quality of the evidence. The data on British trade are different. All the acknowledged weaknesses of the British data notwithstanding, they have proved superior to most others of the same period, for which reason the eighteenth-century British trade has been the focus of repeated archival research. The question was asked recently whether the relatively large share of the total exports attributed to the British traders by historians is not due more to the quantity and quality of the British data than to the actual volume of the trade conducted by the other carriers, some of whom were in the trade much longer than the British.[35] On the other hand, the first 250 years of the trade have been much less studied, the difficulty of procuring archival data being much greater.

Virtually all of these archival researchers have revised upward the relevant component of Curtin's estimates studied. With the first 250 years of the trade still largely unresearched, and estimates of the eighteenth century Portuguese trade remaining unsatisfactory, it is not possible now to state a precise figure based on the surviving archival records. However, the figures published so far by the specialist archival researchers add up to approximately thirteen million people exported.

Some comments need to be made on this figure. First, while the volume of exports in the first 250 years of the trade was relatively smaller than that of the last 150 years, it is still significant that the limited archival studies of the former period all point to a much greater proportionate upward revision of Curtin's figures for that period. Second, even when all the surviving archival records have been discovered and studied, the final figure based strictly on these records will still be only a fraction of the actual numbers exported; the problems of missing data and fraudulent misrepresentation will still make the latter figures difficult to determine. The best that specialists can do on this score is to provide full descriptions of the nature of the archival sources to enable non-specialists to decide for themselves what they consider reasonable additions to estimates based strictly on the surviving records. Third, the published products of the archival researches since the 1970s, based strictly on the surviving records as they are, still fail to support Curtin's figures. His figures have been revised upward, rather than downward as he had expected; and his expected upper limit has been significantly exceeded, even as important segments of the trade requiring proportionately greater revisions are yet to be fully studied.

Interpreting the Impact of the Known Figure on Demography

While archival research to uncover more data for the entire period of the trade must continue, nevertheless, we do now have a relatively solid basis for assessing the impact of the trade on African populations. Apart from the rigorously estimated export figures, micro-regional research has demonstrated beyond reasonable doubt that the Atlantic slave trade seriously disrupted socio-political organizations in Africa. The demographic effects of this centuries-long socio-political disruption has been elaborately documented for West-Central Africa and the Slave Coast of West Africa. Studies of Yorubaland and the Middle Niger Valley

35. Joseph E. Inikori, "The Volume of the British Slave Trade, 1655-1807," *Cahiers d'Etudes Africaines*, 128, XXXII (4) (1992): 686.

also document the disruptive effects. In addition, a large body of evidence now shows that the inter-regional movement of population, associated with slavery in western Africa that was caused by the Atlantic slave trade, as shown earlier in this chapter, had a negative demographic impact. Studies of slave populations in Africa show that they were unable to reproduce themselves socially, because female slaves frequently remained unmarried and when married the harsh conditions of slavery limited reproduction. The incidence of European-introduced venereal disease and its demographic effects in the Atlantic slave trading centers of Central Africa[36] show that these factors deserve to be investigated in other Atlantic trading regions of western Africa as well. The extensive evidence now makes it extremely difficult to deny the retarding impact of the Atlantic slave trade on African populations. Even without using much of the new evidence, and employing the out-dated export figure of eleven million derived from Curtin's estimate, Patrick Manning was still able to demonstrate, through computer simulation, that the population of western Africa would have been twice what it was in 1850 had the Atlantic slave trade not occurred.[37]

But not all historians are willing to accept the implications of the evidence. A counter-factual analysis, based on geographic determinism, has been fashioned to show that African societies would have been unable to sustain the additional population that the Atlantic slave trade prevented. West-Central Africa has been the main focus of this analysis. It is argued that, because of inadequate rainfall and periodic droughts, the population of West-Central Africa reached the maximum level sustainable by the region's resources between 1200 and 1400 A.D. Any increase beyond this level was destroyed by famine and disease. The coming of the Atlantic slave trade helped to maintain the equilibrium between population and resources by removing people who would otherwise have died of starvation.[38]

This argument will not wash. Not a single shred of evidence has been presented to support the claim that the population of West-Central Africa reached the maximum level supportable by the region's resources between 1200 and 1400. On the contrary, archaeological and linguistic evidence shows that new technologies and techniques in agriculture, craft production, and social organization were still being diffused over the three million square miles of Central Africa when the Europeans arrived in the late fifteenth century.[39]

It must be recognized that the settlement of Central Africa by the dominant groups in the region today, the Bantu peoples, occurred relatively recently. The balance of the archaeological and linguistic evidence indicates that the movement of the Bantu peoples from the Niger-Benue region of Nigeria occurred "in the mid-to-late first millennium B.C., only a century or two before the advent of iron."[40] This means a couple of centuries over two thousand years ago, or less

---

36. Harms, *River of Wealth, River of Sorrow*, 182-183.

37. Manning, *Slavery and African Life*, 85.

38. See Miller, *Way of Death*; and Joseph C. Miller, "The Significance of Drought, Disease and Famine in the Agriculturally Marginal Zones of West-Central Africa," *Journal of African History*, vol. 23, no. 1 (1982): 17-61.

39. Vansina, *Paths in the Rainforests*; Christopher Wrigley, "The Longue Durée in the Heart of Darkness," *Journal of African History*, vol. 33 (1992): 129-134. See also the various papers in David Birmingham and Phyllis M. Martin, eds., *History of Central Africa*, vol. I (New York: Longman, 1983).

40. Wrigley, "The Longue Durée," 131.

than two thousand years before the coming of the Europeans to the region. Since the total numbers of the original Bantu peoples who left Nigeria and western Cameroon could not have been very great, certainly not in millions, it is understandable why population densities were extremely low by 1400. Although his interpretations are contradictory in places, the evidence recently published by Vansina is quite helpful on this question. It shows that by 1000 A.D. the settlement process was still in progress, and it was easier to move into empty lands than to adopt new techniques of production and social organization:

> almost everywhere by A.D. 1000 the scale of society was still that of a district composed of four or five villages. One also perceives that even in the second half of the first millennium A.D. communities provided with bananas [plantains] were still colonizing empty lands....It was just as easy and often more attractive to move out of range, to restore security by increasing distance.[41]

The system of production and distribution, social organization, and political tradition all reflected the low population densities, which were generally four persons per square kilometer by 1400. Because settlement in the region was still characterized by sparse populations, hunting and gathering continued to provide a large proportion of the people's food, while farming provided only about forty percent by the fifteenth century. Even by 1900, gathering was still very prominent in the economy of some groups in the region. That gathering and extensive land use systems were a reflection of the extremely low population densities is made unmistakably clear by the adoption of intensive production techniques where market opportunities and other conditions made them a rational choice. As Vansina says:

> The eventual appearance here and there of other field systems deserves particular attention. More intensive farming was found by 1900 in several regions within the area. It was achieved by preparing the ground more thoroughly by mounding and ridging, by applying various forms of green fertilizer, and in places by adding new silt as soil. In most cases such developments occurred in the last few centuries. Most of these techniques seem to have developed for the growing of particular new plants, just as was surmised for the practice of burning. Thus cassava is often cited in connection with mounding or ridging. But in a number of cases intensive agriculture was a response to market conditions that appeared in the last two or perhaps three centuries.[42]

Thus, it is the relatively late peopling of Central Africa that explains the region's low population densities in the fifteenth century, as compared with the much greater densities of West Africa of the same period. The proponents of the environmental explanation of Central African history do not seem to be aware that, both in rainfall and in vegetation, Central Africa and West Africa share identical geographical environments. If the forest lands of Asante, using precolonial agricultural technology that was already in place by the fifteenth century, were ca-

---

41. Vansina, *Paths in the Rainforests*, 254.
42. Ibid., 87-88; also 215.

pable of supporting 130 persons per square mile, as Ivor Wilks has computed (using conservative assumptions), there can be no logical or empirical ground for arguing that the tropical lands of Central Africa could support no more than four persons per square kilometer, under the same conditions.[43] It is also important to note that the tropical forest societies of Central Africa were based on yam and palm oil culture, the same food production system that supported the relatively high population densities of the Igbo people of the Nigerian rainforests.

The implication of the evidence is that the Atlantic slave trade attacked Central Africa at a time when population densities were just building up and when socio-economic and political organizations were still relatively weak in most places. The extremely violent nature of the Atlantic slave trade in the region, which Joseph Miller and others have extensively documented, must have overwhelmed the region's societies that were just being formed. The demographic impact was, therefore, devastating. Hence, Central Africa remained extremely sparsely populated in the late nineteenth century, in spite of its early adoption of imported American crops relative to West Africa, where those crops were not adopted until the late nineteenth century, and even the twentieth century for some areas.

In general, the evidence produced by recent research shows that the population of tropical Africa in the late nineteenth century was far below what the region's agricultural land could support under the existing technology and land use system. Hence, the relatively rapid growth of population from the last quarter of the nineteenth century to the Second World War could take place simultaneously with a phenomenal expansion of agricultural production of export crops without significant food imports and without any change in technology. Let it be said also that all this happened without the benefit of Western medicine; in many cases, it happened in spite of oppressive colonial demand and practices.[44]

How Did the Slave Trade
Affect Africa's Development?

The question of the Atlantic slave trade's impact on the long-term process of economic development in Africa has been the focus of research with increasing conceptual refinement. The main economic questions raised in the literature may be stated as follows: (i) What logical interpretations can we give to the socio-political and demographic impact of the trade in the context of long-term development of land-surplus and labor-scarce agricultural economies, based predominantly on subsistence production? (ii) What impact did the trade have on the process of transforming African peasant craft production into urban industrial production? (iii) How did the trade affect the development of commodity production in Africa for export to the rest of the world? And, tying together the preceding questions in one, (iv) how did the Atlantic slave trade affect the long-term development in Africa of the socio-economic system we have come to know as capitalism? It has been stressed that these questions must be answered, explicitly

---

43. Wilks, "Land, Labour, Capital and the Forest Kingdom of Asante," 500.

44. Inikori, *The Chaining of a Continent: Export Demand for Captives and the History of Africa South of the Sahara, 1450-1870* (Mona, Jamaica: Institute of Social and Economic Research, University of the West Indies, 1992), 18-19.

or implicitly, in the context of the world market and world economy that were evolving during the period. The significance of this point is that once the evolution of the world market and the world economy that started in the sixteenth century had gone through its two stages of formation, the world economic order to which it gave rise allocated functions and distributed rewards to the societies involved in a manner persistently unfavorable to those left behind during the formation process.

One general weakness in the literature is the tendency to compare the socio-economic institutions of precolonial Africa with those which existed in the West after the development of capitalism, and then proceed to explain that the institutions of the West facilitated capitalist development, while those of Africa retarded it. In this way, effects are mistaken for causes. Rather than the predominance of subsistence production being seen as a reflection of limited market opportunity, it is seen as an institutional constraint; rather than the nondevelopment of free wage-labor being seen as a function of the abundant supply of land in relation to population, it is seen as an institutional constraint; rather than the nongeneralized development of private property rights in land being seen as a reflection of the nongeneralized development of commercial agriculture, due to the generally low ratio of population to land and the low level of agricutural production for export, it is seen as an institutional constraint; rather than conspicuous consumption and low rates of productive investment by entrepreneurs being seen as a function of limited market opportunities for capital investment, they are seen as institutional constraints. In this way, the effects that are logically attributable to the Atlantic slave trade are erroneously explained away in terms of a *deus ex machina* — African institutions.[45] If, on the contrary, precolonial African history is compared with periods of Western, Asian, and American history before the evolution of capitalist institutions, more helpful insights may be uncovered.[46]

An economic question that has been the focus of recent research is the impact of the Atlantic slave trade on the development of commodity production for export in western Africa. The analysis is conducted in terms of the Atlantic commerce that evolved from the second half of the fifteenth century. Western Africa and the Americas are presented as competing producers striving to meet European demands for tropical and mineral products. The comparative advantages of both regions are identified, with labor as a major advantage of western Africa and a major disadvantage of the Americas. The Atlantic slave trade is then shown as transferring Western Africa's main advantage to the Americas, which allowed commodity production for Atlantic commerce to be concentrated in the latter at the expense of the former. Once the Atlantic slave trade was firmly established, it generated self-perpetuating politico-military and socio-economic conditions that further retarded the development of commodity production for export in Western Africa.

The consequences of this lost opportunity may be gauged from what happened on the Gold Coast during the years of gold production for export to Eu-

---

45. The best example of works in this category are Peter L. Wickins, *An Economic History of Africa From the Earliest Times To Partition* (Cape Town: Oxford University Press, 1981); and John K. Thornton, *Africa and Africans in the Making of the Atlantic World, 1400-1680* (New York: Cambridge University Press, 1992).

46. As a possible illustration, see Douglass C. North, *Structure and Change in Economic History* (New York: Norton, 1981).

rope, and what happened when the Gold Coast was transformed from a gold to a slave exporting area. The pattern of development associated with gold production in Asante in the fifteenth and sixteenth centuries is broadly similar to that occurring in England at about the same time.[47] The gold trade, first with the Western Sudan and later with the Portuguese, stimulated population growth, urbanization, and internal trade. Wealthy Asante traders, who made their money from the gold trade, invested their wealth in forest clearing for agricultural production. Manufacturing grew and concentrated in the urban centers, away from the peasant countryside. Agricultural production for market exchange by peasants expanded. And there is evidence of an evolving land market. But, as the Gold Coast was transformed, from the mid-seventeenth century, into a slave exporting and gold importing region, there was widespread deurbanization, reintegration of manufacturing with peasant agricultural production, decline in peasant production for market exchange, and even outright depopulation in several sub-regions.

The Gold Coast evidence clearly supports the general argument that by aborting the development of commodity production for export, the Atlantic slave trade retarded the development of the constituent elements of capitalism in Western Africa, in the same way that the demographic and socio-political consequences of the trade have been shown to have operated. The general argument is further strengthened by the evidence showing the response of African societies to the conditions created by the growth of population and commodity production for export from the second half of the nineteenth century to the present. Thus, what some historians see as inherently African institutions were in fact a reflection of the retarding effects of the Atlantic slave trade on the process of long-term economic development on the continent.

Review Questions

1. Why is the study of the trans-Atlantic slave trade controversial? Use one aspect of the debate to illustrate your point.
2. Examine the short- and long-term consequences of the trans-Atlantic slave trade.

Additional Reading

Barry, Boubacar. *Senegambia and the Atlantic Slave Trade.* Cambridge: Cambridge University Press, 1998.

Inikori, Joseph E. *Export Demand for Captives and the History of Africa South of the Sahara, 1450-1870.* Mona, Jamaica: Institute of Historical Research, University of the West Indies, 1992.

Meillassoux, Claude. *The Anthropology of Slavery: The Womb of Iron and Gold.* Chicago: University of Chicago Press, 1991.

---

47. See Joseph E. Inikori, "Slavery and the Development of Industrial Capitalism in England," *Journal of Interdisciplinary History,* vol. 17, no. 4 (1987): 776-778.

Miers, S. and I. Kopytoff, eds. *Slavery in Africa: Historical and Anthropological Perspectives*. Madison: University of Wisconsin Press, 1977.

Rodney, Walter. *West Africa and the Atlantic Slave-Trade*. Historical Association of Tanzania, Paper No. 2. Dar-es-Salaam: East African Publishing House, 1967.

Searing, James F. *West African Slavery and Atlantic Commerce: The Senegal River Valley, 1700-1860*. Cambridge: Cambridge University Press, 1993.

Chapter 18

Euro-African Relations to 1885

Adebayo Oyebade

Introduction

The beginning of the growth of European power in Africa can be traced to the early fifteenth century. To be sure, contacts between Africa and Europe predated this period, having existed in fact, for many generations. Comparatively, however, Euro-African relations before 1400 recorded few significant consequences, either for the people of Africa or for Europeans. Even the almost millennium-long Greek and Roman suzerainty in North Africa produced no profound or epochal legacy for either of the two continents. True, the Roman period brought to the region the influence of Mediterranean civilization and also made Alexandria and Carthage important centers of Christianity. These, however, did not leave a lasting legacy. At the close of the fourteenth century, European relations with Africa were thus of relatively little consequence.

In contrast to the previous centuries, Europe's renewed interest in and subsequent intercourse with Africa from the fifteenth century onwards had long-lasting and revolutionary effects on the continent. By the late nineteenth and early twentieth century, the European presence in Africa had led to the most profound change in the history of the continent—its conquest by Western European imperialist powers. With the exception of Ethiopia and Liberia, the whole continent came under one form of European rule or the other. What was the character of Europe's relationship with Africa that led to European colonial subjugation in the late nineteenth century? This is the question posed in this chapter. It is examined from about 1400 to 1885, the year the European powers divided Africa among themselves in what is known to history as "the partition of Africa."

Europeans in Africa Before 1400

Interactions between the peoples of Europe and Africa may possibly have existed from time immemorial. One early significant European contact with Africa can be dated to the Roman conquest of northwest Africa in 146 B.C. The Roman occupation of this region was achieved after Rome's long drawn-out military contest with Carthage for control of the Mediterranean world. The Roman colonization of the Carthaginian empire in present day Tunisia, and the establishment of supremacy over its environs in northwest Africa was soon followed by the fall of Ptolemaic Egypt in the first century B.C. Egypt's fall signified the subjugation of the entire North African region to the Roman Empire. Over the next centuries the region existed as an integral part of the Roman Empire, useful particularly as a vital source of the empire's food supplies.

However, these early European contacts with North Africa left no appreciable trace, despite the long period of Roman influence. The decline of the Roman Empire, in the fifteenth century, began to show in the erosion of its power in North Africa. The Vandals, an East Germanic people, were the first to exploit this apparent loss of Roman control of its North African territory when they took the region with relative ease. Although the Vandals' rule in Africa lasted a century, the invaders were never able to manage the erstwhile Roman Empire in Africa. The control of North Africa soon slipped to the Byzantines, rulers of the Eastern Roman Empire. Like the Vandals, the Byzantines were never able to exert much influence over the region.

The effective elimination of European influence in Africa was brought about by the Islamic invasion of North Africa. Beginning from the seventh century, the Muslim invaders, motivated by a combination of zeal for holy war and opportunity for booty, overran the whole of North Africa. In a matter of a hundred years, the Islamization of North Africa had been completed, accompanied by a thorough cleansing of any traces of European rule and influence.

The consequence of the Islamic takeover of North Africa was profound for Euro-African relations. A vast Muslim world across the northern stretch of Africa, from the Red Sea to the Atlantic, was for the most part a formidable barrier between Europe and Africa. For almost a millennium, this barrier practically separated the two continents. Europe, during this period, basically turned its back to the Mediterranean and faced inwards. Muslim North Africa, likewise, turned southwards, burning with zeal to spread Islam. Thus, largely shut off from each other by the great gulf of Islam, Europe and Africa developed separately. Save for the frequent clashes between the North African Muslims and the Christians of Southern Europe, Europe and Africa existed in relative isolation from each other until the start of the fifteenth century ushered in a new and entirely different chapter in their relations.[1]

Renewed European Presence in Africa

In the early fifteenth century, Europe renewed its intercourse with Africa on a much grander scale and more enduring fashion. This intercourse was part of a larger scheme of European exploration and expansion. One area of the world where European exploration was particularly important was the American conti-

---

1. For more discussion of early European interactions with Africa, see Norman R. Bennett, *Africa and Europe: From Roman Times to National Independence* (New York: Africana Publishing Co., 1984).

nent, known to the Europeans as the "New World." By 1492, Christopher Columbus, an Italian explorer, had succeeded in "discovering" the American continent for the European world. After this "discovery" Europe began to colonize this vast continent.

European exploration was made possible by two important factors. The first was the achievement of national unity in Europe and the rise of modern nation states. Portugal took the lead in the task of nation building in the late fourteenth century. By 1380, King John I had united under his authority the different principalities in Portugal, creating the first modern nation state in Europe. At the beginning of the fifteenth century, Europe witnessed the growth of fervent nationalism, arising partly out of the effect of the Hundred Years War. The long and weary Anglo-French war, fought between 1337 and 1453, engendered nationalistic fervor which, skillfully exploited by powerful European monarchs, turned into a weapon of national unity. In England, for instance, Henry VII founded the Tudor dynasty in 1485 and began the process of uniting the people. France followed a similar unification process under the successors of Charles VII. Also of importance was the unification in 1469 of the kingdoms of Ferdinand of Aragon and Isabella of Castile through the marriage of the two monarchs. It was the unification of the two kingdoms that laid the foundation for the Spanish nation. Ferdinand and Isabella would later sponsor Columbus' voyage.

The second factor was the great advancement in technology, especially in maritime science. By the mid-fifteenth century, Europeans were building more powerful ships with greater maneuverability. In addition to the new ships, voyaging on the seas was made easier by the development of instruments of navigation, such as the astrolabe and the quadrant. Communication was also greatly improved in the fifteenth century. Of particular importance was the development, in Germany in the 1450s, of the printing press which revolutionized access to information. Information became readily available to more people, especially in distant places.

Exploration of Africa: Early Ventures

The Portuguese were the pioneers in European exploration. Having attained unity and statehood, Portugal at the beginning of the fifteenth century launched Europe on an age of exploration. European exploration of Africa from the fifteenth to the nineteenth centuries would form an important part of the exploration age.

Before European exploration to the New World, parts of West Africa had already been reached. Prior to his famous 1492 voyage to the New World, Christopher Columbus had sailed to the Portuguese post on the Gold Coast in West Africa.[2] Indeed, the experience that the Europeans acquired in their African voyages was to aid them in the exploration of the Americas.

Portugal's pioneering exploration efforts in Africa can be attributed, largely, to the exceptional interest of Prince Henry the Navigator. Son of King James I of

---

2. See Mary Beth Norton, et al., *A People and a Nation: A History of the United States*, 4th ed. (Boston: Houghton Mifflin Co., 1994), 20.

Portugal, Henry played an important role in the initial opening of Africa to the European world. Henry was no stranger to Africa in the early fifteenth century. Indeed, he was part of a 1415 expedition that captured Ceuta, in Morocco, from the Moors. Though his larger purpose was to chart an oceanic route to the wealth of Asia, he also craved access to the riches of Africa. Under his sponsorship, by the 1430s a series of voyages had brought the Portuguese to the Azores, the Madeira, and the Canaries, islands off the Northwest coast of Africa. By 1445, they had set foot on the Cape Verde islands, and found the mouth of the Senegal River. The following years, the Portuguese explored further down the West Coast of Africa. In 1486, Bartholomew Dias rounded the Cape of Good Hope at the southern tip of Africa. Ten years later, Vasco da Gama completed the circumnavigation of the continent and reached India.

The early European exploration greatly enriched Europe's knowledge of the coastline of Africa, from the Mediterranean down the West Coast, around the southern tip, and up the eastern seaboard. Though Europeans, especially the Portuguese, established trading posts along the coasts, rarely did they make any efforts to explore the interior of Africa. They largely confined their activities to the coast.

A number of reasons accounted for the Europeans' inability to penetrate the interior of Africa in the fifteenth century. The first was the natural barrier caused by lack of navigable rivers in several parts of the continent. Many of Africa's rivers, including major ones like the Niger and the Congo, that could have served the course of internal exploration given their length, were simply not navigable all the way along. With rapids and cataracts, such rivers were hazardous to exploration. Aside from non-navigable rivers, there were other geographical barriers, including waterless deserts, impenetrable tropical rain forest, and marshy mangrove forests.

Also of importance was the serious health hazard that unfamiliar diseases posed to Europeans. Parts of Africa were infested by sleeping sickness-causing tsetse flies. Malaria and yellow fever were also rampant in many areas. Before the nineteenth century, there were no remedies for these diseases, and, given the number of European fatalities in West Africa, the region was referred to as "the white man's grave."

For the reasons given above, the exploration of Africa's interior was not vigorously pursued in the fifteenth century. This limited European knowledge of the continent's hinterland. It was not until the late 1700s that Europeans embarked on any sustained inland exploration.

Modern Exploration

The late eighteenth and the early nineteenth centuries were the age of modern European exploration in Africa. A combination of reasons led to this. The primary motive was a desire to tap the wealth of the continent through the establishment of commercial relationships. Many Europeans were well aware of the existence in Africa of a variety of valuable commodities, such as gold and spices, and their overriding reason for embarking on exploration was to open up the continent for trade. Other secondary motives included the desire to spread the Christian faith and European civilization to the so-called pagan peoples of Africa, and the thirst for knowledge in Europe about other lands beyond the seas.

In the late eighteenth century, James Bruce, a British explorer, embarked on the investigation of the Nile River. In 1779 he "discovered" the source of the Blue Nile, and he went on to conduct further exploration in present-day Ethiopia. His activities fired European interests in opening up the African interior. These interests directly led to the founding in 1788, of the African Association, which eventually became the influential Royal Geographical Society (RGS). It was this association that was responsible for the sponsorship of many expeditions.

One of the major explorations of the period was that of Mungo Park in the interior of West Africa. Financed by the African Association, Park, a Scot, set out in 1795 to locate the Niger, the most prominent river running through the heart of West Africa. Park embarked on his exploration from the Gambia, traveling eastwards on the Gambia River, and meeting the Niger at Segu in 1796. In 1805, now sponsored by the British Government, Park undertook a second expedition on the Niger, this time seeking the mouth of the river. He was never able to achieve this feat, for his boat capsized at the Bussa rapids, and he died.[3] Other British explorers took up the challenge of completing the exploration of the Niger, including Dixon Denham and Hugh Clapperton between 1823 and 1825. But it was not until 1830, after more than three decades of European exploration on the Niger, that the mouth of the river was finally reached. This was achieved when Richard and John Lander, on their voyage down the lower Niger, were finally led to the sea.

Perhaps it was in East and Central Africa that the most spectacular European exploration took place. Much of this was the work of Dr. David Livingstone, the best known of the European explorers. Livingstone was a Scottish missionary who had studied medicine at the University of Glasgow, graduating in 1840. He proceeded to South Africa immediately after graduation to work in a mission under the sponsorship of the London Missionary Society. Turned explorer, Livingstone began his more than thirty years' exploration of the East African hinterland in 1841. From Cape Town in South Africa he journeyed northwards, crossing the Kalahari Desert and arriving at Lake Ngani in 1849. In 1851, he reached the Zambezi River in present-day Zimbabwe, and for the next five years he explored the central Zambezi valley. During this exploration he christened the great waterfall on the river, "Victoria Falls" after the queen of England. In 1859 Livingstone explored Lake Nyasa, in present-day Malawi. By that year, the end of the first stage of his exploration, Livingstone had journeyed through Angola, Zambia, Mozambique, Zimbabwe, and Malawi. When he resumed his exploration in 1866, he explored the upper reaches of the Congo River and the area around Lake Tanganyika in present-day Tanzania. In 1871 he reached Ujiji on the lake where the American journalist-turned-explorer, Henry Morton Stanley, met him. Two years later, Livingstone, sick and exhausted by the vicissitudes of his travels, died at Lake Bangweolo.[4]

---

3. For more on Mungo Park's expeditions, see Peter Ludwig Brent, *Mungo Park and the Search for the Niger* (London: Gordon Cremonesi, 1977); Christopher Lloyd, *The Search for the Niger* (London: Colins, 1973), 27-46; and E.W. Bovill, *The Niger Explored* (London: Oxford University Press, 1968), 1-31.

4. For more on Livingstone's explorations, see David Livingstone, *Livingstone's Africa: Perilous Adventures and Extensive Discoveries in the Interior of Africa* (Freeport: Books for Libraries Press, 1971); Reginald Coupland, *Livingstone's Last Journey* (New York, 1947);

Figure 18-1. David Livingstone

The interior of East Africa hosted many other European explorers apart from Livingstone. In 1858, the RGS sponsored the journey of Richard Francis Burton and John Hanning Speke to Lake Tanganyika. The same association also financed Speke and James Augustus Grant between 1862 and 1864 on an expedition down the Nile. However, of particular note among the nineteenth century explorers of East and Central Africa was Henry Morton Stanley. An English-born American, Stanley originally set out to find Livingstone in 1869, having been commissioned to do so by a New York newspaper editor. Stanley found Livingstone after two years of diligent searching. Thereafter, he himself became an explorer, destined for the next ten years to traverse the East African interior. Beginning an expedition late in 1874, he made his way accompanied by a retinue of porters and guides to Lake Victoria, which he circumnavigated in 1875. His most important expedition, however, was his voyage along the Congo River that led him to its mouth.

John S. Roberts, *The Life and Explorations of David Livingstone* (Detroit: Negro History Press, 1971); and George Seaver, *David Livingstone: His Life and Letters* (New York, 1975).

Figure 18-2. Henry Stanley in Africa

Leaving Zanzibar in 1875, Stanley linked up with the river at Nyangwe the following year, and proceeded to follow it to the Atlantic, which he reached in August 1877.[5]

By the end of the nineteenth century, the flurry of European inland exploration activities in Africa had produced significant results. More than ever before, Africa became known to European monarchs, merchants, and missionaries. When Livingstone returned to England after his first exploration, royalty received him with fanfare, and he took a great deal of time to lecture large audiences about Africa. As a result of the explorations, new information about Africa replaced old myths and assumptions. It was learned that the Niger did not, in fact, flow west, but east, emptying its waters into the Atlantic through a delta. Europe was so bombarded with unprecedented information about Africa from explorers, that governments began to take more interest in the opening up of the continent's interior.

European Commercial Enterprise in Africa: Initial Trading Relations

When European mariners, backed by monarchs or independent organizations, embarked on travel to Africa in the fifteenth century, commercial interests

---

5. For more on Stanley's explorations, see Henry Stanley, *Through the Dark Continent* (New York: Dover Publications, 1988), and Dorothy Stanley, ed., *The Autobiography of Sir Henry Morton Stanley* (New York: Greenwood Press, 1969).

provided part of the motivation. Europe longed for unrestricted access to valuable African goods such as gold and ivory. By establishing trading relations with the interior, European merchants hoped to by-pass middlemen, and thereby maximize their own profit.

Euro-African commercial relations, however, predated the fifteenth century. Prior to the Islamization of North Africa in the seventh century, the Mediterranean had served as a commercial bridge between the Maghrib and southern Europe. The conquest of North Africa by the Muslims reduced this volume of trade but did not sever trading contacts altogether. Despite the Muslim domination of North Africa, some commercial exchange continued between Christian Europe and the Maghrib, and as far east as Egypt. Thus southern Europe and North Africa engaged in modest commercial relations, in spite of the religious barrier between them. Europeans continued to obtain African commodities, especially the highly prized gold which was received secondhand from Maghrib traders. North Africans obtained a variety of European goods including manufactured products.

Expansion of European Commerce in Africa

From the fifteenth century onwards, Euro-African commerce assumed a new dimension in at least two important ways. First, the focus of European trading activities shifted from North Africa to sub-Saharan Africa. Second, the volume of commercial exchange expanded as slaves were added to the commodities Europeans sought. By the early seventeenth century, the single most important commodity that Europeans demanded from Africa was slaves. In exchange, Africans obtained firearms and assorted exotic goods.

It was the Portuguese who took the lead in establishing trading contacts with the peoples of the Guinea forest. Prince Henry the Navigator had a keen interest in exploration, but he was also an entrepreneur par excellence. Like many informed entrepreneurs of the time, he saw the possibility of increasing Portugal's prestige with the control of the Guinea trade, especially in gold.

The landing of Portuguese explorers at Cape Verde and at the Senegal River in 1445 opened the commercial gates of West Africa to Portugal. Within a short time, Cape Verde had been colonized and used as Portugal's launching pad for further commercial enterprise in West Africa. The area of the Guinea forest that came to be called the "Gold Coast" particularly commanded the attention of the Portuguese. Its vast gold reserve was so attractive that the Portuguese established a trading post at Elmina in 1482, designed to give them exclusive control of the gold trade. By the beginning of the sixteenth century, Portugal was the undisputed master of European commercial intercourse with Africa. Its trading tentacles extended from the Senegambia area to the Indian Ocean. But Portuguese merchants contented themselves with coastal settlements, establishing trading posts along the coast to ensure their monopoly of the African trade. Although they were largely confined to the coast, they managed to establish some commercial relations with interior states such as Benin. The conduct of the interior trade was, however, firmly in the hands of local African chiefs who dictated the terms of trade and imposed duties on commodities.

By far the most demanded African commodity in Europe in the fifteenth and sixteenth centuries was gold obtained from West Africa. By the mid-seventeenth century, however, the gold trade was struggling in serious competition with the emerging trade in slaves. The dynamics of Euro-African commercial relations were drastically altered. There was a major shift in Europe's imports from Africa. Instead of goods, Europeans began to demand slaves in large numbers.

The Trans-Atlantic Slave Trade

The history of the Atlantic slave trade has been dealt with in the preceding chapter so there is no need here for a comprehensive analysis. The exposition here will simply review some of the important dynamics of the trade, which are helpful in understanding this era of European relations in Africa.

Portugal pioneered the trade in human lives. In the fifteenth century, Portuguese merchants settled in the uninhabited islands called the Madeiras, off the coast of northwest Africa. By mid-century, they had established sugar plantations in the islands to satisfy home demand. Soon the Madeira plantations, worked by a system of slave labor, were stretched to their limits, but Portuguese colonists found land available in the islands of Sao Tome and Cape Verde. The sugar plantation economy was introduced to Sao Tome, which increased the demand for slave labor. With the introduction of large numbers of enslaved Africans into the island in the 1480s, the Portuguese had established an economic system based on African involuntary labor. While sugar flourished in Sao Tome, the Cape Verde islands were unable to sustain the cultivation of the crop. But these islands served a different purpose for the Portuguese—they emerged as a way-station on the Trans-Atlantic route when the slave trade began to flourish.

At the beginning, Portugal dominated the Atlantic trade and was almost solely responsible for the supply of slaves to the Spanish colonies in the New World. It was inevitable, however, that its monopoly of the trade would eventually come to an end. In the 1600s, New World plantations were beginning to demand slave labor at a level that Portugal could not satisfy. Indeed, in the seventeenth century, the Atlantic trade had grown into a large-scale business, producing immense wealth for any nation that cared to participate. Inevitably, other Europeans, particularly the British, the Spanish, the French, and the Dutch were drawn into it.

During the 1630s, the Portuguese lost their pre-eminent position in the Atlantic trade to the Dutch. Holland had in 1621 granted the Dutch West India Company a monopoly of the Atlantic slave trade. In the following years, the company succeeded in wresting the control of the trade out of the hands of the Portuguese. By the mid-seventeenth century, the company had established a strong presence on the West African coast, restricting the Portuguese sources of slaves. However, by the end of the century the Dutch too had begun to drop out of the Atlantic trade.

For most of the eighteenth century, England was in undisputed control of the Trans-Atlantic slave trade. To monopolize the English trade with Africa, King Charles II had chartered a joint-stock company, the Royal African Company, in 1672. This company established almost exclusive rights in Europe to the Atlantic slave trade. It built a number of trading posts on the West Coast of Africa. In particular, the English controlled the region between the Gold Coast and the Bight of Benin, an area that became known as the Slave Coast to English slave traders. Armed with the charter that granted it a monopoly of the slave trade, the Royal African Company had, by the time it abandoned the trade in 1731, transported millions of enslaved Africans to the New World.

The French provided the main challenge to the English trade on the West African coast. Although never as successful as the British, they succeeded in establishing a formidable trading presence on the Guinea coast, especially in the Senegambia region. By the late eighteenth century, according to an estimate, France was transporting between twenty and thirty thousand slaves yearly from Africa to the New World.[6] On the coast of present-day Senegal and Gambia, French merchants established a number of trading posts.

The European slave trade in Africa was by no means confined to West Africa. In East and Central Africa, the Portuguese held an almost complete monopoly of the trade up till its abolition in the mid-nineteenth century. In Kongo, Angola, and the Zambezi valley, a brutal but lucrative slave trade fed the plantations in Brazil.

The Atlantic trade in Africa was in many places conducted with African collaboration. As the European demand for slaves increased, so did African complicity. Then, rarely were European merchants venturing beyond the trading posts established on the coast. The pattern of transaction usually consisted of local African chiefs or traders bringing to the Europeans on the coast their consignments of human goods in exchange for European products. Europeans imports often included textiles, metals, alcoholic beverages such as whisky, brandy and rum, and also firearms.

As the dominant element of Euro-African commercial relations for close to four centuries, the Atlantic trade had profound repercussions for every continent involved. By 1807, when Britain outlawed the trade and instituted anti-slavery naval squadrons to police the sea against persistent slave traders, the European powers had derived immense wealth from the trade. In the New World, European colonies developed, their economy based on a lucrative plantation economy that utilized the labor of enslaved Africans.[7] The New World plantations produced products such as sugar, cotton, tobacco, and indigo in large quantities which increased the demand for cheap and steady labor. The plantation system could not have worked and become the basis of the New World economy without the sweat of enslaved African.

The African share of the wealth accruing from the Atlantic trade was minimal. Participation in the trade by some West African kingdoms such as Asante, Oyo, and Dahomey, brought some benefits to these kingdoms. For instance, the rise of Dahomey to prominence can partly be attributed to the slave trade that played a major role in its politics and economy. However, the slave trade also adversely affected West African kingdoms. Often, the struggle to eliminate competitors brought slave-trading kingdoms into direct conflict with their neighbors. In

---

6. Robin Hallett, *Africa to 1875: A Modern History* (Ann Arbor: University of Michigan Press, 1970), 183.

7. For studies of the New World plantation economy, see Kenneth Stampp, *The Peculiar Institution: Slavery in the Ante-Bellum South* (New York: Vintage Books, 1989); and John Hope Franklin and Alfred A. Moss, *From Slavery to Freedom: A History of African Americans* (New York: McGraw-Hill, 1998).

the case of Dahomey, its southern drive to the coast to control the slave trade brought it into conflict with Allada and Whydah, successfully subjugating them. Dahomey itself soon became a tributary state of Oyo, a powerful Yoruba kingdom to the east. Thus, as the slave trade contributed to the rise of Dahomey, it also spelt its demise.

In East and Central Africa, the debilitating effects of the slave trade on kingdoms and empires were more obvious. The Portuguese slave trade in this region in the seventeenth and eighteenth centuries produced so many internal conflicts that prominent kingdoms disintegrated. These included Kongo, Ndongo, and the state of Mutapa (Monomotapa).

Although the intensity of the Atlantic trade in Africa varied from place to place, Africa lost a great deal in terms of human resources as a result. While the trade lasted, millions of virile Africans were carried away to foreign lands. At first, criminals and prisoners of war formed the majority of the slaves being sent to the Atlantic market. But with the ever increasing demand for slaves in the seventeenth and eighteenth centuries, African merchants and local chiefs began to organize special raids on neighboring groups to assemble enough slaves for the coastal markets. The introduction of firearms encouraged raids and wars that yielded more slaves. The Portuguese slave trading in Central and East Africa resulted in the regions being ravaged by warfare arising from the demand for slaves to work in the Brazilian cane plantations.

End of the Slave Trade and Rise of "Legitimate" Trade

Two factors spelled the demise of the Atlantic slave trade. First and most importantly, there was the onset of the Industrial Revolution in Europe in the late eighteenth century. This rendered human labor on a large scale unnecessary and unprofitable. Secondly, there was the rise of the abolitionist movement in Britain beginning in the late eighteenth century. The opposition to the trade in humans was spearheaded by Christian humanitarian and philanthropic concerns. It is ironic that Britain, which had been the leading slave-trading country, would champion the abolitionist movement.

The loss of demands for slaves, a direct result of the Industrial Revolution, coupled with the relentless opposition mounted by the abolitionists brought about the first victory against the slave trade in 1772. This was the year that the British courts, through Justice Mansfield, declared slavery unconstitutional under British law. In 1807, Parliament outlawed the slave trade completely. The antislavery crusade in the next few decades swept across Europe and America. A year after England outlawed the trade, it was made illegal in the United States. The success of this crusade against the slave trade was largely the work of Britain. Indeed, Britain had to use its naval power to stop persistent traffickers on the seas. By the 1840s, the Atlantic trade was much reduced. A phase in the Euro-African commercial relations was finally coming to an end. But the end of the slave trade posed a new question for the future of Europe's commercial intercourse with Africa. What form of economic exchange would replace it?

Even before the slave trade declined, European merchants were already trading with Africans in commodities other than human beings, commodities whose production increased enormously with the coming of the Industrial Revolution. This was the genesis of an alternative economic venture that became generally known as "legitimate" trade. Former bustling slave markets from Senegambia to the Niger Delta soon became centers where Europeans purchased African products, especially raw materials. While Europeans continued to supply Africans with finished goods, they obtained from the continent products such as palm oil, peanuts, timber, and vegetables. Palm oil produced in the Niger Delta area was of particular importance to the Europeans and it became the principal product obtained from West Africa. Demand for it was high because it was not only used as a machine lubricant in Europe's growing industries, but was also an important ingredient for making soap in English factories. Euro-African trade relations came to be conducted by a new class of merchants. In the coastal strip extending from Lagos to the Niger Delta (known as the Oil Rivers), the so-called merchant-princes established a flourishing palm oil trade with the Europeans.[8]

European Missionary Activities

European missionary activities in Africa represented another major component of Euro-African relations. The Portuguese made the initial introduction of the Christian faith into the continent in the late fifteenth century. In 1490, Portuguese missionaries arrived in the kingdom of Kongo where they succeeded in converting the king to Christianity. The faith, however, did not have a sure footing in the kingdom, for after the death of its baptized Christian ruler, Nzinga Mbemba (also known by his Christian name, Afonso), it declined. In West Africa, the Portuguese attempted to establish a mission in Benin. It did not flourish and was soon moved to Warri, where it existed without much achievement for more than a century. Some Portuguese proselytizing also went on in Fernando Po.

Portugal's missionary activities in Africa before 1800 represented only a half-hearted effort at evangelization. In no part of the continent was a strong foundation laid for the propagation of the Christian faith. The Portuguese, like other Europeans in Africa, were mainly interested in the commercial benefits that the continent could offer. Their preoccupation with the Atlantic slave trade largely accounted for their failure in the task of spreading the faith. By the end of the eighteenth century, European missionary activities in Africa could be summed up as a failure. Wherever the missionaries operated, only a handful of Africans had adhered to the faith; and even for many of the converts Christianity was secondary, or at best complementary, to their traditional African beliefs.

The nineteenth century saw a renewed European evangelization effort in Africa. This revival of interest was a byproduct of the struggle, especially in Britain, to end the Atlantic slave trade. As noted earlier, the anti-slave trade campaign was led by Christian-minded groups of individuals in England who had

---

8. For more on "legitimate" trade, see Robin Law, *From Slave Trade to "Legitimate" Commerce: The Commercial Transition in Nineteenth Century West Africa* (New York: Cambridge University Press, 1998).

suddenly realized the sinfulness of the trade and its degradation of humanity. David Livingstone, during his travels in East Africa, had seen firsthand the horrors of slave trading. To redress the injustice and cruelty meted out to Africans by centuries of European slave trading, Livingstone called for the evangelization of the continent and the introduction of European civilization to its people. The abolitionist movement in England, which included many missionaries, believed in the necessity of taking the gospel and the supposedly superior European civilization to Africa.

In the late eighteenth century the evangelization of so-called heathen peoples and the idea of the "civilizing mission" to supposedly backward lands were tasks European Christendom was more than willing to shoulder. To fulfill these purposes, the last decade of the eighteenth century witnessed the rise of missionary societies of various denominations in Europe, focusing their attention on Africa. In 1787, the Methodist Church in England founded the Methodist Missionary Society, which subsequently established missions in West and South Africa. Another group in England in 1779 established the London Missionary Society, which created a mission in South Africa. The Baptists also established a missionary society that set up missions in many parts of Africa. The Anglican Church in 1799 established the Church Missionary Society (CMS) with bases of operation in West and East Africa. In the nineteenth century other missions were founded. The Basel Missionary Society was established in 1815 and its missions spread over many parts of Africa. The Roman Catholic and the Presbyterian churches were not left out of the missionary enterprise.

One of the most prominent evangelical missionary societies to operate in Africa was the CMS. Its mission in West Africa provides a good case study of the European Christian missionary activities in the continent. Freetown, in the colony of Sierra Leone, was an especially productive theater of operation for the CMS. Founded by private interests in the anti-slavery movement, Freetown was conceived as a resettlement center in West Africa for ex-slaves from England and America, and also for "recaptives," slaves rescued on the high seas by British naval patrols. The missionaries were able to convert many of the liberated slaves who were settled in the colony. The recaptives became a major tool in the propagation of the gospel beyond the colony. Many of them who chose to return to their homelands elsewhere in West Africa were used by the missionaries to spread the faith across the region. This is particularly true of Yorubaland where the returnees from Sierra Leone became known as Saros. One of them, Samuel Ajayi Crowther, originally kidnapped in Yorubaland, returned home to become an important force in the spread of Christianity. Later, Crowther would emerge as the first African Anglican Bishop.

Mission work in other parts of Africa followed the same pattern as in West Africa. The various missionary societies sent missionaries to their mission posts to lead the evangelization work. In East Africa, the main missionary center was Zanzibar, while its counterpart in South Africa was Cape Town. Evangelization in South Africa, unlike other parts of Africa, had to contend with racial divisions. The Boers' brand of Christianity discriminated against the Black population. The evangelicals, whose focus was the Christianization of the local Africans, were opposed to racial segregation, and thus ran into problems with the Boers.

The European missionary effort in Africa had by the 1880s become a force to be reckoned with in Euro-African relations. It had begun to have an impact on the people and the society. Many Africans were beginning to abandon their traditional religious practices and take to the new faith. Also, Christianity had begun to achieve an appreciable geographical spread. Mission churches were not restricted to urban centers on the coast, the traditional base of the Europeans. It was not uncommon in the late nineteenth century to find little bands of converts in the interior managing mission churches.

In one way, the Euro-Christian culture and civilization brought by the evangelicals had a negative impact on African culture and way of life. European missionaries tended to look down on many aspects of African culture as un-Christian and, therefore, discouraged them. Instead, the missionaries encouraged Africans to adopt the supposedly more civilized European culture as a precondition to being a true Christian. Thus, African converts had to take European names as baptismal names. The effect of the Eurocentric missionary instruction was to create a class of culturally alienated Europeanized Africans who rejected many aspects of their culture while assuming a European lifestyle.

The impact of the introduction of Christianity to Africa can be looked at in another light. In terms of social change in Africa, it was the missionaries who set the ball rolling. The missionaries not only established churches; they also built mission schools. These institutions produced the first set of Western-educated Africans, many of whom were trained as mission teachers and catechists. Some of them, as part of their preparation to champion the propagation of the faith among their brethren, saw fit to translate the Bible and commit to writing various African languages. Bishop Crowther, for example, translated the Bible into his native Yoruba language and also developed the Yoruba alphabet.

It needs to be noted, however, that despite the success of the Christian missions, by the end of the nineteenth century Christianity was by no means an established religion. Islamic North Africa remained impenetrable to Christian influence. In West and East Africa, many non-Muslim Africans retained their traditional religion. The seed of expansion of the Christian faith had, however, been planted.

The Road to European Imperialism

The advent of "legitimate" trade, Christianity, and European civilization in Africa in the mid-nineteenth century signaled the beginning of a change in European relations with Africa. Europe's effort to totally uproot the slave trade and replace it with commerce in African produce, and the desire to bring the Christian faith to Africa gave rise in the late nineteenth century to increasing European interference in local African affairs. In no region of Africa was this more glaring than in West Africa, where Britain and France, the leading colonial powers, gradually took over authority.

The piecemeal British takeover of parts of West Africa provides a classic example of the advent of European imperialism in Africa. Britain's imperial designs can be said to have begun to take shape in the late eighteenth century when the colony of Freetown in Sierra Leone was established in 1787. The British government soon took over this settlement from its private management in 1808 when it could barely survive. Thereafter, the colony became the naval base in West Africa for the British anti-slavery naval patrol activities.

From Sierra Leone, Britain's imperial authority advanced to other parts of West Africa. Britain seemed to have believed that the abolition of the slave trade and the provision of opportunities for "legitimate" trade to flourish required a declaration of a protectorate over virtually all parts of the West African coastline, from Freetown to Bonny in the Niger Delta. As a first step toward imposing its authority over this area, the Colonial Office in 1821-1824 took control of the British posts on the Gold Coast which had been managed by private commercial interests. By 1843, the Colonial Office had assumed permanent control of all the British Gold Coast posts. Added to this growing British informal empire were the Danish and the Dutch posts on the Gold Coast, which were acquired in 1850 and 1872 respectively.

In the mid-nineteenth century, the British were tightening their imperial control on the lower West African coast. Under the pretext of fighting the slave trade and promoting "legitimate" trade, the anti-slavery naval squadron was used to extend the frontiers of British authority to the east. Lagos was annexed in 1851 and became a Crown Colony in 1861. A series of annexations from Badagry to the Oil Rivers soon followed. On the Gold Coast, the Danish and the Dutch posts having been acquired, the area was officially declared a Crown Colony in 1874. Meanwhile, Britain was also establishing a strong imperial presence in the Gambia.

The French were no less aggressive in their pursuit of imperial designs in Africa by the middle of the nineteenth century. Senegal, which had been dominated by French merchants since the sixteenth century, grew to become the pivot for the advancement of French power in West Africa. The principal French post in Senegal was Dakar, a strategic outpost that would eventually emerge as the center of the French Empire in West Africa. By 1879, the French had begun to penetrate from Dakar further inland via the Senegal River. Sandwiched between the British colonies of the Gambia and Sierra Leone was the Portuguese territory of Guinea.

Outside West Africa, territories were also acquired by the European powers. In Central Africa, the French acquired Libreville, in present-day Gabon, in 1862. This later became the center of French expansionism in Central Africa. In southwest Africa, the Portuguese owned the colony of Angola with its capital at Loanda, and also a territorial stretch known as Mozambique on the coast of southeast Africa.

The pattern of the European occupation of South Africa was somewhat different. Well before the imperialist designs of the late nineteenth century began to take shape, European occupation of parts of South Africa had been developing. In 1652, the Dutch East India Company established a post at the Cape of Good Hope. Over the next two hundred years, European expansion from the Cape into the northeastern interior was a major feature of South African history. In the nineteenth century, European settlers established permanent settlements in the interior, reaching the Limpopo River late in the century. South Africa's historical reality in the years before the scramble and partition was thus that of the Trekboer expansion into regions in the interior below the Zambezi. This expansion not only led to the Boer's conflict with local people such as the Zulu, but also with the British who were setting up colonies on the coast. By the 1820s, the administration of the Cape Colony had changed hands from the Dutch to the British, and Natal was annexed in 1845. The British exercise of authority over the Boers was unacceptable to many, who chose to migrate further inland. The Anglo-Boer conflict thus greatly affected the pattern of the European occupation of South Africa.

By the last quarter of the nineteenth century, the major European powers had annexed territories in many parts of Africa. Yet European imperial interest in Africa at this point in time was still relatively small. Only a few European powers—Britain, France, and Portugal—had acquired territories there by 1879. Except for South Africa, even these acquisitions were small and often confined to the coast. But this changed dramatically in the 1880s.

The Scramble for and Partition of Africa

In the last two decades of the nineteenth century, the landscape of Euro-African relations altered so drastically that the period could be described as the "scramble for Africa." The 1880s saw not only Britain, France, and Portugal pursuing imperial interests in Africa; Belgium and Germany joined the stampede to acquire colonies, and the "scramble" had started.

Several factors brought this about. European powers had realized the importance of colonies in Africa as sources of raw materials and markets for their nation's finished goods. In addition, defeated and humiliated by Prussia, France wanted to use territorial acquisition in Africa as an escape valve from the psychological effects of the disastrous defeat. Otto Von Bismarck, chancellor of the newly united Germany, hoped that colonial competition in Africa would preoccupy France and wear out its desire for revenge. A recent convert to colonial acquisition, Bismarck himself now wanted a place in the sun for Germany. Its industrial products would find a market and source of raw material in an African empire. It would, therefore, not be left out in the race for territories. By 1885, it had acquired a set of colonies in different parts of the continent: in Cameroon, Togoland, and southwest and East Africa. In less than two years, from 1883 to 1885, Germany acquired a vast empire in Africa not dreamt of even a few decades earlier.[9]

The stage for the scramble seems to have been set by the ambition of King Leopold II of Belgium to acquire a personal empire in Africa. Leopold's dream of territorial conquest overseas dated back to the mid nineteenth century. In the Congo basin he found the opportunity to fulfill this dream. It was the knowledge of the wealth of the area revealed by Stanley's exploration that persuaded Leopold to construct his Congo Free State. Stanley himself was an instrument in this grand imperial design, for he was the one appointed by the Belgian king in 1878 to negotiate treaties with the local chiefs. Leopold acquired the rich region as a personal property. To protect this monopoly, he schemed to establish it as a free-trade area subject to his authority, and recognized as such internationally.

With the unhealthy rivalry among the European powers to build colonial empires in Africa, the road to partition was set. To inject some sanity into the race,

---

9. For general studies on the scramble for Africa, see Reginald Coupland, *The Exploitation of East Africa, 1856-1890: The Slave Trade and the Scramble* (London: Faber, 1968); Raymond Betts, ed., *The Scramble for Africa: Causes and Dimensions of Empire* (Lexington: Heath, 1972); Eric Stokes, *Imperialism and the Scramble for Africa: The New View* (Salisbury: Central Africa Historical Association, 1972); and David Lewis, *The Race to Fashoda: European Colonialism and African Resistance in the Scramble for Africa* (New York: Weidenfield and Nicolson, 1987).

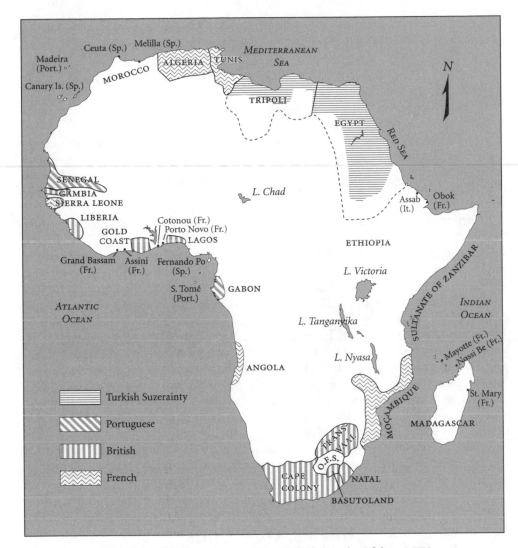

Figure 18-3. European Territorial Claims in Africa, 1879

Bismarck called an international meeting of European powers in Berlin in 1884 to set the modus operandi for territorial acquisitions. The meeting, known as the Berlin West African Conference, met in 1884-1885. By the Berlin Act of 1885, the powers agreed, among other things, that to lay claim on any territory in Africa, a European power must effectively occupy that territory. Thus the conference set in motion the partition of the continent.[10] The Congo Free State was recognized as Leopold's empire. The scramble became intensified and territories were carved out without regard to ethnic divisions. Italy and Spain refused to be left out of the scramble. By the beginning of the twentieth century, virtually the whole of Africa

---

10. For more on partition, see G.N. Sanderson, "The European Partition of Africa: Origins and Dynamics," in J.D. Fage and Roland Oliver, ed., *The Cambridge History of Africa*, vol. 6 (Cambridge: Cambridge University Press, 1985), 96-158.

had been shared out by various European powers. The age of colonialism had set in and a new phase had begun in Euro-African relations.

Conclusion

Africa emerged in the fifteenth century as a fertile ground for European interests. Later, European explorers, merchants, and missionaries traversed Africa, and their activities prepared the grounds for the military conquest and occupation of the continent completed by 1900. In the following years, the onset of colonial rule would follow.

European incursions on the continent before the actual conquest termed 'pacification' had a profound legacy. For instance, European trade in West Africa shifted the center of wealth from the hinterland to the coast. The Atlantic slave trade and the "legitimate" trade that followed led to the decline of the trade across the Sahara with the Maghrib. Instead, the direction of commerce turned southwards toward the coast. By the late 1800s, coastal areas were becoming new centers of power in West Africa.

Although a new class of Europeanized Africans was beginning to emerge in the coastal areas of Africa, in many places the mass of the people remained virtually uninfluenced by any European presence. Except, perhaps, in South Africa, most Africans went about their daily work, oblivious of the Europeans and untouched by their influence. It was not until Europe's conquest and imposition of colonial rule over the continent that Europeans began to exert a direct influence on the lives of the majority of Africans and shape the course of the continent's development. However, Euro-African relations up till 1885 were characterized by significant activities that inevitably led, eventually, to this new stage of relations.

Review Questions

1. What European people had contacts with North Africa before the fifteenth century?
2. What brought about effective elimination of early European influence in Africa?
3. Why was it not possible for early European visitors to penetrate the interior of Africa in the fifteenth century?
4. Assess the importance of Prince Henry the Navigator in the initial exploration of Africa.
5. Assess the contributions of Mungo Park and David Livingstone to the European exploration of Africa.
6. In what ways did the Trans-Atlantic slave trade affect African societies?
7. What impact did European missionary activities have on Africa in the nineteenth century?
8. Examine the factors that brought about the European scramble for Africa in the late nineteenth century.
9. What part did the Berlin Conference of 1884-1885 play in the scramble?

Additional Readings

Ajayi, J.F.A. *Christian Missions in Nigeria 1841-1891: The Making of a New Elite*. London: Longman, 1965.

Betts, Raymond F., ed., *The "Scramble" for Africa: Causes and Dimensions of Empire*. Boston: Heath, 1966.

Crowe, S.E. *The Berlin West African Conference 1884-1885*. Westport: Negro University Press, 1970.

Curtain, Philip et al., *African History*. Boston: Little, Brown, 1978.

Davidson, Basil, *West Africa Before the Colonial Era: A History to 1850*. New York: Longman, 1998.

Hallett, Robin. *The Penetration of Africa: Motives, Method and Impacts*. 1970.

Mannix, Daniel R. *Black Cargoes: A History of the Atlantic Slave Trade, 1518-1865*. New York: Viking Press, 1962.

Oliver, Roland and Oliver, Caroline, eds. *Africa in the Days of Exploration*. Englewood Cliffs: Prentice-Hall, 1967.

Pakenham, Thomas. *The Scramble for Africa: The White Man's Conquest of the Dark Continent from 1876 to 1912*. New York: Random House, 1991.

Index